Publisher's Note

The book descriptions we ask book-sellers to display prominently warn that this is an historic book with numerous typos or missing text; it is not indexed or illustrated.

The book was created using optical character recognition software. The software is 99 percent accurate if the book is in good condition. However, we do understand that even one percent can be an annoying number of typos! And sometimes all or part of a page may be missing from our copy of the book. Or the paper may be so discolored from age that it is difficult to read. We apologize and gratefully acknowledge Google's assistance.

After we re-typeset and design a book, the page numbers change so the old index and table of contents no longer work. Therefore, we often remove them; otherwise, please ignore them.

Our books sell so few copies that you would have to pay hundreds of dollars to cover the cost of our proof reading and fixing the typos, missing text and index. Instead we let most customers download a free copy of the original typo-free scanned book. Simply enter the barcode number from the back cover of the paperback in the Free Book form at www.RareBooksClub.com. You may also qualify for a free trial membership in our book club to download up to four books for free. Simply enter the barcode number from the back cover onto the membership form on our home page. The book club entitles you to select from more than a million books at no additional charge. Simply enter the title or subject onto the search form to find the books.

If you have any questions, could you please be so kind as to consult our Frequently Asked Questions page at www. RareBooksClub.com/faqs.cfm? You are also welcome to contact us there.

General Books LLC™, Memphis, USA, 2012.

ᴥᴥ ᴥᴥ ᴥᴥ ᴥᴥ ᴥᴥ ᴥᴥ ᴥᴥ ᴥᴥ

FROM CHAOS TO THE CHARTER.
A COMPLETE HISTORY
OF
ROYAL LEAMINGTON SPA,
FROM THE EARLIEST TIMES
TO THE CHARTER OF INCORPORATION,
WITH CHRONOLOGY OF
ALL THE PRINCIPAL PUBLIC EVENTS DOWN
TO DATE,
BY
T. B. DUDLEY.
ALL RIGHTS RESERVED.
Printed And Published By
A. Tomes, 43 & 45, Bedford Street, Royal Leamington Spa.
1896.

LIST OF ILLUSTRATIONS.
Pat.

INTRODUCTION. ESCRIPTIVE accounts of comparatively small towns have been depreciated by some as devoid of interest and incapable of profitable study; as fitted but for whiling away unoccupied hours, or, at the best, as being suited only for contracted minds incapable of understanding narratives unfolded upon scales of national grandeur. If it were necessary to quote authorities in demonstration of the utility of local histories, no three names could be cited which would carry greater weight than the Rev. Gilbert White, Professor Freeman and Lord Macaulay. The author of "The Natural History of Selborne" strongly recommends publication of the history of every district, because of the valuable materials which are in this way preserved for the larger accounts of the Counties, and, in his "Old English History," Professor Freeman says: "Every Shire, almost every neighbourhood, has its own contributions to English History. Very few of these could be directly mentioned in a book of this kind, but I hope that the sort of use which I have made of the facts and events special to my own neighbourhood may lead others to deal in the same way with the places and events which more closely concern them. I trust that intelligent readers and teachers will often be able to supplement my references to matters belonging to Somersetshire with references to the same kind belonging to other parts of England." Valuable as are these testimonies, they are surpassed by the more apposite opinion of Lord Macaulay. In his description of Bath he quotes from a local writer, who published a history of the city about sixty years after the Revolution, and of the changes which had taken place within his own recollection. In his younger days, "the gentlemen who visited the springs at Bath slept in rooms hardly as good as the garrets which he lived to see occupied by footmen. The floors of the dining rooms were uncarpeted, and were coloured brown with a wash made of soot and small beer, in order to hide the dirt. Not a wainscot was painted. Not a hearth or a chimney piece was of marble. A slab of common freestone, and fireirons which had cost from three to four shillings were thought sufficient for any fire place. The best apartments were hung with coarse woollen stuff, and were furnished with rush-bottomed chairs." Upon this unassuming and unadorned passage, dealing with subjects usually considered to be but of trifling value, Lord Macaulay makes a remark for which authors of guides and local histories "will ever feel thankful. "Readers," he observes, "who take an interest in the progress of civilisation and of the useful arts, will be grateful to the humble topographer who has recorded these facts, and will perhaps wish that historians of far higher pretensions had sometimes spared a few pages from military evolutions and political intrigues, for the purpose of letting us know how the parlours and bedchambers of our ancestors looked."

The immediate advantages of a local history are comprised, in the rare power it has of focusing the transactions of remote eras within appreciable limits—of imparting to the dry statistics of chronology the warmth and animation of instructive realities—of creating a perspective of centuries, in which the effulgence of the present is enriched by the soft and mellowed splendour of a profusion of antique tints—of encouraging local patriotism, by extending the intelligent range of its observation respecting the parish, the birthplace of some and the adopted home of others—and of disillusioning the minds of all who contemplate progress with feelings of aversion, and change as the inevitable precursor of misfortune. To the attractions of hearth and home succeed those of the parish. Its history is the heirloom of each generation; the common inheritance of each family. The wider the knowledge of its struggles and triumphs, the warmer the sympathy and readier the resolution to promote its welfare by every service at our disposal. Such are the objects this work is designed to promote.

In the following pages 1 make no claim to literary display, nor infallibility of opinion. Doubtless in more competent hands the graces of rhetoric might have embellished many passages now conspicuous for want of ornament, and have given to periods of colloquial simplicity a more stately and rhythmical motion. But, in whatever garb the story is clothed, the progress will be in the same direction, and for the same useful purpose. Dogmatism is laid aside as uncomplimentary to the intelligent reader, and partisanship as opposed to general interests. Some special merit the work may have for its industry in travelling farther back into the vanished centuries than any of its predecessors; for reconstructing the village previous to the Revolution of 1688; for summarising the principal events of its modern life; and for presenting at one view to the public mind a concise but complete account of the rise and progress of Leamington Spa.

Grateful acknowledgements are due to a number of local gentlemen, who have either directed my attention to sources of information of which I was previously unaware, or have generously placed at my disposal books, papers, and plans which I could not otherwise have obtained. During the progress of the work, I expect to receive similar assistance from others. I, therefore, abstain now from individual references, and generally thank all those to whom the public, equally with myself, will be indebted for many valuable and instructive pages.

Belgrave Cottage,   T. B. DUDLEY.
3, Church Terrace,
Leamington.
January, 1896.

CHAPTER I. INCH the date of the primitive village, the record of Leamington has been composed, like the histories of all such towns, of traditions, fables based upon slender facts, facts resting on fables neither few nor slender; guides written with considerable ability, and sometimes displaying scientific knowledge and scholarly attainments; plans, gossip, registers, official and private memoranda, poetry, etc. By carefully sifting this mass of heterogeneous material, we are able to extend the vista of the town and village back through the mists of many centuries and thus secure for the Royal Spa a title in which the ancient and the modern are blended with picturesque and harmonious effect. At least for a century prior to the days of Satchwell and Abbotts, the names of the residents may be recalled, and, by inductive processes of reasoning, the number of the inhabitants and their social condition determined as far back as the stormy days of the Civil Wars. For convenience it may be divided into five periods, each of which possesses its own special distinctions and attractions. The first extends over the many millions of years during which Leamington was, as it were, evolved out of nothing, and, by a series of changes, ultimately acquired that form and consistence now so familiar to our observation. Its testimonies are the stony libraries of the Artesian Wells and the Bore Holes; the rich deposits in the lias beds at Harbury, and Newbold; in the quarries at Milverton and Warwick; and in the polished pebbles and shells found along the banks of the Leam, and at considerable depths beneath the surface of the soil. The second era dates from the time when it first became a place of residence. Ethnography and etymology are

the sole repositories of the evidence relative to the attenuated village in its original state. By the aid of these friendly guides a time in the gray dawn of our national history can be approximately selected when a small band of immigrants settled upon land near the site of the Parish Church, constructed a few mud huts, and called themselves "The Leamingas," namely, "the dwellers on the banks of the Leam." After the lapse of some four or five centuries, the completion of Doomsday Book (1086) marks the commencement of the third principal division of the account of Leamington. Henceforth the historical nebulae increase in number, in clearness, and in interest with each succeeding reign. The chequered fortunes of the estate are traceable from William the Conqueror to Edward Willes and Matthew Wise; and the names and social conditions of the inhabitants are discoverable by a badge of slavery which the Parliament of Charles II. imposed, and the Parliament of William III. abolished. The grant to the Priors of Kenilworth; the Dissolution of the Monasteries in the reign of Henry VIII. ; and the passing of an Enclosure Act, with its Award, are the chief landmarks of this period. For the fourth volume of local history, an examination must be made of the events which transpired between 1786 and 1825. In those thirty-nine years is discoverable much of the initial energy which has won fame and fortune for the town in these more modern times. Drs. Kerr, of Northampton; Johnstone, of Birmingham; Holyoake and Lambe, of Warwick; and Loudon, of Leamington, by their able analyses of the waters, represented the progress of medical science since the discursive allusions of Camden, Speed and Dugdale. Two of the early guide-writers also mention a Dr. Allen, for whom the coveted honour is claimed of having been the first medical benefactor of the Spa; but his place of residence is not given, nor are his writings extant. Satchwell and Abbotts now appear on the scene as the pioneers of the men who, a generation later, spread out the new town like a richly painted canvas among

the verdant pastures and cornfields on the north bank of the Leam. James Bisset, busy as a bee and blithe as a lark, was carolling his humorous ditties into the ears of the modern Leamingas, while the Messrs. Marshalls, Elliston, Merridew, Hewett, Enock, and their music-loving confreres were providing a home for Melody by industriously organising the first of those musical associations which have ever been counted amongst our most cherished recreative possessions.

In this period we also have the exceptionally interesting picture of old Thomas Dawkes, dwelling with contentment in one of the cottages near the church, patiently and laboriously spelling out in his own quaint fashion, "The Short History of the Spa," and vieing with the poetic Bisset for honours as the first historian of modern Leamington. Nonconformity, at that time unfashionable and the subject of social and political ostracism, a seedling from the resultant harvest of Lord Brooke's labours in the seventeenth century, was brought over from Warwick and found a new home at the Spa.

The fifth, and most eventful epoch was ushered in about the year 1825, when, by the establishment of a Board of Commissioners, a scientific frontier was constructed between the decaying village and the growing town. By the creation of this new power the Court of Quarter Sessions and the Parish Vestry were dispossessed of some of their ancient rights and privileges, and the curtain was lowered for ever upon the lights and shadows of a village history of fourteen or fifteen centuries' duration. The town was then in a chrysalis state—putting off the grub and taking on the butterfly—but it was ideally pretty in its original rusticity. Fruitful gardens and orchards were plentiful— burdening the air in the spring with the sweet aroma of their blossoms, and in the golden autumn bending their branches beneath insupportable fruitages of apples, pears and plums. The devious Leam, still unimproved, flagellated by entangling bush and bramble, was chafing with petulance in its narrow bounds at the pebbles and boulders which conspired to obstruct its progress. Close to the Bowling Green Inn was a line of noble elms, with wide-spreading branches and cloud-aspiring tops. The wooden footbridge spanning the river had been supplanted by a structure of brick and stone; but on the site of the Jephson Gardens were fragrant fields, in the hedgerows of which, when the year was young and the May at its sweetest, the juvenile Hampdens and Miltons of the village searched for birds' nests and gathered wild fruits and flowers. ROYAL LEAMINGTON SPA. 7

The old ford, the course of which down to the river ran where letters by the thousand are now posted daily to all parts of the earth, remained. Between thirty and forty thatched cottages kept the village in good countenance. Some of those standing by the Church were conspicuous for their uncompromising Arcadian aspect—their trim little gardens and colonies of bees. Slowly the Parade was lengthening towards Warwick Street. Local colour of dress and dialect was observable in every lane and footpath; while in Clemens Street, the favourite resort of visitors, the smock frocks of the natives commingled with the gorgeous attire of the votaries of wealth, whom fashion had drawn or affliction had driven to the waters. The establishment of the *Leamington Spa Courier,* THE LAST OF OLD LEAMINGTON.

COTTAGE NEAR THE CHURCH, DEMOLISHED JUNE, 188o.

Copied by permission from an Etching by Mr. F. Whitehead.))

in 1828, by which a transient system of paragraph journalism assumed the permanent character of a weekly paper, was a fitting accompaniment to the new Municipal System. It served the practical purpose of bringing the ratepayers into sympathy with the novel experiment which was being made in local government, and provided a much needed organ for the dissemination of useful information respecting local legislation, and for the discussion of questions affecting the interests of the budding borough.

No apology is necessary for introducing, in connection with this epitome, the notes of Thomas Dawkes, Parish Clerk. He dwelt in one of the cottages which formerly occupied the ground at the west end of the Parish Church, the last of which were pulled down in 1880. He was so well known that, by common consent, the group of humble dwellings were distinguished by his name. "Dawkes' Cottages" is a title as familiar to the student of the topography of early Leamington as Satchwell's Post Office, Newbold Comyn, the Manor House and the Parish Church. He was a chronicler in his own fashion; a sort of local Dugdale, who, in the absence of a Leamington journal, made his own reports of the events of his time. His writings are not voluminous, but there is sufficient to create a sincere wish that they had been continued over a longer period, and applied to a greater variety of topics. Posterity is indebted to his unpretentious labours for many historical data, the value of which is enhanced by each successive decade of years.

"The Baths first erected—both hot and cold—at Leamington Priors were by Mr. William Abbotts, in the year 1786, which are called the original Baths, that is, the oldest Baths.

"The first stone in the New Town was laid on Tuesday, the 20th day of September, in the year 1808. The first stone was laid by John Tomes, Esq.; the second by the Rev. James Walhouse, and the third by Benjamin Satchwell, and the bells were set ringing on the occasion; the ringers had £1 16s. for so doing.

"The same year a new Salt Water Spring was found on the North side of the river.

"The New Bridge was begun the same year, but not finished until the following year, 1809.

"The first Market that ever was held at Leamington Priors was on the 5th day of May, in the year 1813. There were 6 stalls with butchers' meat and garden stuff, butter and eggs in plenty, and even loads of greens sold on the first Market day in 1813.

"King George IV. was crowned on the 19th day of July, 1821. Caroline, his wife, died August 7th, 1821.

"The first Petty Sessions ever held at Leamington was on Thursday, the bth day of November, 1823; 5 Magistrates were present. They were to be held every month.

"Lamps lighted for the first time by gas from Warwick was on the 29th day of October, 1823, in the New Town; in number 18 that evening.

"A new piece erected to the Parish Church of Leamington Priors on the South side in the yaar 1816.

"And another large piece was added to it on the North side and erected to the old part in the years 1824 and 1825.

"Mr. John Russell erected a market house in the year 1824, at his own expense; that is Mr. Russell at the Bath Hotel.

"The Leamington Gazette appeared in the Warwick Paper for the first time at Midsummer in 1823.

ROYAL LEAMINGTON SPA. 9

"A new hotel was begun in June, 1818; it is known by the name of the Regent Hotel; tenanted by Mr. Williams, from the Bedford Hotel.

"The Organs in Leamington Churc h and Chapel cost,£330 each, and the playing the first time in the Church was on Christmas Day, 1825, and in the Chapel 3 Sundays before.

"The first brick of Mr. Wills's Bridge was laid on the 1 fth day of April, 1829, it being Easter Monday: the first'brick was by Joseph Hanbott; the ringers had 10s. given them.

"The Duke of Wellington arrived at Mr. Williams's hotel on the 17th day of April, 1829, about half-past 6 o'clock, and he went away again about 4 o'clock on the next day—the 18th day.

"The building over the old established Salt Well was erected in 1804, and the culvert was turned by it about 8 or 9 yards the same year, and not further until the New Bridge was finished; that was by the Cemetery.

"Mr. Russell sunk the price of his ale from 8d. per quart in-doors to 6d. per quart on the first day of November, 1827.

"Trees first planted in Leamington Churchyard on Wednesday, the 5th day of December, 1829, by Mr. Cullis and his men.

"The first stone of the Roman Catholic Chapel was laid on Thursday, the 17th day of April, 1828.

'Mr Russell sunk the price of his ale again on the 18th day of November, 1830, to 4d. per quart.

"The old salt well was rose and repaired from going down 9 steps to up 6 steps in the year 1828.

'The same year there was a Court Leel and a Court Baron held at Mr. Russell's, at the Bath Hotel, on the 14th day of April, 1828. There had not been a Court held at Leamington for upwards of 90 years before.

'The Roman Chapel was opened for the first time on Thursday, the 2nd day of October, 1828.

'A new Chapel towards the Water Mill was begun to be built in April, 1829, called the Independent Chapel. It was opened for Divine Service on Thursday, August the 27th, 1829.

'Service in the Church in the evening at half-past 6 o'clock begun on Sunday, June 20th, 1830. The gas first lighted in the Church on the 15th day of August, 1830; in number 19 lamps.

'King George IV. died June 26th, 1830.

'King William IV. was nominated June 26th, 1830, and ascended the Throne June 28th, 1830, and was Crowned September 8th, 1831.

'He was the Duke of Clarence; he married Adelaide of Saxe Meinengen in 1818; he was bor n August 21st, 1765, and he was Proclaimed at Leamington July 2nd, 1830, with a band of music and 2 flags flying; he was Proclaimed in 4 different places.

'King George IV. was born August 12th, 1762, and died June 26th, 1830, aged 67 years and months. He ascended the Throne January 29th, and Proclaimed January 31st, 1820, and crowned on the 19th day of July, 1821, and was buried July 15th, 1830, at 12 o'clock at night.

Dawkes has omitted to state the number of the months.

"King William the fourth ascended the Throne June 26th, 1830, and he was Proclaimed in London June 28th, 1830; and he was Proclaimed at Leamington July 2nd, 1830, in 4 different places m Leamington, and there were a band of music and 2 Hags, and a great number of people walked in procession; and he was Crowned on the 8th day of September, 1831, and a very grand illumination there was at Leamington Priors on the occasion.

"The Free Masons walked in procession to Leamington Church _on the 14th day of September, 1830, in their full uniform, with a band of music and all their full accoutrements in their Rules and Orders, and the Earl Feris at their head as their leader, and I received 5s. for being Clerk on the occasion.

"The Bathing Institution and Leamington Hospital, the Honourable Charles Bertie Percy in the Chair, he laid the first stone; Doctor Warneford and his Sister gave 1500 Pounds, and it is to be called the General Bathing Institution and Leamington Hospital, after his name; and the first stone was laid on the 10th day of April, 1832, and the amount of the sum is 300 and 8 Pounds, besides Annual Subscribers.

As an illustration of the rapidity of the march of events, and the closeness with which one change treads upon the heels of another, no period can be chosen more instructive than the past fifty years. Within that time three Local Authorities have been extinguished, and two brand new Municipal Institutions, Phosnix-like, have arisen out of the ashes of departed worth. While the number of the governing bodies has thus been reduced, the area of local government has been very considerably extended, by the inclusion of the urban portions of Milverton and Lillington within the sphere of the Municipal domain. Three new churches, four dissenting places of worship, four board schools, a handsome Town Hall, a new Roman Catholic Church, a commodious Post Office, and a Theatre have been added to the numerous list of attractive public buildings previously in existence; besides which, the Warneford Hospital

has been more than doubled in size, and a new cemetery, consisting of twelve acres of land, purchased, and applied to the purposes of sepulture. Extensive as are these statistics of change, they by no means exhaust the list. The acquisition of a bountiful supply of pure and wholesome water, free from the possibility of pollution, takes precedence of the invaluable sanitary arrangements which have distinguished the period under review. The purchase of the Pump Room property was a signal exercise of forethought, by which the credit of the town was pledged in the interests of its health, its amusement, and its recreation. The founding of the College identified Leamington with the higher forms of classical and commercial education; and the establishment of a Philosophical Society introduced a class of lectures, than which none more brilliant have ever graced a public platform.

These parochial and municipal mutations are strikingly in contrast with the unchangeability of the waters. The saline spring, known to Rous in the fifteenth century, and referred to by him as having been famous in the twelfth, has, with lavish profusion, excited the wonder and supplied the wants of many generations. Here, suffering humanity, with its manifold and complex ailments, from every country and clime, has sought the assuagement of wracking pains and the cure of deep-seated maladies. Unlike the mocking mirage of the desert, which aggravates the thirst of the parched traveller by tantalising his vision with an unrealisable expectation, the water has spontaneously responded to every applicant and fulfilled ever-promise. In the catholic dispensation of its intrinsic benefits, no restrictions have been imposed by age, class, or race. Those who drink at the spring in these later times realise all the pristine virtues of the waters.

The progress in the material wealth of the town has been a series of leaps and bounds. The streets and roads, which in 1840, were comparatively few and mostly new, now measure 33 miles in length, and are all well paved, sewered and metalled. The annual revenue has quadrupled; the total sums being £9,598, in 1840, as against £3z53 9s. 6d., in 1895, inclusive of a sum of £10,780 which was raised for Police, School Board, Cemetery, and other Rates. The nett rateable value is £129,210, and the estimated annual rental, £159,279. The amount of the income tax cannot be ascertained, but, on the most moderate computation, it must be very large. When the census was taken, in 1841, the population was 12,812; it is now 27,220. The houses number 6,500; and, although the liabilities upon mortgage of the rates amount to £82,138 4s. 7d., the estimated value of the property, assets, and capital outlay of the Corporation is no less than £186,649 6s. It is questionable whether, in the histories of fashionable watering places, statistics can be quoted more conclusive of popular favour, successful administration and prosperity.

The statistics of the growth of the population from the first Census, in 1801, to 1891, are appended, together with the percentages of increases on each decade, as prepared by Mr. William Bateson, F.S.A.A., the Borough Accountant. From these it will be seen that the largest increase took place between 1831 and 1841.

CHAPTER II. HE origin of Leamington, involved as it is in obscurity, is, nevertheless, attended by circumstances which have justified a distinguished historian in assigning it a place in the early annals of England. Mr. J. R. Green, in "The Making of England," describes it as existing in the form of a quiet township in the gloaming of the seventh century. As the maturity of the oak proclaims a prior existence in the germ-form of the acorn, this "quiet township" of Leamington, in the year 650, gives assurance of a still more remote antiquity as the date of the original settlement. Considering the averment of Rous, in which Camden and other historians of credibility concur, that Warwick was a British town of importance before the invasion of England by the Romans in the year 50; the proximity of Leamington to Warwick and also to Whitnash, a village of undoubted British origin,

we see no reason to question the presence of a small community of ancient Britons, dwelling in rudely constructed huts upon the south bank of the Leam, in the early morning of our national life; nor cause for hesitation in believing that, in all the vicissitudes through which England has passed in the intervening Niagara of centuries, the occupation of this identical site as a place of residence has been maintained in unbroken continuity to the present day. Except such as may be deduced from general considerations, there is no evidence of the tribal nature of the inhabitants having undergone any change in the seventh century, in consequence of the extirpation of the Britons by the Saxons. The phrase, " quiet township," comports more with a British than a Saxon occupation, and it is not incompatible with reason to suppose that after the overthrow of the Britons, the original Leamingas, accepting the inevitable and giving no cause for offence, were permitted to remain unmolested in the chosen home of their forefathers. The place from whence these primitive wanderers came, and their number, are questions which cannot now be determined with precision. The most probable theory is that they were from Warwick, and, with the "native tribe" dwelling in a few huts at Whitnash, formed a three-fold community of kinsfolk, between whom there were constant communications and business relations.

Long anterior to these twilight periods, Leamington was subjected to a series of phenomenal changes in the composition of its soil and the character of its climate. The duration of the formative era—when land was being brought from immense distances by oceanic porterage, and deposited in the order in which we now find it—when the configuration of the surface was constantly assuming new shapes, in consequence of the dynamic force of the internal fires, is estimated at from twenty to thirty millions of years. Difficult as it is to comprehend the lateral extension of land over an area of hundreds of ROYAL LEAMINGTON SPA.

miles, and deposits thousands of feet in

depth, by means of water action; to realise the stupendous eruptive energy which raised the Newbold Hills and the table-lands of Ufton to their present altitudes, we have only to study the object lessons constantly brought within the horizon of our vision in order to understand and accept them as articles of geological faith. About half a century ago, the Local Board of Health spent many thousands of pounds in cleansing out the bed of the Leam, in reducing its contortions, in widening its banks, and in constructing a weir near the railway bridge, at the end of the New River Walk. Fifty years cannot be compared with thirty millions, nor can the feeblest analogy be instituted between the Leam, still characteristically sinuous above the Willes' Bridge, and that boundless empire of water, which, in the chaos of the world's history, rolled with tempestuous force over the site of Leamington, depositing yearly millions of tons of silt and debris; yet, below the weir, the small and sluggish Leam has nearly blocked up the passage of the water, by deposition of silt, brought down from the Southam and Offchurch districts. In the lateral extension of this obstruction towards the Avon we see the way in which Leamington was formed.

Geology is a science far more closely connected with the health of a town than was popularly supposed a quarter of a century ago. From the position of being an intellectual appendage of purely academic value, it has come to be recognised as a branch of knowledge of prime practical importance. This change in public opinion was generally due to the passing of the Public Health Act, 1872—a wise measure, designed to promote sanitation. But it was as much educational in its effects as sanitary. The Inspectors of Nuisances, who had no special qualifications for the discharge of their duties, were superseded by Medical Officers of Health, trained in the studies of water pollution, sewerage, and the suitability of soil for residences. Their reports familiarised the public mind with the new doctrine of sanitary science, and geology was at once metamorphosed from being the toy of the class-room into a health problem for local governing bodies. The increasing interest taken by the public in such questions was strongly emphasised in Leamington in 1875 by another memorable event. The Artesian water supply, with which the name of Mr. Henry Bright, an ex-Mayor of the Borough, will ever be honourably associated, directed attention from the surface of the soil to the strata beneath. The result was the discovery of a treasure which placed Leamington first in its water supply for maintaining health, as it had long been first in its mineral waters for regaining it when lost. An account of the waterworks, with a description of the various strata, of which specimens were carefully collected and preserved by Alderman S. T. Wackrill, first Mayor of Leamington, will be given in due order of time.

By far the best description of the geology of the town and neighbourhood is the following, which we quote from "Reeve's New Guide to Royal Leamington Spa," published in 1839:—

"The town is built upon a light-coloured sandstone series, and appears to be the upper portion of the variegated sandstone at the junction of the variegated marl, if it does not actually belong to the latter; but it is extremely difficult to determine the limits of either, in consequence of the absence of a peculiar limestone observed in Germany, intervening between the variegated sandstone and variegated marl, termed muschekalk. The sandstone is the same as that of Warwick, Guy's Cliff, and many other places in the neighbourhood, and is a good building stone. It contains a few organic remains of saurians, of which several well-preserved teeth, fragments of vertebral and other bones, of different species, have recently been discovered.

"The mineral waters of the Spa are mostly derived from this sandstone rock, at the depth of from thirty to forty feet. In sinking wells, gypsum and rock salt are occasionally met with in small quantities. The hill at Newbold Comyn consists of variegated marl, which has been extensively used in making bricks, surmounted by a bed of gravel, with

sand, and thin seams of light-coloured clay, containing numerous oolitic remains, gryphoe, belemnites, pentacrinites, &c., &c. The London road passes over the variegated marl until it arrives at Ufton Hill, where the western edge of the lias is first seen in that direction; though the nearest point at which the lias is found is at Whitnash, close to the south side of the village, where a narrow tongue of blue clay and rubby limestone is met with, extending from Chesterton camp along Whitnash field to the village.

"On the north bank of the Leam, in the Newbold gardens, there is a thick bed of gravel and clay, in which have been found many bones and teeth of the rhinoceros, horns and bones of deer, &c., Sec., of extinct species, associated with a few fresh-water shells. In the low ground adjoining the Royal Pump Room, in a bed of peat earth, there have been discovered horns and bones of recent species of deer and of other quadrupeds."

No mental measurement can be made of the ages which elapsed during the soil growth of the town; nor can the most vivid imagination picture the extent and variety of the changes which were constantly taking place. Possibly at one time the bed of the River Leam was the summit of a bleak mountain range, and the land we now call the Newbold Hills lost to view in the deep cold recesses of a sunless valley. But besides these physical transformations, there was a change in the climate no less extraordinary. Before the occurrence of the Glacial Drift, the atmospheric conditions of Leamington were almost tropical. A resident population at that period, with average skill in horticulture, might easily have converted the Parade into a magnificent orange grove, and have gathered abundant harvests of spices and gums from the slopes of the hills and the sun-tanned face of the north bank of the Leam. Following the Drift came an atmosphere of arctic severity, and England not being separated from the Continent by water, animals whose habitat was in the Polar regions by instinct followed the cold. The Rev.

P. B. Brodie, an authority universally recognised in archaeology, specifies the elephas primogenias, or mammoth, the rhinoceros, cave bears, and others, as amongst the immigrant species. In an admirable lecture on "Earthquakes," delivered in February, 1880, to the Clarendon Young Men's Christian Association, the late Mr. John Greet, of Church Terrace, thus referred to Leamington in its pre-Glacial-Drift days:— "This mid-England, and therefore, of necessity, the bit of territory immensely interesting to ourselves, and euphemistically styled Leamington, was a steaming morass, covered with rank tropical vegetation, whose lofty groves echoed to the tramp of the giant iguanodon, and was the home and the haunt of the dragon and the turtle."

Ten centuries elapse before we obtain any definite information respecting the early village. In 1086, "Doomsday Book," otherwise called the "Winchester Roll," was completed by order of William the Conqueror. Leamington appears therein under the varied spelling of " Lamingtone," respecting which the announcement is made that it was about two hides in extent, was of the value of £'4, and had two mills of the value of 24s. By modern values and measures, the two hides would be equal to 240 acres, and ROYAL LEAMINGTON SPA.
the £Ar to £285 4s. of our money. One of the mills, it is agreed, stood upon the site now occupied by Oldham's Mill; the situation of the other is uncertain, but the probability is that it was at Newbold Comyn. Mills were important institutions in those days, and often belonged to the Prior, who wielded enormous local influence. He could compel all persons in the parish to bring their corn to be ground at his mill. The monetary values and the two mills seem to point to the fact that Leamington was a place of some consideration at the date of the Norman Conquest. It does not, however, appear to have been paramount in population at any period. In the middle of the seventeenth century, Harbury had nearly double the number of houses, and Radford was almost its equal. Such pre-eminence as it had

would be derived solely from its mills. They represented a trade of considerable importance; heavily laden wains toiling in slowly from the surrounding villages with corn to be ground, and returning with flour for the family and the cottagers. Besides this industry in bread-stuffs, there was the mental merchandise of free intercourse with the surrounding districts—the exchange of news and the conversion of Leamington into an emporium for intelligence from all parts of the county.

In the seventeenth century we have the first intelligence of the inhabitants of the village, and at the same time become acquainted with an oppressive grievance under which they suffered in common with the whole nation. The odious tax imposed by 13 and 14, Charles II., c. 10, on the warmth feebly emitted from the few embers in the grates of the cottagers, was enforced with relentless severity, and sometimes with a callous indifference to the commonest claims of humanity. Upon all persons, rich or poor, there was levied a charge of two shillings per annum for each hearth or stove in the house. This sum, though small, was often raised with difficulty, and in extreme cases by self-denial of the bare necessaries of life. But the financial burden was small in comparison with the unconstitutional burden. For the recovery of this paltry sum of two shillings, the collectors, who were known as the "Chimney Men," were armed with powers almost equal to those wielded by a victorious General over a conquered people. The "Chimney Man" had authority to enter any house, and to go through every room of it at his own will and pleasure; to burst open locked tloors, and a plenitude of distraint in case of non-payment, which was tantamount to absolute confiscation of property. This infraction of the constitutional maxim that "an Englishman's house is his castle" was resented by the people with Curses loud and deep. After the Revolution of 1688, the Tax was declared by Parliament to be "a badge of slavery upon the whole people and abolished." From "a duplicate of all the hearths and stoves retorned att Michael-

mas, 1663," we learn that in the village of Leamington there were about forty-six cottages and other residences. The names of the occupiers and the number of the hearths for which they were liable are subjoined:—

Hearths Liable.—Edward Wills, Gent. 5, Francis Raborne 3, Willm Onley 1, Laurence Nicholls 1, WiUm Cartwright 1, Widd Jackson 2, Robert Johnson 1, Stephen Summers 1, Joan Wardvide 1, Willm Nicholls 1, Thomas Bratt 1, Michael! Summers 1, John Griswold 1, John Onley 1, Samuel Clark 2, George Hill 2, Tarry Wills 3, John Cox 1, Willm Cartwright son 1, Anne Bucknell widd 1, Robert Sherifle 1, John Boddington 4, Hny. E. Bates 1, Willm Wills 1, Thomas Cartwright 1, Richard Onley gent 4, Thomas Lees gent 4, Willm Greswold 1, Edward Rawbone 1, total 49.

HEARTHS Not LIABLE.—William Penden 1, Richard Smyth 1, George Gumby 1, John Anderton 1, Willm Stanley 1, Anne Blithe 1, Edward Heath 1,.Margaret Woodford 1, Catharine Jarett 1, John Smith 1, Walter Anderton 1, John Burwell 1, John Smyfield 1, Walter Rose 1, William Bingham 1, John Ries 1, John Swift 1, total 17.

Our readers will doubtless desire to learn something of the reasons why certain occupiers were not liable to pay the tax. The exemptions are the best barometer we can have of the poverty of the period. By sections 17, 18, and 20 of 13 and 14 Charles II, c. 10, poor people not liable on account of their poverty to pay Church rates and poor rates were exempted from the Hearth Tax; no person inhabiting a house, the full improved rent of which did not exceed twenty shillings a year, was liable to the tax, provided such occupier did not rent any land of the value of more than twenty shillings a year, and was not possessed of ten pounds worth of property. Without in any degree claiming to be mathematically exact, we may take it that in Leamington, upwards of two centuries ago, nearly one-third of the cottages were rented at not more than fourpencethree-farthings a week, and that the occupiers had not ten pounds'

worth of property each, nor allotments or land of the rental of twenty shillings a year.

Besides the burden of the Hearth Tax, the humble Leamingtonians of 1663 had another serious ground of complaint. They were almost immovably tethered to poverty and suffering by a second "badge of slavery." Freedom of contract in respect of wages, now universally admitted to be the right of every class, was strictly prohibited by an Act of Parliament passed in the reign of Queen Elizabeth. The Court of Quarter Sessions for Warwickshire fixed how much the farmers should pay, and the labourers receive. Fourpence a day with food, and eightpence without food, were the average earnings of the majority of the men whose names appear in the foregoing list. Many of them were fathers of families, and the price of wheat was seventy shillings a quarter. Five years before the Hearth Tax was abolished (1685), the Quarter Sessions ordered four shillings a week without food as the payment to the agricultural labourer from March to September, and three and sixpence a week from September to March. Evenemployer who gave more, and every working man who received more, was liable to punishment, but it was no offence to give and receive less. It would be superfluous, here, to dwell upon the straits to which these poor peasants were reduced by the pinching economy necessary to raise the two shillings Hearth Tax for the chimney man, nor need we allude to the anxious and self-denying care with which the little hoard, once obtained, was guarded, even against the inroads of hunger. Nearly a century after the abolition of the tax-, the gloom, wretchedness and misery of those hunger-bitten days loomed luridly in one of Ben Satchwell's verses, and modulated with a pathetic cadence the exultancy with which he contemplated the then rising star of the golden age of the Spa.

"If Muster Abbotts had not done
His Baths of laud and praise,

It must have been poor Leamington
Now, as in former days."

CHAPTER III.

ARIOUS statements have been published by early writers upon Leamington respecting the population of the village previous to the present century. In nothing are they more contradictory of each other, more irreconcilable with facts, and more perplexing to the intelligent reader, than when endeavouring to ascertain its numerical status in the pre-census days. Their estimates of the cottages vary from the minimum of two or three to the maximum of forty or fifty. These are guesses, more or less the outcome of imaginative lotteries, though it must be clearly understood that no blame is imputed to them for negligence, nor are they chargeable with having been actuated by a desire to mislead their readers. As the Census returns do not commence earlier than 1801, beyond that date every writer is left to work out his results in the way which commends itself to his own judgment as best adapted to the desired end. The Hearth Tax Return of 1663, and a Ground Plan of 1783, are the only means for deciding the question, and no reference to either of these being found in any of their works, it is evident that all the writers, from Pratt, the first author of a Leamington Guide, were unaware of the valuable evidence available for the settlement of a point interesting to every student of the history of the town. By way of parenthesis, we may remark that there are two Returns of the Hearth Tax preserved, the earlier one being for the year 1662. But it does not contain the number of the exemptions, nor the names of the residents in Leamington so relieved. Its value, therefore, is less than the one for 1663, which supplies both desiderata. The chief interest in the Return for 1662 consists in the variations of the spellings of the same names, the changes which had taken place in one year in the tax-paying section of the inhabitants; in its mention of the name of the Vicar of the parish, in the curious manner in which the number of the hearths is enumerated, and in the sum being set forth required to be paid by each taxable resident. We subjoin the list:—

Hearths Liable.—Willes Widd, 04 hearths, 8s.; Francis Horne, 03, 6s.; William Oulney, 01, 2s.; Valentine Jackson, vicar, 02, 4s.; Nathaniell Oulney, gent, 04, 8s.; Willm Lees, gent, 04, 8s.; Samuel Clarke, 02, 4s.; John Boddington, 03, 6s.; Thomas Cartwright, 01, 2s.; Wm. Willes, 01, 2s.; Hugh Bates, 01, 2s.; Wm. Cartwright, jun., 01, 2s.; Lawrence Nicholls, 01, 2s.; Robt. Johnson, 01, 2s.; Stephen Summers, 01, 2s.; Micha Sommers, 01, 2s.; Thos. Bratt, 01, 2s.; John Briswold, 01, 2s.; John Onley, 01, 2s.; George Hill, 03, 6s.; Tarrey Willes, 03, 6s.; John Cox, 01, 2s.; William Cartwrightson, 01,2s. ; Anne Bucknall, widd, 02, 4s.; Mary Shreife, widd, 01, 2s.; Richard Sharpies, 01, 2s.; Edward Rawbone, 02, 4s.; William Criswold, 01, 2s.; George Collins, 01, 2s.; total 50.

It will be observed that in both years the number of residences assessable to the tax was the same, namely, twenty-nine, but the total of the hearths was one less in 1663 than in 1662. This diminution is too insignificant to justify any inference as to the

Ji effect of the tax upon the multiplication of hearths, and is referred to only in view of its possessing some possible value in connection with other circumstances. Restriction is the natural effect of taxation, the measure of which invariably corresponds with the weight of the burden imposed. Such a tax in an age of chronic poverty would discourage the proper supply of hearths, stoves, and fireplaces.

Before leaving the Hearth Tax, space must be found for a brief quotation from Macaulay, illustrative of the resentment which rankled in the minds of the people on account of the impost, and the cruelty frequently evinced by the collectors in exacting payment; also to the Act by which it was abolished, noticeable for the fervour of the nation's gratitude and loyalty, and the re-affirmation of a valuable constitutional principle which Magna Charta was not sufficient to preserve against invasion; and lastly, by comparing Leamington in 1663, under the Hearth Tax, with Leamington in 1851, under the Window Tax, indicate

the advance which had been made in the opportunities and privileges of public discussion, petition to Parliament for the redress of public grievances, and relief from oppressive fiscal burdens.

In describing the revenue of 1685, our great historian observes: "The most important head of receipt was the excise, which, in the last year of the reign of Charles, produced five hundred and eighty-five thousand pounds, clear of all deductions. The net proceeds of the customs amounted in the same year to five hundred and forty thousand pounds. These burdens did not lie very heavy on the nation. The tax on chimneys, though less productive, called forth far louder murmurs. The discontent excited by direct imposts is, indeed, almost always out of proportion to the quantity of money which they bring into the Exchequer, and the tax on chimneys was, even among direct imposts, peculiarly odious, for it could be levied only by means of domiciliary visits; and of such visits the English have always been impatient to a degree which the people of other countries can but faintly conceive. The poorer householders were frequently unable to pay their hearth-money to the day. When this happened, their furniture was distrained without mercy, for the tax was farmed, and a farmer of taxes is, of all creditors, proverbially the most rapacious. The collectors were loudly accused of performing their unpopular duty with harshness and insolence. It was said that as soon as they appeared at the threshold of a cottage the children began to wail, and the old women ran to hide their earthenware. Nay, the single bed of a poor family had sometimes been carried away and sold. The net annual receipt from this tax was two hundred thousand pounds."

The impost was abolished by 1 William and Mary, Sess. 1 c. 10, entitled "An Act for the taking away the Revenue arising by Hearth Money." It recited that the King, having been informed that the Hearth Money was grievous to the people, had been pleased to signify his gracious pleasure either to agree to a regulation of it or to the taking away of it altogether, upon which the Commons assembled in Parliament found that it could not be so regulated but that it would occasion many difficulties and questions, and that it was in itself not only a great oppression to the poorer sort, but a badge of slavery upon the whole people, exposing every man's house to be entered into and searched by persons unknown to him. Being filled with a most humble and grateful sense of his Majesty's unparalleled grace and favour to his people, not only by restoring their rights and liberties which had been invaded contrary to law, but in desiring to make them happy and at ease by taking away such burdens as by law were fixed upon them, by which a lasting monument of the King's goodness would be erected in every house in the kingdom, they humbly besought that the said Hearth Money might be wholly taken away.

We have no evidence of the inhabitants of the village adopting any of the wellknown constitutional methods for obtaining relief, such, for instance, as petitioning Parliament, interviewing the Members for the Division, and agitating for a remission of the tax by holding public meetings and passing resolutions. In their day these safety valves to popular discontent were unknown, or much less fashionable than now. They had no parish room in which to assemble, no newspapers from which to seek advice and receive encouragement, no leaders to voice their plaint. Their Town Hall was the village green, whence they were sometimes driven by the logic of rotten eggs, the persuasive force of cabbage stalks, and the inexorable arguments of brickbats. In 1851 we find Leamington, though infinitely more comfortable in its worldly circumstances, less submissive to a tax which restricted the entrance of air and light into dwellings. At a public meeting of the inhabitants, held in that year in the Town Hall, the Window Tax was by resolution declared to be " inconsistent with the laws of humanity, oppressive in its operation, and repulsive to the feelings of the community," in consequence of which it was determined "to exert every means to obtain the total and

immediate repeal of this obnoxious tax. "

The number of the population in the sixteenth, seventeenth and eighteenth centuries is partly a question of trustworthy statistics and partly one of rational speculation. The Hearth Tax Return for 1663 gives the total dwellings as forty-six. The Ground Plan of 1783 does not afford the same exact information, though there is sufficient to show that they could not have varied considerably from the time of Charles II. to that of George III. Thirty-four buildings are indicated, but from these must be deducted the Parish Church, the Well House, several barns, the blacksmith's shop, village stocks, and pound, none of which can be computed as dwelling houses. On the other hand, there are ten sets of cottages varying in number from two to five, which are reckoned only as one each in the total of thirty-four. If an average of three be allowed the total will be about fifty, or four more in 1783 than there were in 1663. Subject to such qualifications as may be adduced from unimpugnable records, the stationary character of the village in the one hundred and twenty years between 1663 and 1783, may be accepted as applicable to a corresponding period of time preceding the first date. Hypotheses founded upon supposititious analogies respecting two distant epochs must necessarily be advanced with some reserve; but, in the absence of evidence to the contrary, the ascertained statistics of the one may justifiably be received as characteristic of the other, if the circumstances of both are known to have been the same. Such was exactly the case with Leamington in its hamlet days. The political and commercial environment was identical in the reigns of Charles I. , William III., and George III. No change had affected its social laws and customs Two forces were constantly acting and re-acting upon the village population, the one to restrain it from rising above the standard of labour, the other to prevent it being unduly depressed below it. For the population required by the local labour market, cottages were provided, but there was no obligation to make

provision beyond that limit. The Poor Laws, which compelled each parish to maintain its own poor, rendered it inexpedient to have a surplus of unemployed, and the means by which the balance was preserved in a state of equipoise between redundancy and scarcity was the cottage accommodation, which kept the population down so as to prevent an increase to the rates, and allowed an expansion sufficient for local needs; what small surplus there was floated away to the towns, the army and navy. Other factors in the prevention of a superabundant population in the villages were insufficient and innutritious food, impure water, insanitary dwellings; absence of drainage; imperfect ventilation, and the occasional prevalence of epidemics, without proper medical supervision being available, such as the Authorities, happily, now provide for every hamlet and village.

The existence of two public houses in Leamington in 1625, is favourable to the supposition of the population being at the time equal to what it was in 1663. William Mills and Margrett Walsgravc were the holders of the licenses, and a collection of four or five two-roomed thatched cottages would have failed to induce them to take out licenses for providing victuals and supplying ale. The following Order by the Warwickshire Court of Quarter Sessions, dated 1625, has the complexion of a report from a somewhat populous, active and independent village community. The two houses, in all probability, were the Dog and Howling Green, famous in the days of Satchwell and Abbotts:—

"An Order for the Suppressing of Wm. Mills ami Margrett Walsgravc, of Lemington Priors, Victualers.

Forasmuch as the Court was this present day informed by a Certificate of dyvers of the inhabitants of Lemington Pryors, in this Countie, that William Mills and Margrett Walsgrave, two victualers, who in the said towne keepe very ill order and rule in their houses, soe that their neighbours are offended and wronged thereby, besydes, as this Court is informed, the said Margrett selleth also without a lycense, in contempt of this Court. It is, therefore, Ordered that the said William Mills and Margrett Walsgrave shall be from henceforth absolutely suppressed from offering or sellingc Ale, beare, or victualls any more, which if they, or eyther of them contynue, Then the Constable there is required to apprehend and attache the bodyes, and them, the said Win. Mills and Margrett Walsgrave, or eyther of them, and them soe attached, to bring or cause to be brought before some justice of peace of this Countic, there to finde sufficient sureties to forbeare selling ale, beare, and victuals as aforesaid, which if they, or eyther of them refuse to doe, then to committ them soe refusing to His Majestie's gaole of this Counlie, there to remaine untill they willingly doe and pcrforme the same. Hereof faile not, as the contrarye you will answere at your perill."

Perhaps the most important part of this Order, as illustrating the character and status of Leamington in the reign of Charles I., is its designation of a "towne." In the legal phraseology of Quarter Sessions' Courts, '"hamlets" and "villages" were not unknown terms; the word "parish" was of extensive use, but it had slight signification so far as population was concerned. The parish was, according to Rlackstone, of ecclesiastical origin; the town was municipal, or civil. The names of "town," "hamlet," and "village" convey meanings of a different character. By "town" is commonly understood a place which contains a larger number of inhabitants than a village or hamlet, and which is of some importance. In the consequence claimed for the application of this term to Leamington during the Stuart dynasty, we do not overlook its primitive signification. We know that "town" is derived from the Anglo-Saxon "tun," and that its original meaning was an enclosed dwelling or dwellings. The " quiet township" of Leamington in the seventh century must, no doubt, be considered in the light of etymology, but since the days of the Anglo-Saxons, language has acquired new force, and names which were once restricted to one idea have become the representatives of many

others. In the days of the Stuarts, the enclosure thought had been excluded from the word, and associations became connected with it of which the Anglo-Saxons had no knowledge. It had come to be known as any number of houses having a regular market, but which was not a city nor a See. There was a third source whence the authority to apply the word "town" to Leamington may have been derived. A parish having its own constable was legally entitled to a greater dignity than other parishes of equal size but without constables. The constable of Leamington, to whom the Order of the Quarter Sessions of 1625 was addressed, must not be confounded with the parish constables of England under the Hanoverian reigns, nor compared with the police constables of the Victorian era. To the functions of both, he added somewhat of the precedence and authority of a mayor, and was locally the great man to whom all turned for guidance. The presence of a constable in Leamington in the early part of the seventeenth century does not necessarily imply a numerous population, but it is more consistent with a large than a small village.

CHAPTER IV. HE third portion of the history of ancient Leamington may be said to have begun in the reign of William the Conqueror, and closed in that of George III. From the Norman to the Georgian era we have a rapid succession of manorial changes, in one of which is discoverable an early indication of the gathering storm between England and Rome which culminated in the dissolution of the Monasteries by Henry VIII. The web and woof of the history of this period are thickly interwoven with change; the situations become increasingly dramatic in their effects, and the records of substantial facts more abundant. Rolls and registers attest in profusion the long line of noble owners who grasped the prize of the estate of Leamington without being able to retain it; whose bitter mortification at seeing it the possession of others quenched in total eclipse the remembrance of the joy they experienced when it was their own. Nothing more vividly portrays the

capricious moods of fortune, the rudimentary condition of authority, the unsettled state of the country, than the changes in the ownership of Leamington at this time. Within the brief space of a little over one hundred years, it was in the possession of eleven proprietors, one of whom held it on two different occasions. Throughout the whole of that period it was in a state of perpetual oscillation between the Court, the Camp, and the Church, the pendulum of events being impelled backwards and forwards by the mandates of monarchs, the arts of diplomacy, the smiles of favourites, the successes or failures of military adventures, and by the mortality of its owners. Its lords included Saxon, Norman and French—nobles of proud and ancient lineage. After passing through a series of vicissitudes, rare even among sorely tried communities; after basking in the genial warmth of a richly endowed form of Ecclesiasticism, and rejoicing in Royal favours of Charters, immunities, and special privileges; and after descending to the depths of poverty, it emerged from its obscurity at the close of the eighteenth century, successively scaled every gradation of local government, and ere the meridian of the nineteenth was passed, gratified its noblest ambition by reaching the summit of municipal pomp and authority.

The first possessor of whom we have satisfactory evidence was Turchill, the last of the line of the valiant Saxon Earls of Warwick. It was one of the forty-eight manors which formed his estate, and was held by him at the date of the Battle of Hastings. He inherited it from his father Alwynus, beyond whom in the history of the village it is impossible to go. The cultivation of the land and the occupation of the dwellings were by his vassals, the produce belonging to its lordly owner. Turchill's absence from the Battle of Hastings (1066) told somewhat in his favour with the Conqueror, and saved him from the immediate confiscation of his estate, but it was a cardinal principle in William's policy to obtain every stronghold for himself or his followers. After seeking in vain to excite Turchill into rebellion by keeping him in a constant state of surveillance, obliging him to repair and rebuild Warwick Castle and hold it fortified in fee, he could brook no further delay. The King accordingly took possession of the Castle, on which the proud and haughty Earl retired, mortified in spirit, to the quiet and secluded shades of the Forest of Arden. William, unable to provoke opposition, could hardly fail to respect the spectacle of fallen greatness which the condition of Turchill presented to his view, and in his favour it remains to be stated that his subsequent conduct towards the man he had so deeply wronged was considerate and generous. Turchill was allowed to retain a considerable portion of his possessions, among which was the estate of Leamington. He had two sons, Siward de Arden by his first wife, and by his second, Leverunia, Osbert de Arden, from whom are lineally descended the Earls of Northampton. Siward became owner of Leamington on the death of his father, but was deprived of it by the King, who had to feed the insatiate greed of his barons, for whom England provided none too much of spoil.

From this date the Earldom of Warwick entered upon another line of descent, anil Leamington became the property of Norman and French knights and barons who had faithfully served the victorious king in his conquest of England. The new owner was Henry de Novo Burgo, or Newburgh, the first Norman Earl of Warwick. He was succeeded by Roger de Montgomery, a French knight, who commanded the main body of William's army at Hastings. As he was credited with having played an important part in the overthrow of Harold, his claims were such as the King could not ignore. Of Roger it is said that he was a man of singular devotion, and that he founded and most amply endowed the Abbey of St. Peter's at Salisbury, where he at length took upon him the habit of a monk, and died in the year 1094. His wife was Mable, daughter of William de Talvaise, a great Baron in Bcleson, who was also one of the supporters of the Conqueror. There were five sons, the eldest of whom,

Hugh, succeeded his father and became owner of Leamington, and at his death, the estate passed to his brother Robert, who was the next link in the historic chain of proprietary we are now tracing. He held it up to the time of the death of William Rufus, when a civil war broke out, the crown being the prize, and the claimants Robert Curthose, Duke of Normandy, eldest son of the Conqueror, and Henry, his youngest brother. Robert, the Earl of Warwick, entered into the family quarrel with zeal, espousing the cause of the elder brother, who was defeated by Henry, and the Earl, taken prisoner, was despoiled of his estates by the new monarch, Henry I., surnamed Beauclerc.

A fresh interest is added to the current of events at this period by the mode in which the proprietorship was disposed. Hitherto it has been the reward of military prowess and successful adventure by flood and by field; now it is pressed into the service of the church, and becomes the guerdon of mitred bishops, of proud priors, and austere monks. ROYAl. LEAMINGTON SPA.

The new King was justly jealous of the extensive prerogative the Pope exercised in England; the Pope was mistrustful and watchful of the ambitions and aspirations of the King. Before a bishop could be instituted to an English See, the ceremonials of investiture and homage had to be observed. Both these functions, derived from Papal authority, were claimed by the King. He resolutely declared that he would sooner lose his crown than forego the right of investiture, to which the Pontiff answered that he would rather part with his head than allow the King to dispense a power which was of the very essence of Papal impregnability. The quarrel, long and bitter, ended in a compromise. The Pope was allowed to retain investiture, but the King obtained the priestly homage as his reward. Henry naturally had a strong feeling in favour of the clergy, and he bestowed Leamington on the Bishop of Lichfield and Coventry, who, residing at the time at Chester, was also officially described as the Bishop of Chester.

View, from a Sketch made in 1828, of old Cottages in High Street, on the site between Packington Place and Church Street. They were purchased by Mr. Henry Mulliner and removed in i860.

In his possession it remained for but a brief period. He disposed of it to Geoffrey de Clinton, which brought it again into the possession of the Warwick family, and made it a Warwickshire property by ownership, as well as by geographical situation, Geoffrey being son-in-law of Roger, Earl of Warwick, the immediate successor of Henry de Newburgh. Another relationship which he had with Warwickshire was that of being the founder of the Castle and Prion' of Kenilworth. Geoffrey, from whom came the powerful line of the Dukes of Newcastle, did not retain possession long before he granted it to Gilbert Nutricius, of Warwick, on payment of ten marks, with a silver cup, and to his wife Agnes a bezantine of gold, Gilbert holding it by the service of half a knight's fee. This ownership was of short duration, and upon its determination, Leamington again reverted into the possession of Geoffrey, at whose death it passed to his son, Geoffrey de Clinton, who, in 1166, presented it to the Priors and Canons of the Monastery his father had built and endowed, about the year 1122, "to the honor of the blessed Virgin Mary," at Kenilworth, "for the redemption of his sins and the good estate of King Henry the First and his own wife and children." This gift of the church and the mill at Leamington to the Priors and Canons of Kenilworth was confirmed by his son Henry, who liberally made considerable additions to it out of his own estate, and obtained from the King immunities and concessions, including the privilege of Court Leet, assize of bread and beer, authority to try and punish malefactors, freedom from county, hundred courts, free warren, etc., etc. The concessions granted by the King were certain to have been by charter, and there is, therefore, good reason for assuming that in the twelfth century Leamington had its Charter of Incorporation, though different in its scope and effect from the one obtained in 1875, and under which the town is now governed. Had the Priory records been preserved, some interesting light might have been gleaned from their pages respecting the special privileges conferred upon the village, and the status it had, in consequence of being in possession of such exceptional favours. Dugdale says:—

"The service of half a knight's fee, by which the said Canons held it (though in the grant there be no mention thereof), was by the bishop passed over to the monks of Coventre; for in 20 Hen., 3, the Prior of Coventre, certifying that knights' fees were held of that monastery, makes instance of half a knight's fee in Lemington juxta Warwick, held by the before specified canons: The like was signified in 36 Hen. 3, which canons, in 7 Edw. I, had a water mill, 3 yard land, and a 4 part, and the half of another mill, here in demesn, as also ix. servants, holding 3 yard land, and 3 quarters, performing divers senile labours; 8 cottiers holding 8 cottages and 8 acres of land; andxi. freeholders, which held 13 yard land and a 4 part wi. h the other half of the water mill; and besides all this a court leet, gallows, assize of bread and beer, by the grant of King Hen. 3, together with the church appropriate, endowed with two yard land: all which was enjoyed by them till the dissolution of the Monasteries."

One of the results of the acquisition of Leamington by the Priors of Kenilworth was an addition to its title, for previously known as Lamingtone, or Leamington, it henceforth was to be "Leamington Priors." Both the time when the change took place and the circumstances attending it are sufficient to refute the theory of the agnomen "Priors" having been supplied for the purpose of distinguishing it from Leamington Hastings. Reserving for consideration in a subsequent chapter the etymology of Leamington and the learned disquisitions of which it has been the subject, we may here incidentally mention that the word is remarkable for the variations it has undergone, both in ancient and modern times. After the Dissolution

of the Monasteries, it still retained the general title of the great religious Order to which it had belonged, and continued to be Leamington Priors down to the early part of the present century. The establishment of the fame of the waters, the salubrity of the climate, and the adaptability of the place to every purpose of a health resort, suggested a more fashionable ROYAL LEAMINGTON SPA. 27 and attractive description. It then became known as Leamington Spa. The greatest distinction, however, was that which her Majesty the Queen was pleased to confer on July 19, 1838, by granting permission to call the town in future "Royal Leamington Spa."

The Monastic Brotherhood for the space of three hundred and seventy-three years held possession of Leamington Priors in undisturbed peace and undisputed right. Whether the times were more favourable for the permanent security of vested interests or the hierarchy at Kenilworth were better skilled in the art of retaining what their secular brethren could not help losing, is an enquiry too remote from the purpose of this history; clear it is, however, that, through the storm and stress of sixteen eventful reigns, their right had never been called in question nor placed in peril. Their tenure had been more secure than that of the Crown of England.

The year 1539 brought an unexpected change to the fortunes of Leamington. Henry VIII. was on the throne, and there was a second quarrel with the See of Rome: this time something more than the question of homage and investiture being involved, for the issue was as to the headship of the Church in England. From the time of Beauclerc the supremacy of the Papal power had rankled in the minds of the English Kings. The King refused to acknowledge the authority of the Pope, abolished the Monasteries with scant notice, without compensation for disturbance or unexhausted improvements, and ousted the Priors of Kenilworth out of their ancient houses and splendid revenues. What was the mode of the cultivation of the land in Leamington during the time of the Priors is not stated. They may have

let it out on rental or have cultivated it themselves. Nor does it appear that they resided here in any numbers, unless the existence of an ancient church be accepted as proof. But between the time when Turchill was its owner and the 26th of Henry VIII., the value had increased from £4. to £S33 15s-4-d-This is important, as showing that the place was free from the stagnation which usually attends small parishes, and which was never more operative than in the period now under review. The possibility is that the Priors hired out such of the land as was not required for their own immediate purposes, and contented themselves with receipt of the revenues. In such a capacity they would be freed from all the anxieties incidental to agricultural pursuits, and would be superior as Leamington lords, temporal and spiritual. By the Dissolution of the Monasteries Leamington reverted to the Crown, and once more entered upon a career of change and vicissitude. For more than three and a half centuries it had enjoyed an unaccustomed repose under the Monks of Kenilworth; it again became the sport of fickle fortune, and had its destinies governed by the currents of Royal favour and family issues, until the time when commerce assumed its supremacy, and distributed it among a thousand owners.

In 1564, it was granted by Queen Elizabeth to the noble and good Ambrose, second son and heir to the late Earl John Dudley, Duke of Northumberland, then attainted. On the 21st of February, 1589, Ambrose died, and having no issue, Leamington gravitated back to the estates of the Crown. One of the earliest grants of the living of All Saints' Parish church now took place. The annexed prdcis of the patent has never before been published, and we have reason to believe that the circumstance of the gift is a new contribution to local history.— 1596. 38th Elizabeth, 22nd April.

Letters patent of this date whereby Her Majesty, in consideration of the good, faithful and acceptable services of her beloved and faithful Councillor John Puckering, Knight, Lord Keeper of the Great Seal of England, before then oftentimes done and performed and upon his humble petition, granted to William Borne, and Jacob Orange, Esqs. *(inter alia).*

All that the Rectory of Lymington with its rights, members and appurtenances, in the County of Warwick, then late in the tenure or occupation of Hugh Lee or his assigns at the annual rent of £4, anil all lands, tenements, glebe lands, tythes and hereditaments whatsoever to the same Rectory belonging or appertaining, or as members part or parcel of the same before that time, held, known and accepted, used or reputed to be with all its rights, members and appurtenances to the late Monastery of Kenilworth formerly belonging and appertaining and parcel of the possessions of the same formerly being, and the advowson, donation, free disposition and right of patronage of the Vicarage Church of the Parish of Lymington, in the county aforesaid, with all its rights, appurtenances to the same Rectory belonging or appertaining, and in as ample manner and form as all and singular the premises before granted to their hands or to the Queen's hands, or to the hands of the Queen's father and brother, Henry the 8th and Edward the 6th, late Kings of England, came or were of right held.

And the Queen granted to the aforesaid Willm. Borne and Jacob Orange that they, their heirs and assigns for ever, should have, hold and enjoy, *inter alia.*

The Rectory of Lymington, with all its rights, members and appurtenances, unto the said William Borne and Jacob Orange, their heirs and assigns.

To the only proper use of the said William Borne and Jacob Orange, their heirs and assigns, in fee farm, for ever to be held of the said Queen, her heirs and successors, as of the Manor of East Greenwich, in the County of Kent. Reserving annually to the Queen, her heirs and successors, for the Manor of Lillington and for the Rectory of Lymington, immediately after the death of Ann Countess of Warwick,,£16 16s. od.

In the ensuing sixteen years there was

no change, but in 1605 James I. bestowed the estate on Sir Fulke Greville, who was afterwards created Lord Brooke. He is described as a virtuous man, an accomplished nobleman, an upright statesman, a writer of repute, and a patron of learning. By his tragic and calamitous death the nation lost an eminently useful public servant, and literature one of its brightest ornaments. On September 8, 1628, he was stabbed by his own servant, whom he had displeased, and who immediately afterwards killed himself. His successor in the title was Lord Brooke, of Puritan fame, the intimate friend of Milton and General of the Parliamentary Militia in the time of the Civil War. His death took place at the siege of Lichfield, where he was killed while fighting for constitutional freedom, civil and religious liberty. The name of the " Puritan Peer" was that which he acquired in the heraldry of public worth, an honoured appellation Wilton has obviously endorsed by referring to him in the pages of the "Areopagitica" in terms of affectionate regard, admiration, and gratitude. From the beginning of the eighteenth century the estate and land of Leamington came into the possession of numerous proprietors. The manorial rights and a considerable portion of the land, with the original saline spring, were acquired by the Earl of Aylesford, the other principal owners being Mr. B. B. Greatheed, of Guy's Cliffe; Mr. Mathew Wise, of Shrubland Hall, and Mr. Edward Willes, of Newbold Comyn. With the establishment of the Spa in the beginning of the present century, the owners found themselves in possession of a veritable El-Dorado of wealth. For the fashionable visitors who flocked to the Spa, it was difficult to provide accommodation, and such was the urgent demand for villa residences that building sites sold readily for prices varying from £1,000 to £4,500 and £5,000 per acre.

An atmosphere of pleasant philanthropic reminiscence lingers round the sale, in 1701, of the Quarry Field, with a little meadow on the west side and one other meadow on the south side.

Owing to this transaction, Leamington was brought into passing association with a celebrated poet, a distinguished physician and a prominent leader in works of practical benevolence. Originally the property belonged to Hercules Beaufoy, of the Manor House, Edmonscote, one of whose sisters was married to Dr. Samuel Garth, author of the well-known poem the " Dispensary." In consequence of his wife's interest in the estate, his signature was necessary to the conveyance. He was one of the first to provide cheap medical attendance for the indigent poor, and in a liberal sense, a share of the honour of founding Provident Dispensaries, now so popular in England, may be awarded to his memory. His marriage entitles Warwick to claim him as a son-in-law, and as one of the vendors of the Quarry Field and its pretty little meadows, he was directly connected with Leamington in its transition period of nearly two centuries ago. The once flowery and fragrant site is now covered with valuable properties, including hundreds of handsome villas, one of which still bears the old name. Among the principal buildings are the fine Wesley Chapel, Dale Street, and St. Luke's Church, Augusta Place. LEAMINGTON PARISH CHURCH EARLY IN THE PRESENT CENTIRY,

With surrounding buildings, the Bridge and gate leading into the meadow where the Royal Pump Room and Baths stand. CHAPTER V. EVERAL statements are to be found in one of the early Guides respecting an Enclosure Act passed in 1767 and an Award made in 1768, affecting the distribution and proprietorship of land on the south and west banks of the river. In the columns of the local press the subject has also been discussed on one or two comparatively recent occasions. The Act and the Award having been the first of the long series of legislative enactments which are inseparably incorporated with the history of the town, renders it necessary that they should find in these pages not only a place, but a full account of their important provisions. Apart from the historic interest they possess by reason of their priority in the order of time, they are noticeable for having brought to a close the last vestiges of the mediaeval system of land tenure in Leamington, and for exercising a marked influence upon the tithing system, the Parish Church, and the fortunes of the Spa. The Enclosure is entitled "An Act for dividing and inclosing the open and common fields, common meadows and commonable lands on the south and west parts of the river Leam, in the manor and parish of Leamington Priors, in the county of Warwick." The preamble sets forth that, "Whereas there are several open and common fields, common meadows, and commonable lands and grounds on the south and west parts or sides of the river Leam, in the manor and parish of Lemington Priors, in the county of Warwick, containing by estimation nine hundred and ninty acres, or thereabouts: And whereas the Right Honourable Heneage, Earl of Aylesford, is lord of the said manor of Lemington Priors and is seized of and intitled unto divers lands and hereditaments in the said Parish of Lemington Priors: And whereas Mathew Wise, of Lemington Priors aforesaid, Esquire, is owner of the Rectory Impropriate of the said parish and intitled to all the great and impropriate tythes yearly arising within the same parish: And whereas Mathew Wise, of the Priory, near Warwick, in the said county of Warwick, Esquire, is intitled to the advowson and right of patronage of the Parish Church of Lemington Priors aforesaid, and the Reverend John Willes, clerk, is vicar of the same church and as such seized of the glebe lands there, containing by estimation three acres or thereabouts, and intitled to all vicarial or small tythes yearly arising, renewing and increasing within the same parish: And whereas the said Earl of Aylesford, Mathew Wise, of Lemington Priors, aforesaid, Edward Willes, Esq., late Chief Baron of his Majesty's Court of Exchequer in Ireland; the said John Willes, clerk, in respect of his glebe land; John Lawrence, Richard Lyndon, Thomas Aston, and John Fairfax, as trustees of charitable lands belonging to the parish of Barford, in the said county of Warwick, are the owners

and proprietors of all the said open and common fields, common meadows, and commonable lands and grounds on the said south and west parts or sides of the river Leam, in the manor and parish of Lemington Priors aforesaid, and the said proprietors or their lessees or tenants are intitled to and do enjoy common or pasture for their cattle at certain seasons of the year, in, over and upon all the said open and commonable lands: And whereas the lands of the respective owners and proprietors of the said open and common fields, common meadows, and commonable lands lie intermixed and dispersed in small parcels in and over the sanie. fields, and are capable of great improvement:

And whereas the said owneTS and proprietors of the said common fields, common meadows, and commonable lands are desirous that the same may be divided and inclosed and specifick shares thereof, or other recompence assigned, divided and allotted to and amongst the proprietors thereof and the said tythes in severalty in lieu of and in proportion to their resyective lands, tythes, common rights and interests therein: But although such division, allotments and inclosure will greatly tend to the advantage of the parties concerned, and be a great improvement to their respective properties and interest in the said common fields, common meadows and commonable lands, yet the same cannot be effectualy established without the aid and authority of Parliament, may it therefore please your Majesty," etc., etc.

The persons named to make the enclosure and apportion the respective shares were the Rev. Henry Homer, of Birdingbury, otherwise Burbery, clerk; John Tomlinson, of Aston; John Watts, of Comb Abbey; Robert Campion, of Woodcot, and John Basely, of Priors Marston. The Commissioners thus appointed for putting the Act into execution were first sworn to make a just distribution without favour or affection to any of the claimants. For the more just and regular division and distribution of the said open and common fields, etc. , it was enacted that they and certain

closes, or pieces of ground, called Midsummer and Lammas Grounds, should be qualited by the Commissioners, or by someone on their behalf, and a true and perfect survey and admeasurement made of all the said open and common fields, common meadows and commonable lands and premises before the ist October, 1768. By the 1st day of January, 1769, or "as soon after as the same can be conveniently done," the Commissioners were to apportion the same lands according to the following directions.

To Edward Willes, Esquire, in lieu of his lands lying in the said open fields, etc., they were to allot one or more allotments (being part of the said land and grounds intended to be enclosed) of lands which lie opposite to and fronting his Mansion House at Newbold Comyn, and as contiguous to a farm house of his, then in the tenure of William Court, as conveniently may be, and to the said John Willes, clerk, they were to allot and set out for him and his successors, the Vicars of Leamington, land which, in their judgment, should be equal in value to the Glebe land, and right of common thereunto belonging; also to Mathew Wise and John Willes, and his successors the Vicars of Leamington, they were directed to assign land equal to two-fifteenth parts of the residue of the tithable lands. For John Willes and his successors the Vicars of Leamington, there was to be made a further allotment of such share of the said two-fifteenths as would be an equivalent and compensation for the final tithes annually accruing from the said commonable fields, etc., and to the said Mathew Wise the residue of the two-fifteenths, in satisfaction of all great and small tithes, moduses and compositions, chargeable upon the land, in addition to which there were to be other allotments of land to the Vicar and Mathew Wise in consideration of their general rights in the Glebe and commonable lands. The Act proceeds:—

"Whereas there are certain messuages, garden allotments, orchards, and ancient incloses on the south and west parts or sides of the river Leam belonging to some of the proprietors of land in the said open and common fields, etc., be it further enacted that the said Commissioners allot such part of the said open and commonable fields as would otherwise be allotted to such proprietors, unto and for the said Mathew Wise, and John Willes, clerk, and his successors the Vicars of Leamington, such plots and parcels of land as in their judgment shall be thought a full compensation to the said Matthew Wise and the aforesaid Vicar respectively for their several and respective tythes, moduses, and composition arising within, or payable out of or in respect of the said messuages, gardens and orchards and ancient inclosures."

And it was further directed that such allotments were to be made and laid contiguous to the other allotments of the said Mathew Wise and the said John Willes, clerk, in consideration of which allotments, the said messuages, gardens, orchards, and ancient inclosures were to be for ever discharged from all tithes whatsoever.

The succeeding clause deals with a class of residents other than the petitioners or claimants whose names have been mentioned. These persons, respecting the number of whom no information is supplied, are described as "being proprietors of one or more close or closes, commonly called by the names of Midsummer and Lammas closes, lying within or adjoining the said fields." If they were desirous of keeping the same, upon notice to that effect being given the Commissioners within a specified time, such close or closes were not to be thrown into Hotch Pot with the rest of the lands and grounds. And in the event of notice being given that these proprietors of Midsummer and Lammas closes wished to retain their own property, it became the duty of the Commissioners to formally allot these closes to their respective owners, "provided they should think it consistent with the general partition and division of the lands intended to be divided and enclosed." This discretionary power was, however, governed by the important provision that nothing contained in the Act was to ex-

tend, or to be construed as extending, to prejudice, lessen, or defeat the right and title of the said John Willes, clerk, and his successors, Vicars of Leamington, "to any oblations, Easter offerings, or surplice fees whatsoever arising or becoming due to him or them, but the same were to remain due and payable to him and his successors the Vicars of the said Parish Church, Leamington."

All lands allotted to the Vicar and his successors were to be inclosed and fenced round the outer boundaries in such manner as the Commissioners should direct "by and at the expense of the several other owners or proprietors of the said open and common fields, etc., and of the proprietors of the said messuages, gardens, orchards and ancient inclosures." The proportion to be paid by each was a matter within the discretion of the Commissioners. After the fences were erected, the expense of keeping them in repair was to be borne by the Vicar and his successors. Other persons to whom lands were inclosed and allotted under the Act were to inclose, hedge, ditch, and fence them at their own expense. After providing for the making of roads, etc., it was directed that the award of the Commissioners, "containing full particulars of the allotments made," should be signed and sealed and inrolled by the Clerk of the Peace for the County of Warwick, or in one of His Majesty's Courts of Record at Westminster " to the end recourse may be had to the same by any person or persons interested in the same intended inclosure (for the inspection and perusal whereof one shilling shall be paid and no more)." The Award, or a copy, signed by the Clerk of the Peace or other proper officer, for which twopence per sheet of seventy-two words was to be paid, was at all times to be admitted and received in all Courts as legal evidence.

Authority was given the Commissioners, and they were required "to ascertain, set out and appoint both public and private roads or ways through the new inclosures and allotments, so to be made, as aforesaid, with the assizes and breadths thereof so as such public roads

and highways shall be and remain sixty feet broad, at the least, between the ditches, (except bridle and foot ways, in case any such shall be set out); which said public roads and highways shall at all times for ever thereafter be repaired and kept in repair by and at the expense of the inhabitants of the said parish of Lemington Priors, in such manner as the other roads or ways within the said parish were repaired and kept in repair before the passing of the Act, and as by the laws of the realm the same ought to be repaired and kept; and in case any private road shall be set out, the same shall be for ever repaired and kept in repair by such persons as the Commissioners shall appoint." After the setting out of such roads it was to be unlawful for the public to use any other roads or ways over the inclosures for foot, horse, cattle or carriage traffic.

In case of contumacy on the part of any allottee, the Commissioners had power to appoint a Receiver to act for him, and to elect Guardians for such as were incapacitated. It was also enacted that the new allotments were to be in bar of all former rights, and from and immediately after making the said divisions and allotments, and the completion of the said Award or instrument in writing, "all right of common belonging to or claimed by all and every the same owners and proprietors or occupiers of messuages, cottages, or tenements, lands, grounds, and other hereditaments, within the manor and parish of Lemington Priors, aforesaid, in, over and upon the said open and common fields, common meadows, and commonable lands, grounds, and premises intended to be inclosed as aforesaid, shall cease, determine, and be for ever extinguished." The remaining clauses relate to questions of a subsidiary, though not altogether of an unimportant nature. For example, the public notice which the Commissioners were required to give of the time, place, and business of their meetings throws a curious light upon the uses to which the pulpits of parish churches were occasionally put in the old times, when printing and the press were but imperfectly developed. They were imperatively directed "to give public notice in the Parish Church of Lemington Priors upon some Sunday, immediately after Divine service, of the time and place of the first meeting of the Commissioners for executing the powers hereby vested in them, at least fourteen days before such meeting, and also give like notice of every subsequent meeting (meetings by adjournment only excepted)."

The provisions for enforcing a rigid observance of the Award were at once prompt and stringent. If a villager allowed his cattle "to go, depasture, or feed on any of the said commonable lands" after the right of common had been extinguished as prescribed in the Act, it became lawful to impound such cattle and impose a fine of ten shillings. From the time of the passing of the Act the lands became vested in the Commissioners; no trees nor hedges could be cut down without their permission; the nature of the crops and cultivation were to be under their direction, "any usage or custom of stocking wild cattle, sowing, cropping, or otherwise managing the tillage to

C the contrary, notwithstanding." On October 10, 1768, all leases at rack-rents ceased, the lessees being entitled to such compensation as the Commissioners should allow for their privilege of growing, cutting, and housing or stacking on their respective farms.

In addition to the specific and particular statutory abolition of common rights which accrued from the making of the Award, another mode of extinction by public notice was directed. The Commissioners were given authority "by a note for that purpose in writing under their hands, to be affixed on any one of the doors of the Parish Church of Lemington Priors aforesaid, to extinguish all rights of common in and over the said open and common fields, common meadows, commonable lands and grounds and premises hereby directed to be inclosed, and then and from and after the time to be mentioned and expressed in such notice, all such right of common shall cease and the same is hereby declared to be utterly extin-

guished."

The Act concludes with a saving clause in favour of the Earl of Aylesford, lord of the manor. Nothing contained in its provisions was to " prejudice, lessen, or defeat his right, title, or interest in the seigniories and royalties belonging to the said manor, and he and his heirs hereafter were to enjoy all rents, services, courts, perquisites, and profits of courts, and all other royalties, rights, and privileges belonging to the manor (excepting rights of common, and the soil and inheritance thereof), in the same manner as though the Enclosure had not been made."

The residence of Benjamin Satchwell. the first Postmaster, with (;ate leading into the fields at the rear, known as the Shell Levs. The cottage stood in New Street, on the site number 2. now occupied by Mr. Madeley Burman, Corn Factor. It was taken down in 1871, Mr. John Blakemore being the owner of the property.

CHAPTER VI. HE Award commences by reciting the general terms of the Enclosure Act, and refers to Edward Willes, Esq., late Chief Baron of His Majesty's Court of Exchequer, Ireland, when the Bill for Enclosure was presented, as since deceased; states that due notice had been given of the first and other meetings; that the Oath prescribed had been taken by the Commissioners, and the lands "properly qualitied" by John Tomlinson. Having perused "and well-considered the said survey, and the several qualitys of the lands intended to be inclosed," and also the "messuages, tenements, and antient inclosures hereinafter allotted and set out in exchange, in accordance with the directions of the said Act;" and "having also heard and duly informed ourselves of the rights and claims of all parties interested in the said open and common fields, common meadows, and commonable lands and grounds, and settled and determined the same and all other matters relating to the Enclosure, the aforesaid Commissioners, by this present Award or instrument, written on parchment, and signed and sealed," awarded and divided the said lands, " containing together in the

whole by statute measure 867 acres, 1 rood, 25 perch, and also the several messuages and old inclosures allotted in exchange," as follow:—

To the Earl of Aylesford two several allotments, containing 21 acres, 3 roods, 3 perch, being (1) a plot of land in Innidge Meadow, 3 acres, 3 roods, 19. perch, and a part of an old inclosure, 1 rood, 2 perch, called Court's Home Close, bounded northwards by the river Leam; eastward and southward by the first allotment to Ann Willes, widow and relict of the said Edward Willes, and the other part of the old inclosure belonging to her, called Court's Home Close; westward by a small part of the road leading to the Mill. (2) A piece of land in Gravel Pit Field, 17 acres, 3 roods, 24 perch; bounded northwards by lands allotted to the Vicar of Lemington, etc., and the turnpike road from Warwick to Southam: eastward and southward by the second allotment to Ann Willes; westward by the allotments to Richard Lyndon and the Vicar, etc. These Awards were "in full recompense, compensation, ami satisfaction for, and in lieu and discharge of all lands and grounds and right of common of and belonging to the said Earl of Aylesford in the lands inclosed, and also of a parcel of old inclosed land, called the Ham, which, before the execution of the Award, belonged to him, but was allotted to Ann Willes (by, and with the consent ami approbation of the said Earl and Ann Willes, signified in writing), in exchange for the small part of the old inclosure, Court's Home Close, and so much of the lands of Ann Willes, in the open and common fields, etc., as was of equal value thereto, which were taken from her and added to his allotments.

The allotments to John Willes, " and his successors, the Vicars of Leamington," were (I) a plot of ground in Gravel Pit Field, 5 acres, o roods, 32 perch, bounded northward by the turnpike road; eastward and southward by lands belonging to the Earl of Aylesford in Gravel Pit Field; westward by lands allotted Richard Lyndon. (2) A parcel of land in Innidge Field and Innidge Meadow, 24 acres, 2 roods, 0 perch, bounded northward by the first allotment to Ann Willes and the Leam; eastward by the Leam, and kinds allotted John Lawrence; southward by the turnpike road; westward by the first allotment to Ann Willes. The hedges, mounds, ditches, and fences of these allotments were to be made by the other proprietors, according to their respective interests, but maintained and kept in repair by the Vicar, etc., from the time of the Award. (3) Another allotment, described as "all that messuage or tenement, with the barn, garden, and premises thereto belonging, then or late in the tenure or occupation of Susannah Bradley, containing 13 square poles," bounded northward by a farm-yard of Ann Willes; eastward by the town street; southward and westward by antient messuages and gardens of Matthew Wise, which said messuages, etc., before the execution of the Award, belonged to him, and, together with other lands of his in the open and common fields, etc., of the yearly value of £1 4s., were taken from him and allotted John Willes, etc., (with the consent of Matthew Wise, of Lemington Priors, John Willes. and Matthew Wise, of the Priory, Warwick) in exchange for the messuage called the Vicaridge House, with the garden and piece of ground thereunto belonging. These two plots were awarded John Willes, etc., out of the open and common fields, etc., and also the said messuage, "in lieu of, and in full recompense, compensation and satisfaction for and in bar and discharge of the Glebe lands and right of common belonging to the Vicaridge, and the vicarial or small tythes yearly arising out of the open and common fields, etc., and also of all the vicarial and small tythes, moduses or compositions arising and payable in respect of the several messuages, gardens, orchards and antient inclosures belonging to the proprietors of the land inclosed, a list of which is given in the schedule annexed, and also of the Vicaridge with its appurtenances, allotted Matthew Wise in exchange, as recited. The Commissioners explained that I acre, part of the first al-

lotment to John Willes, etc., on the east side thereof, was "in lieu of the Glebe lands and right of common belonging to the Vicaridge; and I acre, 25 perch adjoining the last-mentioned acre was in lieu of the vicarial tythes arising from the several messuages, gardens, orchards and antient inclosures belonging to the proprietors of lands in the open and common fields, etc.; and 1 other acre thereof in lieu of the lands and grounds, of the yearly value of £1 4s., taken from Matthew Wise and given John Willes, etc.; and the residue of the first allotment, and the whole of the second, made to John Willes, etc., were for such share of the two-fifteenth parts or residue of the tythahle lands, as the Commissioners adjudged an equivalent and compensation for the small tythes arising from the enclosed fields, etc., which were to be "for ever discharged from the payment of all vicarial or small tythes, moduses and compositions, and all other payments whatsoever usually made in lieu thereof."

The subjoined plots of ground, containing 472 acres, 2 roods, 36 perch, were allotted Matthew Wise, of Lemington Priors:—(1) All that lot of land on the north side of the turnpike road, 97 acres, 1 rood, 6 perch, including an old enclosure belonging to him, called Raven's Close, I acre, 3 roods, 13 perch, and an old enclosure, belonging to Ann Willes, called the Ham Meadow, 2 acres, 2 roods, 31 perch, allotted (with the approval, in writing, of Ann Willes and Matthew Wise) in exchange for lands of his in the open and common fields, etc., of equal value, which were taken from him and added to the allotments made to Ann Willes, bounded northwards by the river Leam, the garden of Matthew Wise, and by the road from his house to the Parish Church; eastward by the garden of Matthew Wise, by a close toft allotted him in exchange for another close awarded John Lawrence, by the farm yard of Matthew Wise, by the piece of land belonging to the Vicaridge House, by an old inclosure belonging to William Abbotts, and by an old inclosure belonging to Matthew Wise; southward by the turn-

pike road and Warwick Common Field; westward by Warwick Field and the stable yard of Matthew Wise. (2) A lot of land on the south side of the turnpike road, being the whole of Malian's Hill Field, High Dadley Field, and part of Mathecroft Field, 186 acres, 2 roods, 20 perch, bounded northwards by land allotted as Charitable Lands of Barford, and the turnpike road; eastward by lands allotted John Lawrence; southward and westward by the Common Fields of Whitnash and Warwick and by the lands allotted to the trustees of the Charitable lands belonging to Barford Parish. (3) The plot of land called Nabbs's Lammas Closes, 4 acres, 3 roods, 20 perch, bounded northward by antient enclosed lands of Matthew Wise and John Lawrence; eastward by a lane Mr. Matthew Wise resided at the Manor House, now the Manor House Hotel, not at Shrubland Hall, the present seat of the family.

called Watery Lane, being part of the land allotted Richard Lyndon; southward and westward by other parts of the allotments to him. (4) A piece of ground on the north side of the turnpike road in Sidenham Meadow, and a small part of the Sidenham Field, 13 acres, I rood, 8 perch, bounded northward by the Leam; eastward by Radbrook; southward by the turnpike road; westward by an allotment to John Lawrence. (5) A parcel of land on the south side of the turnpike road, being part of the Sidenham Field, the whole of Church Hadeland Field, and part of vvhitnash Hill Field and Gravel Pit Field, 170 acres, 2 roods, 22 perch; bounded northward by the turnpike road; eastward by antient enclosed lands within the parish and manor of Radford Semeley; southward by Whitnash Common Fields and land allotted Ann Willes; westward by other lands allotted her. The foregoing "lots, plots, pieces or parcels of land or ground," allotted Matthew Wise out of the open and common fields, etc., and the antient inclosure called the Ham Meadow included therein, were " in lieu of, and in full satisfaction and compensation for, and in bar and discharge of all Impropriate or Great Tythes, moduses or compositions, yearly arising and renewing out of and from the said open fields, etc, and of the said tythes, etc., in respect of messuages, gardens, orchards and antient inclosures lying on the south and west parts or sides of the river Leam, belonging to proprietors of lands in the said open and common fields, etc. , (particularly mentioned in a schedule annexed) and also of the lands and grounds of Matthew Wise, and right of common thereunto belonging, in the said open and common fields," after deducting land of equal value of the antient enclosure called the Ham Meadow, allotted to Ann Willes in exchange for the Ham Meadow, and also, after deducting lands of the yearly value of"l 4s. , allotted John Willes, etc., together with the tenement, barn, garden, and premises in the tenure of Susannah Bradley, in exchange for the Vicaridge House, garden, and land thereto belonging, and appurtenances allotted to Matthew Wise, and also of the common belonging to six cottages of his, " situate, standing, and being in Lemington Priors aforesaid." The part of the last-mentioned allotment in Sidenham Field, Radbrook Furlong, and Church Hadeland Field, 94 acres, 1 rood, ig perch, was allotted " as and for the residue of the two-fifteenth parts of the tythable lands and grounds" not before allotted to John Willes, etc., and four lands on the south side of Fallow Furlong, in Church Hadeland Field, 3 roods, 20 perch, were allotted "in lieu of and in full compensation of all Great and Impropriate Tythes, moduses, or compositions in respect of the said messuages, gardens, orchards and antient inclosures" belonging to the proprietors of lands in the said open and common fields, etc., which payments were for ever to be discharged. The Vicaridge House, with garden and a piece of ground, 1 rood, 38 perch, bounded northward by the farm yard of Matthew Wise; eastward by the town street and gardens of Mary Reading, spinster, and William Abbotts; westward by the first allotment to Matthew Wise. This allotment was made to him (with the written consent of Matthew Wise, of the Priory, War-

wick, and John Willes) in exchange for the messuage, barn, garden and premises in the tenure of Susannah Bradley, and lands of his in the open and common fields, etc., of the yearly value of"i 4s., which had been taken from him and given to John Willes, etc. An old enclosed close of pasture, with the appurtenances, lately belonging to and occupied by John Lawrence, called Satchwell's Close, 1 rood, 26 perch, bounded eastward by the road from the house of Matthew Wise to the Parish Church; southward by his farm yard; west and north-westward by the first allotment to Matthew Wise. This Award (made with the approval, in writing, of Matthew Wise and John Lawrence) was, in exchange for a close of pasture and its appurtenances, known by the name of the Bancroft, formerly occupied by William Jervis, and afterwards by John Lawrence, and now allotted in exchange for the close of pasture allotted Matthew Wise.

The Commissioners awarded Ann Willes the following 194 acres I rood, 34 perch:—(1) A plot of land in Innidge Meadow and Innidge Field, the other part thereof being a Lammas Close, called Shell Leys, 97 acres, 1 rood, 31 perch; bounded northward by a house and garden belonging to John Brookes, by antient inclosures belonging to Matthew Wise and Ann Willes, by the first allotment to the Earl of Aylesford and the river Leam; eastward by the second allotment to John Willes, etc.; southward by the second allotment to the Vicar, etc., by the turnpike road, and by antient inclosures belonging to the said Ann Willes; westward by antient enclosures belonging to Matthew Wise and Ann Willcs; by the town street at a gate leading into an old inclosure belonging to Ann Willes, called the Round Close, and by the first allotment to the Earl of Aylesford. The Commissioners ordered that a watercourse should for ever be carried and conveyed from the town street of Lemington Priors down the lane leading to Innidge Field, being part of the last-described allotment, in, over and through the allotment to Ann Willes in Innidge Field and Innidge

Meadow, to the river Leam, to be maintained and kept by her and the owners and proprietors of the last-described allotment for the time being. (2) A plot of ground, 97 acres, o rood, 3 perch; bounded northward by the second allotment to the Earl of Aylesford, by the turnpike road, and by the fifth allotment to Matthew Wise; eastward by the same allotment; southward by Whitnash Common Field; westward by lands allotted Richard Lyndon and the second allotment to the Earl of Aylesford. Both of which allotments, out of the open and common fields, etc., were "in lieu of and in full satisfaction and compensation and discharge of the lands and grounds belonging to Ann Willes, and right of common after deducting therefrom so much of the land belonging to her, as, with the small part of the inclosure, Court's Home Close, was of equal value to the land called the Ham, allotted her; and also of the old inclosure, the Ham Meadow, which had belonged to her but was granted Matthew Wise, with the consent in writing of all parties, in exchange for lands in the open and common fields, etc., belonging to Matthew Wise, and of equal value to the old inclosure called the Ham Meadow taken from Matthew Wise and added to the allotments of Ann Willes." (3) One common belonging to a cottage of Ann Willes. (4) A piece of old inclosed land called the Ham (exclusive of the fishery thereunto belonging). 3 roods, 38 perch, bounded on all sides by the river Leam. This was allotted with the consent of the Earl of Aylesford and Ann Willes, and was in full satisfaction of the exchange of land, Court's Home Close.

John Lawrence had awarded him the following:—(I) A piece of land in Malian's Hill Brickiln, and Rinill Field, 67 acres, 3 roods, bounded northward by an antient inclosure belonging to him, by lands allotted Richard Lyndon; eastward by an antient inclosure also belonging to John Lawrence, and lands allotted Thomas Aston, by lands allotted Richard Lyndon, and by Whitnash Common Fields; southward by Whitnash Common Fields; westward by a public road awarded and set out through the second allotment to Matthew Wise. By the request of John Lawrence, this allotment was made him in full satisfaction and discharge of his lands and grounds and right of common in the open and common fields, etc., to which he was entitled under the last will and testament of his late uncle, Robert Lawrence. (2) A plot of land in Sidenham Meadow and Sidenham Field, 8 acres, 16 perch, bounded northward by the Leam; eastward by the allotment to Matthew Wise; southward by the turnpike road; westward by the second allotment to John Willes, etc., and the Leam; such allotment being in discharge of all the lands of his in the open and common fields, etc., but not mentioned in his first allotment. (3) An old inclosure of pasture called the Bankcroft, formerly in the tenure of William Jervis and then of John Lawrence, 2 rood, 24 perch, bounded northward by the turnpike road; eastward by antient inclosures belonging to Thomas Aston; southward by lands allotted him; westward by an antient inclosure belonging to John Lawrence; which allotment was made with the approbation of John LawTence and Matthew Wise, and in exchange for a close of pasture before the execution of the Award belonging to John Lawrence, but which had been allotted to Matthew Wise in exchange for this allotment to John Lawrence.

Richard Lyndon had an allotment in the Brickiln and Rinill Fields consisting of 67 acres, 3 roods, 7 perch, bounded northward by land allotted Thomas Aston, by antient inclosures of Richard Lyndon and Sarah Dickens, by the third allotment to Matthew Wise, by the town street; eastward by an antient inclosure belonging to Matthew Wise, by the third allotment to Matthew Wise, by the first allotment to John Willes, etc., the second allotment to the Earl of Aylesford, the second allotment to Ann Willes, and liv the Common F'ield of Whitnash: southward by the said Common Field, and by the first allotment to John Lawrence, by lands allotted Thomas Aston, by the third allotment to Matthew Wise, and by an antient inclosure of John Lawrence; in full satis-

faction of his lands and right of common thereunto belonging in the open and common fields, etc.

A plot of land in Brickiln Field, I acre, I rood, 10 perch, was allotted Thomas Aston, bounded northward by antient enclosures of John Lawrence and Thomas Aston; eastward and southward by the allotment to Richard Lyndon; westward by the first allotment to John Lawrence, in satisfaction for all the lands and right of common thereunto belonging to him and lying in the open and common fields, etc.

The grant to the trustees of Charitable lands belonging to the parish of Barford was a piece of land in Machecroft Field, 8 acres, I rood, 5 perch; bounded northward by the turnpike road, eastward and southward by the second allotment to Matthew Wise, and westward by Warwick Common Field, in full satisfaction and discharge of all the lands belonging to the parish of Barford lying in the said open and common fields, etc.

Respecting the "public and private roads and ways" directed in the Enclosure Act "to be ascertained, set out, and appointed," the Commissioners ordered:— That the ancient public road leading from the north-east corner of Malian's Hill Field, over the second allotment to Matthew Wise in Malian's Hill and High Dadley Field, on the east side of the same fields to a gate at the south-east corner of High Dadley Field leading into Whitnash Common Field, should be and for ever remain of the breadth of 60 feet in every part thereof, as it was then marked and staked out, and be used and continued as a publick waggon and drift road, or highway; the grass and herbage growing thereon for ever to remain for the benefit of Matthew Wise and the owners of his second allotment for the time being.

They further directed that the ancient publick, but then turnpike road leading from the north-east corner of Warwick Way Furlong in Malian's Hill Field, between the first and second allotments to Matthew Wise into Warwick Field, should be and for ever remain of the breadth of 60 feet in every part, and be used as a publick, waggon, drift or high-

way.

Also that the antient publick, but then turnpike road leading from the place where that part of the turnpike road is inclosed and enters the Sidenham Fields, over the field called Sidenham Field to Radbrook, should be and for ever remain of the breadth of 60 feet, and be continued as a publick, waggon and drift, or highway.

A new footpath or highway was to be made from the north-west corner of Gravel Pit Field, in, through and over the first allotment to John Willes, the second allotment to the Earl of Aylesford, and the allotment to Ann Willes on the west side of these several allotments, to a stile leading into Whitnash Common Field on the south-west corner of Whitnash Hill Field, and that it remain for ever of the breadth of 4 feet in every part, and be continued as a publick path or footway; the grass and herbage growing thereon being reserved for the several persons through whose allotments the pathway leads and the proprietors of the allotments respectively.

Lastly, the expenses incurred in obtaining the Act of Parliament, and of the surveying, admeasuring, planning, valuing, dividing and allotting the open and common fields, etc., and the preparing and inrolling the Award, and all other charges, amounting to the sum of £571 6s. 6d., were thus appointed to be paid by the allottees:— REFERENCES.

1 The Mill and Cottage in Mill Yard, still standing. 2 Richard Court's Farm House, on site of Brighton

House, Mill Street.

3 Old Post Office, Benjamin Satchwell's Residence, behind the site of Mr. Alfred Blakemore's Furniture Warehouse. 4 Cottages and Gardens, now Burying Ground. Chapel 5 Farm Buildings & Riokyard, site of Lady Huntingdon's b Thomas Abbotts' Farm House, site of Mr. Reynolds'

Furniture Repository. The kitchen remains.

7 The old Parish Church. 8 Dawkes' Cottages, in present Churchyard, and near Old Well 9 The Old Well, on waste land by the roadside. 10 Barns A farm

buildings of Thos. Abbotts with orchard adjoining. 11 House in Church Lane, afterwards used as ironmonger's shop by Mr. Flavell.

12 The Old Vicarage in Church Lane, on site of Messrs. Avery's shop. 13 House opposite Vicarage, still standing. 14 Cottages near the Vicarage. 15 The old Bowling-Green public house. 18 Cottages on site of Mr. Franois' butoher's shop, with Tailor Brown's house at the oorner, and other cottages facing the London Road. 17 Farmer Whitehead's residence, now the George Inn. 18 Buildings in rear of Whitehead'!

Farm, now standing.

19 Parish Poor House, and Parish Field. 20 Tidmas' Cottage. 21 Boyes' Cottage. 22 Cottages in rear of pond (present Town Hall). remains. 23 Cottages in Savage's Yard, one of these 24 Smith's shop. The village stocks and the Pound were in close proximity. 25 The Cottages of Kingerlee and others. 26 Residence of Farmer Lewis. 27 The Dog Inn, residence of William

Abbotts, originator of Leam'tn Baths 28 Cottages in Bath Lane, ocoupied by Mr. Wise's labourers.

29 Cottages occupied by labourers, near the Chapel in Spencer Street. 30 Bobbins' Cottages, still standing. 31 Woodbine Cottage, residence of Mr. 32 Abbotts' field and cottage. Robbins. 33 Well House. 34 Cottage occupying site of present

Gordon House.

Re-printed By Permission-Fro *This rcftrs to the old Town Hall, Hick St*

John Parry, of the Borough of Warwick, gentleman, was appointed to "ask, demand, sue, recover," and receive the said several sums, the same to be paid before the 1st Jany., 1769. The Award was signed on the 22nd of December, 1768, "at a public meeting, held at the house of Simon Hinton, commonly known by the name of the 'bowling Green House,' " of which meeting "we caused due notice to be given in the Parish Church of Lemington Priors."

In the foregoing synopsis, the phrase "Vicar, etc.," is an abbreviation for "John Willes and his successors the Vicars of Lemington," and "open and common fields, etc.," for "open and common fields, common meadows and commonable lands and grounds." All the measurements were exclusive of roads, and each allottee, excepting the Vicar, was required at his own cost to make the hedges, mounds, ditches and fences rendered necessary by the land awarded him. The boundaries of the allotments have been given upon the advice of residents more competent than ourselves to estimate correctly their real historic value. Frequent references are to be found in the boundaries descriptive of one allotment to the allotments of other allottees. To make these clear and readily accessible, we have supplied the figures in parentheses.

Subjoined is the schedule of messuages, gardens, orchards, and ancient inclosures, discharged by the Award from future payment of all tithes, in consideration of the grants to Matthew Wise and the Vicars of Leamington:—

The Mill House, and Stable, occupied by Frances Satchwell, widow, and a small part of Court's Home Close, belonging to the Earl of Aylesford, 1 rood, 6 perch. Messuage, buildings, garden, brickyard and close, belonging to and occupied by Frances Satchwell, I acre, 1 rood, 1 perch. Messuage, yard, and garden belonging to and occupied by William Webb, 3 perch. Messuage, yard and garden, belonging to and occupied by Thomas Roberts, 8 perch. Messuage, outbuildings, yard, and garden, occupied by Susanna Bradley, and belonging to the Rev. John Willes, Clerk, 13 perch. Messuage, outbuildings, yard, garden and land, belonging to and occupied by Matthew Wise, 2 acres, 2 roods, 13 perch. A toft, called Satchwell's Close, occupied by Matthew Wise, I rood, 26 perch. A yard, barn, rickyard, etc., occupied by Matthew Wise, I rood, 23 perch. Messuage called Vicaridge House, with outbuilding, garden, and land thereto belonging, I rood, 38 perch. A piece of ground, lately two closes, called Bancroft, in the occupation and belonging to John Lawrence, I acre, 3 roods, 1 perch. Yard, barns therein, garden, piece of ground whereon stood two messuages, which have lately been destroyed by fire, in the occupation of John Lawrence,

I rood, 32 perch. An orchard adjoining the Watery Lane, in the occupation of John Lawrence, 2 roods, II perch. Messuage with out-buildings, garden, yard, rickyard and close, belonging to and in the occupation of Simon Corbett, 1 acre, 3 roods. A close of antient inclosed land, lately planted with fruit trees, belonging to and occupied by Matthew Wise, 2 acres, o rood, 20 perch. Four messuages, with the outbuildings, yards, and gardens adjoining together, the property of Matthew Wise, and occupied by Mary Rose, Richard Righton, John Ratnate and John Watts, 1 rood, 26 perch. A barn, and close of land thereunto adjoining, called Nan Willes's Close, belonging to and occupied by Matthew Wise, I acre, 3 roods, 16 perch. Two barns, two yards and a close or parcel of ground adjoining thereto and also to the last-mentioned close, called Nan Willes's Close, in the occupation of Matthew Wise and William Jervis, 1 acre. Messuage, outbuildings, yard, garden, and rickyard adjoining a close called Shell Leys, occupied by William Jervis, 1 acre, I rood, 2 perch. Messuage and outbuildings called the Bowling Green House, with the garden, bowling green and land thereto belonging, occupied by Simon Hinton, 3 roods, 24 perch. Messuage, outbuildings, yard and garden in the occupation of Thomas Amjon, 12 perch. Messuage, outbuildings, gardens, yards, rickyards, close or parcel of land thereunto adjoining, and belonging with the osier bed adjoining and occupied by Thomas Abbotts, 2 acres, 3 roods, 38 perch. Messuage, outbuildings, garden and land belonging to Thomas Makepeace and in his occupation, I rood, 39 perch. Barn, outhouse, yard, garden, belonging to and in the occupation of Thomas Abbotts, I acre, 3 roods, 27 perch. Messuage, outbuildings, garden and close of land belonging to and in the occupation of William Tredgold, the elder, 1 rood, 37 perch. Two closes called Raven Close and the Ham Meadow, 4 acres, 2 roods, 4 perch. Messuage, outbuildings, yard, garden and rickyard belonging to and in the occupation of Ann Willes, 1 acre, o rood, 18 perch. Close of land belonging to the last-mentioned tenement adjoining Shell Leys, occupied by Ann Willes, I acre, o rood, 29 perch. Messuage, outbuildings, yard, garden, rickyard and close, being the remainder of Court's Home Close, in the occupation of William Court, 3 acres, o rood, 36 perch. A piece or parcel of land called the Ham, allotted in the Award to Ann Willes, 3 roods, 3 perch. Messuage, outbuildings, yard, orchard, garden and rickyard, belonging to John Lawrence and in his occupation, 1 acre, o rood, 30 perch. Messuage, outbuildings, yard, garden, orchard and land, belonging to Thomas Aston and occupied by Robert Evans, 3 roods, I perch.

The witnesses to the signing of the Award were Thomas Abbotts, John Parry, and Robert Abbey, servant to Job Baseley. The following certificate of acceptance was handed to the Commissioners:—

"We whose names are hereunto inscribed, being the proprietors of, or persons interested in the several messuages, tenements, gardens, lands and antient inclosures in and by the written Award or instrument in writing, allotted in exchange as therein is particularly mentioned, do hereby severally and respectively signify and declare on each and every of our consent and approbation to all and every the exchange and exchanges therein mentioned. Witness our hands this twenty-first day of December, in the year of our Lord one thousand seven hundred and sixty-eight: Matt. Wise; Ann Willes; Matt. Wise, Lemington Priors; J. Willes, Vicar; John Lawrence."

The last paragraph of the Award certifies that notice of the first meeting of the Commissioners was given in the Parish Church, on Sunday the 13th day of March, immediately after Divine Service, to be holden at the house of Simon Hinton, known by the name of the Bowling Green House, on the 3ist day of March, 1768, at which first meeting, immediately before commencing business, the Commissioners separately took the following Oath:—

"I, A.B., do swear that I will faithfully, impartially and honestly, according to the best of my skill and judgment, execute the several powers and trusts reposed in me as a Commissioner for dividing and allotting and inclosing the open and common fields, common meadows and commonable lands lying on the south and west parts or sides of the river Leam in the manor and parish of Lemington Priors, in the County of Warwick, and join with the other acting Commissioners in making just and proportionate allotments thereof to the several parties interested according to their respective rights therein, and that without favour or affection to any of them."

On September 29, 1769, the Award was inrolled by T. Beardsley, Clerk of the Peace for the County of Warwick.

CHAPTER VII.

N the dilapidated archives of antique Leamington there is no treasure more richly archaic than the Award, authorised by the Enclosure Act, 8 Geo. III., formulated, signed and sealed in 1768, and inrolled in 1769. It at once determined a public patrimony in waste lands which was venerable before the fame of the waters reached Rome in the twelfth century; before the foundations of the Parish Church were laid in an earlier age, and ante-dated by many generations the first form of local government in England. Legislatively, the Award was associated with at least six centuries of English history, in the revolving years of which the enclosure of commonable lands had been carried on with tireless zeal, and upon a scale of surpassing magnitude. From its modern aspect emanated iridescent beams, luminously prescient of the approaching advent of an age of prosperity, beneath the benign influence of which a Royal borough, with gardens of fadeless beauty, fountains at which health satisfies its cravings, the chosen home of fashion, wealth, and culture, would supplant the blowing woodlands and the breezy heaths on the banks of the Leam. The story of these annexations is one of centuries of conflicts in which there were many truces but no peace; in which Parliament was repeatedly compelled to in-

tervene, at one time in the interests of lords of manors; at another in defence of those of the public. The barometer of legislation from the thirteenth to the nineteenth century on enclosures has ranged from partial sanction to large approval, and from limited restriction to perfect prohibition.

The first enclosures were made under a claim that all unenclosed waste land belonged by constitutional right to the owners of adjoining enclosed lands. This doctrine gave rise to an exciting paleozoic controversy, in which the jurists of the Middle Ages found ample scope for the exercise of their acumen and the display of their abilities. To compose the strife, Parliament passed the Statute of Merton in 1235, by which enclosures of waste lands were legalised, provided in each case sufficient pasture was left for the public use, with proper egress and ingress. The principle was confirmed by the Statute of Westminster the second in 1285; but the compromise effected was not of permanent duration. In 1642, an enclosure of waste lands at the Soke of Somersham, near St. Ives, Huntingdonshire, by the Queen, led to loud complaints by the tenants, and a Parliamentary enquiry by Committee. Mr. Hyde, afterwards ennobled as the Earl of Clarendon, was chairman, and Oliver Cromwell one of the members. Cromwell, at this time, a plain Huntingdonshire farmer and Member of Parliament, had not commenced the toil of that acclivous path which conducted him to the dazzling and perilous heights of the Lord Protectorship. The enquiry took place in the Queen's Court, where between Hyde and Cromwell there were many stormy scenes. Clarendon has left an account of Cromwell's conduct in language very peppery, and strongly pickled with contempt and reprehension, but Carlyle tells the story in another way. "Cromwell knew this Soke of Somersham, near St. Ives, very well; knew these poor rustics, and what treatment they had got, and wished, not in the imperturbablest manner, it would seem, to see justice done to them." Enclosures by special Acts of Parliament were established in the reign of Queen Anne, the first being passed in 1710. It was under this system that the Leamington Enclosure Act and Award were obtained. Encouraged by Parliament, and fostered by the increased value of the land, the Enclosure Bills rose from hundreds to thousands, and commons of vast extent were absorbed all over England.

VIEW OF MILVERTON EPISCOPAL CHAPEL, Popularly known as the "Pepper Box Chapel," with the fields in front at the time of its erection in 1835-6. It was purchased by Mr. G. F. Smith, builder, Milverton, and pulled down in 1880.

Open and willing as was the ear which Parliament lent to these applications, it was soon discovered that the improved productivity of the soil and the higher wages permanently secured to one section of the labouring class were not unmixed blessings. In 1775, a change for the worse was observed in the general condition of the rural population, one of the causes for which was assigned to be " the loss of privileges by the enclosure of commons." To prevent further deterioration and secure improvement, Parliament had recourse to two remedies, not immediately, but after prolonged deliberation and delay. The first was to cast upon the ratepayers the cost and responsibility of providing land in substitution for that which had been lost by enclosure. The Act 59 Geo. III., c. 19, ss. 12 and 13, passed in 1819, gave permissive power to churchwardens and overseers, with the consent of the vestry, to obtain by purchase or lease not more than twenty acres of land, to be rented to the poor on reasonable terms. In 1831, by 1 and 2, William IV., c. 42, the quantity was increased to fifty acres. We need not stay to explain that this optional benevolence was not attended with the desired result. The second and more equitable plan was included in the General Enclosure Act, 8 and 9 Vict., c. 118, s. 50, which created for the holders of freehold cottages, and all residents who had been users of commons and waste lands for twenty years, a title to compensation in case of enclosure. This confirmation of the doctrine laid down

in the Statutes of Merton and Westminster was expanded upon still more popular principles by the General Enclosure Act, 8 and 9 Vict., c. 118, ss. 31, 108, wherein all special qualifications of time, property and usership were extended in favour of the prospective interests of the whole of the inhabitants of the parish, and what was equally important, in the new code of claims, recreation appears for the first time as a legitimate object for which to make provision. Before commons and waste lands could be enclosed, the sanction of the Enclosure Commissioners had to be obtained, and one of the powers conferred upon them was that of requiring "the appropriation of an allotment for exercise and recreation for the inhabitants of the neighbourhood." The sizes of such allotments were to be four, five, eight, or ten acres, according to the population. The idea in the mind of Parliament seems to have been the establishment of public parks, free for all, as the best possible form of compensation for the losses some had sustained through enclosure. Small parks having thus been conceded to small towns, large parks could not be withheld from the cities and the boroughs. The density of the populations, and the rapidity with which all open spaces were coming within possession of the golden tentacles of commerce, rendered it necessary that they should be exempted from the enterprise of the speculative builders. In 1866 the Metropolitan Commons Act prohibited the enclosure of commons within the Metropolitan area, a restriction which was applied to Lammas lands by an Amending Act in 1869. But the most beneficent measure was reserved for 1893. 1he Commons Amendment Act of that year sequestrates the whole of the waste lands of England from enclosure, except upon the hardly possible condition of proof that it is for the public benefit. And such advantage, it is material to note, must be local and special in its effect, not general nor remote; something resulting from the enclosure, immediatelv and directly.

In the completion of this cycle of statutory enactments on the enclosure

system, it will be seen that the Mertonian acknowledgment of public rights in waste lands has survived every modification of the law, and, like an imperishable seed, has flourished, no matter what the nature of the soil in which it was sown. But while resisting decay, its development has been essentially affected by modern ideas, and its course directed into new channels. " The early legislation aimed solely at physical results, but the inspiring motive of the wholesale enfranchisement of rich and poor, and the prohibition of all future encroachments, is furnished by recreative, health, and aesthetic considerations. For the public losses have not been confined to mere questions of ownership. The Fine Arts and the Muses were greatly impoverished by deprivation of idyllic treasures of priceless value—Claude-like landscapes in the presence of which artists, tourists, and travellers loved to dwell "in the sweet of the year," and fondly lingered until the days grew short and the shadows long; groves, carpeted with flowers of many hues, and canopied with foliage, in colour and motion like an emerald sea beneath the sunlight of spring; in autumn glowing with the brilliance of burnished gold; woods whispering welcomes and vibrant with the melodies of birds, to whose matins and vespers rills and rivulets responded with symphony and tinkling orchestral accompaniment; winding rustic lanes, broad-belted with gorse, wild ferns and grasses, and shaded with centenarian oaks, festooned with mistletoe and ivy: undulating heaths, amid whose sweet odours the poor wandered in quest of health, and the enrapt artist in search of those delicately sun-wrought tints, the faithful transfer of which to canvas has ever been one of the proudest ambitions of genius. It is quite as much for the conservation of these collections of natural treasures as for the material improvement of the masses that Parliament has wisely appointed limits, within the bounds of which they are for ever sacred from trespass and appropriation.

Travelling far from the Leamington Award as this greatly abbreviated account of the enclosure system may be considered, it is necessary, in order to comprehend clearly how far the distribution and allocation of the land enclosed harmonised with the spirit of legislation, which, as shown, was always favourable to an enlargement of the advantages of the public. It may be further observed that the subject in itself is an important branch of knowledge, and that the dullest page in English history is not the one on which is unfolded the story of the enclosure of commons. In consequence of the peculiar position of the village, the widespread distress among the poorest sections of the rural population, partly traceable to the loss of common rights of pasturage, does not appear to have reached Leamington. Long before the effects of the enclosure in this direction could possibly become manifest, a new state of things had arisen. The immediate result of the Award was the improvement of the local labour market to the extent of more employment, and possibly at better wages; and by the time the work of fencing, ditching, draining, hedging, and road making for the new allotments was finished, visitors were beginning to arrive, and the village had fairly started out with brisk steps on its journey towards Municipalisation. The enclosure was perfectly legal in form, and the distribution bears the impress of honesty of purpose, but the notice to the publicwas made when not many would hear and but few understand its import. One, plainly written or printed and affixed to the church doors, the plan afterwards adopted for intimating to the public that the land was enclosed, would have been more satisfactory than a verbal statement to the small congregation just as they were leaving their seats and retiring from the church But the Enclosure Act did not oblige the Commissioners to supply those ample preliminary particulars at present compulsory in such cases. A formal announcement, penurious in words almost to beggary, and frugal of information almost to total abstinence, would have been a sufficient compliance. The chief cause of the comments which the Award has occa-

sioned is the disregard shown of the public interests. There was sufficient land to compensate the reasonable claims of all parties, without excluding from participation in its benefits the most necessitous classes. A moderate allowance for the free use of the tenant farmers and the cottagers Public notices of projected Enclosures must now be inserted in the local newspapers for three months.
would have secured a feeling of gratitude, and have prevented discontent. The Statute of Merton was as efficacious in 1768 as in 1235, and an application to the Commissioners under its provisions would probably have led to a different arrangement—one more consonant with the spirit of the progressive legislation which had preceded it; more agreeable to the villagers of that time, and the burgesses of this, and in no way injurious to the rights and vested interests of the promoters of the Enclosure. It has been well remarked by the *Leamington Chronicle* that, "although the Award was not obtained from motives altogether unselfish, some credit is due to the landlords of that day who reaped a rich reward from its operation, and their successors, for having willingly assisted in the various schemes of improvement which were carried out when the dawn of Leamington's prosperity set in." Whatever diversity of opinion may exist as to the policy of the Award, few will deny that
Lord Aylesford, by his dedication of the Old Well to the free use of the poor for ever, and Mr. Edward Willes, by the concession to the town of the Jephson Gardens, upon nominal terms, have earned a warmth of gratitude which has been properly acknowledged on all occasions and by all parties. The late Mr. Matthew Wise on several occasions subscribed liberally to the church and other institutions, and for many years was a member of the old Board of Commissioners. It should also be borne in mind that there may have been money compensation to the tenants, which sometimes accompanied the Enclosures of Commons, in which case the cause for complaint would be small, if it exist-

ed at all. The most satisfactory point is to know that the change in the circumstances of Leamington at the time prevented any serious losses to the public, and though some were made richer, the town in a few years was none the poorer.

One result was beneficial to all. The commutation of the tithes, in consideration of the grant of land, proved to be a relief welcome in *every* home, and was as much an advantage to the Church as to the parish. The tithing system was an incubus upon the business of the farmer, deprived him of a considerable amount of the profits of his trade, and in rural parishes was the yeast which kept in a state of perpetual fermentation a feeling of hostility to the Church. When we remember the many taxes and charges then imposed, and the poverty of the time, we can imagine that the parishioners of Leamington in 1768 may have readily considered exemption for ever from the exaction of tithes a sufficient compensation for the loss of their rights and privileges in the open fields and commonable lands.

A concise description of the allotments will, no doubt, prove more serviceable to our readers than the technical details of the Award. The first to Lord Aylesford was the field between the old Mill and the Willes Road; the second, the farm in Mill Street; the third, the land recently sold for building new houses in Clapham Terrace; the land on the east side of the Warneford Hospital, purchased by the Governors of that institution; and the land beyond the canal, just bought by the Corporation for a Recreation Ground. The first allotment to the Vicar was the land on the west side of the Hospital, which became known as the Parish Field, and being sold a few years since to Mr. Councillor William Dawkes, he erected thereon the houses forming Camberwell Terrace; the second, the Allotment Gardens abutting the Radford Road, and the meadow rented by the Corporation, and third, the Vicarage, now number 8, Church Street, occupied by G. Main and Co. The first allotment to Mr. Matthew Wise was the land between the New

River Walk and the Old Warwick Road; the second, the Shrubland Estate; third, the land on which Flavel's Kitchener Works stand, and surrounding streets; fourth, the meadow beyond the Allotment Gardens on the Radford Road, and fifth, the Sydenham farm. Mrs. Ann Willes's first allotment consisted of the land forming Leam Terrace, New Street, and Russell Terrace; the second was Rushmore farm. No information can be obtained of the third, the boundaries being omitted from the Award. The fourth was the large island opposite Newbold Comyn. The locality of John Lawrence's allotment was the Whitnash boundary; the grants to Richard Lyndon were near the Cemetery and the Windmill, and the one to Thomas Aston in Grove Place. The lands allotted the Barford Charity were on the Old Warwick Road, near Myton. These sites may vary a little from the actual boundaries, but substantially they will be found correct. It is to Mr. Councillor William Dawkes, an excellent authority in all matters respecting the history of the town, that we are indebted for these and many other interesting particulars.

With the view of imparting variety to a topic from which brevity has been excluded by novelty and importance, we conclude this chapter with a few selections from the well-stored magazine of ancient Leamington. The little bridge which feebly spanned the Leam in the old times was frequently a source of trouble to its owners, the County. It appears in the Orders of the Court of Quarter Sessions as the "Lemintone and Leminton Bridge," new orthographical variants of the many spellings Leamington has undergone. At the Trinity Quarter Sessions (23 Charles I.) there was a minute to this effect:

D

"The Court was informed that there issues, amounting to the sum of 47s. and costs, imposed upon the inhabitants of the Hundred of Knightloe for not repayring Lemintone Bridge in this countie; that the said sum was levied upon the goods of Richard Hanyood of Dunchurch, and ought to have been upon the inhabitants of the whole Hun-

dred. It was ordered that a levy be forthwith made on the said Hundred, and that the said R. Hanyood be repaid the said sum, together with such reasonable costs and charges as he had expended in this behalf." Several boroughs and towns in the County in 1651 refused to pay their proportions to the repairs of Leminton and Edmonscote Bridges, in consequence of which they were reported at the Easter Quarter Sessions of that year. Orders to repair the bridge "at the charge of the whole County" were made at the Trinity Quarter Sessions, 1669; Michaelmas, 1669; Easter, 1679; Trinity, 1679; Easter, 1684; Trinity, 1684; Epiphany, 1696; and Trinity, 1709; and at the Epiphany Sessions, 1709, it was Ordered, "That Edward Willes be reimbursed certain monies expended by him for the bridge." Another order to repair was made at the Easter Sessions, 1718.

In F. White & Co.'s "Warwickshire" for 1850 the origin of the Barford Charitable lands is thus described:—

"John Beale, by Will, 1672, gave £60, which was laid out in the purchase of land in Leamington Priors. By the award of the Leamington Inclosure Act, dated December 22nd, 1768, a parcel of land, containing 8a. ir. 5p. (was granted) to the trustees of Charitable lands in the parish of Barford. By an indenture of bargain and sale, 26th August, 1807, two closes of the above land, containing 7a. 2r. 27p. of the yearly value of £12 were exchanged for 8a. 3r. 2op. of land of the yearly value of £20 situate in the parish of Kenilworth. A small portion of the Leamington (land) was taken previous to the exchange for the purpose of the Warwick and Napton Canal, for which the company pay an annual rent of £1 14s. 8d. to the trustees. The land in Kenilworth is now let for the annual rent of 20, which sum and the £1 14s. 8d. are applied towards the maintenance of a free school at Barford."

Until the site and quantity of the land originally purchased are known, no opinion can be expressed of the nature of the bargain the trustees made.

SOᶠTH VIEW OF BENJAMIN SATCHWELL'S COTTAGE IN NEW STREET. The small wheel and weight under the gable

represent a contrivance of Satchwell's for turning his spit. CHAPTER VIII.

N the 14th of January, 1784, occurred one of those events which are often the pivots around which the histories of communities revolve. Two men, then in comparatively humble circumstances of life, emerged from their native obscurity—their "hoddin gray and a' that"—advanced to the footlights, and, with realistic success, played the leading characters in the fourth Act of the village drama. Impartially has posterity awarded them the " od'rous chaplets " of the " Founders of the Spa," but one, with a self-abnegation rare in the annals of biography, has ascribed to the other the whole of his own share of the merit. Since 1730 the fame of the Leamington water had been gradually widening in the adjacent villages of Whitnash, Tachbrook, Radford, Cubbington, Offchurch, and Milverton. Frequently were there to be seen on Sundays, men, women and children trending their way across the green fields, when the bells were chiming for church, for supplies from the spring, which at that time spontaneously flowed in large quantities from a fissure in the rock into an open ditch. Thence it found its way to the river across the land now forming the west end of the churchyard, and the site of the Post Office. At the spring they filled their earthenware pots, their bottles of wood and leather, and after exchanging accounts of the cures they had experienced or known, returned home, treasure laden, to their expectant families. This small export trade was accompanied by a local faith of enormous dimensions. From two to three quarts per diem is the quantity Dr. Short estimates to have been imbibed by the villagers. Better testimony to the perennial store could not be desired by the most enthusiastic believer in the Spa, and after applying to his report the customary grain of salt, sufficient remains to prove the non-injurious effects of the water, even when taken generously without medical advice. The enclosure of the commonable lands, the rearrangement of the various properties within their area; the pilgrimages to the shrine from places far and near, combined to paint for the village a future spanned by the bow of hope and promise. But, for the realisation of this hope, and the fulfilment of this promise, baths were needed. To that subject Benjamin Satchwell and William Abbotts applied themselves with zeal, with perseverance, and happily with success.

Of the time when the Satchwells immigrated to Leamington, and the part of the country where they had previously resided, history is silent. The Hearth Tax Returns for 1662 and 1663, show that they were not here in those years. It is at a vestry meeting held on Oct. 20th, 1702, we make our first acquaintance with the familiar and popular name. The "mounds" round the churchyard needing repairs, a meeting of the "freeholders and inhabitants" was convened to take the subject into consideration. Joseph Previous to the appointment of the Board of Commissioners in 1825, there was no wall round the Churchyard. The enclosure, described as " mounds," consisted of heaps of stones, palings, the walls of cottages, etc.

Satchwell was present, and was one of ten who signed the decision at which the meeting arrived. He also appeared at vestry meetings held in 1710 and 1712, on both of which occasions he again signed the minutes. A reference to dates leaves small room for doubt that this Joseph Satchwell was the grandfather, and the first of the family who settled in Leamington. The important local position of the Satchwells may be inferred from their having filled the office of estate bailiffs to the lords of the Manor from the beginning of the seventeenth century. Socially, they were not many degrees below the vicars; but they were much more exalted than the churchwardens, who in ST. LUKES CHUKCH, HOLLY WALK.

Built as a Congregational Chapel in 1849, and opened for public worship on October 25 of that year; purchased by St. Luke's congregation (Church of England) in 1X1)5. The dedicatory services were held on

February 16, 1896.

village life usually rank next in dignity to the clergyman. In their hereditary office they were the intermediaries between the tenants and the agent; from their decisions in labour questions there was no appeal to the estate office at Offchurch. A front pew in the gallery of a parish church has from time immemorial been looked upon as the visible sign of parochial respectability and influence. This was one of their possessions.

They resided at the Mill, where probably Ben's father, William Satchwell, was born, somewhere about the year when grandfather Joseph was sitting in the assembly of freeholders and inhabitants at the vestry meeting of the Parish Church. The Mill continued to be their home until after the Award in 1768, when Ben, who was married in 1764 to Mary Whitmore, took his widowed mother to his cottage at the end of New Street, and provided for her comforts during the remainder of her life. The family consisted of five sons and a daughter: Joseph, born December 8, 1726; Thomas, February 7, 1729; William, February 18, 1730; Benjamin, "ye younger son of William and Frances Satchwell, on the 3rd and baptised the 16th of January, 1732;" John, July 8, 1736, and Man', March 16, 1737. Ever since the days of Homer, the nativities of famous men have been prolific of disputes and rival contentions, but Satchwell stands pre-eminent in having been the subject of controversy in respect of the end as well as the beginning of his life. 'Three places have been suggested as possessing the honour of his birth, and two deaths are assigned him separated by an interval of five years (1810 and 1815). He also belonged to a generation one of whose years consisted of nine months only.

The materials bequeathed to posterity of his life are scant, and rather adapted to an outline than a portrait in detail. The colour of his eyes and hair and the tones of his voice; his gait and address and the food to which he was most partial; the number of hours of sleep he found necessary and his experience of the effects of tobacco, with similar minutiae which biographers collect with

avidity and readers consume as sweet morsels, are lost, irrecoverably. But all the essentials have been preserved. Devotion to the welfare of the village, a desire to make himself useful among his neighbours; conciliatory and philanthropic in his disposition; filial affection very strongly marked, and a faith in the efficacy of the water which bordered upon superstition, were the main elements of his nature. He wrote poetry, but of what kind we are unable to say, as sufficient is not extant to justify an estimate of its merits or defects. Only two examples have come under our notice; one the verse which has already appeared in these pages; the other being a dedicatory poem to his friend Mr. Pratt. The quality of his song has been compared by one of his admirers to that of a bird in a state of freedom, "warbling its native wood-notes wild." This eulogium must be taken on credit, for the public arc not likely to ever have an opportunity of forming an opinion as to his general powers of versification and illustration; his sensibility to the delights of honeyed cadences; nor his capacity for expressing himself in graceful and tuneful numbers. Before he had reached the age of fourteen his father died, and to prepare him for the battle of life, young Ben was apprenticed to Edward Whitehead, of Offchurch, a shoemaker in a small way of business. The choice seems to have been wisely made, for the master having some literary taste, fostered in the apprentice the latent desire to become a scholar. The books accessible to the lad were few, but of those he made the most and the best use. Small rewards of money were given him from time to time by his master for the satisfactory progress he was making in his trade and self-tuition. With the funds thus acquired he replenished his small library, and when unable to make further purchases, borrowed old newspapers and books, which were gladly lent him by the villagers.

In 1753, his indentures of apprenticeship having been completed, he returned to Leamington, and went to reside with his mother at the Mill. He was master of a trade, useful though humble;

he was tolerably proficient in reading, writing, and arithmetic; his mind was thoroughly furnished with an excellent store of general knowledge which qualified him for the position of the village oracle. That tide in the affairs of men, which, taken at the flood, leads on to fortune, had now reached him. The village, containing an estimated population of nearly three hundred, was a field ample for his industry and enterprise. The respect in which the family was held brought him customers in plenty, whose confidence he repaid by a character of workmanship which earned for him the title of an "honest mender of boots and shoes." His learning, his resource, and his manly common sense, constituted him the adviser in general to the villagers; the unanimously-chosen arbiter in local quarrels. Often while the great wheel outside his shop was churning the placid waters of the Leam into billowy surf and foam, "Master Ben," as he was familiarly styled, was holding Court within, listening with presidential dignity to his neighbours' disputes, and amicably pouring oil upon the troubled waters which threatened to embitter the life of the village. Between 1753 and 1764, the date of his marriage, he had saved the very handsome sum of £200, £70 of which he lent to a man named Brooks, on mortgage of the cottage in New Street and the land at the back, afterwards named Satchwell Place, and by subsequently advancing another £50, he became owner of the property in fee simple.

Among his friendships, which were many, one was assimilated to a family relationship in its closeness, durability and intensity. William Abbotts, often confused by the Guideographers with Thomas Abbotts, the farmer who occupied the farmhouse where the Post Office and Reynolds's Furniture Repository are, was landlord of the Black Dog, a snug little country public on the south side of the turnpike road opposite Church Street. He was born at Long Itchington in 1736, and had the misfortune to lose both his father and mother while he was quite young. An uncle, who was keeper of the woods at Bird-

ingbury, belonging to Sir Theophilus Biddulph, took him under his care, and at his death left him some landed property in Lillington Lane, whereon the first baths were erected. Shortly after the death of his uncle he removed from Birdingbury to Leamington, and became the landlord of the Black Dog. Between Satchwell and Abbotts there was an affinity on one subject which blended their natures and made them more like brothers than neighbours. Friendships based upon reciprocal benefits and worldly considerations are liable to be snapped asunder by the most trivial misunderstandings, and to degenerate into implacable hatreds, but the sharers of a germinating faith rarely become estranged. Satchwell's imagination had been fired in early life with the belief that the village would be superseded by a town, to the importance of which he could prescribe no limits. In his fervid vision, the cottages were already potentially the palaces of the future; the narrow lanes and footpaths, wide streets thronged with visitors from every country; gorgeous shops were taking the place of hedgerows, and mansions, terraces and parades were rising with magical celerity in all directions over the pastoral meads of the village. With his mind imbued with this rosy dream, he was an enthusiast, and in Abbotts found a listener, responsive,

Facsimile of Satchwell's signature, from a Valuation for Administration in the possession of Mrs. Wilks, No. 8, Church Terrace. Mr. G. W. Grove, 7, Warwick Street, ironmonger, also has a Deed of Conveyance signed by Satchwell.

appreciative and sympathetic. The ideal of the one immediately became a co-partnership with an unlimited liability of service devolving upon the principals. There were many exciting conversations on the subject in the cosy parlour at the Dog Inn; much prospecting in the fields and lanes for a second spring, and schemes, projected with a feeling of confidence in their success resolved themselves into airy nothings when submitted to practical tests.

But the speculative, the distant, and,

it might be, the impracticable, were not allowed by Satchwell to exclude public work, immediate and realisable. The side-lights of tradition reveal him to us as ceaselessly busy in solving problems which have a fascinating interest for the superior intelligence of the present age. It is with no ordinary feelings of surprise we see him towards the end of the eighteenth century setting in motion the rude machinery of some elementary form of village government and controlling and regulating its movements; establishing a Friendly Society; reporting for the London and Coventry papers every local event likely to improve the prosperity of the village, chronicling in ecstacies of delight imaginary and real cures effected by the waters, and writing poetry, of which we may reasonably believe there is much that is worse in the world and a great deal that is better. No account has been handed down of the pleasant evenings spent at the Dog Inn, but from what has been transmitted to us of the customs of rural life in the pre-railway days, it is not derogatory to believe that on many a winter's evening Mr. Matthew Wise walked over from the Manor House to smoke a friendly pipe with the village patriot, philosopher, and oracle, and even the Squire from Newbold Comyn, on rare occasions, might have been of the company. The year 1784 was an important one in Satchwell's life. His and Abbotts's great dream had been unfulfilled. No second spring had been found, and no baths were as yet possible. But the labour of years was about to be rewarded by a rich harvest of health, wealth, and prosperity. On the 14th of January, the two worthies were engaged in conversation in Lillington Lane (Bath Street), probably talking over their many failures, strengthening each other's faith and hope, and devising new plans for future operations in their search for an additional fount of health. They must have been there frequently before, but now, for the first time, their attention is directed to a strange motion in the water of the ditch by which they were standing. Over one particular spot bubbles were rising in rapid succession and exploding on the surface. Around, the ordinarily lazy stream was industriously glassing itself into an infinite variety of fantastic eddies and miniature vortices. Could it be possible that this was the consummation of a life-long aspiration? A brief examination was sufficient to answer that important enquiry. Tasting proved the new water to possess every palatal characteristic of the older spring; and an analysis confirmed its therapeutic worth. On that memorable day, the fortunes of modern Leamington were made; how, will be related in subsequent chapters.

CHAFFER IX. HE nomenclature of a town is an old mint from which have been issued the worn and polished coinages of its ancient and moder n history. Ineffaceable marks of dutiful loyalty, impulses of patriotism, traces of political faiths, courtesies to noble families, indications of local topography, and glimmerings of antiquarian lore are promiscuously intertwined with well-earned expressions of popular gratitude, and playful ebullitions of humour, legend, and imagination. What the judiciously compiled index is to the volume, the names of the streets, roads, bridges, fountains and river are to Leamington. As marginal notes, they express in condensed form the emotions of past and present generations.

Taking first into consideration the modern titles, we have several derived from special local circumstances. In this list must be classed Bath Street, Bath Place and the Bath Hotel, as mementoes of the street where Satchwell and Abbotts discovered the second spring in 1784, and by the latter the first baths, hot and cold were erected in 1786; Priory Terrace, Church Walk, Church Street and Church Terrace are so named on account of their proximity to the old Parish Church of All Saints; St. Mary's Crescent, and St. Mary's Road bespeak the immediate locality of St. Mary's Church; Trinity Street and Trinity Street East are derivatives from Holy Trinity, and St. John's Road and Terrace from St. John's Church; Mill Street is the street leading to and from the Mill; Brook Street is so called because of its

being built on the margin of the Milverton brook; Grove Street stands where a grove formerly existed; Binswood Avenue and Place are the sites of an ancient wood of very considerable extent; the Avenue Road and Avenue Station (L. & N. W. Ry.) commemorate the splendid horse-shoe avenue of elms which in former times graced the approaches to the old Manor House; Leam Terrace, Leam Street, Upper and Lower, and Leam Terrace East indicate their contiguity to the Leam; Springfield Street is the locality of springs of abundance of fresh water; the Holly Walk, Street and Holly Street East, owe their names to the celebrated holly trees which at one time flourished in the locality. The title of George Street is doubtful, and Dale Street ambiguous. The former is claimed to have been indebted for its name to the George Inn, to which it was at one time, a much frequented thoroughfare, but considering that George IV. visited Leamington in 1819, it probably belongs to the loyal category, where we have elsewhere placed it. Dale Street has been attributed to the dell which was situated on the north bank of the river, and commencing near the Adelaide Bridge extended in wild and romantic luxuriance westward towards the Avon. The Guidists and some of the oldest inhabitants still living, speak in rapturous terms of the sylvan charms of this highly favoured spot, with its babbling brook hard by making "sweet music with the enamel'd stones"; its shady bowers and mossy banks, and its weird cave, over which legend had cast its apocryphal mantle. Here the monks of the old times are reported to have descended into a subterranean passage, where, "far from the madding crowd's ignoble strife," they kept "the noiseless tenor of their way" to the distant Priory of Kenilworth. But as a James Dale was one of the early owners of property in the locality, it is quite as likely that Dale Street took his name as that it was called after the dell near the river.

The titular evidences of the loyal feeling of the borough are the Victoria Bridge, Victoria Colonnade, Victoria

Terrace, Victoria Road; Victoria Street; Queen Street; VIEW OF THE I.F.AMINGTON HYDROPATHIC ESTABLISHMENT As it appeared when erected by Dr. John Hitchman in 1862. The property was purchased in 1884 for the ' Midland Counties' Home for Chronic and Incurable Diseases." The opening ceremonial took place on June 27, under the presidency of Lord Leigh.

King Street; Augusta Place; Adelaide Bridge and Road; Charlotte Street; Clarence Street and Terrace; Albany Terrace; the Alexandra Fountains; the York Promenade and Bridge; Regent Street; George Street and Place, and Windsor Street. These are all expressive of a sentiment of loyalty, and several of them are connected with Royal visits.

Names bestowed as marks of courtesy and respect to the nobility and others include Althorpe Street, Aylesford Street; Beauchamp Avenue, Hill, Square, Terrace and Street; Bedford Street; Bertie Road and Terrace; Brunswick Street, Chandos Street; Clarendon Avenue, Crescent, Place, Square and Street; Dormer Place, Eastnor Grove; Euston Place; Gordon Street and Passage; Gloucester Street; Hamilton Terrace; Brandon Parade; Hyde Place; Lansdowne Circus, Crescent, Road and Street; Leicester Street; Norfolk Street; Packington Place; Percy Terrace; Portland Street, Place, Road and Street; Russell Terrace and Street; Somers Place; Tavistock Street, Villiers Street and Villiers Street North; Willes Road and Terrace; Wise Street, etc.

In the glitter of this star-shower of respectful amenities, one name is conspicuous by its absence—a name possessing stronger claims than many included in this local honours list. The visit of the Honourable Mrs. Leigh, in September, 1788,—"a truly patroness visitor from Stoneleigh Abbey," who "expressed great satisfaction at the supematurality of the water, and the convenience" of the baths—heralded the long bright summer of Leamington's prosperity, in which the gilded butterflies of fashion arrived from every country and every clime in welcome swarms. For nearly forty years Lord Leigh has led or supported each good cause in the town, presiding at the annual meetings of most of its public institutions, and, with unvarying liberality, contributing to their needs. With the name of Leigh standing first in the list of noble visitors who, for more than a century have bountifully fed the springs of its prosperity, and the latest amongst those who have almost dedicated themselves to its service, the town has inadvertently omitted to honour it with a garland such as it has profusely bestowed upon strangers.

The small tower in Tower Street, once one of the most conspicuous objects south of the Leam, but now hidden from view by loftier and more pretentious buildings, is responsible for the belief that here the Wesleyans or the Roman Catholics held their first services. A brief examination of the semi-ecclesiastically looking structure will suffice to show that it was not designed to be a place of worship, and never was used for such a purpose. Public utility of another kind was the sole object for which it was built. Most of the land in this part originally belonged to Mr. Booth, of Coventry, who, early in the history of the town, erected thereon a large number of houses. For the convenience of his numerous tenants and the public, a tower was built upon one of the houses and supplied with a public clock. The street takes its name from the tower, which still remains.

The High Street is a topographical title. Its length between the eastern boundary of the parish at Radford and the western at Myton has now three names, the Old Warwick Road and the Radford Road being the other two, but its ancient title was the public way when it was nothing more than a narrow road, bounded on each side with common land, full of mud-ruts, and in the winter season of little service for traffic. During the ownership of the Priors, travellers and all other persons using it would be liable to pay for the privilege a heavy toll to the religious confraternity at Kenilworth. Under an Act passed in the reign of Queen Mary, every peasant in the village was bound to give one week's free labour in each year in road-

making and repairing. At the time of the Enclosure in 1768, it was the turnpike road, and this name was probably applied to it in 1763 by legislation, which then look cognisance for the first time of all main roads in the country. In the beginning of the century, it was known as the London Road and the High Street, both of which titles it retained until 1840, when the latter, being employed in the Guides, reports and public documents, became the only name by which it was known. The Commissioners in their Award ordered it to be widened to the extent of sixty feet from Bath Street to a point near the Radford brook.

Satchwell Place and Abbotts Street are patronymic, the former having been bestowed by Miss Satchwell, the first and only Leamington Postmistress, and daughter of Ben Satchwell, in affectionate remembrance of her father, and the second taking its name from William Abbotts, the founder of the first baths. Clemens Street obtained its name from an owner of land on which it is built, and Covent Garden Market from a market formerly held there.

Beaconsfield Street and Northcote Street belong to the names of courtesy and respect, but they are also political, and therefore constitute a separate department in the vocabulary of local nomenclature.

Guy Place and Street are legendary; Guy's Cliffe Road is topographical. We also have Warwick Street (the street directly communicating with Warwick,) Lillington Road, Rugby Road, Radford Road, the old and new Warwick Roads; Kenilworth Road the Tachbrook Road, and the Lillington Lane of the time of the Award, all of which are topographical.

Spencer Street is a pathetic tribute to the memory of a distinguished Congregational Minister, who, in the beginning of the century, occupied a position analaous to that of Mr. Spurgeon towards its close. The Rev. Thomas Spencer, in 1810, was appointed by the Committee of Hoxton Academy, in which institution he was a student, to preach for several weeks to the congre-

gation in Newington Chapel, Liverpool. His extraordinary talents and amazing popularity resulted in a call from the church to be its pastor, which he accepted, and entered upon the duties of his office at twenty years of age. The congregation rapidly increased, and in three months from the date of his settlement in Liverpool, the foundation stone of Great George Street Chapel was laid. Before the completion of the building, in which accommodation was provided for the multitude who thronged to his ministry, Mr. Spencer was drowned while bathing in the Mersey. The intelligence of his death was a shock felt throughout the whole of the Free Churches of England, and for years was the topic of a general regret. Dr. Raffles, who succeeded him in the pastorate, wrote his biography with the pen he left on his study table when he went to bathe, and seated in the chair he vacated. At the time of the building of Spencer Street Chapel, in 1836, the street had no name. As a compliment to the Rev. Alfred Pope, the first minister, the choice was left with him, and that of Spencer Street was selected as a testimonial to a young minister whose genius resembled a meteor in its brilliance and duration, and whose untimely death produced a melancholy interest unexampled in the obituaries of eminent divines.

This account is doubted by an old resident, who says the land forming the street, and the Manor House belonged to Mr. Matthew Wise. Where the street is there was formerly a road leading from Bath Street to the Manor farm barns, with a footway from the Manor House to the Parish Church. Mr. Wise removed to Shrubland Hall, and the Manor House was occupied by Mrs. Acklow in 1818. She was stepmother to Lord Althorp of the Spencer family, who, during her more than twenty years' residence, frequently visited Leamington. From this he is inclined to believe that the name is complimentary to the Spencer, family, and belongs to the titles of complaisance. Mr. Ebenezer Goold, who is our authority for the foregoing paragraph, distinctly recollects the naming of the Chapel and the street, and has no misgiving as to the purpose of its application. He was a youth at the time, attending Spencer Street Chapel, and well remembers how interested Mr. Pope was in the subject and his expressed desire to have the Chapel and street named after the Rev. Thomas Spencer. We have referred to the Guides, Directories, etc., without meeting with the designation earlier than 1836, the time of the building of the Chapel. It does not appear in " Fairfax's Guide" of 1832, nor in the list of voters for the same year, nor in "Moncrieff's Guide" of 1833. It is first mentioned in "Merridew's Guide" of 1837, m connection with a brief description of the Chapel. The absence of the name from the Guides until the date of the building of the Chapel agrees with the evidence of the rate-books which, by the courtesy of Mr. George Rogers, the Assistant Overseer, we have been permitted to consult. Spencer Street is not referred to in the rates made for 1831-2-3-4 and 5. The first mention of it is in the rate for 1837, which would be twelve months after the opening of the Chapel, on which occasion the preachers were the Revs. John Angell James, Birmingham; James Parsons, York; and William Jay, Bath. There were only five houses in Spencer Street at the time, the tenants being Mrs. Smith, Daniel Goodman Squirhill, Mrs. Ely, William Fairfax, and Edward Clark.

Many of the old names have disappeared from the map; some have been changed once and others oftener. The Parade was first known as Lower and Upper Union Parade, because it united the Old and the New Towns. In 1860, the word "Union" had ceased to be applied to it, and now its whole length is only described as "The Parade." The original names of Warwick Street and Regent Street were Upper and Lower Cross Streets, both of which were derived from their crossing the Parade. The first name of Clarendon Avenue was associated with Newbold Comyn, but at the time the villas were erected on the north side they all had a south aspect, and it was accordingly called the

South Parade. This appellation was correct until the south side of the street was built upon, when the aspect was as much north as south. The misnomer was corrected in 1882 by giving it the title of Clarendon Avenue. The old Lillington Lane commenced at the point where the railway bridges are in Bath Street, and proceeding over the Victoria bridge, continued along the Parade to Regent Grove, thence into Clarendon Street, where it lost itself in Crab Tree Lane. It has now four names, as enumerated. The town street mentioned in the Award was the road leading out of the turnpike (High Street) along Church Street and Church Terrace to Farmer Court's farm in Mill Street, and onwards to the Mill. Orchard Street, changed to Bath Place, had its first title from the beautiful orchard belonging to Mr. Matthew Wise which occupied the site of the Music Hall, Bath Street. Printers Street, now West Street, was where the first printing office was established in Leamington.

Entertaining as the details of the early history of the town are, they would have lacked a special charm without those services which Art has voluntarily contributed to the treasury of its literature. Sufficient acknowledgement has not been made of the productions of O'Neil, Roe, Brandard, Rider, Olerenshaw, Squirhill, and Wood; Jackson and Hisset, who have left some fine examples of the thatched cottages; John Merridew, whose views of old Leamington excel in number and variety while they equal in merit all who preceded or followed him; Mr. Whitehead and Mr. Varney, the Parade. It is a satisfactory sign of the increased interest now manifested in our local history to find that these works generally are being highly prized, and that the canvases of the latter, rich in colour, and distinctly artistic in every detail, are finding their way into the halls and drawing rooms of the wealthy classes. The present generation of Leamingtonians may congratulate themselves upon the labours of the Artists, whose illustrations impress upon the retina of the mind a far more vivid idea of what old Leamington was like than it is competent for language to

convey, in its most delightfully graphic moods and tenses. Of Art in its modern aspect, as represented by a distinguished school of photographers, and the salutary effect their productions have had upon the prosperity of Leamington, we shall speak on another occasion.

The value of the Award as a repository of names in the village era is scarcely inferior to the account it has preserved to us of the enclosure of the commonable lands. They were mostly proprietary, and for centuries may have been changing as new circumstances arose. Court's Home Close; the Innidge Field and Meadow; Raven's Close; Malian's Hill Field; High Dadley Field; Mathecroft Field; Nabbs's Lammas Closes; Satchwell Close; the Bankcroft, and Rinill's Field, were proprietary, while the Gravel Pit Field; Watery Lane; Church Hadeland Field; Malian's Hill Brick-kiln; Shell Leys and Round Close were descriptive. The Ham was the larger of the two islands in the river above the Willes bridge, the Sidenham Meadow and Field being the northern part of Sydenham Farm with the land cut off by the canal, extending to the Radford Road. There are various theories as to the origin of the word, which in Anglo-Saxon is "him," meaning a home or dwellings. Newbold Comyn, anciently an estate separate from Leamington, comprised four lordships, or manors, and according to Dugdale, had its mill, which is held by some authorities to have been upon this island. In that case the name might be taken as indicating that the island, the meadow and the fields were the home of the mill, and the place where the miller and the labourers resided. Other speculations are that the name may have originated from the contour of the island resembling a ham, or to its having in some remote age formed a peninsula with the land on one of the sides of the river, in which sense it is still in use in Worcestershire. Both these conjectures must be dismissed as wholly untenable, seeing that the Saxons were in the immediate neighbourhood in considerable numbers during the Heptarchy. It is more consistent with historical evidence and the exercise of a rational judgment to accept the name as the sign of the home of an early generation, who probably were Saxons, and retainers or vassals of Offa, King of the Mercians, when he was in occupation at Offchurch. Sidenham Field and Meadow, now Sydenham farm, may be names deduced from the island. Radbrook is the only exchange for Radford we have seen.

The etymology of the name of the town is a theme fertile in speculations of a literary and antiquarian nature. From no writer has it received the special attention it deserves, though several have referred to it in a cursory manner, by quoting it as illustrative of some principle of interpretation of obsolete terms, or have assigned to it a meaning in harmony with a particular aspect of locality or language. For the more comprehensive examination of the subject, and the greater diversity of ideas which appear in the following comments we must acknowledge our obligations to Mr. Edward Cookes, a gentleman who has a deep interest in the welfare of Leamington, which, as man and boy, he has known for nearly three-quarters of a century. His researches, of which we make a full use, invest with new attractions a subject usually dry, and substitute for its threadbare garments an attire representative of the learning of one age, and the rude and superstitious imagery of another.

The root or stem of the word Leamington is widely diffused through the languages of Europe, and is frequently met with in the initial forms of compounds, as "leam," "lem," "lym," "lim," and "Ien." It is nearly always associated with rivers, lakes, or streams, either as a name descriptive of such waters, or as the appellation of a place situate upon their banks, or at a short distance. In the United Kingdom we have the following instances:—(1) Leamington Priors, Warwickshire, a borough on the banks of the river Leam; (2) Leamington Hastings, also in Warwickshire, on the left bank of the Leam, deriving its name therefrom; (3) Lower Lemington, Gloucestershire, a parish in the Shipston

union, where there is a branch of the Stour; (4) Lemington, five miles from Newcastle-on-Tyne, but standing near the Tync; (5) I.imington, in the Yeovil Union, on the banks of the river Yco; (6) Lemington, a township in the Alnwick Union, Northumberland; (7) Lymington, Hants., on the river Lymington, which flows into the Solent; (8) Lyminge, Kent; (9) Leamside, Durham, situated about a mile from the river Wear; (10) Leneham, in Kent, on the river Lea; (11) Lemsford, near Hatfield, Herts.; (12) Limerick on the Shannon; (13) Limene, a river in Kent. In foreign countries the name is freely employed descriptively of towns and places, and is recognisable without difficulty in spite of the strange dress in which its terminologies are clothed. As examples, we may quote the following:—(1) Lem, a small village in Jutland; (2) Lem-vfg, also in Jutland; (3) Lemforde, close to the Dummer Zee, betw-een Osnabruck and Bremen; (4) Limberg, in the Duchy formerly part of Holland; (5) Lemburg, the capital of Gallicia, Austria. This list may be very considerably extended by consulting the many standard works in which are enumerated the names of the principal cities, towns and rivers of the world.

The variety of costumes in which we meet with the word in other English towns and in foreign climes is not greater than the changing verbal fashions it assumes at home. In "Domesday Book" we have it spelt "Lamintone," in the Rous Roll of the fifteenth century, "Lemyn," and in the grant of the living of the Parish Church to William Borne and Jacob Orange by Queen Elizabeth, "Lymington." The Warwickshire Court of Quarter Sessions, in their Order of 1625, suppressing William Mills and Margaret Walsgrave, Victuallers, render it "Lemington," a form of spelling adopted in the Enclosure Act and Award, of 1768; but in many of the resolutions respecting the repairs of the bridge, passed by the Court of Quarter Sessions from, 1650 to 1750, the style is " Leminton" and "Lemintone."

The universal employment of the word suggests a common source of ori-

gin, and an identity of purpose in its application. What that origin is supposed to be, and the sense in which we may understand the meaning of the name Leam-ing-ton, given to the town, we will endeavour to explain. There are four theories as to the first syllable of our tripartite title—Leam. Dugdale considered the fountain of derivation to be Greek. In his Antiquities of Warwickshire he observes:—

"At Emscote it is that Avon is enlarged by the confluence of Leame, which, having its head in Northamptonshire, about Braunston and Daventre, entreth Warwickshire betwixt Wolfhamcote and Willoughby. Touching its name, I mean the etymologie, it may seem to be derived from the Greek word *limne,* which signifieth a pool or lake, for our ancient Saxon language is affirmed by very learned men in both to have its originall from the Greek. Neither is this conjecture improbable, for as much as this river is of a muddy disposition, having some standing holes in the nature of lakes or ponds in sundry places thereof. And we find at this day that divers of those artificial rivers in Cambridgeshire, antiently cut to drayn the Fens, do bear the name of Leame, as Watersey Leame, New Leame. Merton's Leame, etc., being all muddy channells, through which the water hath a dull and slow passage."

There are also advocates of the Celtic and Anglo-Saxon origin; others look upon a derivation from the two founts as possible. Mr. Rihton Turner favours the Celtic source, and assuming his view to be correct, we have "Leam" from the British or Celtic "leamh," which means "the elm tree river." Leamington, therefore, would be the town standing near the river deriving its name from the large number of elm trees growing upon its banks. This theory derives support from the abundance of elms which formerly flourished in the county. At one time it was a common form of speech to refer to the elm as " the Warwickshire weed." The Rev. George Miller,.on the contrary, makes a strong claim for the Anglo-Saxon theory. "Leam " he derives from " lam," the Anglo-Saxon term for "mud," and "loem," the equivalent for "loam." These make Leamington mean "the loamy town near the muddy Leam." None can say this idea is opposed to well-known facts—the soil has a large admixture of loam, and the river, if not muddy, is nothing. Mr. Edward Cookes supplements these learned conjectures with another: the Welsh word "llwyr," a "platform," coincides with " Hem" and "llym," "sharp," or, "llamn," to leap in the sense of "limb" from "shooting, or extending," which in AngloSaxon is "lim" and in Danish, "lem." The "Leam," in his opinion, might be considered as a limb of the Avon, into which it empties itself at Portobello. The luxuriance of these suppositions is amplified by derivations from other sources representing the import of the name of the river to be, "foliage," "crown of a tree," "a broom," "a rod of twigs," "a sound true voice," "a ray of light;" "to shine," and "gentleness and softness," in which last sense it has been interpreted as denoting "a gentle flowing river." The second syllable— "ing," sometimes rendered "eng"—is in Anglo-Saxon and Danish, "a meadow." In Bosworth's Anglo-Saxon Dictionary the signification given is "a young man, a son, a descendant, progeny, and offspring." Upon this the question has been asked whether "Leaming" may not be accepted as applicable to "Leam's descendants," and the complete form, "Leamington," as meaning "the town where the posterity of the original 'Leamingas' have their abode." Dr. Johnson, formerly of Malvern, an eminent linguist and antiquary, is firmly opposed to every derivation theory, whether from language or circumstances of site. He considers that as the "Leams" and "Lymns" are so widely distributed, the meaning must be more general than would be the case if they referred to elm or other sorts of trees. "It would not be," he imagines, "an out-of-the-way appellation to call a stream or streamlet, an arm of water, an arm or hand of the river. The vivid imagination of an early race might see in the streams falling into the river or sea the fingers of a hand. Leamh Abhaim might

become Leam-Avon, Leam-an, and Lemyn by easy stages, and mean Avon's hand, or Avon's arm; or Leamyn might be referred to as Leamh-an, i.e., arm of the water, or water arm." As an etymologist, he holds this to be the better view of the meaning of the word. There is another explanation to be mentioned. It concedes the elm tree theory of Mr. Ribton Turner, and the muddy river and loamy soil of the Rev. G. Miller, as principles of origin, but with a new process of nomination. In "The Saxons in England," by John Mitchell Kemble, revised by Walter de Gray Birch, there appears a long disquisition on "The

E

Mark," and "Men of the Mark." According to his authority, England, on the advent of the Saxons, was mainly forest land, and was settled by the Saxons in this wise: a group of the invaders would make a clearing of the forest, or perhaps occupy a clearing already made; this they termed their mark. The occupants of that space were also called "the Mark," that is, by the men of that mark. The different groups of settlers acquired distinctive names, which were usually formed from those of the principal residents by the termination "ing." The Mark men were also sometimes named from local circumstances, the termination "ing" still being used. Kemble is of opinion that all the topographical names with "ing" have this origin, and he expressly includes Leamington in the class. The Mark men of the spot called Leamington were the Leamingas, Leamington being their "t6n" or enclosure.

The intermediate syllable does not provide the same abundance of materials for speculative controversy. By the majority of scholars it is accepted as meaning "a meadow." Leamington originally was contained in a meadow, and when, in the efflux of time, it exceeded the limits of one, other meadows provided for it the necessary accommodation. In 1880, there was an entertaining correspondence in *Nottt and Queries* upon this particular subject. An enquiry having been made as to the force and

meaning of "ing" occurring in the word Leam-ing-ton, numerous answers were furnished by readers of that journal. One was "the town on the meadow by the Leam or muddy river," and another, given as the more frequent interpretation, "son of," "inhabitant of;" "land of," the "homestead of, or on the Leam." It has been asked whether Leaming might not be properly construed as signifying Leam's descendants or Leam's tribe, and not the town in the loamy meadows on the banks of the muddy river. In reply to these and other conjectures, the correspondent who started the discussion replied that the "Domesday" form was "Lamintone," and in Dugdale's "Warwickshire" (1665) it was "Leminton." The "g" in the modern spelling he considered to be intrusive, and the middle syllable being due to a case-ending of the river name " Leme," the meadow theory was one which the five correspondents who had adopted it would have to give up. The interpretation of the last syllable, " t6n," is accepted by all etymologists as the equivalent for "town."

It was a maxim with Camden to be "scepticall" rather than critical in etymology. The present is a case where the exercise of that prudential virtue is to be commended. The age when the river was named was precedent to the settlement of the aboriginal Leamingas. Language was then in an elementary state; words were meagre and sterile compared with the profusion of ideas with which they became enriched in later times by invasions, by conquests, by the admixture of tribes, the commingling of races and the amalgamation of tongues. Dugdale was not infallible, but his erudition was sound, and always under the guidance of sensible and moderate opinions. We prefer his derivation, and upon a review of the various theories, regard the meaning of Leamington as: Leam, a pool or lake; ing, a meadow, and ton, a town, i.e., a town standing in a meadow on the banks of a pool or lake, called the Leam.

CHAPTER X. HE lines of the historical perspective of All Saints' Parish Church, gradually approaching each

other, coalesce in a region of fable beyond the mists of that turbulent period
when the first Plantagenet ascended the
English throne. When it was built, by
whom, and under what circumstances,
are questions for which the most diligent search has provided no answer.
Concurrent opinion has assigned its
foundation to the twelfth century—a
speculation, the accuracy of which we
see no reason to doubt. There were
churches in almost every parish, and it
is incredible that Leamington, which
had been a township from the seventh
century, should have lacked in the
twelfth what was a common possession.
All conjectures respecting its early history disappear in the succeeding century, from which time the stepping-stones
provided for the historian are sufficiently close for continuous progress and re-
liability of narration. Originally it was
a chapelry belonging to Leek Wootton,
and, according to the veracious and
ever-helpful Dugdale, was "therewith
confirmed to the Canons of Kenilworth
by Ric. Peche, Bishop of Coventre, in
Henry the Second's days, and appropriated to them by G. Muschamp, his successor, in King John's time, in Anno
1291, 19th Edward I. It was valued at
vi. marks over and above a pension of
xx. shillings then issuing out of it to
the Abbey of Malmesbury; and the vicaridge at xx. shillings." In the "Valor
Ecclesiasticus" (Henry VIII., 1534-5)
it1s referred to as the Church of the
parish of " Lemyngton Priors, in the gift
of the Abbot and Convent of Kenilworth," John Corney being vicar perpetual, worth, in tenths, offerings and
emoluments of other kinds, £6 10s., of
which xxxiii. shillings and iv. pence
were received of the same Abbey in
pension, but from which there had to
be deducted a payment of 13s. iod. for
some purpose not explained. Here we
must leave for a time this much trav-
elled path of dry and ancient statistics.
The relationship in which the Parish
Church stood to the village, by providing in its vestry a shelter for popular
forms of self-government while in a
rudimentary stage, is of transcendent
importance.

For several centuries the village church
was the senate as well as the sanctuary
of the parish. Supremacy in things secular and ecclesiastical was its prerogative. Time, changing all else, has modified its ecclesiasticism, and shorn the
vestry, formerly the seat of local government, and the parochial expression
of imperial authority, of every vestige
of temporal power. There are some old-
world institutions which command respect, there are others which call forth
no feelings but pity, derision or amusement. The primitive vestry, as the an-
cestral home of the Corporation of
Leamington, merits admiration for its
conservation of principles of representative government imported into Britain
by the Saxons, Jutes and Angles, and
left by them as a priceless heritage to
a conquered race. But while proving an
ark, wherein an enfeebled form of popular control rode in safety over a flood
of national bigotry, intolerance and superstition, the vestry added nothing to
its intrinsic value nor subtracted from
its inherent worth. What had been received was preserved with scrupulous
care, and when posterity in the nineteenth century demanded its patrimony,
the estate which the vestry had to convey was neither diminished nor improved. In its possession, representative
government was as unexpansive as the
demonstrations of Euclid and the laws
of arithmetic, but when transplanted into the more bracing atmosphere of Improvement Commissioners, Local
Boards of Health, Boards of Guardians,
School Boards, District and Parish
Councils, and the Council Chambers of
Corporations, its native energy, diffusive spirit, and sufficiency for every
public need were immediately conspicuous. Custom and precedent were no
longer permitted to trammel invention
and enterprise, nor a reverential regard
for the past to shut out from view the
necessities of the present. Each eminence gained revealed a still distant territory for legislative conquest, the power for which has been liberally supplied
by successive enactments. The beneficial results are well known. Expanded
to almost imperial magnitude, our local

government system has become a vast
organisation, comprehending within the
wide compass of its duties everything
appertaining to the health, peace and
comfort of rich and poor. None would
desire to go back to the drowsy
parochialism which ruled Leamington
down to the year 1825, but it should not
be forgotten that the vicar who left his
study, the squire the contemplation of
his rent roll, the yeoman his farm, and
the labourer his plough, for the vestry a
hundred years ago were the prototypes
of the members of the present Corporation, and that from the humble assembly
at the Parish Church has descended the
more influential and powerful Council
at the Town Hall.

The Church of All Saints had, in the
village era, a distinctness and a stability
which contrasted with all its surroundings. From whatever point of view the
parish was surveyed it was the most
conspicuous object. The dwarf cottages
at its base, built with a lavish wealth
of timber, made it appear much greater
than it really was; the hill on which it
stood gave it a commanding view over
the loftiest buildings in the neighbourhood. The level of the streets being
much lower than at the present time, rel-
atively, the church occupied a more elevated site.

The first improvements which interrupted the repose of the original Church
are vaguely reported to have taken place
in 1624 or i6z6, the Rev. H. Clarke being vicar. It were vain now to seek for
definite particulars of the changes alleged to have been made at that period.
Moncrieff, in his "Guide," published in
1818, says it "appears to have been either re-built or materially repaired," and
mentions as his authority " some dates
and names in the interior and on the exterior of the Church." Students of eccle-
siology in Leamington will never cease
to regret the absence from his pages of
transcriptions of these dreams in stone.
Neither Pratt, who wrote in 1814, nor
Bisset, in 1816, nor the Rev. W. Field,
whose work appeared in 1815, makes
reference to this interesting alphabet of
local Church restoration. John Merridew, who had a strong and healthy

digestion for archaeological food, published an " Improved edition of Moncrieff" in 1837, one of which improvements was the omission of all allusions to alterations during the vicariate of the Rev. H. Clarke.

According to report, at some time, either towards the close of the last, or at the commencement of the present century, the interior of the Church was renovated after the same fashion as Malone in 1793 improved the bust of Shakespeare in Stratford-uponAvon Church, by effacing the glowing colours of ancient art with a coating of modern white paint. "The good old Saxon arch capitals, between the nave and chancel, were destroyed and renovated with painted deal wainscoat." The date of this obliteration has been given as the year 1800, when William and F.dward Treadgold completed their contract for re-pewing and re-seating the Church, and supplying a new pulpit and reading desk, but their estimate contains no allusion to alterations of the fabric. By virtue of a Faculty granted in 1781, a gallery was erected on the north side of the Church, containing three pews, one of which was appropriated to the use of the inhabitants of the farmhouse belonging to Mr. Matthew Wise. The Saxon arch capitals may have been removed on either of these occasions, for Church improvers and restorers do not always rigidly adhere to the limits of the licenses obtained from the Consistorial Courts. The farmhouse referred to stood on the site of Reynolds' Furniture Repository, Stubbs, after remarking in his " Constitutional History" that the vestry was representative ot the "gemot" with which it was once identified, says its importance cannot be exaggerated when we look further on and see in these local gatherings the chief element in the organisation of the borough system of later date.

and was then in the occupation of Thomas Abbotts. After the Rev. Robert Downes succeeded the Rev. John Wise, in the living in 1821, he pure hased this farm with its yard and buildings from Mr. Wise, demolished the house, and erected on the site the Priory, which

continued to be the residence of the vicars of Leamington down to 1877, the year of the Rev. John Craig's death. The other two pews were allotted, one to the Rev. Edward Willes and was occupied by himself and his family, and the other to John Campion, residing at the farmhouse near the Campion Hill, and also holding the tenancy of the Mill, as the successor of Mrs. Satchwcll after she went to reside with "Ben" in New Street. His name has been transmitted to posterity in connection with one of the Newbold Hills, from the summit of which panoramic views are obtainable over a vast expanse of country rich in tone-colours and variegated landscape; with pastoral aspect of straggling villages, peaceful farmsteads, and distant gray churches, and crowned with a magnificent sweep of a verdure-clad horizon, in which is distinguishable the lofty crest of the historic Edge Hills bathing itself in the fathomless blue of cloud and sky. From a portrait over the fireplace in the newspaper reading-room at the Free Library, the venerable face of Edward Willes looks down upon the readers with its accustomed benignant expression.

From different sources we have been able to ascertain what were the size and position of the Church and the character of its surroundings in 1781. The nave exactly filled the space between the present four Evangelist columns, the Chancel extending fifteen and a half feet eastward. The Churchgoers of the present day who occupy sittings within the area of the Evangelist columns are worshipping upon the site of the ancient village Church, where probably some thirty generations of Leamingtonians have preceded them. Every portion of the interior of the Church outside the columns is of nineteenth century origin, dating not farther back than 1816. On the site of the clergy-vestry, choir-vestry and the clock tower, there were a "barn, stable, stone wall, and gate," belonging to John Corpson, one of the early landowners, and nearly opposite the Post Office stood the cottage of the Dawkes family, occupied in the seventeenth century by Daniel Dawkes, great-

grandfather of Thomas Dawkes—from whose verdant memoranda we have already made numerous extracts—and ancestor of Mr. W. G. Bloomfield, 22, George Street; Mr. E. I. Bloomfield, Parish Clerk, 19, Church Street, and Mr. Councillor W. Dawkes, 13, Radford Road. One other old building near the Church calls for passing mention. Where the wooden belfry stood on the west side there was a barn which originally belonged to John Morcott.

The improvements of 1799 were entrusted to Messrs. Treadgold, builders and timber merchants, carrying on an extensive business in Church Street. Their shops, offices, and yards were at the back of Sussex Cottage, No. 23, now occupied by Mr. F. E. Fessey, Assessor and Collector of Taxes. The original estimate and contract, in the possession of Mr. W. T. Barter-White, of Cotswold House, 19, Regent Street, and obligingly lent for the purpose of this history, will prove of interest to builders and contractors, as showing the cost of materials a century ago, and to the general public for the information they afford of the heavy pressure of taxation on trade which existed in the good old times. The total amount of the estimate was £103 5s. 7d., and to give it legal effect, it was necessary that the contract should be written on a sheet of paper bearing impressed stamps of the value of four shillings, and the receipt for payment on another, having a stamp value of one shilling. In these times a sixpenny and a penny stamp would be sufficient.—

"An Estimate for newly re-pewing with Oak the whole Body of the Church and erecting a New Pulpit and Desk. 6 Square of Oak flooring for the bottom of the Pews at 3 10s. per square, *£21*; 328 Feet of *l* Inch Oak Wainscot for front of Pews at 13d. Per Ft., 17 15s. 4d. ; 574 Feet of Square Wainscot for Do. at 9d. Per Ft., £21 10s.; 331 of Wale Do. at 8d. Per Ft., *£11* 0s. 8d.; 34 Feet of Plinth at 7d. Per Ft., 19s. iod.; 189 Feet of Oak seating at 8d. Per Ft., £6 6s. ; 30 Feet of bearers for Do. at 6d. Per Ft., 15s.; 99 Feet of Oak Desk boards at 7d. Per Ft., *£2* 17s. 9d.; 30 Feet of

Coping for Do. at is. Per foot, £1 10s.; Hinges, screws and nails, £2 15s.; Pulpit and Desk, 16 16s; total, "103 5s. 7d.

"We whose names are hereunto affixed do solemnly engage and Contract (in the presence of a Meeting held in the Parish Church of Leamington Priors in the County of Warwick) to repew completely with Oak the Body of the aforesaid Church and Erect in the same a New Pulpit and Desk agreeable to the above estimate. Witness our hands this 30th day of March, 1799. Contractors' names: William Treadgold; Edward Treadgold. Witnesses present when this was signed: E. Willes; Jno. Wise."

William Treadgold died in 1801, and Edward in 1839, after which the estate, which comprised many valuable properties and building sites in the Old and New Towns, was sold by Mr. George Carter, of 42, High Street, an auctioneer, then in a flourishing state of prosperity. The sale, which commenced on the 29th of October, at the Bath Hotel, and was continued for several days, would call for no further notice here, except for the fact that one class of property offered to the public opened the floodgates of an agitation which knew no slumber for thirty years; gave rise to the bitterest feud which the Parish Church has ever witnessed, and repeatedly obscured the Local Board of Health when engaged in some of the most important of its work. Modern churchgoers will read with wide-eyed astonishment that announcements such as the ensuing were not of uncommon occurrence in the catalogues of the early Leamington auctioneers:—

Lot 14. A Pew of 3 sittings, being No. 8 in the West Gallery.

Lot 15. A Pew of 6 sittings, being No. 47 in the West Gallery.

Lot 16. A Pew of 6 sittings, being No. 42 in the North Aisle-

The majority of the " pues," as an old writer quaintly describes them, were held as private property, and, when offered for sale by public auction, invariably excited a spirit of eager competition among the parishioners. Seldom has the persuasive mood of eloquence been more powerfully exhibited than

when the auctioneers of the last generation were tendering these bargains to the highest bidder. Nor has the topography of the interior of the Parish Church been subject to more critical examination, or the advantages of situation canvassed with a finer sense of appreciative discrimination. Not a single advantage of position was overlooked. The eligibility of one pew for seeing and hearing; the seclusion afforded by another for faded gentility; the freedom of a third from draughts; and the facility provided by a fourth for quietly tip-toeing out at the door before the collector arrived with the plate, were considerations which made a pew fifty years ago more valuable than a share in the gas company now. In the churchwardens' accounts, from Easter, 1839, to Easter, 1840, it is recorded that a "small pew in the west gallery" had been sold for £3b, the balance, after deducting £$ 14s. 8d. for alterations, fittings up, etc., being £30 5s. 41L, and at the meeting, when the accounts were passed, it was admitted that the sittings had become " very valuable property, and as investments had paid 11 or 12 per cent, interest."

The sale of pews, which was originated in 1816, in circumstances of exceptional difficulty, was abolished by the Court of Arches in 1871. The enlargement of 1816 took place when the population could not have been very much in excess of 1,000 inhabitants. There were no funds, and to enable the Vicar and the Churchwardens to carry out the work the Consistory Court of Lichfield granted a Faculty, authorising them to dispose of the additional seats, nineteen in number, by sale. The story of the delegation of such a power would be doubtful, were it not supported by Mr. Alfred C. Hooper, Registrar of the Consistory Court of Worcester, in his statement before the Parish Church Pew Commissioners, who met in February, 1870, and adopted and repeated by them as a correct version in their subsequent report to the Consistory Court of Worcester. In fairness to the three vicars (the Revs. John Wise, Robert Downes and ohn Craig), the churchwardens who served under them, and the parishioners

who invested their money in what proved to be an illegal transaction, it should always be remembered that they had the sanction of a Court in whose decision they were justified in reposing confidence.

The number of new seats, according to the early "Guides," was 120. We have given 19, which was the total of the additions Mr. Hooper mentioned to the few Commissioners.

In 1824, more money was required for further enlargements, and the population being small and scarcely above 3,000, the prospect of raising it by public subscription was remote, if not out of the question. Recourse was therefore had to the sale of pews by issuing the following notice:—

"Conditions of Sale of the new pews in the Parish Church of Leamington Priors. The first applicants will have the preference of situation, as all the pews will be sold on the same terms if purchased before the 2lst of December, 1824. The Pews to be sold (if purchased before the day above mentioned) at 10 guineas per sitting, one half of the purchase money to be paid at the time of taking the Pew; the other half on *From a photo, hy Buttock Bros., The Parade, Leamington.* THE PARADE,

Showing the Regent Hotel with the portico built in front in 1849, and also the elms and laburnums on the south side previous to the demolition of the Denby Villa and the clearance of the site in 1882 for the erection of the Municipal Buildings.

possession being given. N.B.—The expense of procuring a Faculty is included in this sum. Any purchaser refusing or omitting to make good the second half of the Purchase money at the time the Pew is ready for occupation or within one Calendar Month after that time to forfeit the sum advanced and to lose all right and claim to the Pew. All purchasers to sign their names to these conditions at the time of taking their Pews, as an acknowledgment of their compliance with them. The Pews will be ready for occupation on or before the last day of June, 1825."

This appeal, in which the legality of

the sale of pews is taken for granted, succeeded. Sittings were purchased wholesale and farmed out at fabulous prices. The Parish Church, national in design, and parochial in administration, was being gradually sold in sections, not to churchmen, nor parishioners, but to the public. In effect the new shareholders were enclosing and partitioning the Church among themselves in the same way as the commonable lands had been enclosed and appropriated by others. Churchmanship was not a necessary qualification for ownership, nor was it requisite that purchasers should be parishioners. The names of Nonconformists, who never went to Church, and non-residents who seldom came to Leamington, were prominent in the list of proprietors. Including £1,000 which Mr. Downes expended, under the sanction of a special resolution of the vestry, and nearly £700 worth purchased by the late Mr. John Oldham's father, and which were left by will to his son, there could not have been less than from £2,000 to £2,500 invested in those properties at the time of the sale of the Treadgold pews, in 1839. That sale was followed immediately by an agitation for the abolition of the system. Mr. C. Meredith protested against it in vestry; in Merridew's *Chronicle* it was assailed with vigour; and, in 1855, the feeling of the town was directly reflected by the Venerable Archdeacon of Coventry, on the occasion of his Visitation, calling upon the churchwardens to do their duty and put an end to the practice. Some years afterwards a Pew Redemption Committee was formed, with the view of arranging with those who had been led to believe that they were the owners of the pews. Negotiations failed, and to relieve themselves from the contentions of rival parties, and the church from the strife which had existed for many years, Messrs. Walter Watson and Alexander Johnson, Churchwardens, in 1870, requested the Consistory Court, at Worcester, to appoint a Commission to examine all claims, and re-allot pews according to law and the requirements of the parishioners. The Commissioners appointed were the Revs. James

Reynolds Young, Rector of Whitnash, and John Wise, Vicar of Lillington; Messrs. John Ogden Bacchus, John Panton Gubbins, and Frederick Acton Colville. The two principles on which they proceeded were the disallowance of all claims of proprietary interest by reason of purchase, and provision for the needs of those attending the church. The Rev. John Craig, who had purchased Mr. Downes's pews for,£1,100, and claimed to have spent £7,000 of his own money on church improvements, opposed the Commission on several grounds, the principal being the allegation of a Faculty of 1826, which Mr. Hooper said did not exist, and the absence of consecration of the land on which the north transept was erected. Mr. John Oldham also opposed the allocation, in consideration of the pews purchased by his father with the sanction of the vestry, in 1825, and Mr. William Savage, because of the pews which had been in the possession of his family for three hundred years. The Consistory Court dismissed all the objections, but directed that better accommodation should be provided for Mr. Savage and his family than the Commissioners had made. On an appeal to the Court of Arches, the Dean confirmed the finding of the Consistory Court, and in so doing handed back to the parish, pews which had been alienated through an irregular Faculty for nearly fifty years. The result gave satisfaction to the public, but a strong feeling of sympathy existed for those who had lost considerable sums of money through an erroneous impression produced by the Faculty of 1816, and especially for.Mr. Craig, whose purchase, in consequence of his exchange of livings with Mr. Downes, had not been entirely voluntary, and whose liberality in church improvement was well known. An offer of £joo, made to him previous to the litigation, entitles the Pew Redemption Committee to the credit of having desired a settlement which would not have entailed the loss of all his money; but their peremptory rejection of his proposal for arbitration, after the decision of the Consistory Court in their favour, and before the

hearing of the appeal in the Court of Arches, was considered by his friends as depriving them of the peculiar lustre of exercising magnanimity and generosity when elated with victory. The case was one of immense importance to the parishioners, and to all who take an interest in the maintenance of the comprehensive basis of the old parochial system. A decision adverse to the churchwardens would have vested the right of sale of portions of parish churches in the Consistory Courts, and have opened the door to commercial speculation in pews upon an extensive scale in every parish church in England.

CHAPTER XI. ROM the time of the erection of Abbotts's Baths there were indications of a new effervescence of local life, but that was not the only novelty of the year. Nonconformity, now represented by numerous influential congregations and chapels, among which may be named, as of the finest in the kingdom, the Wesley Chapel, Dale Street, and the Congregational Chapel, Spencer Street, found in the Rev. James Moody, the youthful pastor of Brook Street Chapel, Warwick, an energetic and successful home missionary. The Rev. J. Sibree, in his history of "Independency in Warwickshire," speaks of some memoranda in the congregational records of the period respecting the expenses incurred in these early services at Leamington, but does not mention the amount, nor the nature of the payments. Bisset, who came about 181 2, and was consequently in touch with many people who were living at the time of Mr. Moody's visits, clearly points, in the following jaunty quatrain, to a public house as the place in which some meetings were held:—

"Till the meeting-house lire began to appear, The good folks called Dissenters were happy;
And thought it no sin to preach at an Inn
   Where, on week-days was sold the 'brown nappy.'"

The services conducted by Mr. Moody are represented as having been held in a barn, in a cottage, and at a public house. There is no positive information as to which of these theories is to be relied on in preference to the others. Bisset's verse, however, had no reference to Mr. Moody's services, for he says in explanation of the circumstance to which he alludes, "Till the Chapel in Clemens Street was built, A.D. 1816, the Congregation assembled in a room at the Oxford Hotel, now called 'the Blenheim.'" Those meetings did not take place earlier than 1813.

There were two public houses in Leamington—the "Dog," and the "Bowling Green "—and if Mr. Moody selected the former for his ministrations, as by some is supposed to have been the case, the landlord was William Abbotts, who resided there until 1793, when the " New Inn " was ready for occupation. The theory of the services having taken place at a public house is not improbable, seeing that nowhere else could sufficient accommodation be obtained. It is unlikely that Abbotts would refuse to hire one of his rooms to the Dissenters, notwithstanding his churchmanship and possession of a pew at the Parish Church. His mind has not been shown to have been tainted with sectarian bigotry; on the contrary, his activity in promoting the welfare of the parish, and desire to make it popular, suggest a disposition tolerant of the opinions and conveniences of others. The pre-existence of Nonconformity in the village is incapable of the same degree of proof as the visits of Mr. Moody, but that it was present in an assertive and sturdy form in the days of the Hearth Tax (1662) is not a gratuitous assumption. The most gratifying circumstance attendant upon Mr. Moody's local inauguration of the principles of Independency is the absence from the village of that spirit of persecution which was rampant in the rural districts, and to which the itinerant and unmitred Bishops of Dissent had to submit with heroic patience. At a time when preacher-baiting was by no means an isolated diversion, and Long Itchington was pelting Nonconformist parsons out of its village, the Rev. James Moody was preaching at Leamington without interruption, annoyance or molestation.

Leamington, in the months of April and May, 1791, was heavily scourged with a visitation of smallpox, the most remarkable circumstances of which were the promptitude displayed by the parish authorities in applying the remedial measure of inoculation, THE CONGREGATIONAL CHAPEL, CLEMENS STREET,

After it became the second Theatre of Leamington. It was erected as a Chapel in 1816; was sold in 1849 for a Theatre, and was re-purchased in 1866 for use as a Congregational Chapel.

and the strict conformity of the course of the disease to those laws which medical science had prescribed as its natural direction and effect. The introduction of inoculation into England from Turkey, about the year 1721, by Lady Mary Wortley Montague, led to enquiries which showed that the average rate of mortality in cases of smallpox was one death of every five or six persons attacked, but of those who were inoculated not more than one in five or six hundred. There were twenty-nine cases of natural smallpox in the village, resulting in six deaths—precisely the number predicated by the collectors of smallpox statistics. One hundred and twenty-four of the villagers were inoculated, all of whom recovered and were found to be proof against the contagion.

The duty of providing for the public a means of ascertaining the time has been acknowledged by the parish authorities from a very early period. Of this the more ornamental than useful sun dial on the south side of the church tower was an instance. In the seventeenth century the novelty of a clock was introduced, as much to the delight and wonder as for the convenience of the inhabitants. We may feel certain that the majority had never seen a clock before, and for some time it would prove as great an attraction as the church or the parson, however popular he might be. The maker was Nicholas Paris, of Warwick, probably a foreign immigrant who had learned the art of clock-making abroad. He afterwards improved the clock, and subsequently entered into a contract with the Churchwardens for keeping it in repair, a copy of which we subjoin.

"One bond of the penalty of ten pounds dated the I ith day of December, 1678, and made by Nicholas Paris to John Lees and Edward Rawbone, and conditioned as followeth: Whereas the above-named Nicholas Paris did heretofore, at the charges of the inhabitants of the above-said parish of Lemington Priors, make for them one Church clock, which he hath lately altered and put in order at their charges: Now the condition of this obligation is such that, if the said Nicholas Paris shall from time to time during his natural life, as often as need shall require, upon every reasonable request to him to be made by the Churchwardens of the said parish for the time being, or by either of them, well and sufficiently repair and put in order the said clock in all things except only cords and such repairs as the said clock shall at any time need by reason of any hurt to be done to the same by any person or persons, other than the said Nicholas Paris, his servants, or agents, or if the Churchwardens of the said parish of Lemington Priors for the time being, or one of them shall not yearly during the natural life of the said Nicholas Paris pay unto the said Nicholas the summe of one shilling between the Feast Day of St. Michael the Archangel and the Feast Day of the Nativity of our Lord yearly, at the now dwelling house of the said Nicholas Paris, in Warwick, above-said, for keeping the said clock in repair as aforesaid, then this present obligation shall be void, or else shall remain in full force and virtue."

After fulfilling the terms of his contract with exemplary fidelity for thirty-eight years, during which time we may rest assured the grateful churchwardens cheered and sustained him by the punctuality of their annual payments, the good old clockmaker died in 1716; but whether from the infirmities of age, the burden of wealth, or the cares of office, does not appear. At a vestry meeting, held on the 20th of December in that year, it was decided to cancel, and deliver up the bond to his son, Thomas Paris.

A brief reference, while on this subject, to an ingenious clock, introduced into Leamington in the early part of 1857, will provide entertainment without involving a waste of space. The tradesman to whose enterprise the thanks of the public were due for the opportunity of seeing something approaching the ingenuity of the Orrery of Wimborne Minster, reduced to the scale of an ordinary house clock, was Mr. F. White, then in business in Regent Street, as jeweller. The clock in question was very simple in construction, and showed, on one dial, without the aid of hands, the time of day at no less than forty-four different places in both hemispheres. It was sold at a moderate price, and combining utility with amusement and curiosity, was extensively patronised by the public.

The interest of horology is carried much farther back than the seventeenth century by the old clock at the Regent Hotel Mews. In no town in England is the elementary stage of clockmaking more vividly contrasted with its perfect development than in Leamington. The turret clock at the Regent has the reputation of an age between three and four hundred years. The companions of its youth were the antiquated hour glass, the sun dial, and the clepsydra of the period of Julius Caesar. All the modern achievements of science in adaptability and excellence of mechanism, artistic finish, electrical contrivance, and arrangements which render it proof against the interruptions of the extremes of temperature find perfect expression in its near neighbour, the clock in the Town Hall tower, presented by Mr. Councillor Bright, during his Mayoralty. The Regent clock is reported as from Stoneleigh Abbey. The late Mr. Simmonds, of Warwick, consulted in 1860 touching its manifold infirmities, accepted its reported age as correct and advised daily attention and unremitting care on the part of the Local Board of Health as indispensable for the continuance of its functions. Assuming the story of its longevity to be well-founded, it must have been marking time at the Abbey when Charles I., weary and dejected, turned away from the frowning

battlements of Coventry and sought an asylum in the classical abode of Sir Thomas Leigh. Mention must not be omitted from this reference of a circumstance which may have some bearing on the probable age of this clock. In 1154, an Abbey of Cistercian Monks was founded at Stoneleigh, and continued in a state of impressive Monastic splendour until the unceremonious dissolution of the Monasteries by Henry VIII. in 1539. About the eleventh century, the clepsydra—a water-clock introduced into Britain by Julius Caesar—began to give way, in the presence of numerous improvements in clocks moved by weights and wheels, discovered and first applied in the monasteries of Europe. These inventions would, in the very nature of things, be carried from the principal conventual institutions of one country to another, and especially to powerful and influential confraternities like the Cistercian Order which flourished in great pomp at Stoneleigh. The Regent clock has no name of a maker, and possibly we may regard it as one of the manufactures of the Monks and Priors while they were in residence at the Abbey. Should the statements which have been publicly made of its age, and never contradicted or called in question, be verified by further research, its destination should be, not the miscellanies of the marine store dealer, but the future Museum of Leamington.

Once more we must temporarily lay aside the attractive subject of the Parish Church, the settlement of an important principle of parish law in respect of pews to which it had incidentally given rise, and the diverting story of its clock history, for the consideration of two other topics, both nearly associated with old Leamington, but differing in their effects on the modern history of the town. The physical aspect of the village having been so often described, and being so much a staple commodity of common tradition and everyday conversation, renders any minute literary photography of its lanes and cottages in these pages a work of supererogation. Even if there had been no such informa-

tion vouchsafed to the public, the illustrations we have published would suffice to convey to the mind of the reader a more vivid idea of the village rusticity than would be possible by the employment of the most flexible and copious vocabulary. But while it is unnecessary to particularise, a general portraiture will not be out of place. The chief characterisation of the village was that of seclusion from the outer world. It was self-contained, and influenced largely by the prevalent superstitions, from the effect of which not even the courses of agriculture were excepted. North of the Leam there were only three residences—Newbold Comyn, the farm house of the Campions, and a small hut in the Quarry Field. All the land formed parts of farms in various occupations. The principal buildings in the old town were the Church, the Manor House, the farm houses, the "Black Dog," and the "Bowling

Green Inn." The latter occupied the site of the Guernsey Temperance Hotel, now owned and conducted by Mr. Councillor Charles Purser. One of its rooms being the largest in the village, and the only one suited to public meetings, was dignified by the name of the "Assembly Room." The Bowling Green was the land in front, bounded by Regent Place, Bath Street, High Street, and Church Street, and it was from this place that the famous aeronaut Green made the first balloon ascent in Leamington in 1825. In the village era, the Green, which was a favourite resort for the recreation of bowling, was enclosed by a thick, high hedge, with tall spreading elms growing at intervals along its course, the branches of which in summer sheltered the lanes and the players from the burning rays of the sun. The land enclosed by Regent Place,

Bath Street, Gloucester Street and Church Street was the well-stocked garden belonging to the Inn, and on the south side of the Bowling Green was an unenclosed piece of land, with a pond in the middle, the fishing rights of which belonged to the public. The original bridge which spanned the Leam. had a steep ascent, whether approached from the town side or the fields on the north bank. At a not very remote period, the traffic was so limited, that a mere ford across the river at the most convenient place was probably all that was required. Tradition says that at one time the communication was by means of stones placed at intervals in the shallow parts of the stream. The structure which stood on the site of the Victoria Bridge was, until 1809, only wide enough to admit one carriage or vehicle at once, and if a foot passenger were on the bridge at the same time and proceeding in the contrary direction,.there were angular spaces left to enable him to step aside while the cart, wagon, carriage, or whatever it might be, passed along. Near the old Town Hall in High Street, there was a duck pond fed by the Whitnash brook, and in Bath Street, the water in an open ditch flowed past the Old Well down to the river.

Within a stone's-throw of the Church were several heavily-gabled farm houses, in the moss-grown eaves of which twittering sparrows kept noisy concert from "incense breathing morn" till "dewy eve;" adjacent rickyards, flecked with the snowy plumage of poultry and pigeons, and capacious barns, from which, in the autumn months, the sounds of the discriminating flail reverberated ceaselessly through the village. In the long winter evenings, the old-fashioned horn lanthorns flitted like fire-flies about the folds, the lanes, and paths, emitting just sufficient light to reveal the surrounding Cimmerian darkness. Near the bottom of Court Street was the inevitable village smithy. Not "under a spreading chestnut tree," but beneath the shadows of umbrageous elms, did the perspiring smith, amid constellations of sparks, shape the fruitful ploughshare on his melodious anvil. The land on the north bank of the river was artistically brocaded with woods and copses, dingles and dells. One of the most beautiful of the old groves was inadvertently omitted from our list of local descriptive names. Where the New Town Hall, the Denby Buildings and the Theatre Royal stand, was a collection of the finest elms in Warwickshire,

interspersed with majestic oaks and soaring pines, flanked with holly trees from two to three feet measurement in the girth, and in later days, jewelled in the Parade with masses of golden laburnum, and lilacs, mauve and white. The remembrance of this splendid anthology, and its proximity to the Regent Hotel, has been preserved by the appropriate compound title of Regent Grove.

There were two Bowling Green Inns, not at the same time, but in succession.

The Guernsey Temperance Hotel wa, the second, and stands on land which was anciently called the Town Close; the earlier Inn occupied a site in High Street between Bath

Street and Church Street, and adjoining it was an open space, where on May 5, 1813, was established the first of the four public markets which Leamington has possessed.

It was continued on Wednesdays, with some success, for several years during the season. The original "Bowling Green house," as it was named in the Award, is

F sententiously described by the Rev. W. Field, who wrote while it was standing, as "small and comfortable." One of its principal attractions was the commodious Green, which, kept in admirable order, was a favourite resort for the farmers and gentry. "In Whitsuntide week," says Moncrieff, they held "a grand feast and festival, when all the members walked in solemn procession to the church, where an appropriate sermon was preached on the occasion, after which the day was finished in the exhibition of various rural sports on a stage erected in the green, at the southeast corner of the inn, when the Tolletts, Strutts, and Douces, that chanced in the midwhile of their antiquarian and Shakespearean researches to visit the natal shire of their favourite bard, were frequently gratified by the appearances and performances of troops of Morisco, or Morris dancers, those most fascinating remembrancers of our old Knglish sports. These merry wights, with their bells, sticks and handkerchiefs, were wont to contend for the silken prize of pink or blue, which it was the enviable

province of the fair and virtuous Mayday Queen of the village to award; we know not if they had, as in the olden time, their Dramatis Personae of Fool, Friar, Hobby-horse and Maid Marian, and however rude and imperfect their exhibitions to the researcher into the amusements of the days gone by, they could not but have proved highly interesting."

This local version of Milton's "L'Allegro" was characteristic of the "small and comfortable" for many years after the dawn of the present century. Readers of Miss Prickett's admirable novel, "Warwick Castle," will remember the sleepless night Lord Montague passed at Sinker's hotel on his arrival in "Lemmington." "It was, unfortunately, the assembly night, and this festive meeting being held in a ball-room, at another Inn, exactly opposite to our bedchamber at the hotel, the windows of which were all thrown open for air on account of the sultry heat of the weather, the continued repetition of the music, added to the changing steps of the dancers as they pursued their amusement till a very late, or rather early hour, entirely banished sleep." The next day was " devoted to the arduous task of lodging-hunting, and after having perambulated every corner of this rapidly increasing village, and found our search unsuccessful, for not a single cottage appeared untenanted, we at length obtained a conditional promise of a house then occupied by some of the Gordon family, who were expected to leave the place upon an excursion to Cheltenham. " The ball at the Bowling Green Inn which deprived Lord Montague of the solace of "Tir'd Nature's sweet restorer, balmy Sleep," may have been the memorable occasion when the celebrated Dr. Samuel Parr, of Hatton, led off a country dance with her Grace the Dowager Duchess of Gordon.

p " The house then occupied by some of the Gordon family " was Gordon House, situate in Gordon Passage, leading from New Street into Russell Terrace. It is a three-storied plain brick dwelling, with two large bay windows on the ground Hoor. At the time of the Gordon resicience these looked out upon a spac ions lawn into George Street, which had not then been formed. Tin-erection ot surrounding properties in George Street. Kussell terrace. New Street and Gordon Street, and the provision of more attractive residential properties north of the river, caused this one e celebrated residence to deteriorate in value. For many years it has been occupied by Mr. Thomas liagshaw as a marine store, and last month i August, it was sold by Messrs. J. Staite & Sons, by public auction, to Mr. Madelcy liurman, who is also the owner of the site on which Men Sate hwcH's t ottagc stood. Gordon House, the residetu e of one of the oldest aristocratic-families in the early years of the century, may be seen from the Russell Terrace end of Gordon Passage.

The Guernsey Temperance Hotel was built in 1825, the year of Green's balloon ascent, by Joseph Parsons, on land purchased from Edward Treadgold, and described as "part of the Town Close. " When completed, it was licensed and opened under the title of "The Rowling Green Commercial Inn." The second landlord was Mr. Burridge, and he was succeeded by Charles Liebenrood, a son of George Christopher Liebenrood, at that time proprietor of *The Royal Leamington Spa Courier.* Owing to rival hostelries, the business was not a success, and on Mr. Liebenrood relinquishing the tenancy, the house was closed for a considerable time. The next occupant was Mrs. Meeks, who had previously kept a second-hand furniture shop in Ben Satehwell's Cottage, New Street, and who was the last resident in that famous dwelling. She re-opened the Inn as a Temperance Motel, and continued the business until 1873, when Mr. Councillor C. Purser, the present owner and occupier, acquired the property.

As an illustration of the healthy conditions of Leamington and their influence upon longevity, we may mention that there are now living, hale and hearty, several old men and women who wen- included in the third census of 1821, and some of whom were present at the balloon ascent from the Bowling Green

in 1825. It would be difficult, if not impossible, to collect all their names and ages, and an imperfect list might lead to the inference that we had selected some in preference to others. We must, therefore, content ourselves for the present with a reference to one who appears to be the senior, and publish later on the best list we can obtain. Mr. William Clarke, 3, Cross Street, now eighty-six years of age, was working in the fields at Leek Wootton, and as there was a good deal of talk in the village about the balloon, and speculation as to what it might be, he and two women left their work and came to Leamington to see the ascent. When they returned, the cottagers came out and plied them with questions, for they had never seen a balloon, and had no idea what it was like. Clarke's description was graphic and original. In reply to enquiries, he said it was " as big as a wheat-stack, and was made of silk. It was filled with smoke; covered with a cabbage net, and under it there was a big clothes basket in which the man sat." Green, who has the credit of having been the most successful and experienced of European aeronauts, was the first who employed coal gas instead of hydrogen, the inflating medium used by all his predecessors. The ascent from Leamington was among the early demonstrations of the superiority and greater economy of the new system. CHAPTER XII. ODERN Leamington has even-reason to be gratified for the success which has attended the growth and prosperity of its many well-conducted Friendly Societies. A large saving to the rates, an improvement in the standard of health, the prevention of disease, and the encouragement of thrift among the working classes have been the direct results of the movement.

The establishment of the parent Friendly Society in Leamington took place nine years after the enclosure of the commonable lands. On Whit Monday, 1777, Ben Satchwell convened a village meeting, at which was started "The Fountain of Hospitality," a philanthropic club, the objects of which are fully set forth in the following paragraphs.

The name will doubtless appear to most readers bombastic, if not grotesque, but to such as are acquainted with the inflated and high-sounding titles of Friendly Societies in the last century, it will be admired for its comparative modesty and obvious propriety of language and sentiment. Proud as the Odd-Fellows, Foresters and members of other kindred friendly organizations must feel when they contemplate the beneficent work they have accomplished, and the noble edifice which they have reared by the simple process of combined effort, it cannot fail to increase their satisfaction to find that the principle of unity for their own and each other's good was adopted and practised in the form of club-life before Leamington had the least title to be called a borough, and that they occupy the first place in the chronological order of public institutions. We transcribe from the Book of Rules the description of this interesting association:—

"The Fountain nf Hospitality supported by select Pillars of Gratitude: Beautified with Humanity and also embellished with Regulations to conduct a Friendly Society, holden at Leamington Priors in the County of Warwick. United in a bond of peace, and good will, to glorify (iod, to comfort and assist each other as Christian Brethren to provide for the sick, the Lame, the Blind, the Prisoners, the Widows, the Orphans, the Infirmities of old age and to Bury the dead.

Comprised by B. Satchwell & Co. We then that are strong ought to bear the Infirmities of the weak.—*Rom.* 15, vers 1.

"General Meetings of the Society. I. On Whitsun-Monday. 2. First Monday, on or after the 24th day of June. j. First Monday on or after the 29th day of September. 4. First Monday on or after the 20th day of December. 5. First Monday on or after the 25th day of March: all annually.

' N.B.—The Committee meet on the 14th day next after every meeting aforesaid."

In the rules, which are styled the " Articles of Agreement," the appointment of a "Warden," or as he would be called in these modern times, a "Sick Visitor," is first provided for. He was to be elected by the Stewards of the "Leamington Priors Association" to visit any brother who fell sick, and report upon his state and condition in writing at the end of every twenty-eight days, under the penalty of forfeiting sixpence for each and every neglect. He was to pay the sick brother the sum of shillings per week, the same to be repaid to him by the Society on demand.

At the annual meeting on Whitsun Monday, May 16, 1785, it was declared that many of the original rules had been found of little or no use, in consequence of which they were revoked, while those which had been adjudged useful and necessary were retained "in full force, and power and virtue," with some additions which were considered to be required.

The rules prescribed that at all times thereafter every person who intended to be a brother of the society should first give notice in writing and send one shilling with the same to some brother, setting forth his Christian and surname, age, occupation and place of abode, but such writing was not to be deemed any notice until the same had been read and laid before a general meeting of the society. On all occasions when a brother was chosen, the question was to be determined by the impartial method of voting by ballot in a general meeting and in the presence of one steward, or deputy steward, and one clerk with nineteen other brothers at least, a less number voting to be null and void. And whenever twenty-one members or upwards as aforesaid voted for a new brother and the majority appeared in favour of the candidate, it was the duty of one of the clerks to enter in the books the day and date of the election, and the true number of votes for the candidate and against him, or forfeit one shilling for every neglect, and one steward and one clerk were to attest-the same or forfeit sixpence. After a member had been chosen as aforesaid, the stewards and committee had fourteen days to enquire and receive information touching the character of such member elect, and if any reasonable objection appeared that such person was not qualified, one of the clerks was to write against the votes of the election thus: "T.J. is not qualified for a member of this society, and, therefore, is excluded by the committee," the same being attested at the meeting by five of the committee at the least, or pay a fine of twopence each for neglect. On confirmation of the election, the new member had to contribute five shillings to the cash box, but if rejected the shilling sent with the application was returned. No one could be elected a member under sixteen nor over thirty-five years of age; the following were also ineligible: felons, soldiers, sailors, militia, Jews and other aliens. The place for holding the general meetings was for the members to determine, but if no selection was made, they were to take place alternately at the two public-houses, known, the one by the sign of the Dog and the other by that of the Bowling Green.

The hours for commencing business were six o'clock in the evening in summer and five in the winter months; members' contributions one shilling and sixpence each and threepence to be spent in ale, but of this sum one shilling and sixpence was to be applied in eating, and two shillings and sixpence for committee refreshments. On Whitsun Monday, " our great feast day," the Fountain was much given to demonstration and hospitality. The thirty members of which it was composed assembled at the Club House in High Street at eight o'clock in the morning, and after transacting business, marched to Church at eleven, accompanied by a "band of music," for whose services the sum of two shillings and sixpence was payable out of the funds. In this Church Parade, *every* member was to appear "in a decent manner, with a wand, or some emblematical instrument or order." Ten shillings and sixpence was allowed the Vicar for preaching the sermon, and one shilling the Parish Clerk for his attendance. Returning to the Club House on the conclusion of the service, to the merry strains of the band, they were re- galed with a bountiful feast, for which each member paid one shilling and one shilling for ale; a penny being also due from each member for the clerks, one penny for the cooking and another for the waiting. A sum of one and sixpence was reserved for refreshments at the next committee meeting.

With what absorbing interest would a full report of these proceedings be now studied! Ben Satchwell's few remarks on opening the Lodge; the subjects brought forward for discussion; the results of the year's working; the names, addresses and occupations of the thirty pioneers of the Friendly Societies movement in Leamington; the strength and composition of the band and the music they discoursed; the small crowd of villagers who lined the streets; the menu, the toast list, and the Vicar's sermon, would furnish a delectable page of reading. The personality of the trombone, who, with ballooned-cheeks spoke in tones which shook the thatch of the cottages; the big drum with stately step beating rhythm and earnestness into the movement, and the dominating clarionet, would add to the interest of local musical memories.

According to rule, the business of the Society was concluded at four o'clock in the afternoon, but there was nothing to prevent the devotion of an extra hour or two to the cause of enthusiasm, a renewal of pledges of friendships and convivialities. The benefits of membership were an allowance of three shillings per week during sickness for members who had been enrolled twelve months, and five shillings after membership of two years. An old age allowance of one shilling weekly was granted for members sixty years of age who had been on the books twenty years; two shillings at sixty-five with twenty-five years' membership, and three shillings at seventy years of age and thirty years' membership. When the funds in the cash box were below twenty pounds, a levy of threepence per member might be made.

We have no information of the duration of the society's existence, but on such a basis it could not have been immortal. All Fountains must soon run dry which have no better sources of supply than the contributions specified in its rules. But the efforts of Satchwell are not to be judged by nineteenth century standards. He had not in his possession the carefully prepared tables of actuaries which make the establishment of a solvent Friendly Society now an easy task, nor could he call to his aid a single experimental test as to the proportion which should exist between contributions and benefits. The soundness of his society does not call for discussion in this place. It is his motive rather than his method with which we have to deal. In the lofty and capacious gallery of illustration which the history of Leamington has filled with noble and beautiful pictures, there is no scene more captivating than the sight of these thirty hob-nailed Knights Hospitallers, clad in homely fustian and serviceable cordurov, groping with sterling probity of purpose for workable ideals of self-help, amidst gross statistical darkness, and seeking a harvest from a soil barren of philanthropic husbandry and experimental science. Actuated by the single desire of enhancing the welfare of all, they were unconsciously assisting in laying the foundation of a movement destined to outlive every form of ridicule, to flourish in spite of all kinds of opposition; to acquire renewed strength from those errors of judgment which are unavoidable in new movements, in our own time to wield an influence respected by the most powerful Governments; and to be locally represented by a roll of membership which includes the most reflective and thrifty of the working classes of Leamington and many of those who by loyal devotion to its interest have won for themselves the highest positions in the administrative departments of the borough.

The remaining events we shall have to notice before proceeding with the history of the present century are made up of sunshine and cloud, storm and calm. What was the local effect of the Civil Wars is not discoverable from any work we have seen, though it is not impossi-

ble that Charles and Cromwell had their adherents; that Cavaliers and Puritans scowled at each other as they passed in the lanes of the village, that Leamington was represented in the armies which fought at Edge Hills in 1642; among the Royalists who were defeated with Prince Rupert at Marston Moor in 1644, and the Roundheads who were victorious under Cromwell at Naseby in 1645. We need not be reminded that these are suppositions, for we present them only in that light. Under the circumstances, Leamington could not have been an indifferent spectator of the great struggle between the Parliament and the King, nor have remained impassive, with the echoes of war resounding upon its borders, the tramp of armed hosts at its doors; with the powerful inducement of higher wages being obtainable by righting than by working,

With the Wooden Belfry and the boundary wall before the improvements of 1888. The New Post Office is also shown. The Belfry was taken down in 1889, and the Porch at the west end removed at the same time.

and with the martial spirit inculcated from the pulpit as the first of religious duties. In a list of Warwickshire Ministers in 1648, who had signed the "Solemn League and Covenant," are "Thos. Glover, Preacher at Lemmington Priors; Benjamin Spicer, Minister at Milverton, and Henry Smitheman,-Minister of Lillington." They were probably Presbyterians, and practically recruiting sergeants for the Parliament. Opposed to the Church and to prelacy, the extirpation of which was one of the leading principles of the Covenant, they rank as the first Nonconformists in Leamington and the immediate neighbourhood, though their Nonconformity differed materially from that which passes under the same name in these days. CHAPTER XIII. HE Vestry, as we have explained, was the village Parliament, of which the vicar was "Mr. Speaker" during his tenure of office, or, to use a title better suited to our present form of local government, "his Worship the Mayor." Its franchise was democratic, and its doors were thrown wide open to the parish-

ioners. At the threshold there were no Revising Barristers to bar the way, nor political agents to ask questions which would have made the farmers and the labourers fumble in their thatch for hours before they found the proper answers. Singly it had a wider range of administrative authority than any of the existing governing bodies, but compared with their collective powers, it possessed merely the shadow of strength.

Its transactions are recorded in an old register at the Parish Church, for the perusal of which our thanks and those of the readers of this history are specially due to Mr. Sidney Flavel, ex-Mayor and Vicar's Warden, and Mr. C. I. Blaker, the Warden for the Parish. But for their permission, several ingots of pure historic gold, wrought with patient care and skill, and with qualities of malleability which will enable the antiquarian artist to manufacture numerous leaves of unalloyed auric wealth, would have been absent from these pages.

The book consists of two parts; one being a transcript of minutes from an older register which had been lost; the other containing the results of what has the appearance of a competition in original methods of spelling, by the ancient parish clerks, each one of whom has succeeded so well as to make a conscientious award of the prize an extremely difficult task. The transcript has every excellence except that of legibility. To the ordinary reader it bears a close resemblance to a battalion of Runic characters in a state of fuddle, each letter trying to look very sober, and with comical effect casting imputations on the sobriety of its neighbours. Without pledging ourselves as to the result, we are inclined to think that a page of this might be found very useful as a tourist ticket, or inspire with heart of hope a despairing claimant to the great Jennens's estate. The period to which these minutes apply, extends from 1646 to 1702, and by collecting them in the kaleidoscope of our observation, we learn who were the local aristocracy two centuries ago; make the acquaintance of the yeoman class of that period; ascertain the nature and mode of transacting public business, and discover a more considerable distribution of land among owners and tenant farmers than is to be gained from any other source. Independently of the inherent value of these records historically considered, their worth as the earliest account we have of public meetings and official gatherings in Leamington scarcely admits of exaggeration.

It appears that previous to 1678, the parish documents were kept by Mr. Edward Willes at Newbold Comyn, but on the 5th of November in that year he attended a vestry meeting and "delivered up out of his hands ten several writings hereunder menconed belonging to the inhibtants of the parish of Lemington Priors, and the same were thereupon laid up in the box which is within the Church of Lemington Priors aforesaid. " The box had two locks and two keys, one of which, with the agreement and consent of the inhabitants of the said parish, was to be kept in Leamington Priors and the other in Newbold Comyn. The writings referred to, as well as a number of others, are believed to relate principally to the old system of apprenticing boys by the parish; the settlement of poor residents in their own parish, and other duties now discharged by Boards of Guardians. Upon these no comment is required, and the selection of one will serve as an illustration of the rest: "One bond of the penalty of £40, dated 1 3 June, 1646, made by Richard Rawbon and John Olney to Peter Willes and Thomas Cartwright, condiconed to save the parish harmless from Robert John Johnson." The interpretation which has been placed upon this is that Johnson was the apprentice, and Rawbon and Olney, two householders, who became sureties to the churchwardens, or overseers, for his diligent and honest service to his master, and responsible for any claim to which misconduct on his part might give rise. There are many other of these bonds, all couched in the same formal terms.

One of the writings which Mr. Willes gave up to the Vestry was a lease dated November 30th, 1677, showing the poverty and rent of some of the cot-

tages. The minute sets forth that it was made by "Tarry Willes to John Corpson, Samuel Clark, John Lees, Thomas Savage and George Eborn, of the little cottage or tenement with thappurtenances, in the occupacon of Anne Smith, widow: To hold from the day next before the date hereof for the term of sixty years (if the said Anne Smith shall so long live), without impeachment of wast, and from and after the death of the said Anne Smith, for the term of six months, without impeachment of wast, under the yearly rent of one shilling, payable on the 25th of March."

The contract of Nicholas Paris, of Warwick, for keeping the Church clock in order, which we have published, is among the other records, and the following report of the meeting in 1702 for repairing the mounds round the churchyard:—

"The Parish of Lemington Priors in the County of Warwick. Memorandum: That upon the twentieth day of October, 1702, after consideracon of the best evidence that could be had touching the repairs of the mounds of the Churchyard in Lemington Priors, it is concluded and agreed upon by the freeholders and inhibtants of the said parish that the said mounds ought to be repaired at the charges of the occupiers of the houses and lands hereinafter menroncd in the manner following, vizt:—

"On the east side of the Churchyard, begining at the north end of the mound from Mr. Corpson's wall, the lands of Edward Willes, the elder, gent, in Newbold Comyn, which was his ancestors estate are liable to repair the first three yards and an half. The lands of the Honble. Dame Charlotte Beaufoy, widow, and of the said Edward Willes in Xewbold Comyn, which were the lands of Sir Henry Beaufoy, knight, deceased, are liable to repair the next three yards and an half, The lands of Robert Fisher, Esq., in Newbold Comyn, are liable to repair the next seven yards thereof. Forty acres of Mr Samuel Clark, which were heretofore the lands of John Morcott, are liable to repair the next four yards thereof. Twenty acres of Francis Cassmore, now in the occupacon of

Thomas Middleton, which were also heretofore the lands of the said John Morcott, are liable to repair the next two yards thereof. Fifty acres of Mr. John Lees and fifty acres of Edward Willes, the younger, gent, being in all one hundred acres, which were heretofore the lands of the said John Morcott, are liable to repair the next ten yards thereof. Twenty acres, late of Tarry Willes, which were heretofore the lands of— Jaggard are liable to repair the next two yards thereof. Thirty acres of John Corpson, gent, in the occupacon of George Yardley, heretofore the lands of John Olney, are liable to repair the next three yards thereof. Forty acres of the said Robert Fisher in the occupacon of the said Thomas Middleton, heretofore the lands of Thomas Mans, are liable to repair the next four yards thereof. Four score acres of Booth Allestre, Esq., in the occupacon of Edward Rawbone, heretofore the lands of John Rabone, are liable to repair the next eight yards thereof which end at the gate. The gate is to be repaired by the Churchwardens at the charge of the wholl parish. Twenty acres heretofore the lands of Widow Cox whereof part is now the land of the said John Corpson, other part is the land of Stephen Nicholls, gent, in the occupacon of William Bodington, and the rest is the land of Sarah Mallery, widow, in the occupacon of James Webb, are liable to repair the two yards mound between the said gate and the wall of the house of the said John Lees, heretofore called Morcott's parlour wall.

' The south side of the Churchyard is mounded with the houses and pales of the said John Lees, which he is to repair.

"On the west side of the Churchyard, begining at the south end of the mound from the said pales of the said John Lees, where formerly stood a barn of the said John Morcott, thirty acres of Robert Lawrence, late the lands of William Hobday, and heretofore the lands of William Freeman, are liable to repair the first three yards thereof. Twenty acres of the said Robert Lawrence, late the lands of Thomas Naseby, and heretofore the lands of John Freeman arc liable to repair the next two yards thereof. Forty acres of the said Booth Allestre, late in the occupacon of John Cox. and now of Edward Rawbone, being heretofore lands of William Booth, are liable to repair the next four yards thereof. Three score acres, late of the said Tarry Willes, heretofore the lands of Henry Jaggard, are liable to repair the next six yards thereof. Twenty acres of the said John Corpson, in the occupacon of George Yardley, heretofore the lands of Rowland Anderton, are liable to repair the next two yards thereof. Forty acres of the said Samuel Clark, heretofore of George Alcox, are liable to repair the next four yards thereof. Twenty acres of the said Robert Lawrence, heretofore the lands of the said Henry Jaggard, called Padmore Ground, are liable to repair the next two yards thereof. Fifty acres of the said John Corpson, heretofore lands of Thomas Holbage, are liable to repair the ST. Mary's Church, Ekected 1839.

First incumbent, Rev. Dr. Marsh. The site of the church was presented by Mr. Willes; opening service and consecration, July 27, 1839.

next five yards thereof. Thirty acres of the said John Corpson, in the occupacon of the said George Yardley, heretofore the lands of Quintan Ward, arc liable to repair the next three yards thereof. Eight acres of John Summers, heretofore the lands of the said Quintan Ward are liable to repair the next one yard thereof. Ten acres of Mr. Thomas Savage and others, in the occupacon of John Reading, heretofore the land of John Man, are liable to repair the next one yard thereof, which ends at the gate. The gate is to be repaired by the Churchwardens at the charge of the wrholl parish. Ten acres of the said John Corpson, in the occupacon of William Olney, heretofore the lands of Thomas Egleston, are liable to repair the next yard on the north side of that gate. Fifteen acres of Richard Bicklcy, heretofore the lands of Robert Belt, are liable to repair the next one yard and an half thereof. Fifteen acres of the said Francis Cassmore, in the occupacon of the said Thomas Middleton, heretofore the lands of the said Robert Bett, are liable to repair the next

one yard and an half thereof. Four score acres late of Hercules Beaufoy, Esq., in the occupacon of John Russell, heretofore the lands of Thomas Cartwright, are liable to repair the next eight yards thereof, which end at a cotage in the occupacon of Mary Pen, widow, which cotage, standing close to the Churchyard, doth supply the last five yards of the mound on the west side of the Churchyard, which five yards, if the cotage did not hinder, ought to be repaired as followeth, viz.:— The house, or cotage of the said Thomas Savage and others, in the occupacon of the said John Reading, heretofore the house of the said Henry Jaggard, called the Mill House, is liable to repair the first yard thereof, lying next to the said last-menconed eight yards. The cotage of the said Stephen Nicholls, in the occupacon of the said William Bodington, heretofore the lands of Robert Swane, is liable to repair the next yard thereof. The cotage of the said Robert Lawrence, in the occupacon of Sara Greenway, widow, heretofore the lands of the said Thomas Holbage, is liable to repair the next yard thereof. The cotage of the said John Corpson, in the occupacon of the said William Olney, heretofore the land of the said William Freeman, is liable to repair the next yard thereof. The cotage of the said Francis Cassmore, in the occupacon of the said Thomas Middleton, heretofore the land of the said Robert Bott, is liable to repair the next yard thereof, which endeth at the house of Daniel Dawkes.

"'The north side of the Churchyard, begining at the west end thereof, is mounded by the house and hedg of Daniel Dawkes so far as his ground goes, which he is to repair, and from thence to the barn, stable, stone wall, and gate of the said John Corpson, do make the rest of the mound on that side, which he is in like maner to repair.— (Signed)—Edw. Willes, sen., Robert Lawrence, Robert Campion, John Summers, J. Richard Onley, Joseph Satchwell, Edward Rawbone, John Cave, John Corpson, William Duffing."

The income of the Parish Church has from time immemorial been largely de-

pendent upon charges made on lands and agricultural produce. These were termed "Vicar's Tythes," and previous to the Award of 1768 they were collected on both sides of the river. On the south they were abolished by the Award, Mr. Wise and the Vicar being compensated by grants of land out of the open and commonable fields for the loss, by the former of the Greater, and by the latter of the Lesser tithes. This adjustment did not affect the land on the north of the" river, where the Vicarial Tithing system continued as before, but there Mr. Matthew Wise had no tithing interest. On February 11, 1796, Mr. John Bird viewed the lands in Newbold Comyn, and made a valuation of the payments due from the farmers to the Vicar of Leamington as tithes. From this document we gather full particulars of the several scales of tithes imposed, the names of the fanners occupying the land, and the sizes and nature of their holdings.

"A valuation of the Vicarial Tythes of Newbold, in the Parish of Leamington Priors.

"Lands belonging to Bertie Greatheed, Esq., held by Mr. Perkins, computed to contain 60 acres (including 12a. of meadow), part in turf and part in tillage, reckoned to Summer and sheer 40 sheep, Tythe of which is 4 Fleeces, and at 4 shillings per fleece amounts to 16s. Also thought to breed 20 Lambs, Tythe of which at 10d. per Lamb is £1. It is likewise presumed that the 12 acres of Meadow will produce annually, upon the average, one Tun of Hay to the Acre, but, supposing the same to be grazed one year in a many, or that the Crop be damaged by a Flood, or by bad weather, under these circumstances it is supposed that 15 hundred to the Acre may be a fair calculation, the Tythe of which is i hundd. to an acre, and 2s. ad. per cwt, conies to £2 9s. 6d. Besides the above, it is thought there will be due for tythe, calves, or for dry cows or other feeding Cattle, or for extra stock after Harvest, etc., commonly called Agistment, Tythes, after ye rate of 3d. per Acre, amounting to (for sixty Acres) 15s. Whole vicarial Tythes of Mr.

Perkins's farm, £5 os. bd.

"Lands belonging to the Rev. Edward Willes, in the occupation of Mr. Court, computed to be about 160 acres, viz: 25 meadow, 66 pasture, and 69 in tillage, supposed to Summer and Sheer 90 sheep, Tythe, wool t) Fleeces, and at 4s. per fleece comes to £1 16s. Also supposed to breed 45 lambs, Tythe of which, at tod. each lamb is £2 5s. od.; likewise the Tythe of 25 acres of Hay, at 15 hundred to the Acre, and at 2s. gd. per hundred amounts to£5 3s. od. Besides Tythe of Calves and Agistment, etc., at 3d. per Acre (160) £2. Amount of Tythe on Mr. Court's farm, 11 4s. od.

"Mansion House and Gardens with 30 acres (computed measure) of good Greensward ground, judged to be worth not less than 30 shillings an Acre, yearly upon the average. Tythe laid at 3s. per acre, £q ios.

THE LEAMINGTON COLLEGE, BINSWOOD AVENUE. Established 1843; foundation stone of the College laid in 1847 by Dr. Jephson.

"One Pingle of pasture land belonging to Rev. W. Willes but in the holding of William Abbotts, situate near the Bridleroad leading towards Warwick, said to be about two acres, valued at 30 shillings an acre. Tythe laid at 3s. per acre, 6s.

" Pinglc " is an obsolete term, but frequently used in former times as descriptive of small enclosures of land. Barclay, Worcester, Johnson, Bailey, Todd and other lexicographers generally define it as meaning " a small croft or enclosure." The word was the subject of some enquiry and disquisition in " Notes and Queries" in 1874, and again in i88H. when a correspondent contributed the following dialect version from Miss Baker's 11 Northamptonshire Words and Phrases ": "A clump of trees, or underwood; not large enough for a spinney. This sense appears to be peculiar to us." The use of the word in Bird's survey of the land in Xewbold Comyn might either mean that the land had originally been covered with trees or that it was simply a croft, or an enclosure with some kind of fence. There are no means of ascertaining which of these

interpretations is applicable.

"A Farm belonging to the Karl of Aylesford in the holding of Mr. Campion, said to contain 280 acres, viz.: 165 acres pasture and seeds, 30 of meadow (including some small pieces) and 85 in tillage, computed to summer and sheer 180 sheep. Tythe 18 Fleeces which at 4 shillings per fleece comes to £3 12s. Also to breed e)o Lambs, Tythe 9 and tod. per Lamb is £4 10s. Hay ground 30 acres supposed to be mowed yearly and to bear 15 hundred to the acre Tythe of which 45 and at 2 and 9 comes to £b 3s. qd. There is likewise presumed to be due for Tythe of calves and for keep of dry cows or other feeding cattle and for extra stock kept after harvest (commonly called Agistment Tythes) Fruit, Eggs, etc., after the rate of 3d. per acre amounting to £3 10s. Amount of Mr. Campion's Tythes, £17 15s. oxl.

"Tythe of Mr. Sinker's Close and garden (half-an-acre) 2s.

"Tythe of Mr. Vm. Abbotts's Close and Homestal, one acre, 4s.

"Leamington Glebe.—Vicarage House, Hovel, Garden, etc.; Wm. Russell, Tenant (annual value) £2. One close of pasture near the village in the occupation of Mr. Shaw, said to contain 5 acres, valued at 50 shillings per acre, amounts to 12 10s. Mr. Thomas Abbotts, one Lay close, about 3 acres at 25 shillings an acre, "3 15s.; one meadow (part Lays) about 12 acres at 35 shillings, £21; one piece of pasture about yj acres at 45 shillings,,£21 7s. 6d.—Total amount of Glebe, £do 12s. 6d.; ditto of Tythe, £30 2s. 3d. £')') 14s. ad."

We have already spoken of the wages paid in Leamington in the seventeenth century to the farm labourers; those of the artisan class were on the same starvation scale. In "Archrcologia," 1794, there is the following Order of the Warwickshire Court of Quarter Sessions for workmen's wages, the date of which is stated by an excellent authority to have been somewhere about the year 1682:—by the Day.

With Meat and Drink. Without.

A dayry Maide or Wash Maide..........
.... 1 10 o

These minimum doles of wages were earned by the maximum hours of labour which human nature could endure, before they were paid.

"All artificers and labourers, being hired by the day or week, shall betwixt the midel of the months of March and Sept., be and continue, att their work att or before five of the clocke in the morning, and continue att worke, and not depart untill betwixt seven and eight of the clock att night, except it be in the time of breakfast, dinner or drinkinge; the which times at the most shall not exceede above two houres and a halfe in the day, that is to say, att every drinkinge an halfe hour, and for his sleepe, when he is allowed to sleepe, the which is from the midst,of May to the midst of August, halfe an hour att the most, and att every breakfast an halfe hour, and all the saide artificers and labourers, between the midst of September and the midst of March, shall be and continue att their worke from the spring of the day in the morninge, untill the night of the same day, except it be in the time above appointed for breakfast and dinner uppon to loose one penny for every houre's absence, to be deducted and dcalted out of his wages that shall soo offend.

"Every person givinge above the wages appointed shall suffer ten days in prison and forfeit five pounds. Every person taking above the wages appointed shall suffer one and twenty days imprisonment. Every retainer, promise, gift and payment of wages contrary to the Statutes, is utterly void and of none effect.—(Signed)—John Mordaunt, Charles Halt (Holt), John Clopton, Regneld Horster, Edward Hinton; Basil Fieldinge, Charles Howsham, Thomas Clarke."

It has been thought that the price of provisions being low, these wages were equal for a decent livelihood. Such a delusion is dispelled by Macaulay's remarks on the state of the working classes at the Restoration. "The great majority of the nation lived almost entirely on rye, barley, and oats." The hours of work amounted to eighty-seven a week, reckoning from five o'clock in the morning till half-past seven in the evening, and after deducting fifteen for meals and rest, thete were seventy-two hours of manual labour for wages which brought to their tables a diet "almost entirely of rye, barley and oats." We have only to contrast this state of things with the present condition of the working classes in order to see the progress they have made and the share they have obtained of the increased prosperity of England within the last two hundred years.

CHAPTER XIV. OMMOTION and alarm, such as had never disturbed the serenity of the village since the days when the Saxon hordes were marauding in War-wickshire, were the local results of the battle at Edge Hill. Richard Baxter, the Puritan, was preaching at the time at Al-cester, a distance, as the crow flies, of seventeen miles from the scene of action. In his diary is the following note: "Upon the Lord's Day, October 22, 1642, I preached at Alcester for my reverend friend, Mr. Samuel Clarke. As I was preaching, the people heard the cannon playing and perceived the armies were engaged.... Next morning, being desirous to see the field, I went to Edgehill." Leamington, by the same mode of measurement, is ten miles from the battle-field. This shorter distance is, however, considered by some to have been counterbalanced by the difference in the character of the two routes, the spur of the Burton Dassett range intervening between Leamington and Edge Hill, whereas the country between Edge Hill and Alcester is free from such obstruction. Much would depend on the state of the weather and the direction of the wind. The former is thus described: "The ground was wet and miry, but the day was fair overhead" Though the Burton Dassett Hills might have retarded the sound of the roar of battle, they could not have rendered inaudible, in fair weather, at a distance of ten miles, sounds which were distinctly heard in a slightly varying direction at seventeen. Imagination need not be laboriously exercised in respect of the feelings produced by this near approach of the car of the Juggernaut of War. Among the

rustic congregation filing out of the Church on the afternoon of that eventful day; in the cottages and tap-rooms of the public-houses, and beneath the Bowling Green elms, upon whose tops the autumnal tints were gathering, the one topic of conversation would be the issue of the conflict, and the possible course in which the tide of war would roll.

The air, soil, water, and scenery of a locality, are the four great natural agents wheh most directly affect health and longevity. In the possession of these momentous adjuncts, Leamington is more happily situated than any other town in England. As antiquarian subjects, they may with propriety be included in these notes on the ancient order of things, for, unquestionably, they are older than the nation, and even than the race. Making due allowance for the elevations and depressions in the site of the town during the formative era, the atmospheric revolutions of the Glacial epoch, the decrease in the humidity of the climate consequent upon the clearances of the primeval forests, and the adoption of an extensive system of drainage, we might almost apply to them a sentiment borrowed from Byron's description of the Ocean, and say that "such as

G creation's dawn beheld" they are at present. But in one respect they differ from all other subjects in the same category. The moated castle and the ivy-mantled tower, where "the moping owl does to the moon complain," are of small consequence to the dwellers beneath their shadows, in comparison with the nature of the atmosphere breathed, the water used for domestic purposes, and the character of the soil upon which life has to be sustained. The justness of the ancient classification to which we assign these topics may be illustrated and defended by the recital of a witticism of an American lady, who, while on a visit to Leamington, maintained with the dominant pride of her country the superiority of everything in America to all she had seen in England. Warwick Castle having been pointed out to her, and its history of a thousand years ex-

plained, the remark was confidently ventured that America, being a young country could boast of no such antiquity. "I guess our Rocky Mountains will beat your Warwick Castle in antiquity by much more than a thousand years," was the triumphant and conclusive answer.

A celebrated musician, in an inspired invocation to "Gentle spring," with its "Ethereal mildness," has evoked from his lyre a song so fresh and melodious that, once heard, it can never lapse from memory. From the days of Lucretius and Haydn, the spring-time of the year has had irresistible attractions for poets, painters and musicians, but for the scientist has been reserved the higher duty of appraising the effect upon health of the climate in all seasons, and of guiding those who have means, to resorts where disease may be obliterated, chronic maladies assuaged, and vigorous health maintained. It is the province of the meteorologist to almost weigh and count each particle of moisture in the air; that of the geologist to discriminate between soils clayey and gravelly, porous and impervious; and for the chemist and physician to investigate, the former by researches in the laboratory and the latter by observations in the sick chamber, the effects of these varied conditions upon health and disease. The right of Leamington to precedence as a home for the athlete and an asylum for the afflicted, rests upon no shadowy foundation. Statistics which cannot be controverted, and authorities beyond the reach of cavil and the imputation of self-interest, are its testimonies. As the best history which it is possible to write of Leamington would be lacking an essential quality of excellence without some special allusion to these subjects, we propose in this chapter to consider them in a sense and manner somewhat proportionate to their importance and the space at our disposal.

The geological formation has already been alluded to by a quotation from Reeve's "Guide,"of 1839. The information there contained was ample, at that period, to meet the technical wants of the few who turned to the page of geology for curious entertainment rather than useful knowledge. Neither Reeve nor his contemporaries were aware of the subtle influences which the strata of a locality exercise upon the health of the residents, nor of the inexhaustible supply of excellent fresh water reserved in the vast subterranean reservoirs of the Permian and Keuper strata for the future use of the borough. To other instructors we must look for the more edifying knowledge of this branch of geological science. In October, 1877, on the occasion of the Congress at Leamington of the Sanitary Institute of Great Britain, the President (Dr. W. B. Richardson) and a party of ladies and gentlemen visited the Warwick Museum, where they were received by the Rev. P. B. Brodie, the ablest and most eloquent expositor of the geology of the Midlands, and the Nestor of Warwickshire palaeontologists. In the course of a specially instructive address, characterised by his customary lucidity, he strongly emphasised the connection existing between the health of a district and the nature of its soil, and particularly mentioned that the red sandstone formation and the water bearing stones of the Permian and Keuper strata were geological conditions favourable COTTAGES IN HICH STREET, on the site of the premises No. 40, now occupied by Mr. Henry Savage, wheelwright.

in cases of pulmonary affection, including consumption. The formation on which the town stands is of the character he described. It was at this Congress that most valuable compliments were paid Leamington for its cleanliness, healthiness, and low rate of mortality, one of the speakers remarking that it enjoyed as large a meed of health as any town in England, and adding in felicitous terms that statistics showed it to be making rapid progress towards an early realisation of Dr. Richardson's ideal City of Health— Hygeia. The scholar and the sanitarian thus unite their testimonies to the healthfulness of Leamington in terms qualified by no reservation, and admitting of no deductions on account of exaggeration in sentiment or language. The subsoil is composed of gravel intermixed with loam and sand; porous, and conforming to that state of dryness which Dr. Thorne-Thorne, of the Local Government Board, in his valuable remarks to the Medical Book Club at the Warneford Hospital, on July 10, 1890, declared to be the first requisite in a thoroughly healthy dwelling. The soil, in its composition and arrangement, forms the best foundation for healthy residences and provides for the most efficient sanitary administration. By enforcing compliance with an excellent code of by-laws, and carrying out extensive drainage, sewerage and water works, the various governing bodies have turned these natural advantages to the best possible account. On the principle of an ounce of fact being worth a ton of theory, we may mention that the percentage of mortality in Leamington compares favourably with that of any other town in England. In 1894, the annual death rate from all causes, including old age and natural decay, as certified by Dr. S. Browne, the Medical Officer of Health, in his able report to the Corporation, was only 136 per 1,000 of the population. There was no death from enteric fever, and the mortality from the whole class of zymotics was the very small return of o'3 per 1,000.

The prophylactic influences of Leamington, natural and artificial, are best exemplified in the annual reports which have been presented to the Corporation by the Medical Officers of Health since the passing of the Public Health Act, 1872. These registers of the history of the health of the Borough may be consulted by all who are seeking the restoration of lost health, or having good health in their possession, are desirous of retaining it unimpaired. A casual reference will enable them to see in the uniformly low death rate, and the almost total eradication of mortality from zymotic diseases, that while the extrinsic beauties of the town give it a title to be called "The Garden of England," it possesses the higher and more important claim of being regarded as "The Temple of Health."

In support of the foregoing statements, a few statistics from the reports of the late-Mr. J. S. Baly and Dr. S. Browne, the past and present Medical Officers of Health for the Borough, may be advantageously quoted. An examination of the death-rates of inland watering-places from 1879 to 1896 shows Leamington to be invariably among the two or three towns which have the healthiest record. Its position occasionally varies, but never with the effect of bringing it low down in the list. The highest local death-rate in the period named occurred in 1871 and 1891, when the return was i9'4 per 1,000 of the population, and the lowest, lyb, was in 1894. These divergent percentages emphasize the importance of climate. The meteorological report for 1891, furnished by Mr. J. Barnitt, is as follows: "The rainfali was abnormally heavy in the third and fourth quarters; the mean temperature was below the average of the last 27 years; practically there was very little sunshine and almost no summer." "Without doubt," Mr. Baly remarks, "these conditions were important factors in raising our mortality." The climatic influences of 1894 were of an entirely opposite character. "The mean temperature was slightly above the average, and the month of April i'S warmer than usual. The rainfall was about the normal average; though the number of rainy days was unusually large; in no single month was it very high or very low." Omitting from consideration these explanations, and accepting the returns since 1851 as indicative of the general standard of the health of the town, the results will be seen to be satisfactory. The average death-rate for the ten years ending 1861 was 18'c)6 per 1,000 of the population; 1871, 19/4; 1881, 17-6; and from 1882 to 1895, inclusive, 16 5. These registers have more than an arithmetical value. To fully comprehend their import it must be borne in mind that 170 per 1,000 is a healthy standard, and coincident with the steady improvement of which they are the eloquent exponents, zymotics have been practically extinguished. The death-rate from these highly dangerous diseases in 1S74 was r8 per 1,000; in 1880, 2-4; in 1885, o'6;

in 1890, 04; and in 1895, 0 2. Only one case, which was imported into the town from another place, has occurred since the date of the last report. If the immunity of the past ten months be maintained through the present and next month (November and December), the report for 1896 will contain the lowest death-rate ever recorded in Leamington, and a total freedom from zymoticdiseases of local origin.

These conspicuous advantages are greatly enhanced by a water supply which is the envy of many towns. The water provided for the public, to be satisfactory, should be abundant, and free from the possibility of contamination. In both respects the supply of Leamington is beyond complaint. The source whence it is drawn is estimated by Professor Ramsay, of the Geological Survey Department, the greatest authority in England, to consist of from five to ten square miles of Keuper and Permian water strata, capable of yielding as many million gallons per day. In the droughts of recent years, prudence has dictated to the Corporation the propriety of preventing waste, but in no instance has necessity imposed upon the householders the restraint of its fair use, even to the extent of a spoonful. The analyses are numerous, and by men habitually engaged in water inspection. They are by Dr. Horace Svvete, Public Analyst for Worcestershire; Dr. Bostock Hill, Borough Analyst for Leamington and for the County of Warwick; Dr. J. C. Thresh, Medical Officer of Health for Chelmsford, and Professor Tidy, Professor of Chemistry, London Hospital, and Medical Officer of Health for Islington, with whom, each of the other analysts concurs in the following report: "I am of opinion that as a dietetic water, it is in every respect of excellent quality, and for wholesomeness leaves nothing to be desired."

Scenery, always a most important element in the establishment of health and enjoyment of life, is distinguished around Leamington by every variety and charm of sylvan grace and beauty. And if any visitor, wisely prolongs his stay for a few weeks or months, he will find in the environment, delightful country walks amid scenes of enchanting loveliness. These, without exhaustive labour, will lead him by easy stages to rural villages, recalling the glories of Goldsmith's " Sweet Auburn " before the days of its decay and desertion; to fields wherein the flora of England exist in a greater variety than in any other county, and to places of historic interest like Kenilworth and Warwick, Coventry, Offchurch, Edge Hill, and the shrine of Shakespeare at Stratford-upon-Avon.

The principal qualities of the climate of Leamington are its salubrity and its freedom from humidity, or to speak with accuracy, the very small quantity of moisture with which the atmosphere is charged. A dry air is conducive to health, and immunity from disease; damp and moisture are inimical to the former and promotive of the latter. The town stands 195 feet above the sea level, and surrounded as it is by an open, undulating, wooded country, the air is always fresh and healthful. Its inland position protects it from the violence of gales resulting from atmospheric disturbances, to which towns situated nearer the coasts are constantly exposed. A valuable series of meteorological tables, compiled by Messrs. Jones and Barnitt, chemists, 86, Parade, for thirty-five years, give the following important and highly favourable results: average rainfall from 25 to 26 inches; average mean temperature, about 45 degrees.

The existence of a medicated atmosphere is a question which Dr. Francis William Smith, of 1, Bertie Terrace, Milverton, has discussed with affirmative vigour of language and reason. He has devoted much valuable time to an investigation into the character of the saline waters, and has frequently employed his pen in publicly announcing the powerful influence they exert in curing diseases. Two extracts from a letter contributed by him to the *Leamington Spa Courier* on June 11, 1881, are appropriate to the question we are now considering. "From whence come these waters? From the ground in and around the town, which in almost every part is impregnated with saline salts. Does this saline-impregnated soil impart nothing to the atmosphere around? I assert that it does. It produces a health-giving, medicated atmosphere which those who live in it cannot help breathing. I daresay most of your readers have been by the sea-side, and I daresay many of them have noticed deposits of salt on brick walls—everywhere, in fact, and also possibly, the different effects which sea air produces upon different metals, such as silver and steel. Have any of them, I wonder, observed, in the spring time especially, the salt on the walls and the strange effects of the atmosphere upon metals in Leamington? And do they suppose there is no cause for this? Let me tell them that the secret lies in the medicated saline earth and medicated atmosphere. What is the experience of most, we will say, healthy people when they come to reside in Leamington? Is it not a feeling of lassitude—general sleepy feeling? Did they never experience the same feeling by the sea-side? I know they have, and afterwards, in both cases, the feeling gives place to one of renewed vigour. I have said that the inhabitants of Leamington cannot help breathing this pure medicated air."

One objection has been urged against the climate of Leamington. An opinion prevails that it is relaxing, and conducive to a feeling of enervation with consequent incapacity for exercise and labour. Over the boundless empire of delusion, fashion rules with an authority, to the omnipotence of which the countless martyrs of imaginary ailments render slavish fealty. The air of Leamington is debilitating in the same way as wholesome food is debilitating, when a man refuses to take sufficient and prefers to starve on crumbs at a table bountifully spread with the good things of life. More of the air, not less, was the specific with which Dr. Jephson worked wonders in the cure of ennui and the re-establishment of health. The fallacy of ascribing to the climate what is attributable to a refusal to appropriate its benefits was ably refuted by Dr. George Wilson, Medical Officer of Health for Mid-Warwickshire, in the course of a lecture on "Air in its Relation to Life and

Health," delivered in the Public Hall, Windsor Street, to the Philosophical Society, on March 8, 1877. Speaking of Leamington, he said: "Its broad, clean, and beautiful streets, shaded, as they are, in many places, with handsome trees; its leafy gardens, open squares, and elegant terraces, all contribute to render Leamington exceptionally attractive as a health resort and place of residence. Indeed, I have heard travellers say (and American travellers, when they do start, run over most of the civilized world) that Leamington, taking it all in all, is the most beautiful town they have ever visited. But on the present occasion, the special question will be— what about the air of the town? Well, on this point I have specially consulted Mr. Jones, of the Parade, who, as most of you know, has for many years taken the trouble to make daily meteorological observations, and he has kindly supplied me with the following broad results for your information: "The climate is mild in winter, and not too hot in summer; it does not suffer from cold north-easterly winds; there are no extremes of temperature, and the rainfall is moderate." And these, I take it, are all of them most favourable indications of its salubrity. But as it is not to my interest in any way to advertise Leamington as a health resort, I am in a position to state publicly any opinions to the contrary, and during a three years' residence in the town, the only complaint against it which I have heard, or which I myself could make, is this—that in summer and autumn the climate is a little too relaxing. Now, I am free to confess that not long after I came to Leamington, I did experience something of this relaxing complaint, and whenever I began to feel that work and study became unusually burdensome, I joined the chorus and complacently blamed the climate. But after a time I began to discover that the complaint was in reality a purely contagious disease, and that as a matter of fact there are so many idle people about Leamington when the hunting and dancing season is over, that they don't know *(From a photo, taken iv:.ih the Magnetium Light, by Mr F.*

L. Spieei, Leamington). CURIOUS OLD STONE, IN RELIEF, IN THE VAULTS HENEATH THE NORTH TKANSE1T AT THE PARISH CHURCH; height, Id inches; width, 20! ditto; thickness, to ditto; breadth of borders on each side, ditto; height of letters and borders, j ditto. what to do with their spare time, and take loo little exercise to fill it up. So you see the relaxing objection does not hold good." The valuable meteorological tables tor Leamington date from 1861, when they were originated by the late Mr. Samuel Urwick Jones, chemist, Parade. After his retirement from business in 1875, they were continued by his partner, Mr. J. Barnitt, who gratuitously supplies a yearly statement for the annual report of Dr. S. Browne, the Medical Officer of Health. Quoted by writers of eminence and extensively read, the influence on the prosperity of the borough of these irrefutable criteria of its healthfulness must have been considerable.

Closely allied to the subjects named are numerous branches of collateral importance for which this page has no space. The mineral waters, which are among the heritages of antiquity, would have been included in these remarks were they not reserved for a future chapter. The collections of the opinions of eminent medical men and other authorities on the health conditions of Leamington; a comparison of the statistics of the borough with those of other fashionable resorts, and a complete summary of all the attractions provided for visitors and residents, is a work for the enterprise of the Mayor and Corporation. Such a publication, ably edited, and circulated by thousands, would be a profitable investment for the town and a boon to the afflicted all over the world.

At the close of the seventeenth century (1693), the Bishop of Lichfield and Coventry held a visitation at the Parish Church, on which occasion a Terrier was laid before him of the property belonging to the Vicarage of All Saints. The following is a copy of this ancient document:—

"A true Terrier, or Inventory of all Glebe Lands, Meadows, Gardens, Orchards, Houses, or Portions of I ithes which belong to the Vicarage of Lemington Priors, in the Diocese of Lichfield and Coventry, as followeth:—Impris: the Dwelling House, Two large Bays and Tyled. Item: One Barn, one Bay of Building. Item: One Croft or little Close; A Garden taken out of it and joyning to the Dwelling House. Item: in one of the Commonable Meadows Eight Poles wanting four foot. Item: in another Meadow comonly Sydnam Meadow, what is left at the Upper End, when all the Meadow is measured. Item: reserved from there Majestys as a Debentur at the Audit, £ 13s. ad. Item: all privy Tithe which properly belongs to a poor Vicaridge. Item: the Church yard belongs to the Vicaiidge.—In Witness whereof We, the Minister and Churchwardens have set to our hands. —Hum. Joans, Vic; Currey Willes, George Yardley, Church Warden,.—This Copy agrees with the original Terrier now remaining in the Registry of the Bishop of Lichfield and Coventry. Exhibited at the Bishop's visitation, held in the year 1693.—Examined 20th of March, 17G8, by W. Buckeridge, Deputy Regr."

The individual life of the parish is nowhere carried back to a period so remote as in the annals of the Church. Dugdale, and Dr. Thomas, in his "Continuation of Dugdale's History," have collected such of the names of the Vicars from 1315 to 1730 as were accessible to their researches. Their list, valuable though it be, is generally considered incomplete, but no idea exists whether the omissions are few or many. In quoting their table, we have added one name not to be found in any other history. The Rev. Valentine Jackson was Vicar in 1662, and is included in the Hearth Tax Return for that year. During the three years he was in office as Churchwarden (1891 to 1893), Mr. Robert S. Whitehouse, of Portland Lawn, applied himself with zeal and success to the long-neglected work of bringing down to date the names of all who had held the living of All Saints from the fourteenth century. In the following list we gratefully utilise the information thus accumulated, which, with the name of Valentine Jackson we have added, makes it the nearest approach to a perfect roll of the Vicars of Leamington which has been published. 0 " Joans " and "Currey " are probably clerical errors for "Jones" and " Tarry."

Ecclesiastically, the parish of Leamington Priors was originally in the Diocese of Coventry and Lichfield, but somewhere about the year 1837 it was transferred to that of Worcester, of which it now forms a part. The register of the curates licensed since this rearrangement is a necessary part of the history of the Parish Church, and represents an important element in local life during the past half-century. A glance at the following list, collected by Mr. Whitehouse, will awaken echoes of sermon and service long since gone by, and recall voices and figures once familiar to every parishioner.

CHRONOLOGY TO 1800. 1OO6.—Leamington owned by Turcliill, the last of the Saxon Earls of Warwick. 1086.—" Domesday Book" published containing description of Leamington Leamington in the possession of Roger de Montgomery, a French knight. 1100.— Granted the Bishop of Lichfield, Coventry, and Chester.

1166.—Presented by Geoffrey de Clinton to the Priors of the Monastery of Kenilworth. Takes additional name of "Priors" in consequence. 1240.—The estate passed over to the Monks of Coventry. 1315.—Henry de Keton (Dom), the first Vicar of

Leamington mentioned by Dugdale. 1480.—Supposed time when John Rous compiled nis Roll and made reference to the mineral waters of Leamington. 1492.—Richard Bennet, Vicar of Whilnash, also

Vicar of Leamington. 1531.—Memorial brass inserted in the north wall of

Whitnash Church as a monument to

Richard Bennet, who held the two livings of Leamington and Whitnash. 1539.—Richard Willes, of Ufton, and William

Morcote, of Leamington, purchased Newbold Comyn.

Dissolution of Monasteries; Church property

went to the Crown. 1564. — Granted by Queen Elizabeth to Ambrose

Dudley, the "good Earl of Warwick." Richard Willes died, possessed of Newbold

Comyn, having married the heiress of W.

Morcote.

1572.—Queen Elizabeth visits Warwick, but is said to have been unable to pass through Leamington in consequence of the bad state of the public way. 1586.—Camden's "Britannia" published, with references to Leamington waters. 1589.—Ambrose Dudley dies without issue, and

Leamington reverts to the Crown. 1596.—Speed's " Theatre of Great Britain "published, and the mineral waters again the subject of notice.

Queen Elizabeth granted the living of All Saints to William Borne and Jacob Orange. 1605.—James I. bestows Leamington on Sir Fulke Greville, the "friend of Sir Philip Sidney." 1624. — Jubilee year of the Rev. Henry Clarke's

Vicariate of All Saints. 1624-6.—Reported enlargement of the Parish Church.

1625. —Order of Warwickshire Court of Quarter

Sessions suppressing William Mills and Margaret Walsgravc, licensed victuallers. 1648.—Thos. Glover, "Preacher at Leamington Priors," is in the list of Warwickshire Ministers who supported "The Solemn League and Covenant." He is not mentioned by Dugdale as one of the Vicars, and, therefore, must be looked upon as a dissenting Minister, probably of the Presbyterian persuasion. 1656.—Dugdale's "Antiquities of Warwickshire" published, in which allusion is made to the Old Well. 16O2-3.—All inhabitants of the village, except those exempted on account of their poverty from paving church and poor rates, taxed two shillings yearly for each hearth and stove in their dwellings. Fuller's "Worthies of Great Britain" published, containing another notice of the Leamington waters. 1663.—There were 46 houses in the village. 1669.— John Lees and Thomas Cartwright over-

seers of the poor. 1678. —Edward Willes attended vestry meeting on the 5th of December, with "ten several writings belonging to the inhibtants of the parish." These, it was agreed, should be deposited in a box having two keys; one to be kept in Leamington Priors, and the other at Newbold Comyn. Nicholas Paris, of Warwick, on the Ilth day of December, contracted with John Lees and Edward Rawbone to keep the church clock in order during his natural life for the sum of one shilling a year, to be paid between the Feast Day of St. Michael the Archangel, and the Feast Day of the Nativity of our Lord. 1679. —John Lees and Edward Rawbone, Church wardens.

William Cartwright and Dunsmore Heath,

Overseers.

1682.—Order of Warwickshire Court of Quarter Sessions regulating wages and hours of labour made and published somewhere about this year.

1689.—Dr. Guidot published his treatise on the mineral waters. 1693.—A Terrier, or Inventory of property belonging to the Parish Church, prepared and submitted to the Bishop of Lichfield and Coventry. 1693.—Daniel Dawkes appears to have been in office either as Churchwarden or Overseer. In one of the apprenticeship bonds, he is named with three others to whom it was made. 1700.—The land of Leamington began to be dispersed amongst numerous proprietors. 17CH.—Edward Willes purchased the Quarry Field. 1702.—Meeting of freeholders and inhabitants on October 2nd, at the Parish Church, to consider the state of the mounds round the churchyard. Joseph Satchwell supposed to be the first of the Satchwell family who settled in Leamington attended Vestry and signed minutes. 1705. —" Alice Harding, being excommunicated and denied Christian Burial, was buryed in a garden," January 13. 1706. —The tenths, 13s. per annum, were discharged by

Act of Parliament, and the clear yearly value thereof returned to the Governors of Queen Anne's Bounty was £lb 10s. od.

CHRONOLOGY T 1724.—Warrant to "disturb" John Milton, who there-1 uon left the parish, laid up in the parish chest. 1727. —Edward Willes bequeaths to the poor of

Leamington Priors,£5, to be distributed anion;; theni at the discretion of his executors.

1728. —Daniel Dawkes " died ye I2th and was buried ye 14th day of July."

1730.—The continuation of Dugdale's Warwickshire, by Dr. Thomas, published with further allusion to the Old Well. 1732.—Benjamin Satchwell born at the Mill, on

January 3.

1736.—William Abbotts born at Long Itchinglon. 1740.—Dr. Short's treatise on Leamington waters published. 1740. —William Satchwell, Parish Clerk, died October

"ye 22nd, and was buried ye 24th."

1768.—Enclosure Act passed.

First meeting of the Commissioners held at the Bowling Green House, kept by Simon Hinton, March 13.

Award signed at a public meeting held at the

Bowling Green Inn, December 22.

1760. —Award inrolled by T. Beardsley, Clerk of the

Peace for the County, September 20.

1773. —The first flood, of which any report exists, took place this year. 1774. —At the General Election, which lasted eleven days (from October 20th to 30th) there were six persons voted for the village of Leamington,'viz., William Abbotts, Thomas Field

(Warwick), John Lawrence, William Perkins, William Trcadgold and Matthew

Wise.

For Lillington, one voted, namely, John Coles,

clerk in holy orders, residing at Warwick.

Milverton ditto, two, viz.: Richard Newbury,

and Thomas Thompson.

At this election there were in Warwick 310

votes, and in Kenilworth 135.

1775. —Another flood, when the water in the river rose to a very great height.

1777. —Benjamin Satchwell started a Friendly Society called " The Fountain of Hospitality." 1778. —William Abbotts renovated the Black Dog

Inn, and added two bay windows fronting the turnpike road. 1 781.—Faculty granted by the Consistory Court of Lichfield for the erection of the north gallery in the Parish Church containing three pews.

1783.—The King's tax of 3d. on each funeral commenced October 2nd this year. Abraham Kingerlee, whose interment took place on October 4th, was the first buried under the new charges. The entry in the Parish Register is " received 3d. for tax." The number of voters on the Parliamentary Register for i8yo is 3.356.) 1800. — Cuttlinued. 1784.— Satchwell and Abbotts discover the second spring in Bath Street, January 14. Dr. Kerr, of the Northampton Infirmary, and Dr. Allen visit Leamington, and express favourable opinions of the curative power of the waters.

Dr. Holyoake, physician, Warwick, offered

Lord Aylesford £1,000 for a building lease of the ' scite" of the Old Well, which w is refused, his lordship remarking the water should never be locked up from the poor.

1786. —Rev. J. Moody, Pastor of Brook Street

Chapel, Warwick, began holding services in Leamington.

Abbotts commenced building the first baths on the site now occupied by Francis and Son's drapery establishment, Bath Street.

1787. —Baths completed and opened for public use. 1788. —The Hon. Mrs. Leigh, of Stoneleigh Abbey, visited Leamington, and was much pleased with the waters and the baths.

Satchwell, Abbotts, and the inhabitants publicly thank Dr. Allen for his services in making the virtues of the water known.

1789. —Frances Satchwell, Benjamin Satchwell's mother died and was buried March 24. 1790. —The third spring discovered at the south-west corner of Bath Street, on land belonging to Matthew Wise, and baths erected on the site of

the present Alexandra fountains.

William Abbotts commenced building the New Inn, Lillington Lane, now the Hath Hotel, occupied by Mr Thomas Welch. This is the oldest hotel in Leamington, and was the first of the new houses erected in the old town.

1791. —Visitation of small pox; 29 persons were attacked with the disease, 0 of whom died: 124 of the villagers were inoculated, and escaped the contagion.

1793. —William Abbotts removed to the New Inn,

and Thomas Sinker succeeded him as landlord of the Black Dog.

1794. —Dr. Lambe, an eminent physician, residing at

Warwick, published an analysis of the Leamington waters in the 5th volume of the

Transactions of the Manchester Philosophical

Society.

1796. —A valuation of the Vicarial tythes in Newbold made by Mr. John Bird.

1797. —Certificates for using hair powder were obtained by Thomas Abbotts for his daughter; Margaret Dolphin for infant; Thomas Sinker for wifi and family; Matthew Wise for Martha and Bridget, wife and daughter, and household; and Edward Willes for family. 1799. — William Treadgold and Edward Treadgold entered into a contract with the Rev. John Wise and Edward W illes to reseat the body of the Church and supply a new pulpit and reading desk for the sum of,£103. 5s. 7d. 1800. — lhe Parish Church reopened for public worship after Improvements. CHAPTER XV. HEN the year 1800 dawned it was upon many encouraging signs of approaching prosperity. The new Baths and Inn; Wise's Baths at the comer of High Street; the bay windows with which Abbotts had smartened the Dog public house, and the improvements at the Church, were instalments of the coming town. But after the village had passed away, two influences were to remain as its humble contribution to posterity. All the seeds of nineteenth century greatness had been sown, and for the ingathering of an abundant harvest nothing was needed but the patient development of the policy which had been successfully inaugurated. The first great factor which the town of 1825 inherited from the hamlet of 1784 was the medical opinion obtained of the value of the water, and the second was the impulse the labour of Satchwell and Abbotts had given to the work of local improvement. Still, granting every claim which can be consistently advanced on behalf of the learned cobbler and the patriotic publican, and generously placing in the scale a handful of additional laurels as a tribute to the special grace which belongs to lowly merit, the fact remains that the patronage of Drs. Allen, Kerr, and Lambe dissolved the village fabric long before it would otherwise have taken place, and paved the way for the arrival of the borough in the nineteenth instead of the twentieth century. Satchwell and Abbotts had not the power of influencing public opinion, and especially that section which is represented by wealth, culture, and fashion. What they lacked the physicians possessed, and promptly at this juncture in the history of Leamington they came to its aid.

After the discovery in 1784 of the second spring, Satchwell was unusually active and hopeful. A report of his, which appeared in *The Coventry Mercury* for September u, 1788, contemplates with exuberant gratitude the events which were then taking place. "We can with pleasure say many persons of distinction have graced our salt baths already this summer. Such numerous genteel visitors, with carriages, etc., daily resort to this place that in a short time it must wear off the aspect of a country village. On Monday last, our said baths were honoured with a truly patroness visitor from Stoneleigh Abbey, the Honourable Mrs. Leigh, who expressed great satisfaction at the supernaturality of the waters and the great convenience." The list of these genteel visitors, which he kept in a book, has been lost. So have most of his poetic effusions; his ambitious work, "The Rise and Fall of Troy," a poem he had composed while cobbling boots and shoes; and another of a less imaginative kind, entitled "Astronomi-

cal Characters and their use with Explanatory Figures," a production which has been described as long, but not unskilful, and one showing how naturally his mind was disposed for study. A large collection of materials for the history of the village, made by him in the course of years of study and research, has also passed away into the abyss of oblivion. Though a complete account of those who complimented Leamington by their occasional visits between 1784 and 1810 is now beyond the reach of the historian, many names are to be collected from the early "Guides" and other publications of the period. The Dukes and Duchesses of Bedford and Gordon; the Earls of Longford and Ludlow; Lord Frederick Montague; Bishop Jebb: Dr. Parr, Vicar of Hatton; Dr. Allen; Dr. Kerr, of the Northampton Infirmary; Dr. Winthorpe and Dr. Lambc, both of Warwick;

Dr. Yates; Dr. Johnstone, of Birmingham; James Perry, the proprietor of the *Morning Chronicle;* the Rev. James Wallhouse; and Walter Savage Landor, the poet, then residing at Warwick, were among the number.

Between the years 1784 and 1810, a visit to the cottage in New Street and a chat with Satchwell was accepted as the best way of spending a happy hour at the Spa. Sitting in the chimney corner, the great Dr. Parr whiled away many an afternoon, smoking his pipe, and, for the moment, forgetting the elegance of his Latinity in the village rhymer's rude imitations of Homer and his vague astral speculations, in which there may have been more astrology than the discoverer of the law of gravitation would have allowed. There also came Mr. Perry, deeply interested in Ben's schemes for making the world acquainted with the health-giving qualities of the Leamington water, and placing at his service the columns of the extensively circulated *Morning Chronicle.* With an air of great probability it is believed that Dr. Parr and he were frequently in conference over the embers in the cottage grate, respecting the policy of the paper, and that other visitors were of a much higher social grade: people whose

names are in the first line of the English nobility, who rode in splendid equipagei, with coroneted panels, drawn by velvety steeds, and attended by powdered servants. Those who wore patches came when those who wore pearls had left. Against Farmer Court's barn across the way were assembled the wearers of rags and tatters; the representatives of the infirmities and misfortunes of the village. To them Ben gave willing audience, and, pitying their distresses, of his own bounty bestowed coins that restored food to tables which were often bare and cupboards which were never full. His influence was unbounded. Says one, who was a frequent visitor, he seemed to be "master of the place," to which Moncrieff adds, "he was a very ingenious, persevering, spirited man; in a different sphere of life he might have raised himself to greatness, and founded a kingdom elsewhere as he founded a village here." His position as co-executor with Jeremiah Alder and Richard Lythall to the estate of John Purden, farmer, of Radford Semele, was one of many proofs of the respect in which he was held in the neighbouring parishes; the confidence reposed in his integrity, and his readiness to respond to all who sought his assistance. The estate was administered in 1798, and from papers preserved the work of distribution appears to have devolved principally upon him. The allocation of the respective shares to the widow and eleven children was made with that minute regard to detail which was the habit of his life, an excess balance of one penny, after payment of all claims, being set down with scrupulous care. To his incessant labours in the public interest were added the cares of a large family and the support of his aged mother. There were eleven children, three of whom died during his lifetime, namely, Elizabeth, after whom the next daughter was named; Keziah, and George. In the Parish Church Register they appear in the following order: Hannah, baptised 6 August, 1765; Elizabeth, ditto, 24 July, 1767; buried 19 October, 1769; David, baptised, 19 June, 1768; William, ditto, 25 February, 1770; Elizabeth, ditto, 15

March, 1772; Ann, ditto, 1 January, 1774; Thomas, ditto, 20 November, 1775; Joseph, ditto, 21 February, 1778; Keziah, ditto, 29 October, 1780, buried, zz October, 1787; George, baptised, 10 March, 1782, buried 11 June, 1782; and Phcebe, baptised, 30 November, 1783. When Abbotts's Well was discovered in 1784, the family circle consisted of eleven persons—eight children, the mother and father, and the grandmother, who died and was buried March 24, 1789.

A large increase in the number of aristocratic visitors, and a demand for lodgings greatly in excess of the accommodation furnished by the cottages, were the auspicious circumstances of the first year of the century. The three Inns were constantly full, and the humblest dwellings were besieged by people who were willing to pay the rent of a country mansion for two or three rooms which had been previously worth as many shillings a year. One of the visitors has left an interesting description of the village from 1800 to 1820, the dates of his first and last visit; an important testimony to the efficacy of the water, and an illustration of the manner in which the opinions of Dr. Kerr were influencing the public mind in favour of the newlyestablished Spa. He was an old man, named Wrench, who had made a competence in London as a harness maker. His wife was afflicted with erysipelas in the nose, and biliousness, for which she visited Bath, but without obtaining relief from drinking the waters. The mineral wells of Tunbridge were next tried, with results equally disappointing, no improvement in the health of the invalid having accrued from their use. Being told that a great physician at Northampton (Dr. Kerr) had written a book showing the Leamington waters to be a sovereign and infallible remedy for cutaneous eruptions and visceral diseases, he resolved to bring his wife to Leamington and test their efficacy. His description of the state of things when he first arrived in the village applies to the year 1800. The cottages were scattered irregularly in High Street, the Warwick Road, and

near the church. The river was crossed by a wooden foot-bridge. "On the rising ground over the river, where now stands the new town, but one erection was visible, amid all the golden corn-fields and wild heaths, and that a hut 'composed of half wicker and wood.' In the distance, amid the woods on the uplands, and as far as the eye could reach, the Leam—little, narrow, fleet, and sluggish—ran noiselessly along through the meadows, almost hidden by overhanging brambles, weeds, and rushes. Where the Victoria Bridge now stands he saw a ford beside the railed bridge. Then a rivulet ran through the meadows where the High street is, to supply a fishpond near the church; and another stream ran thence through Bath Street to the Leam. He put up at the Bowling Green Inn, that he might be near Abbotts' Bath (opened in 1786 by the advice of Dr. Kerr), but the accommodation for a day's stay was so poor that he was half inclined to try old Sinker's house in the High Street, where the ' Royal' afterwards stood. The charges for dinner were more than the economical old gentleman liked to pay, but then Mr. Boniface said he could not compete with the houses in the county town, as he had to pay for the butcher's meat and groceries being sent from thence. 'Humph,' thought my ancient, with an eye to business, 'if there's summit in the waters to cure all the ills that flesh is heir to, here's an opening for a general huckster.' And he was a good mind to build a shop at once, but he didn't." The reestablishment of his wife's health is thankfully recorded in his diary. They had to pay a shilling a pint for the saline water, which was taken out of a dirty stone basin in the ground. In a fortnight, Janet's health was improving, the redness was disappearing gradually, and her appetite much stronger, and after a month's course of drinking the waters she was much better in health—indeed, as well as she could expect at her age. "Wherever I go," said old Mr. Wrench, " I will sound the praises of the new Baths." The quantity Mrs. Wrench drank was one quart daily.

In 1803, the Earl of Aylesford visited

the village and stimulated the work of local improvement by enclosing the Old Well in a respectable building of stone. Previously, the water flowed into an open ditch, where at one time it was collected in a tub, and others in jugs and basins. A benevolent clergyman of independent means must be mentioned in this place for his philanthropic disposition towards the poor, his disinterested zeal in public work, his hearty co-operation with Satchwell and Abbotts, the halo that gathers round his memory as one of the two men who commenced the movement which led to the establishment of the Warneford Hospital, and also for the share he had in this, the first, improvement of the Old Well.

The Rev. James Walhouse, an early benefactor, a few years before the spring was enclosed, as a visitor made his acquaintance with Leamington. Charmed with the scenery of the village and neighbourhood, and impressed with the medicinal value of the waters, he selected it for his adopted home. One of the objects he earnestly desired to see accomplished was the erection of a suitable building over the Well, the provision of which by Lord Aylesford was due to a movement in the village of which he was the acknowledged leader. Pratt, in his very diffusive work of 1814, has a remark illustrative of the public spirit due to the energy of Satchwell and Abbotts. "In June, 1803," he observes, "the spring being disgustingly dirty, a subscription for its improvement was intended, and Lord Aylesford, being first applied (to) for his consent, made an offer of erecting a building over it at his own expence, which, the year following, was set about, with the intention of having a cold bath below the spring for the use of the poor; but the water, owing to the new Baths since erected, not rising to its former level, and decreasing in quantity, the Baths exclusively for the poor were of necessity laid aside." Were the subject left in this form, we should feel justified in crediting Mr. Walhouse with active participation in the local agitation for improving the Well. The information furnished by Dr. Loudon, whose "Practical

Dissertation on the Waters of Leamington" appeared in 1830, makes scepticism on the point impossible, and, at the same time, places in its own proper niche of honour, a name, without which the list of the benefactors of Leamington can never be considered as complete. In his remarks on Abbotts's Well and Baths, he says: "This spring was the only one which existed in the place for several years, An inherent faculty of art perception, developed to perfection by study and travel, placed in the front rank of qualified judges of scenery, the late Mr. John Burgess, Associate Member of the Society of Painters in Water Colours. In 1870. a sketch of his life, by Signor Rosario Aspa, exhibiting much animation of style, vigorous thought, and critical acumen, was printed and published by Mr. Joseph Glover, J.P. , then proprietor of the *Leamington Courier.* Writing to a friend on November 4, 1870, Mr. Burgess thus expressed himself on the subject of the scenery round Leamington: "I have had some delightful drives, and have visited some villages within some five or six miles of this place that I had not seen before, though I have been here 30 years. 1 am more than ever impressed that there is scarcely anything so good as this neighbourhood in all England." Nathaniel Hawthorne, in "Our Old Home," speaks to much the same effect. "The chief enjoyment of my several visits to Leamington lay in rural walks about the neighbourhood, and in jaunts to places of note and interest, which are particularly abundant in that region. The high roads are made pleasant to a traveller by a border of trees, and often afford him the hospitality of a wayside bench beneath a comfortable shade. But a fresher delight is to be found in the footpaths, which go wandering away from stile to stile, along hedges and across broad fields and through wooded parks, leading you to little hamlets of thatched cottages, ancient solitary farmhouses, picturesque old mills, streamlets, pools, and all those quiet, secret, unexpectedly yet strangely familiar features of English scenery that Tennyson shows us in his idylls and eclogues. These by-paths

admit the wayfarer into the very heart of rural life, and yet do not burden him with a sense of intrusiveness." Pratt, discussing the.-esthetic beauties of Leamington, was of opinion that it would come to be known as the "Village of Painters." so many artists and amateurs were to be seen, pencil in hand, at work in every direction of Kenilworth, Stoncleigh, Offchurch, etc.

H for in sinking it the water of the Old Well fell several feet below its former level, and, from neglect, was almost inaccessible for use until the beginning of the present century, when the Rev. Mr. Walhouse, one of the earliest patrons of Leamington, settled in this place. It is, in fact, to the exertions of this gentleman, with the lord of the manor, that the community is indebted for rescuing the Old Well from oblivion and for the handsome building which at present surrounds it." The elimination of this interesting circumstance from the past history of the borough has obscured the credit which belongs to Mr. Walhouse for having practically given the spring to the public without the interposition of any payments. It has also been misleading as to the principal event of the time by attributing the enclosure to an accidental visit of the lord of the manor, whereas it was the result of a local movement with the spirit of which Lord Aylesford generously complied. Dr. Loudon is not alone in his praise of Mr. Walhouse. Four years before the publication of his work, Sarah Medley sang the merits of Satchwell, Abbotts, and Walhouse, as of men worthy of honour in the Pantheon of local benefactors. After alluding to the brilliant galaxies of "rank, wealth, and taste" accustomed to assemble in Satchwell's cottage, and paying a tribute to " Poet Satchwell's much-respected name," she says:

"Abbotts and Walhouse, honoured names we join,
And wreaths of praise well-earned for both entwine.
Founders of Leamington! your generous aid,
In the chang'd scene, how amply now display'd!

Hence where the hovel stood, immur'd in smoke,
Where lay the thorny glebe for years unbroke,
Sudden we view with pleasure and surprise,
Superb hotels and noble structures rise:
With aspect fair and numerous now they stand,
Meet to receive the Princes of the land."

Mr. Walhouse resided sometimes at the Bowling Green and occasionally at the Dog, but he was invariably in the seat of honour at the *table d'hole* at the lastnamed hostel, presiding over a company of guests, who usually averaged about twenty-four. On these occasions he seldom missed an opportunity of pleading the cause of charity. When the cloth had been removed, and the walnuts and the wine brought in, his custom was to inform visitors of the benevolent projects of Satchwell for the assistance of the poor. These brief but eloquent appeals were followed by collections, the proceeds of which were handed to Satchwell, the founder, treasurer, and secretary of the Leamington Spa Charity.

CHAPTER XVI. HE time of the enclosure of the Well is the date of the commencement of all local improvements of a public nature, for though Lord Aylesford defrayed the whole cost, and the property belonged to him, it was dedicated to the interests of the village, and the town, which was soon to follow. Abbotts's and Wise's Baths were private speculations, in the benefits of which residents and visitors could not participate without payment; the original Well, on the contrary, was as much a public institution as the Free Library, the Jephson Gardens, and the Pump Room Grounds are at the present day.

The public interest awakened by the erection of the New Inn in 1793; the ambition of the inhabitants to record their names as contemporaneous with that event; the music and processions on anniversaries; the bell-ringing on September 20, 1808, when the first stones of the New Town were laid, and again on April 16, 1829, when a commencement was made with the Willes

Bridge on the site of the old Mardyke bridge, and the flags and processions on proclamation days, forbid us to think the inauguration of the first building over the Well was permitted to pass without some suitable demonstration. The villagers were at no time accustomed to take their pleasures sadly, and we may well believe that an occurrence of such uncommon importance was celebrated with an *eclal* in every way appropriate to the occasion. According to report, Mrs. Hopton, Ben Satchwell's daughter, had the honour of laying the foundation stone, a proof of the esteem in which the family were held.

The year of Lord Aylesford's visit is also noticeable as the one in which we gather the earliest information of the rateable value of the village. The total sum raised for all parochial purposes, including poor and highway rates, was £336 8s. iod., at 4s. 4d. in the pound. From this it would appear that the net rateable annual value of the parish was, in round figures, about £1,500. The growth of the town in ninety-three years will be seen by comparing this amount with *£1 29,210*, the present rateable value. It is interesting to note that in the same year a rate of 7s. 4d. in Lillington parish produced 236 os. 3d., and one of 3s. 6d. in Milverton, *£182* 19s. 3d. There is no similarity between the incidence of local taxation in the two periods of 1803 and 1897, the present rates being applicable to a variety of subjects for which no provision had to be made in the former period. Considering the very limited character of local government in 1803, the small return the ratepayers received for their money, and the additional payments which had to be made for Church rates and window taxes, the position of the inhabitants at the commencement of the century will be seen to compare disadvantageous!y with that of the present generation.

The accompanying illustration of the original structure and its surroundings is one of the most valuable of the period. The open space on the south side is now occupied by the *Courier* Printing and Publishing Offices, and in the background is seen a section of the old

boundary round the Churchyard, commencing at the pales which adjoined the houses of John Lees, as mentioned in the vestry minutes of 1702. The thatched cottage, partly shown on the same side, stood near the site of the establishment of Mr. F. C. Rolls, draper, 11, Bath-street, and was occupied by Widow Webb, who had charge of the Well; the timber-framed house on the north side, with its high pitched roof, was the homestead of Farmer Abbotts. The arrangements made by Lord Aylesford for securing the free use of the water for the poor must not be omitted from notice. The sale of the site, it will be remembered had been refused to Dr. Holvoake, and a promise made that the free use of the water should be reserved to the public for ever. This feudal tenure, which had become one of the Aylesford traditions, as we have seen, had nearly lapsed through neglect, but it was now confirmed by the Earl, whose new building permitted of no restrictions as against the public. This time is selected by all the "Guide" writers as the occasion when the old pump was first introduced, the handle of which was placed outside against the north wall for the poor. The precaution Lord Aylesford adopted in favour of the public was the common-sense plan of leaving the avenue to the spring as open and free as were the streets of the village. Where there was no gate leading to the steps, and no door leading to the Well, it was impossible to prevent the gratuitous use of the waters.

Both Satchwell and Abbotts experienced something of those difficulties which fall to the lot of such as take their places in the van of progress. Their work was far from being all sunshine. A reluctance by the principal owners to sell land on the south of the river for new buildings thwarted their efforts and impeded the extension of the village for nearly thirteen years—from 1793, the date of the building of the New Inn, by Abbotts, till 1806, the time when Robbins discovered the fourth spring on land forming the site of the present Victoria Colonnade. This obstacle was accompanied by another which, at one

time, threatened to involve Abbotts in a heavy pecuniary loss. At first, the Warwick County.Magistrates refused to license the New Inn, two public-houses, in their opinion, being sufficient for the reasonable needs of the village in its normal state. The control exercised by the Magistrates over the public-houses a hundred years ago. and the stringency with which the Licensing Laws and applications for new licenses were administered and examined, are the chief points of interest in the decision. Abbotts ultimately succeeded in obtaining his license, the Magistrates, no doubt, being influenced by the lack of accommodation which the village provided for visitors, and the great convenience it would be for invalids to have lodgings near to the Baths. The inability to build houses was a more serious difficulty. Dr. Lambe's treatise, published in 1794, is reported to have had a favourable result in Lancashire, and to have brought cotton lords as visitors in abundance. To them it was a luxury beyond the roseate dreams of romance to leave their factories, their spindles, their bobbins, and their reels, for a holiday on the banks of the Leam: to drink before breakfast the water from the spring while the buzz and sparkle of the gases were fresh in the glass, or new milk in the farmyards warm from the pail; to loiter near the old Mill, listening to the noise of the wheel; or from the rustic bridge in the Lillington Lane, to watch the evanescent foam speeding its way on to the Avon; to ramble among the heaths and fields on the north bank, disturbing hares in their forms and larks in their nests; to gather nosegays of wild flowers in Warwick Stieet, and curiously wrought grasses in the Parade; to dine wisely and well at Sinker's; drink old port from the cask which always stood in the bar corner at the Bowling Green, and at night to sleep in cottages with thatched roofs and latticed windows, partly covered with clematis, the sweet-scented eglantine, roses, and honeysuckles. But to supply the requirements of these visitors, more houses were needed. Insufficiency of accommodation caused many to engage rooms at

Emscote and Warwick. The only difficulty was to find building sites, for though of land there was plenty, none was to be had.

"Middleton and Loudon give 1797 as the date of Dr. Lambe's Analysis; Field and others, 1794.

By reason of this phase of the history of the time, a special local interest belongs to Satchwell Buildings, Satchwell Place, an unassuming row of four houses, once the most prominent object near to the Parish Church, now hidden from view by the more costly residences in George Street, the comfortable and wellappointed villas in Leam and Russell Terraces, and the less expensive but conveniently situated properties in Gordon and New Streets. Those who are acquainted with what transpired after the erection of the New Inn will recognise in these Buildings a record of unselfishness at a time when self-interest was in the ascendant: a singular display of energy when indolence was more profitable, and a preference.

ST. PAUL'S CHURCH.

Foundation Stone laid, May 15, 1873, by William Willes, Esq., Newbold Comyn; opened by the

Bishop (Dr. Philpott), May 14, 1874. in opposition to long-established maxims of worldly wisdom, of public over private advantages. A few speculators had come to the village, and Satchwell, with their aid, had endeavoured to meet the difficulty by enlarging several of the cottages and re-furnishing others. This proved nothing more than a temporary relief, and, offers of large sums for small plots having been repeatedly refused, he resolved on a further remedy. The garden land at the back of his cottage, which had come into his possession in the manner described, he gave to his married daughter, Mrs. Ilopton, who was assisting him in the business of the Post Office. Upon the site she erected, in 1807, Satchwell Buildings. They were also known as Hopton's Boarding Houses, and, until Copps's Royal Hotel was built, they provided the largest amount of accommodation of any of the lodging and boarding houses in Leamington. The situation was singularly

pleasant, and the views, in every direction, extensive, diversified, and charming. Six thousand mansions, villas, and houses have been erected in Leamington since the date of the Satchwell Buildings, not one of which has been more happily placed in regard to surrounding scenery. As far as Warwick, the view in front was an uninterrupted expanse of wood and meadow, and included two objects for which many a nobleman would pay a very large sum to have in the perspective from his drawing-room windows—Warwick Castle and Church. At the back were the Shell Leys, the groves of Newbold Comyn, the distant woods crowning the heights of Ufton, and the Leam meandering sluggishly round the islands and among the meadows. They were in great request by the nobility, and for years after Michael Copps had reared his gorgeous Royal Hotel in High Street, the fashionable life of the town gravitated to Satchwell Place as naturally as it turned its footsteps towards Clarendon Square at a subsequent period.

Strong reflections on the conduct of the chief owners in refusing to dispose of their land have been frequently made, and a desire to preserve the privacy of their own dwellings from public intrusion has been mentioned as the motive of their opposition to the village becoming a place of fashionable resort. We do not consider it has been by any means satisfactorily established that they were averse to the utmost development of which the village was capable. Local prosperity was their interest more than of any other class. An influx of thousands of visitors meant a demand for land which they alone could supply. As monopolists they followed those instincts of self-interest which have influenced men in all ages, and will continue to regulate the principles of barter and exchange to the latest times. Visitors were arriving in hundreds, and the village had suddenly been placed in competition with the older health resorts of Cheltenham and Bath. With a rising market, it was policy on their part to sell slowly, or not at all; to wait a few

years before parting with their estates. They had no objection to make hay, but they preferred to do so when the sun was shining brilliantly in the approaching summer of Leamington's prosperity, rather than in the spring-time of its history.

William Abbotts died in 1805, respected by all who had the pleasure of his acquaintance, and regarded by Satchwell with brotherly affection. Of him we know much less than of his venerable friend. Nothing has been preserved of his personal appearance; no portrait such as we have of Satchwell. That he was of a practical turn of mind goes without saying; that his baths exercised an influence for good on the fortunes of the village is shown by the praise Satchwell has lavished on his memory. The "Leamington Salts," of which he was the first manufacturer, won the approbation of the leaders of medical opinion, and, for more than half a century, were a testimonial to his enterprise. The memoranda of the visits of Mr. and Mrs. Wrench contain one reference which portrays him as a model landlord and bath proprietor. "Grandma was particularly fond of Mr. Abbotts, who treated her with kindly attention and did his best to court her favour. In later years she often spoke of his civilities at the baths," Satchwell was one of the mourners who attended the funeral, and many of the other inhabitants were present in token of the respect in which they held the memory of the deceased. Over his last resting-place in the village Churchyard, a tombstone—the size and character of which contrasted with its humble surroundings—was erected by his daughter, with the following inscription: — "Behold the Tomb of William Abbotts, who died the First of March, 1805, aged Sixty-nine. First Founder of the celebrated Spa Water Baths at this place, in 1786. He devoted his whole time and fortune to accommodate the public, and lived to see his benevolent works merit the approbation of the most eminent Physicians.

In Peace 1 rest—pray be so kind,
Improve the works I leave behind.
May Invalids (made whole) agree

To praise the Lord—instead of me."

The *Warwick Advertiser,* of February 15, 1806, distinguished him as the founder of modern Leamington: "A handsome tribute has lately been paid to the memory of the public-spirited person who first drew the attention of the neighbourhood and the public to the sanative qualities of the Lemington waters, by the erection of a well-executed grave-stone in Lemington Churchyard, the workmanship of Messrs. Sprawson and Cakebread, of Harbury." A copy of the inscription follows, in which "spa water" is rendered "spaw water." A further acknowledgment of Abbotts's services to the village, couched in terms expressive of sincere admiration, appeared in "Beck's Directory" for 1840: "This worthy individual, in conjunction with his friend, Benjamin Satchwell, deserves to be particularly recorded in the annals of the town, whose early prosperity was first promoted, and afterwards fostered and extended through a series of upwards of twenty years with the most unremitting vigilance and assiduity, by these two fathers of the village. The character of Abbotts (as well as that of his colleague) appears to have been perfectly free from any taint of selfish or sordid principle in the energetic endeavours he made for the welfare of his native place; many opportunities which must have existed for the appropriation of property to no inconsiderable amount, were by him wholly disregarded, and not only so, but a comfortable income, which his industry had amassed for his latter years, was entirely and without reserve devoted to the projects of a sanguine and judicious judgment. Uniting great simplicity of manners with a "penetration that was not slow in anticipating the probable result of his enterprise, Abbotts, by a combination of circumstances, became the instrument of effecting a change equally singular and fortunate to the interests of Leamington."

The history of his Baths admits of a brief narration. When established in 1786, the accommodation afforded was small, and "rude in the extreme."

There was one reservoir for warm salt water and another for cold. After the death of her husband, Mrs. Abbotts carried on the business until April, 1806, when she transferred both the Inn and the Baths to her son-in-law, William Smith; but from the public notice of the change of proprietorship it appears that she continued to superintend the business at the Baths while Mr. and Mrs. Smith attended to the Inn. The Baths were then improved; enlarged in 1815, and, at the same time, arrangements were made for supplying the indigent poor at a nominal charge. There was a second enlargement in 1836, the old structure being demolished, and a new edifice, more in accordance with the changed condition of the town, erected on the site. The new building and arrangements comprised eight baths for hot or cold bathing, and the same number of shower baths. The first douche bath was supplied, and also a vapour and hot air bath. Mr. J. Goold was in occupation in 1841, at which time they were known as "Goold's Original Baths and Pump Rooms," and were described as '' Saline and Sulphurous." Ten years later Mr. and Mrs. Gardner were the Managers. Mr. W. Wood, who had previously held the Victoria Baths in the Victoria Colonnade, became the tenant of the "Original Old Spa Baths" in May, 1858. In 18S1, they were the property of Messrs. Stock and Co., Birmingham, for whom Messrs. White and Locke, auctioneers, were the local agents. The last change took place in 1867, when they were purchased by E. Francis and Sons, drapers, 34, 36, 38, Bath Street. The semi-circular plate-glass window at the corner of Bath Street and Abbotts Street encloses the site on which the most interesting of the historic baths of Leamington once stood.

CHAPTER XVII. REAT as were the expectations of prosperity resulting from the discovery of the second spring and the building of Abbotts's Baths, the prospect of an immediate realisation was at one time far from being bright The real obstacle was the difficulty in obtaining building land, but in 1806 the effect of this obstruction began to diminish, and eligible sites were more

easily obtained. This change was caused by the resolution to build a new town, on the north banks of the river where the owners were willing to sell their estates. With the commencement of this important movement, a slight enlargement of the village had taken place in the direction of Clemens Street. Satchwell Buildings, erected in 1807, were followed by the building of a house at the corner of that street. Hopper mentions it as the first new private residence in the Old Town, and 1808 as the year in which it was built. At a very early period in the history of Leamington it was applied to business purposes, and one of the first tradesmen who occupied the premises is reported to have been Mr. James Bird, wine and spirit merchant, who founded there the successful trade he afterwards transferred to 118, Parade, and now carried on by Mr. James Brown. The (fete when he became tenant as a grocer and wine and spirit merchant in Clemens Street was 1821. Merridew gave his place of business as 11, Lower Parade in 1837. In the year 1842 the house was in the occupation of Mr. Henry Butler, butcher, and the demolition of this and other properties took place when the street was widened and generally improved for the building of the railway bridges. The situation was at the bottom of the street, on the west side, but it projected out into the roadway a considerable distance beyond the present line of the shops and houses. Standing at the Bath Hotel and looking towards Clemens Street, the house almost completely obstructed the view of the whole of the street. A few other buildings in the same locality were erected in comparatively rapid succession. One adjoined it in High Street, and another, built at the opposite corner by Mr. Thomas Palmer, draper, was, years afterwards, absorbed by Copps's Hotel. But previous to the dates of these buildings, a house, to which very considerable interest attaches, had stood on the site of the present Crown Hotel. It was a small building, but it was the original The houses occupied by Bird and Palmer are shown in the illustration on page no. The dwelling forming the south-west corner of High Street and Clemens Street was the residence and business premises of the former; the balconied house at the south-east corner belonged to the latter. The narrow street between the two properties was the commencement of Clemens Street. village school; the first local seat of learning; the Athens of old Leamington; and the ancestor of our modern School Board system. In the course of a few years, additional houses were erected in the neighbourhood, and gradually Clemens Street and High Street rose out of the meadow, with outlines much the same as at present, but in many respects differing in the number and character of the buildings, and, most of all, in the crowds of visitors who already thronged the streets and filled every lodging-house in the village. To the principal of these dwellings we shall advert in subsequent chapters. Meanwhile we must direct attention to the beginning of another movement of still greater importance—the invasion by the builders of the groves and heaths on the north bank, and the creation of a new town.

By the preparation of plans, general arrangements, negociation, and the adoption of a scheme, the New Town in reality dates from 1806. Terms of purchase as to land having been made, on Tuesday, September 20, 1808, the first building was commenced by the laying of three stones, one by John Tomes, Esq., a rich banker at Warwick, and the other two by the Rev. James Walhouse and Benjamin Satchwell. It was not to be expected that an event so promising for the future greatness and prosperity of Leamington would be passed over without some marks of public rejoicing. Dawkes says "the bells were set ringing on the occasion; the ringers had £1 16s for so doing." A dinner at the New Inn, or the Bowling Green; a procession round the village, led by "the band of music," with the Fountain of Hospitality, and a service at the Parish Church, most probably belonged to the gala proceedings of the day. In what part of the New Town these stones were laid it is impossible to say with absolute certainty. The Golden Lion, Regent Street;

Mclia's Stores at the north-west corner of the Parade and Regent Street, and the properties from 59, Parade, occupied by Mr. Walker Boshell, antique dealer, to 71, the premises of Messrs. Powell Bros., confectioners, which Mr. W. Dawkes mentions as the first block of houses built in the new town, are claimed as the localities. It can only be said modern Leamington began on one of these sites, and that the happy auspices under which the stones were laid have been followed by a degree of prosperity far exceeding the expectation of all who participated in the rejoicings of the time. It ought, however, to be stated that the claim for the last-named site is supported by Mr. Councillor Dawkes, on the authority of his father. Guided by what his father on several occasions had told him, he believes the house, 69, now in the occupation of Mesdames Kolsch and Marsh, milliners, to have been the first building erected in the New Town. Field reports the following "as a memorial of honourable distinction and as a record of an interesting fact:—George Stanly, mason, of Warwick, laid the first brick of the first house, erected at new Leamington, October 8, 1808." "This house," he says, "which was built by Mr. Frost, of Warwick, stands at the corner of Upper Cross Street, opposite the Assembly Rooms, and it is with no more than a well-deserved compliment to the first bold adventurer in a new and untried path, that a street running parallel with Union Street, only as yet in part formed, has, in honour of him, been named Frost Street." The street referred to is Bedford Street.

Before proceeding further in chronological order, it becomes necessary to notice a series of very remarkable events, simultaneous in their origin, and all belonging to the year 1806. The discovery of two new springs; the erection of two sets of Baths; the commencement of a great philanthropic movement; the renovation and reorganisation of the existing hotels, and the preparation for a new town, were the principal schemes of local aggrandisement in that auriferous period. To two of these interesting subjects—the foundation of

a new settlement, and the improvement of Abbotts's Baths—we have already alluded; the others shall be briefly sketched.

BATH STREET IN THE COACHING DAYS. Russell's Bath Hotel, 1826, with the luggage office; the elms and oaks along Spencer Street and Victoria Terrace, and Robbins's Baths near the Bridge.

The most important work of Satchwell's life was reserved for 1806, the year following the death of his friend Abbotts. There seems to have been an artistic arrangement in the events of his career, commencing, as they did, with some very humble efforts, directed towards the improvement of the condition of his neighbours, and culminating in a movement which, to-day, stands prominent among the noblest charitable institutions of England. The Leamington Spa Charity, founded by him, is admitted in the annual report of the Warneford Hospital for 1873, to have been the seedling plant which grew into the Dispensary and Infirmary of 1816, and that from this institution came the Hospital of 1826. Actively co-operating with him, in the establishment of the Charity, was his constant friend, the Rev. James Walhouse, correctly described by Pratt as having been amongst the "most early, indefatigable and unwearied patrons of the institution." The rules were few, but absence of voluminous details is compensated to the full by their comprehensive spirit, their perspicuity and the benevolent design which illumines every word. The object of the Charity was to provide free baths for poor people from any part of England. Visitors, subscribing, became members of the General Committee, and had the right to vote in the appointment of a Select Committee to manage the Charity. In order to be admitted on the books, candidates had to obtain certificates from a medical man, and a respectable friend or parish officer, as to their illness and circumstances. After approval by the local medical staff, they were entitled to the privileges of the institution for one month, during which time they had a weekly allowance, free baths, and medical attendance. In special cases the physician in charge of an invalid, or the Committee, had power to extend the time of benefit, and to pay the cost of the patient coming to Leamington and returning home. The following gentlemen deserve to be mentioned for their services to this most useful organization:—.Medical Establishment: William Lambe, M.D., London; John Johnstone, M.D., Birmingham; Sir Christopher I'egge, M.D., Oxford; William Kerr, M.D., Northampton; R. Chauner, M.D., Burton. Resident Physician: Amos Middleton, M.D. Surgeons: Mr. George Birch, and Mr. Franklin. President: Isaac Wilkinson, Esq. Vice-President: Dr. Middleton. Satchwell continued to discharge the arduous duties of his offices until his death, after which time his son-in-law, Mr. Richard Hopton, became treasurer. When it is stated that in the course of ten years the Charity gave two thousand free baths to poor invalids, sufficient will be said to prove its utility, and to explain the feeling of pride with which the Warneford Hospital Committee, in 1873, claimed for their own institution, through its descent from this Charity, a date of origin coeval with the rise of Leamington.

Two years—1804 and 1810—are generally quoted as having been the dates of the establishment of Mr. F. Robbins's Baths, but it was on Monday, July 5, 1806, they were opened to the public. They were near the bridge on the south side of the river, surrounded by trees, and had at the rear some gardens, and a copse which fringed the bank of the stream as far as the Adelaide Bridge. Along this was an erratic footpath, forming one of the most delightful walks afforded by the village in the spring and summer seasons and early autumn. Robbins's Baths, with their rustic associations, are shown in the illustration we give of the Bath Hotel, for many years their nearest neighbour. This was the fourth spring of saline water possessed by the village, but the supply was increased a few months later by the discovery of a fifth in High Street, on land, the property of the Rev. William Read, Baptist Minister, Warwick, who at once proceeded to construct a

building for hot and cold baths. "Read's Baths" was the name they derived from their owner. Mr. Read was appointed to the Pastorate of the Baptist Church at Warwick in 1804, and was the seventh minister from the time of the Revolution. A list of his predecessors in the office is given in "Field's History of Warwick." The spring was on the premises of Messrs. G. and M. Rayson, confectioners, 12, High Street, and is still in existence, though the Baths have been closed several years and the drinking fountain discontinued. These Baths passed through the usual vicissitudes of private bathing institutions, there being frequent changes of ownership, the name following those of each of the proprietors. At one time they were known as "Lee's Baths." It was here the first Turkish Baths in Leamington were established in September, 1861, by the late Mr. James Hudson, who advertised them under the name of "The Royal Leamington Turkish Baths." The energetic proprietor, in his public announcement of what was a great novelty in those days, expressed the reasonable hope that his efforts "to supply a want much required in Leamington will meet with the support its importance demands." Turkish Baths were not then appreciated, and the large expense he had incurred brought him in no adequate returns.

THE OLD WIND MI I.I. AND COTTAGE, TACHBROOKE ROAD.

The same year Sinker, stimulated by the examples of his neighbours, and assured of success by the urgent demands for accommodation daily received by him from visitors of quality, enlarged his hotel and made the rooms "very elegant for those who wish to experience the efficacy of these saline waters." Lodging-houses were being furnished, and a plan prepared for a "new street with a magnificent Assembly Room." This evidently referred to a proposal to commence the New Town on the north side of the river by widening the Lillington Lane from the bridge to the corner of Regent Grove, and carrying the Parade through the cor n and clover pastures as far as Clarendon Avenue. The "magnif-

icent Assembly Room" was either the Royal Pump Room or the old Assembly Room which occupied the site from the south-west corner of the Parade and Regent Street and extended back into Bedford Street. These were not erected until 1813, but it is clear that as early as 1806 one of them was in contemplation. It is to this project of colonising the northern slope we must look for an explanation of the first widening of the bridge— a necessary accompanying condition to the investment of capital and the vigorous development of this spirited scheme. The social change in the village is indicated by the transformation of the Dog public-house, where the farmers and labourers had been accustomed to assemble time out of memory, into a select private Boarding House, and the aristocratic character of the guests, by a head waiter being required, middle-aged, one who had served in the capacity of a butler preferred, "disposed to keep everything in the neatest order," and, "as the wine will be entrusted to his care," Mr. Sinker " must have an unexceptionable character from his last place." The change of proprietorship at the New Inn was attended by a corresponding spirit of enterprise. Under the new management, the establishment was entirely renovated and arrangements made in every way calculated to enhance the comforts of visitors.

The sale of the Wind Mill on the Tachbrooke Road, formerly spelt "Teachbrooke," might be passed over without reference, were it not for one or two circumstances of special interest. It appears to have been the first sale of freehold property by auction in Leamington in the present century; the description of the situation and condition of the cottage are landmarks of local and general social progress. The age of the Mill was probably one of centuries, and, in its day, the owners, men wielding power and authority in parish affairs. Mr. Bromwich is named in the advertisements as the owner and occupier, and "Lemington, near Warwick," as the locality. With the Mill were also sold one acre of land, and a cottage which the discreet auctioneer did not omit to inform the public was "tiled." A tiled roof in Leamington was a luxury in cottage architecture, of which auctioneers made as much as possible; it will readily occur to the reader how in the Terrier of Parish Church property presented to the Bishop in 1693, the vicarage dwelling-house was said to have had "two large bays and tyled." The Wind Mill, cottage, and garden were sold at the Star and Raven Hotel, Warwick, on Wednesday, October 29, 1806, by Mr. J. Loveday.

The first medical treatise on the waters by a local author was published in 1806. It was from the pen of Mr. Amos Middleton, a young practitioner rising into notice, at the time M.R.C.S., but afterwards M.D.; the father of the medical profession in Leamington. The title of his work, which was printed and published by Mr. Henry Sharpe, the proprietor of the *Warwick Advertiser,* was as follows: "A Chemical Analysis of the Leamington Waters, with a Practical Dissertation on their Medical Effects: Illustrated by Cases to prove their efficacy in the cure of Scrofula and Scorbutic Humours, to which are added Instructions for cold and warm bathing." It had, as it deserved, a very large circulation, and among those contributory influences which began to fill the sails of Leamington with the gale of prosperity, it was far from being the least. In 1814 it had reached the third edition, which, revised and enlarged, was dedicated to Dr. Kerr, "as a small tribute of gratitude for your professional kindness and assistance; as a slight remembrance of old family friendship, and as a general token of respect for your acknowledged medical talents; your eminence as a physician, and your strenuous exertions in the investigation, in the support, and in the recommendation of these particular waters." His aim in publishing the work, he tells us, was "to put into the hands of the invalid a short and easy, but condensed and comprehensive, account of all that is necessary to be known as to the nature of the Leamington waters, or observed as to the method of using them." In this purpose he cannot be said to have failed.

Middleton's directions for drinking and bathing are the most valuable chapters of a large number of the old "Guides."

The initiative of the broad and level roads and streets, to which Leamington owes much of its deservedly high reputation, was commenced in 1808 and finished in 1809. Like the old Romans, the early Leamingtonians were sensible of the advantages of good roads. No sooner was the first stone of the New Town laid than public attention was directed to the state of the bridge. Authorities differ respecting the form and material of the old structure, and we question whether any means are available for reconciling their conflicting statements. By one we are informed there was only a wooden footbridge across the river; by another that it was a low, ancient bridge, consisting of a single arch, spanning a more contracted stream than that which now flows under the Victoria Bridge. The usual rail fence lined the approaches. In consequence of its narrowness, "the rule of the road was for drivers going towards Lillington to take the bridge in preference to any vehicle advancing in an opposite direction, while the latter crossed by the ford, which still existed, descending from the site of the Jephson Gardens Lodge and ascending by the waterway recently filled up alongside the Post Office." Whatever might have been the character of the bridge, all concur in describing it as narrow and more calculated for keeping the two sections of the town separate than for uniting them into one harmonious whole. It was the property of the County, and from time immemorial had been the sport of storms and floods, a great expense to the ratepayers, and constant source of irritation to the local farmers. The new bridge was substantially the present structure, amplified by enlargements in 1839. It was built of stone, consisted of three arches, as at present, and provided for two vehicles to pass at the same time instead of limiting the accommodation to one, as was formerly the case. The prompt response of the County Authority to the local application for improved communication was an official recognition of the growing importance of the

place.

Satchwell's unaffected simplicity, his earnest desire to please all the visitors, and his intelligence made him a special favourite. In a former reference we regretted the vacant page on which posterity would have wished to see his personal appearance faithfully delineated. We have since been favoured with a report which advances the portrait towards completion. He was, says the writer, "very prepossessing. The silver locks that fell over his shoulders imparted a venerable look which his ruddy and cheerful countenance belied, and this happy state of health and innate peace remained with him to the last. Several portraits were taken of him at this time by ladies who were desirous of perpetuating his memory among their friends; one, which was engraved in 18z9, was drawn, however, many years previous, when age weighed but slightly upon him, and time had not left those traces upon his countenance which afterwards invested him with such patriarchal grace." The honour of promoting the public convenience by improving the local postal system, and inducing the authorities to establish a branch post office in the village at a very early period of its history, is a flower in the garland with which Time has rewarded his many-sided labours. Leamington was originally part of the Warwick postal district, the deliveries of letters from which were late in the day, and the time allowed for reply by return only about an hour and a half, or two hours. It is not known when he first became officially connected with the service, but his original labours were, it is almost certain, of a voluntary character, and in the humble capacity of collecting letters from visitors, and taking or sending them to Warwick to be posted. His assiduity in minimising the discomfort which the imperfect machinery of the village imposed on patrons from populous towns leads to this conclusion. This assistance would be greatly esteemed, and his selection for the office of district postmaster followed as a matter of course. The appointments were then at the disposal of Members of Parliament for the Counties and Boroughs, and all that was required to elevate Ben to the position of being representative of the Monarch, as he had long been of the million, was a recommendation from some of his numerous aristocratic friends. His popularity, intelligence, and trustworthiness marked him as the most suitable man for the post.

Early in the morning of Saturday, December i, 1810, Satchwell breathed his last, and there passed away from local life the most interesting resident of the previous half-century. A month or five weeks before his death, he was in good health and spirits. The beginning of his illness was a slight inflammation of the chest, which, gradually increasing in intensity, baffled every remedial measure. The greatest care was bestowed upon him, and frequent medical consultations were held. Around his bed were gathered those many indissoluble friendships which his long and useful life had garnered. On one side was the Rev. James Walhouse, with the skill of a professional nurse, and the tenderness and affection of a brother, ministering to the wants of his afflicted friend; on the other was Dr. Kerr, who, on hearing of his illness, had driven over from Northampton, bringing his vast stores of medical knowledge and his wide experience as a voluntary contribution to the agencies which were being employed for his recovery; at the foot stood Mr. George Birch, the medical attendant, painfully conscious that he was contending with two formidable foes—the ravages of an insidious disease, and the infirmities of age. Covering the table were various delicacies, such as tempt the appetite of the sick chiefly by their novelty, contributed by sympathisers of every class in the village, in the vain hope of recruiting his shattered health. Daily growing weaker, he called to his bedside the members of his family, and having tranquilly arranged his affairs, joined with them and a select circle of personal friends in the Sacrament, and shortly afterwards peacefully went out with the ebbing waters of the old year, and quietly "crossed the bar." The news of his death produced a darkness in

every cottage so gross as to be felt; and in the village a void which made it a strange place, even to those who had known it all their lives as their home.

The *Warwick Advertiser,* in its obituary notices on December 8, 1810, thus referred in appreciative terms to the memory of the deceased: — " On Saturday morning last, deeply regretted by his neighbours and friends, Mr. Benjamin Satchwell, in the 78th year of his age, senior inhabitant of Leamington Priors. He contributed with honest zeal and laudable assiduity to raise the name of the Leamington Waters to their present eminence, and his ' rustical roundelays,' and homely but well-meant gratulations will be held in remembrance by many of the first families in the kingdom, whose arrival at the Spa he seldom failed to commemorate in some loyal and complimentary effusion."

He was buried in the Churchyard, near the south porch, with every sign of public respect and grief. A long train of mourners attended the funeral, and mingled with the hot scalding tears of his family were the sobbings of many he had befriended, and heavy sighs of sympathy by those who, above him in social circumstances, valued him as their friend, and treated him as their equal. An expensive altar tomb was erected over his grave by his daughter, Miss Satchwell, in August, 1812, inscribed as follows:— "This sacred tribute of a Daughter's love and Duty is raised to the Memory of Benjamin Satchwell, of Leamington Priors, who departed this life December 1, 1810, aged seventy-seven years." On the opposite side were the subjoined lines, composed by Mr. Pratt, author of the "Gleaner," and the first "Guide" to Leamington, which appeared in 1812.

"With kindred dust beneath this stone doth blend,
The ashes of a Patron and a Friend:
Thy Friend, thy Patron, Leamington whose zeal,
Recording Time and Truth shall long reveal.
Lowly as his, thy birth, unknown to fame,
But thy fair youth his latest age pro-

claim.
Thy copious fountains sparkling high with health,
Thy growing greatness and thy future wealth,
Thy proudest villas and each cot's recess,
Bid thee the grave of humble Satchwell bless.
His the clear head in Nature's volume taught,
And his the wisdom sage experience bought;
His the strong powers of Body and of Soul,
And his the honest heart to crown the whole.
Reader, who'er thou art whom sickness brings,
Or more consuming sorrow, to these springs,
Or, if gay pleasure lure thee to the scene,
Where Nature spreads the charms of loveliest green.
Thou, too, shouldst hail the unassuming tomb,
Of him who told where health and beauty bloom,
Of him whose lengthened life improving ran,
A blameless, useful, venerable man."

Enough has been said to excite a feeling of admiration of a lasting character for Satchwell, without attempting anything approaching a minute analysis of his nature, his work, or the motives which kept him in constant action. He stands at the head of the Friendly Societies' movement in Leamington, and in a subordinate capacity, was the first of its journalists. In that small group of men who endowed the village with every energy COPPS'S HOTEL, HIGH STREET, THE MARKET, AND WISE'S BATH, 1822.

they possessed, he was a central figure, and his rank is first in the postal service. Posterity, from thoughtlessness, has allowed his tombstone to fall into a discreditable state of decay, and Time has rendered undecipherable the inscription which expressed the veneration and esteem in which he was held by his contemporaries. But we are not without hopes of seeing this oversight remedied by the collection of the few pounds necessary for its restoration, and the tribute which was earned by lowly worth preserved for many generations to come. Should this be realised, we would suggest to those who take the work in hand the propriety of placing on record his valuable services to the cause of the afflicted poor by founding the Leamington Spa Charity.

A flutter of delight in the village was caused in 1808 by the visit of a family, whose association with early Leamington is historic. Their Graces, the Duke and Duchess of Bedford, out of respect for whom one of the principal streets was named a few years afterwards, and the palatial Bedford Hotel, built in 1811 on the site of the London and Midland Bank, 12b, Parade, derived its title, arrived with a large attendance of servants. This seems to have been their first patronage of the Spa, and from the following paragraphs, which appeared in the *Warwick Advertiser,* in May and August, we think it not improbable that they stayed at the New Inn, Bath Street.

"The Duke and Duchess of Bedford intend to visit Leamington Spa in a short time, where lodgings are engaged for their accommodation. The well-known salubrity of the waters; the commodiousness of the baths, and the late charming weather, have already induced many of the admirers of rural retirement and elegant society to repair to this delightful spot."

"This Spa could never boast a more numerous or a more fashionable company—His Grace the Duke of Bedford and his amiable Duchess, with a princely retinue, arrived at the Baths on Tuesday evening, where three of their children and their attendants have been for more than a week past. The frankness and affability of these noble personages is not less conspicuous upon this rural spot than it is in the brilliant circles in which they generally move. His Grace, we understand, highly approves of the water."

To the following earliest collected and published list of visitors who were in the village at the same time, a certain degree of curious interest belongs, though the names do not represent anything like the total number for the season:—

"The Right Rev. the Bishop of Limerick, and Lady; Major Warburton; Rev. Archdeacon Warburton and Miss Warburton; Gore Townsend, Esq.; Lady E Townsend and the Misses Townsend; R. Dyott, Esq., and Mrs. Dyott; M. R. Boulton, Esq.; Captain Adderley, R.N., and Mr. Adderley; Captain Corsley and Mrs. Corsley; Rev. Mr. Pickering; Rev. Mr. Pearson: Mrs. and Misses Pearson; Ed. Watts, Esq.; Mrs. and Miss Watts; Rev. M. Portington; Rev. Mr. Latton; Rev. Mr. Knapp and Mrs. Knapp; Mr. Pickard; Mr. Wheelwright; Miss Jordan; Mr. J Hodgson; Mr. J. G. Gamble; Mr. Rolls; Mrs. Hallway; Mrs. Floyd; Mrs and Miss Dearman; Miss Board; Mr. Tooke; Mrs. Perry; R. Clark, Esq. , and Miss Clark; Mrs. and Miss Umbers; Rev. Mr. Cotton; Mr. Cotton, jun. ; Miss Fox; Mrs. Hollis." These names are the return for May 14, 1808 The Rev James Walhouse and Dr. Lambe are in the list for May 28; Dr. Kerr and Lord Egremont in those for June.

A youth, for whom Fame had in store a chaplet of immortality; who, after winning the golden sceptre of empire on the stage, was to spend the calm sunset of his life in promoting the cause of education amongst the agricultural labourers, visited the village early in the century. William Charles Macready, the great tragedian, in his "Reminiscences," thus refers to the occasion:—

' Birmingham was the most important of the towns of which my father held the theatres, and there we soon arrived. The summer months were passed there, diversified by a short stay at Leamington, then a small village, consisting only of a few thatched houses— not one tiled or slated—the Bowling Green Inn being the only one where very moderate accommodation could be secured. There was in process of erection an hotel of more pretension, which, I fancy, was to be the Dog or Greyhound, but which had some months of work to fit it for the reception of guests. We had the parlour and bedrooms of a huckster's shop, the best accommodation in the place; and used each morning to walk down to the springs across the churchyard with our little mugs in our hands for our daily draught of the Leamington waters."

There are good and sufficient reasons for believing those writers to be in error who mention 1808 as the time when the Macreadies were in Leamington; one is, the description does not agree with the state of things in that year; the other, that in the chronologically arranged " Reminiscences," the Spa holiday is reported as having taken place before the death of Mrs. Macready, his mother, at Sheffield, on December, 3, 1803. The time of the visit is a subject for intelligent conjecture, but it must have been much earlier than 1808, at which period there were many houses in Leamington with tiled and slated roofs.

An advertisement in October, headed "Leamington: New Buildings," for brick makers, pump makers, well sinkers; persons willing to sink cellars and get out foundations for a number of houses; and another, of land to be let on building leases, "near the baths, and in the centre of the village," are some of the straws which indicate the direction and force of the gale of prosperity which had arisen. The date of the commencement of Clemens Street is clearly stated by another notice that 'a new street is laid out and begun upon this land, leading from the village to the canal, and there is great probability of its being completed in the course of another summer or two.' "Brick-kilns are opening on the said lands, and as the canal from Birmingham and Warwick to London goes through the premises, building materials are conveyed to the spot with the greatest facility." These brick-kilns were in Court Street and Grove Place.

"Oon Maister Toone," to quote from a quaint description of the rise of Wesleyan Methodism in Leamington, in other words, Mr. John Toone, settled here about the year 1809. He was a native of Stoneleigh, and by trade a builder. Connected with the rise and progress of the town for the space of sixty-six years, and a prominent man in public affairs, a brief notice of his life forms a part of this work. His first place of business, there are reasons for believing, was in the New Town, and his workshop and timber yard, on land in Warwick Street, lying between Satchwell Street and Park Street. The present shops and houses were not then built. As he was a Wesleyan Methodist, we regard him as one of the small congregation, who, in 1817, worshipped in a loft, in Barnacle's Yard, in Satchwell Street, where, and when, the cause of Wesleyan Methodism in Leamington took root. In 1829, he built the Mill Street Chapel, and in 1840, the Leamington Brewery. In 1834, he was occupying a part of the land mentioned, on which there was a cottage directly opposite Guy Street. But his residence was the house and shop in the Parade, now occupied by Mrs. Roake, furniture dealer, and numbered 37. It was in this house the Wesleyans assembled in 1834, and decided to enlarge the Portland Street Chapel at a cost of £600. Mr. Toone had a builder's shop at the bottom of Satchwell Street, in Regent Street, the site of which is that of Mr. T. F. T. Parkinson, pawnbroker, number 101. He was one of the early Parish Constables; and also qualified as a Commissioner, for which Board he carried out at various times important sewerage contracts. His personality was distinguished for its originality, and in the later years of his life for its venerable characteristics. Tall and erect, his face a picture of health and happiness; wearing a low crowned hat, and spectacles, through which he beamed contentedly on his generation; a beard of snowy whiteness, "descending swept his aged breast;" such was the patriarchal appearance of old John Toone in the hardy winter of his time. He died March 13, 1875, aged eighty-seven.

A valuable piece of land in Highstreet, about two acres in extent, opposite Mr. Wise's garden and baths, was brought into the market in December, 18oq. The description agrees with the situation of Wise Street and Bath Place. HATH STREET, HATH HOTEL, THEATRE,

AND ASSEMBLY ROOMS, 1822. The views on pages 131, 134, 141, and 142, are copied by permission of Mr. Frank Glover, of the *Leamington Spa Courier,* from an exceedingly interesting work by Mr. J. C. Manning, M.J. I., on the growth of the town, entitled "Glimpses of our Local Past, incidental to the Rise and Progress of Royal Leamington Spa." Mr. Manning's contribution to local history is written in a most entertaining style, and is a valuable addition to the literature of early Leamington. For the illustration on page 137, entitled "Leafy Leamington," we are indebted to the Rev. W. Field's "History of Warwick," a standard book, composed in the talented author's best style, and indispensable to every student of the history of the County town. In the accompanying description the date of Robbins's house and baths, by a press error, appears as 1800 instead of 1806." CHAPTER XVIII. ITHERTO the advancement of the town has been principally the work of individual enterprise. We are now drawing near to the period in which new forms of activity will be brought into play. To supply the public needs, syndicates, or companies were necessary, and under the influence of their energy, large buildings will presently be raised, and give a powerful impetus to the growing popularity of Leamington. A rapid survey of the chief events of 1810 is all for which we can find space. The total number of visitors in the previous year was reported to have been no less than 1,500, exclusive of servants, children, and other members of families, who probably numbered an additional 2,000. There were not at the time more than sixty or seventy cottages and houses in the village, a large proportion of the occupants of which, in the old town, were so poor that the Overseers exempted them from paying rates. Every coach that arrived was laden with visitors, many of whom, we are informed, were poor invalids who had sought the benefit of the waters in distressed circumstances, having been liberally relieved from a fund established for such a laudable purpose. They re-

turned to their homes restored to health, and sincerely grateful for the assistance they had obtained from that beneficent institution—the Leamington Spa Charity.

The sixth spring was discovered this year. It was on the north side of the river, and the event led to the building of the Pump Room and Baths.

It was somewhere about this time that a large quantity of land on the north of the river was disposed of, thereby sensibly accelerating the work of developing the New Town, and freeing the land in the old village from obstacles which reluctance to sell had thrown in the way of would-be investors. It consisted of a farm of sixty-five acres, belonging to Mr. Greathead, of Guy's Cliffe, and was occupied, we believe, by a Mr. Perkins, at a rental of £70. The exact situation is not stated, but it is not unlikely to have included the greater part of the Parade. Between £40,000 and £50,000 was the sum realised by the sale; a moderate price compared with the average amounts paid for eligible sites at this period; "dirt cheap," contrasted with the £4,000, and in some cases £5,000 per acre, given a few years later, but fabulously extravagant by the side of £60, the value of land when Abbotts erected his baths in 1786. And now the effects began to appear of that bond of unity which had existed between the ancient borough of Warwick and the village from the date of discovery of the second spring; a mutuality of sentiment and an identity of interest which have subsisted to the present time, and of which there is no reason to fear a dissolution throughout the succeeding ages of time. In every stage of the history of Leamington, for at least twenty-five years following the analysis of the waters by Dr. Lambe in 1794, the fostering helpful care of Warwick is observable. Smith, on taking to the New Inn, in 1806, acknowledged the services of the medical men of the borough, who appear to have seconded the labours of Lambe by every means in their power. Warwick was not without ample rewards for these services. For years the overflow of visitors to Warwick exceeded those who remained in Leamington. The hotel keepers, the tradespeople, and those having apartments to let, reaped a golden harvest which more than reimbursed them for the local trades then decaying and passing away.

"The Leamington Building Society" appears to have been a Warwick Institution, designed for purchasing land for houses, and assisting in the development of early Leamington. No precise information can be gleaned of the details of its work, the only source of information being its public notices, which, though meagre, bear this construction. The mode of subscription differed from that of any existing building societies. Members entered their names for one or more shares, and, as money was required, a call of so much per cent, was made by order of the Committee. When a house, or several houses were built, they were disposed of by ballot among the members. On March 8, 1810, a meeting was held at the Black Swan, Warwick, and eight houses erected at Leamington were distributed among the members by ballot. Mention is made in several of the "Guides" of a row of twenty houses having been built by a syndicate in Union Street, below the Assembly Rooms. This Society was most probably the syndicate referred to, and the houses balloted on the date mentioned, a part of the row. On the same day five shares in the society were sold by auction.

One of the early " musicianers," Mr. Owen Owen, settled in Leamington in July as a teacher of "that delightful and most fashionable instrument," the pedal harp. Particulars were obtainable at Mr. Olorenshaw's Library, High Street. Mr. Owen specially desired correspondents to pre-pay their letters, a not unreasonable request, seeing the cost was 7c!., 8d., and 9d. each.

The list of visitors in July contained a hundred and sixty names; in August they were to be counted by several hundreds, those old patrons, the Duke and Duchess of Bedford, being again amongst the number.

On August 4 and 6, appeared at the Bowling Green Assembly Room, Master and Miss Smith, "the celebrated musical phenomena," the latter being also described as the " first female violin performer in Europe." No report exists of the concert, but, as this was the first occasion on which the inhabitants assembled to listen to artistically rendered music, it is a noticeable event. Another point is the evidence it affords of the fame of the village at the time—artists beginning to include it in the list of places to be visited; and, lastly, it is interesting to note that the violin to hear which the concert was given should in our own day have become a popular part of education.

The Pump Rooms, with the original cottage roof, erected at the north-west corner of the Bridge, in 1813; Robbins's House and Baths, at the south-west corner, built in 1800 (the site is now occupied by the establishment of Merridew and Sarson, wine and spirit merchants, and the houses in the Victoria Colonnade);house and farm buildings, at the south-east corner (the land from the Old Well sloped down to the river); the Bridge, as completed in 1809; the old Parish Church, previous to the improvements in 1816; and the woodland scenery on the site of Victoria Terrace and along the bank of the river at the back of Spencer Street Chapel.

Another historic visit took place in November of this year. There are frequent references to the residence of the Duchess of Gordon and her daughters at Gordon House, but excepting that she led off the dance one evening at the Bowling Green Inn with Dr. Parr, nothing further is reported. It appears, however, that it was health rather than pleasure which brought her to Leamington, and that she was one of a crowd of illustrious patients who have derived signal benefit from the Leamington Waters. The following is from the *Warwick Advertiser,* Nov. 17, 1810:—

"The Duchess of Gordon left Leamington on Wednesday, the 7th instant, for London, after expressing herself highly satisfied with the waters, and declaring that she had received more benefit from the use of them than she could possibly have expected, even from the flattering representation of the Duke of Bedford, by whose recommendation she was induced to visit them. Her Grace left Leamington a month ago, for a few days, to fetch the Duke of Manchester's daughter, who came down with her and returned in perfect health. The reports we may expect to have made in the fashionable world from so high and distinguished a character in fashionable life as the Duchess of Gordon, and the influence her Grace has acquired among all ranks, not less by her affability and goodness than by her high station and family connections, will, we have no doubt, another season fill this wonderfully improving place, beyond anything we have yet witnessed, and we hope speedily to see Leamington crowded with such gay and splendid parties as will set it upon a level with any watering place in the kingdom."

Numerous anecdotes of the wit, vivacity, and condescension of the Duchess, current in the last generation, have evaporated from local memory. One alone remains, and this may be quoted as a useful lesson to people who, arriving late at service, thoughtlessly disturb congregations. In this predicament her Grace found herself on a certain Sunday at the Parish Church—every pew full and the service considerably advanced. Respecting the example in punctuality of the villagers and visitors, and declining to disturb the humblest worshipper, she seated herself on the lower steps leading up to the singers' gallery, where she remained throughout the whole service.

The leading events in 1811, were the completion of the Bedford Hotel, and the commencement of the New Assembly Rooms. Both were called into existence by the special circumstances of the time. Visitors were numbered by thousands, the majority of them moving in circles of rank, wealth, and culture. For these there was no accommodation such as they had a right to expect; no assembly room for balls and festive gatherings, no hotel in which they could obtain rooms furnished after the style of their homes, and service at the table equal to the best which their own establishments could provide. The Bedford was finished in the month of October, and on the 25th was opened for the reception of visitors. The proprietors were Mr. and Mrs. Williams, who for many years had been in service as butler and housekeeper at Guy's Cliffe. What is known as the house-warming took place on Saturday, December 4. The popularity of the hotel, and the powerful patronage ensured, are seen in the number and quality of the guests. There were one hundred and twenty-eight gentlemen present, representing the leading families in the county. The dinner, we are informed, was one "abounding in excellent wine and every delicacy of the season, dressed in the highest state of cookery." The chronicler of the time says: "Appropriate toasts and songs enlivened the evening. which was prolonged to a late hour with the utmost gaiety and conviviality. Besides the gentlemen who were present, many of the most distinguished nobility and gentry of the county, who were unable to attend in person, took tickets to express their wishes for the prosperity of the undertaking." The Stewards were Sir Charles Mordaunt, Bart., M.P.; Lord Middleton; Sir Gray Skipwith, Bart.; Sir James Lake, Bart.; Bertie Greatheed, Esq.; Eardley Wilmot, Esq. Tickets, including wine, dessert, etc., were one guinea each.

Mr. Franklin, a surgeon, whose name frequently occurs in after years as Dr. Franklin, was one of the early residents. An advertisement of his in 1811 announced that he was residing at number 8, New Town, where he intended practising the different branches of the profession, and " trusts that strict attention will entitle him to the Support and Patronage of those Friends who may please to favour him with their confidence. Physicians' Prescriptions carefully prepared.''

The Golden Lion, Regent.Street, which has the reputation of having been the first house built in the New Town, was offered for sale bv auction at the George Inn, Warwick, on June 29, 181

2, by Messrs. J. and R. Loveday, Auctioneers. The landlord was Mr. James Miles. Two "newly-built" houses near it, occupied by Messrs. Tew and Lawrence, were also included in the sale In addition, a piece of building land, adjoining the Golden Lion, and fronting Cross Street (Regent Street) fifteen yards, and another, fronting Hill Street, twenty-four yards, and Cross Street, eighteen yards, were included in the sale. These particulars point to Miles as the first landlord of the Golden Lion, and to Hill Street having been the original name of Satchwell Street, or some other street in the locality.

Raffling was a perfectly legal mode of disposing of articles in 1812, and announcements were regularly made in the papers of the prices paid per ticket and the prizes given. But household property, seldom if ever, passed from one owner to another through the ballot box, except in the case of members of Building Societies. The following notice, dated June 13, 1812, is the only one of the kind which has come under our notice:—

"Freehold Premises: Leamington Spa.—To be Raffled for at the Bedford Hotel, at Leamington, aforesaid, as soon as the tickets are disposed of, of which due notice will lx; given in this paper.

A Moiety, or equal half-part of that substantial new-built Dwelling House, with the out-offices and garden belonging, being number 26, Union Street, Leamington aforesaid, at present untenanted.

The Premises comprise an excellent dining room in front, back parlour; kitchen and pantry, on the the ground floor; very good drawing room and bedroom on the first floor, three exceeding good bedrooms and a closet on the second floor, and four exceeding good attics; excellent cellaring, large brewhouse, and other convenient out offices.

Tickets (of which there will be 100 in number) may be had at Five Guineas each, by applying to Mr. Williams at the Bedford Hotel, aforesaid, at which place the rules and regulations for governing the raffle may be seen, on or before Thursday next, and from thence to

the time of raffling.— *Warwick Advertiser"* CHAPTER XIX.

HE erection in the green fields, on the north bank of the river, of a commodious building for balls, concerts, entertainments, and fashionable reunions, ushered in a new era of extensive building speculations, greatly assisted in swelling the influx of visitors, and gave to the town a social tone, which, as yet, it had not possessed. The exhilarating effects of cheerful society, and the invigorating influence of social gatherings are preservatives of health and powerful restoratives to recovery from various classes of disease. Before a place of assembly was provided, visitors who resorted to the waters hastened back to their homes and friends, on being relieved, or cured. Afterwards, a large proportion decided to stay, to make Leamington their home, and to invite their friends to join them.

The origin of the old Assembly Rooms belongs to 1810 by inception, and to 1811 and 181 z by building, completion and inauguration. In November of the first named year, the idea was thus made public, and steps taken for raising funds:—" Notwithstanding the buildings and improvements at Leamington have been carried on during last summer with uncommon energy and spirit, they have not kept pace with demands for lodgings and other accommodation; in consequence, some new streets have been laid out, and a subscription has been opened to erect an elegant Hotel with extensive and beautiful Assembly Rooms at the top of the new buildings in Union Street." The next reference to the project occurs in the subjoined advertisement, published in the *Warwick Advertiser,* February 9, 1811.

"To Architects, Leamington Spa, Warwickshire. A Premium of Twenty Guineas will be paid for the most approved ground plan and elevation for erecting Public Rooms at this much admired wateringplace. The plot on which the rooms are proposed to lie built is a Corner Situation, and contains 50 feet on the East—189 feet on the North (fronting Two principal streets)—50 feet on the West, facing a back street, and 189 on the South—adjoining Land already built upon—such Part only of the above Land to be used for the building as may be deemed necessary." Application to be made to the office of Messrs. Tomes and Heydon, Warwick; plans to le sent before the First Day of March next.

The scheme was successful, and the building, which became known in after years as the Upper Assembly Rooms, to distinguish it from the Parthenon, or Music Hall Assembly Rooms, in Bath Street, was opened on September 24, 181 2, with a ball, for quality, number, and brilliance, not surpassed, and very rarely equalled, in the subsequent history of the town. Sir Gray Skipwith, Bart. , officiated as steward, and there were upwards of three hundred guests and patrons present, including the Earl of Aylesford, Lord Chet wynd, Lord Clonmell.the Hon. Mr. Verney, Sir Charles, Lady, and the Dowager Lady Mordaunt, Lady Lavvley, Lady Peele, Mr. Dugdale, M.P., General Broadhurst, Colonel Crump, Mr. Bertie Greatheed and family, Mr. Townsend and family, Mr. Lucy and family, Mr. Dewes and family, Mr. Wise and family, Mr. Sheldon and family, etc. The building, to which we shall have occasion to refer later on, was for more than half a century the focus of the social side of Leamington. In 1878, it was sold and converted into the present range of shops.

The year 1813, opened more brightly for the prospects of Leamington than any of its predecessors. All was bustle and excitement. The builders were accumulating

Clemens Street, 1815, showing Blenheim Hotel, on the east side, where the Independents held their services before the first chapel was built in 1816 wealth; the landowners were making fortunes. The service of coaches had been increased, and visitors were daily swarming into the town. The Bedford Hotel and the Assembly Rooms were powerful magnets of home comforts and social delights, which strengthened the health attractions of the waters. Three other institutions were still required—a market, a theatre, and bathing accommodation which would compare with Bath and Cheltenham. The necessity for a public market does not now exist. Every article of food, drink, apparel, and luxury is supplied by the tradespeople at prices the cheapness of which excites wonder and removes all cause for complaint. But in 1812, the state of things was different. The increase had been in dwellings—not in shops. Bisset, who came as a visitor in 1811, and as a resident in 18i2, says it was not possible to obtain a beef steak or a roll in the village. Warwick, at this time, was the general provider for Leamington.

A small memorandum book of forty-six pages, such as would now be purchased at any stationer's shop for three-pence, contains the particulars of the rating system in force in 181 3, a list of the occupiers of land, the annual value of their respective holdings, and a complete register of the ratepayers of the period. This is preserved with jealous care at the office of Mr. Rogers, Bedford Street, and forms part of the mountainous archives which Time, and the poor rates, have patiently piled on the shelves. Few as are its pages, they furnished space for two rates which were collected, and one which went no farther than the imagination of the Churchwardens and Overseer. The reason for their indulgence in theoretical rates is obscure, unless we are to believe that it was a mild form of recreation with which they passed away the long winter evenings.

There were twenty-two occupiers of land in 1813, whose names and assessments are subjoined:—Messrs. John Campion, £352; Thomas Abbotts, £204, and Vicarage, £32; William Court, £193 ; Thomas Court, £170; George Whitehead, £1b2 ; Matthew Wise, including mansion, £137; Edward Willes, do. do. , £jb; Richard Reading,,645; — Walton, £22; Elizabeth Smith, £14.; Thomas Sinker, £13; Joseph Hiorns, £12; William King, £11; Elizabeth Abbotts, ,10; James Mackie, £10; Walton and Smallbone, £6; Mary Shaw, £5; William Olorenshaw, £8; Thomas Palmer, £3; William Benton, £j; and Edward Treadgold, £3.

On April 3, 1813, a levy of 3s. in the pound was made by George Whitehead, "overseer of the poor of Leamington and Newbold Comyn." Thomas Abbotts and John Campion, who at the time were filling the office of churchwardens, signed it, and Messrs. C. G. Wade and George Boswell, two Justices of the Peace, saw and allowed it on the 10th. It produced £$ 16 8s. 6d., nearly as much as a rate of 4s. 4d. realised ten years earlier. There were eighty-one ratepayers, whose names we reproduce. They constitute the first complete Directory we have of modern Leamington. No streets are mentioned in this rate:—

Thomas Abbotts, Elizabeth Abbotts, Richard Ambler, Joseph Brookhouse, George Birch, Richard Brown, William Benton, Henry Butler, N. S Bayley (Baly?), John Campion, Emma Cromblehome, Thomas Court, William Court, Richard Court, George Commander (senior), George Commander (junior1, William Commander, Joseph Dollm, Mrs. Edwards, John Evens, Francis Franklin, Thomas Fisher, David Frost, John Kenton, Mrs. Harris, Edward Hughes, Joseph Hiorns, — Hickling, Ann Kearney, George Kitchen, William Key, William King, Benjamin Keen, Samuel Letts, William Lewis, James Locket, James Leigh, James Mackie, James Miles, John Morris, — Mills, William Moody, William Olorenshaw, Thomas Olorenshaw, Thomas Palmer, John Pirkens, William Page, John Paine, William Perry, George Reading, William Reading, Francis Robbins, Richard Reading, Richard Sanders, Elizabeth Smith, Mary Shaw, Thomas Sinker, William Smith, Elizabeth Satchwell, Mary Satchwcll, William Savage, Mrs. Surcombe, John Tomes, Edward Treadgold, Thomas Thompson, Thomas Verron, Henry Williams, Richard Walton, Matthew Wise, Rev Edward Willes, Edward Wareing, Mrs. Willson, George Whitehead, William Webb, John West, John Williams, Walton and Smallbone, Thomas Worrall, Miss Walker, Robert Radford.

In the rate book we also have the particulars of a levy at is. 6d. in the pound, made on the ist day of April, 1814, by Thomas Abbotts and Richard Brown, overseers of the Parish of Leamington Priors, for money expended from Easter, 1813, to Michaelmas, 1813. This is the first rate in which appear the names of the streets of the old and the new towns, the entries in the previous rate having been in alphabetical order.

The following are not classified:— Matthew Wise, Rev. E. Willes, John Campion, Thomas Abbotts, George Whitehead, Thomas Worrall, Richard Walton, Thomas Court, Richard Reading, Thomas Sinker.

High Street.—John Russell, William Large, William Fowler, Thomas Thompson, William Alder, Rev. William Read (house and baths), William Olorenshaw, William Webb, Thomas Palmer. — Fisher, Michael Copps, George Kitchen, George Commander, William Townsend, William Key, Esther Kingerlee, Joseph Kingerlee, Wrilliam Savage, Mary Bayliss, Richard Ambler, John West, Elizabeth Griffiths, William Steat, William Hobbs, Joseph Tidmas, John Nicholds, Robert Radford, John Paine, Thomas Whale, Mary Thorneycroft, John Green, Richard Pinfold, Edward Gunn, John Hollick, Richard Brown. Of the thirty-five residents in High Street in this year, twelve are marked off as too poor to pay rates. Grandfather of Mr. James Brown, Wine Merchant, l'arade.

Church Street.— Mary Shaw (Bowling Green Inn, here described as a "lodging house"), Eli Hiorns, Joseph Hiorns, (rated house, wharf and two sites, one occupied by Crump and the other by Freeman), John Knight, John Fenton, Joseph Polton, William Benton, Edward Treadgold, Joseph Wood, John Gardner, Mary Flowers, Ann Griffiths, William Stiles, — Wright, Esq. Six of these were excused from paying rates on account of their poverty.

Mill End.— Mary Satchwell, Elizabeth Satchwell, Phoebe Satchwell, James Leigh, William Worrall, and Richard Court.

Clement Street.—Ann Kearney, Elizabeth Willson, John Hicklin, Thomas Veamon, Joseph Parsons, George Arnold. George Reading, William Holmes, Thomas Olds, James Tilley, John Penn, William Merry, Thomas Olorenshaw, Thomas Worrall, Stephen Probett, Rev. — Morgan, Mrs. Tinnery, Richard Booth, David Mackie, William Moody, William Page, Thomas Castle, John Key. Three returned as poor.

Bath Street.—Francis Robbins (baths, two houses, Woodbine Cottage, stables and three cottages), Mary Lewis, Mrs. Holding. Elizabeth Abbotts (house and land), Elizabeth Smith (bath house, stables and land), Thomas Bradshaw, Benjamin Keen, Mary Webb, James Lockett, Joseph Dolfen, John Evens, William Lewis, Frances Cummens, George Commander, Stephen Cuningham, Mrs Surcombe, John Walton, Edward Wareing, William Allen, John Cox, Theatre Five are described as poor, and, therefore, are not charged with the rate.

Gloucester Street.—Henry Butler, John Seers, Samuel Letts, William Smith, William Spires, John Wincott, Thomas Dawkes, William Warmsley (Wamsley?). Thomas Lord.

Union Parade.—Isaac Wilkenson, Samuel Perkens, John Parks, William Parks, William Orden, Mrs. Gill, Thomas Atkens, Mrs. Wickes, Charles Lawrance, John Clark, John Williams, N. S. Bayley (Baly?), John Morris, Mrs. Harris, George Birch, Emma Cromblehome, John Morris, Francis Franklin, Joseph Brookhouse, Edward Hughes, John Tomes, Richard Sanders, Mrs. Edwards, Doct. Middleton (house and land), Henry Williams, Publick Rooms (Assembly Rooms).

Upper Union Street.— Daniel Frost, William Smith, Mrs. W. Webb, Miss Walker, John Clemens, John Taylor, Mrs. Clark, Mrs. Rackstrow, Rev. Mr. Trotman, Robert Webb, James Bissett, Mr Rackstrow.

Cross Street.—Richard Doughty, James Leigh, James Miles, William West, Joseph Smith, George Walton, Thomas Smallwood, Stephen Peasnall, Thomas Dunkley, James Billingham, Charles Wood, William Betts, Thomas Taylor, Richard Ballard, James Parsons,

Charles Lawrance, Thomas Tew, Richard Rousam, John Barnwell, George Elliott, — Cole, John Saul, Richard Pratt, William King (house, land and stables), William Smith (house and garden land).

Bertie Greathead, Esq., for brickyard; Hicklen and Mackie, ditto.

The resolution to have a market was adopted early in the year, and was thus made public by a notice, dated April 24, in the *Warwick Advertiser:*—

"Leamington Market. The public are respectfully informed that a MARKET will be held at Leamington on Wednesday, the Fifth day of May next, and every Wednesday after during the Season, when every accommodation will be provided by the Inhabitants, who beg to solicit the Assistance of the Neighbourhood to supply necessaries for the convenience and comfort of the Visitants"

Reporting on May 8th, the inauguration, the *Advertiser* said:—

"On Wednesday last, pursuant to public advertisement, the first Market was opened for the accommodation of the numerous Visitors who resort to the Salubrious Springs of this rapidly rising village. It was held in the open Space nearly opposite Sinker's Hotel. Proper Stalls and other conveniences were provided for those who attended on the occasion, and we are happy to add that there was a good show of Meat, Vegetables, Eggs, Poultry, and other articles usually needed at such places of public sale. If this newly established Market should be continued and sufficiently encouraged, there is no doubt it will answer the good intention of those who first instituted it, and prove a great public benefit."

The second of these weekly markets was held on the izth, and notwithstanding the popular attraction of " the Great May Fair Day," al Warwick, there was a tolerable supplv of the usual necessaries, which sold at reasonable prices.

An extensive development took place this year in the Ranelagh Gardens, which at the time were known as "The Leamington Nursery and Pleasure Grounds." They are reported to have been laid out in 1811, and probably the first occupier was Mr. Mackie. They were ten acres in extent, and were liberally planted with choice trees, flowers and shrubs. There does not appear to have been in the early arrangements much artistic taste displayed, but they were conveniently situated at the time for visitors, for whom they were a pleasant resort. In 1813, Mr. Mackie was joined in a partnership by Mr. James Brown, who, first as a pupil to Mr. Baldwin, gardener to the Marquis of Hertford at Ragley, and afterwards as gardener to the Rev. H. C. Morewood, of Alfreton Hall, Derbyshire, had attained professional rank in the cultivation of flowers and landscape formation. Their successor was Mr. John Cullis, who came into possession in 1814, when he is said to have planted with his own hands the trees which now form the beautiful Linden Avenue, on the north side of the Pump Room Grounds; one of the most effective pictures in the centre of the town, but capable of improvement along the borders. Under the care of Mr. Cullis, the gardens reached the zenith of their prosperity, and for many years, during the season, they were much frequented by fashionable people, for whose pleasure a band had been engaged to discourse popular music. The original idea was that they should be a permanent attraction, and doubtless this would have been realised, had not circumstances arisen which frustrated the object in view. The gradual movement of the town northward, and the dedication, afterwards, to the public of the more convenient and superior Jephson Gardens, detracted from the value of the Ranelagh Pleasure Gardens as a place for recreation, and caused them to decline in general favour. Mr. Cullis continued in occupation until 1849, during which time he was active in bearing his share of the public work of the town, and at one time fi'led the office of Churchwarden. His death occurred in the year named, and the property was then offered for sale by private treaty, application to be made to Mr. William Russell, auctioneer and estate agent, Spencer Street, and in 1851, by auction,

at the Bath Hotel, "with two pews at the Parish Church." Mr. Thomas Mander occupied them in 1857, having at the same time the shop, No. 48, Bath Street. Mr. Parsons and Mr. John Hugh Hawley were also tenants, the last-named being Head-master of the Brunswick School, and a strenuous supporter of the Free Public Library, on the Committee of which he sat for many years. Mr. Crump followed, and in 1891 Mr. Greenfield, nurseryman and florist, 17, Bath Street, took the tenancy, of which he is the present possessor.

K CHAPTER XX.

UALIFIED by past and present successes for making further progress, the attention of the town was now directed to the subject of its recreations and amusements. This feeling found a tangible expression in the erection of a Theatre, for which preparations had been made by the provision previously of a temporary structure. It has been stated that the original Temple of the Drama in Leamington was a very primitive building somewhere at the rear of the Crown Hotel, and that the strolling players of the old times were in the habit of using it for their histrionic performances to houses composed for the most part of smock-frocks. Scarcely anything would be more calculated to enhance the interest of the history of the village than a reliable account of its Sock and Buskin life in the pretheatre days, all the more so as some very eminent names have been mentioned as probably included in the list. The temporary theatre to which we have made reference —and it is the only one respecting which we have been able to find any authentic information— was fitted up in August, 1813, and was possibly that to which Bisset refers as being situate at the back of Read's Baths, High Street.

The Theatre itself—the first of the three Leamington has had —was erected in Bath Street, immediately opposite the Bath Hotel. The site is now numbered 15, and is occupied by the shop and premises of Mr. John Collier, bookseller and stationer. It had a light ornamental verandah in front of the door, forming a shelter, in wet weather, for the oc-

cupants of carriages entering and leaving the building. When full, and with ordinary prices, it was capable of holding about £30, but on the occasion of the visit of Charles Kean, in 1825, the receipts were £')j. As will be seen, it was a neat and elegant structure, comparing with insignificant effect to the present noble Theatre, in Regent drove, but at the time of its erection, an architectural addition of striking prominence and importance. It was opened on Tuesday, October 26th, 1813, from which date the story of the stage in Leamington takes its rise, and with varying fortunes has been continued to the present time. The following address issued to the public by Mr. Simms, the proprietor, is of interest, as being the first theatrical advertisement ever published in Leamington.

J. SIMMS most respectfully informs the Nobility and Gentry of Leamington, its Vicinity, and the Public in general, that he has repeatedly promised the enquiring Public, that the New Theatre should be o1ened during the present season; and that it may be free from Damp (which is chiefly the result of Plastering, he has declined that part of the Finishing, as well as the ornamental Painting and other embellishments, 'till after the close of the present season. He trusts that he shall have some portion of Credit for his exertions, in preparing a more commodious Place of Amusement, in so short a Period; and he begs they will accept of the attempt in providing the rational and interesting Amusement of the Drama, as an earnest of his future Spirit and Liberality; assuring them that by the beginning of next Season, the Theatre will be completely finished, and in a Style of Decoration not inferior to any one out of the Metropolis; when he flatters himself he shall be honoured with that Support and Patronage a discerning Public are ever ready to confer on those who endeavour to merit their Favors.

An Occasional Address, by way of Prologue, on the Opening of the Theatre, (written by Mr. Bissett,) will be spoken by MISS SIMMS. On TUESDAY next, October 26, 1813,

Will be presented, Dr. Franklin's celebrated Historical Play of
THE EARL OF WARWICK.

King Edward IV Mr. Waylett, Jun.
  Earl of Suffolk Mr. Waylett.
  Earl of Pembroke Mr. SMOLLETT.
  Duke of Clarence Mr. Povey.
  Duke of Buckingham Mr. Spendal.
  Earl of Warwick Mr. WallIS.
  Margaret of Anjou Mrs. Godwin.
  Lady Clifford Miss Simms.
  Lady Elizabeth Grey Mrs. Swendal.
  End Of The Play,

"Lilla Of Leamington," (written by Mr. Bissett), will be sung by Mr. Povey.

A Grand Transparent Scene of Britannia In The Temple Of Fame! with the Song and Chorus.

A Song By Miss Godwin.

Comic Songs by Messrs. Swendal and Smollett, to which will be added the laughable Farce of FORTUNE'S FROLIC.

  Robin Roughead Mr. Simms.
  Snacks Mr. Swendal.
  Mr. Frank Mr. Waylett.
  Countrymen Messrs. Smollett And Povey.
  Rattle Mr. Waylett, Jun.
  Dolly Mrs. Swendal.
  Nancy Miss Godwin.
  Margery Mrs. Godwin.

Boxes, 3s.; Pitt, 2s.; Gallery, is.

Doors open at Six o'clock, and begin at Seven.

% Tickets or Places for the Boxes to be had at the Theatre, from Ten till One, on the Day ot

Playing; and at Mr. Rackstow's, Union Street, Leamington.

Days of Performing:—Tuesdays, Thursdays And Saturdays.

On Thursday, the 28th, the Comedy of
WILD OATS, or the Strolling Gentleman, With the HUNTER OF THE ALPS.

Were the space at our disposal equal to the supply of material, several pages might be filled with a most entertaining collection of facts, incidents and occurrences of this early home of the theatrical life of Leamington. But necessity, not inclination, compels us to be brief. Here, stars of the first magnitude shone with all that peculiar effulgence which belongs to the possessors of ge-

nius; which no external influence can supply where it is absent, nor obstacle suppress where it exists. The first of these was Robert William Elliston, an actor of brilliant powers, who was, at one time, lessee of the Theatre Royal, Drury Lane, London.

The Old Theatre, erected in 1813, on the site of the premises of Mr. John Collier, Bookseller and Stationer, No. 15, Bath Street, and opened on Tuesday, October 26, in the same year.

It has long been the fashion to represent his association with Leamington as beginning with the year 1816, and resulting from a casual acquaintance he made with the place when passing through, as a coach passenger, to fulfil some engagement. There is an excellent reason for believing that his introduction to the Spa took place at an earlier date, and that he made many friends and obtained popularity though the agency of the Theatre. In July, 1815, he was on the boards at the Bath Street house, and again in August of the same year. He also played three nights in the month of September following, on one of which he sustained the character of *Hamlet*; and in October he was again before a Leamington audience. He would, therefore, be tolerably well acquainted with the Spa long before the stage coach journey of 1816, in which year he was in frequent request at the Theatre, playing *Charles Surface* early in October, and towards the close of the month, acting for the benefit of Mr. Simms. Another eminent man, who appeared at the Theatre, was Joseph Shepperd Munden, one of the old magnets of comedy, a friend of Elliston's, who, when the Theatre came under his management at a subsequent date, engaged him to play twelve nights to the Leamingtonians. The manager had his wine, and the actor his brandy and water in the green room. Before leaving the town, Munden sent for his bill at the next tavern—fourteen glasses, as many shillings. On being asked to contribute 3s., El lis ton refused, as Munden had drunk his wine; "but," retorted Munden, screwing his features up to the very point of exaction, "sip-pings, remember sip-pings," allud-

ing to Elliston's occasional visits to his glass while he was playing his part.

James Bisset, who settled in Leamington in the young years of the century, was one of the most remarkable men of the period. By birth he was a Scotchman; by training and commercial education he belonged to Birmingham; by adoption and selection he was a Leamingtonian. Addison has mentioned a class of men who, infusing a spirit of mirth and good humour into a community, are worth £500 a year. Bisset was of that class. Cheltenham knew his value, and offered him *£100* to go there; as a stranger, he came here, and helped to build up the town. But it was the Leamington waters which won. lie was the proprietor of a Museum in New Street, Birmingham; figured largely among the City Fathers, and, in addition to a lively disposition, he was of an enterprising turn of mind, an author, and ingenious in the arts and sciences. In a manuscript autobiography, he thus explains the reasons which brought him to Leamington:—

"In the summer of 1811, I took Mrs. Bisset ami my eldest daughter, who were both unwell, to try the Baths at Leamington Priors—a small village, then scarcely known, ab:ut two miles from Warwick. I had never before heard of the Spa, but, finding the waters amazingly efficacious, I began to project some arrangements for the accommodation of visitors who might be induced to try the virtue of the Spa. The place was then an obscure hamlet, with only a few very poor and detached cottages, with about three public-houses. In the spring of 1812, I engaged a large rjom which had been built for an Assembly Room; and as a spirit of speculation began to manifest itself at the Spa and a range of very line houses were begun across the river Leam, in what they called "the New Town," I opened a Picture (iallery and Select News Room at the Spa, leaving Mrs. Bisset to conduct the Museum and my other concerns in Birmingham, and most happily succeeded in everything, far beyond my most sanguine expectations. There was not a house in Clemens Street beyond my Gallery, which was the only building on the east side of the street. Bath Street was a very nanow, dirty lane, and there were only four houses from the corner of Clemens Street all the way up the Warwick Road. There was a temporary Theatre at the back of Read's Baths, which, in general, was well attended. Mr. J. Simms, manager. I had lodged at Mr. Fisher's during the season, and, being pleased with Leamington, Mrs. Bisset and the children came over to see me, and they being likewise satisfied with the situation, I took the lease of a house in Union Street, New Town, and. having returned to Birmingham to settle my affairs, Mrs. Bisset and I bid adieu to the Toyshop of Europe and came to reside here in March, 1813. We opened the Gallery in Clemens Street as usual, and the Museum was kept by Mrs. B. at our house in Union Street. Both my establishments answered extremely well, and the longer I resided at the Spa I liked it the better. The place began to enlarge exceedingly, and the waters were held in high repute. A new suite of Baths and an elegant Pump Room were begun, and a superb Assembly Room was built. Several new hotels were opened, as also many new lodging and boarding houses; butchers' and bakers' shops were established; for a short time previous to this you could not obtain a beefsteak nor a hot roll in the village."

The special event of 1814 was the opening, in the month of July, of the Pump Room and Baths. They were commenced in 1813, but according to a report, were not finished in even' detail until 1819, when the Regent Hotel appeared to bear them company. The spring was discovered in 1810, at which time there seems to have been an idea floating in the mind of the village that a bathing institution, on a scale far surpassing anything yet attempted, was a necessity no longer to be deferred. The lapse of time between the date when the water was found, and when the work of the building commenced, is probably to be accounted for by the judicious application of tests respecting the quantity of the supply on which reliance could be placed At the other wells (Abbotts's,

Wise's, Read's, and Robbins's), the buildings appear to have followed almost immediately on the finding of the mineral waters. An entirely different course was taken with the spring on the north bank of the river, near the bridge. There was a delay of about three years. It was proposed, to quote the words of Moncrieff, "to erect on this spot, baths which should excel all that had been built in England, and rival, if possible, the Thermae of the Ancients." The contemplated outlay was large, and as the success of the new Institution would wholly depend on an abundance of water, the first step to be taken was to ascertain, by prolonged and repeated pumpings, the nature of the yield. Of all the sites which offered, the one chosen was the best adapted for the convenience of the future town, which already was shaping itself in broad and intelligible outline, in the formation of the Parade, Warwick and Regent Streets. Beyond a brief reference contained in the manuscript work of Bisset, in the possession of the author of this history, nothing is known of the nature of the ceremony at the foundation-stone laying of the building, and it is only by this means that we are able to supply an item of interest in connection with the rise of one of the most important public buildings and movements of the town. He says:— "When the foundation stone of the new Colonnade was laid at the Royal Pump Room, I gave two superb silver medallions of his Majesty to be put under the corner stone of the North Pillar. The Rev. Dr. Rees delivered an impressive and appropriate oration, and Mrs. Opie and a large assembly of the people stood on the rafters of the Pump Room and sang 'God Save the King' in full chorus. The Right Hon. Lord Sandon was one of the party." The event was one of the greatest importance in the history of Leamington, and whoever undertakes to analyse those influences which powerfully assisted the progress of the early Spa will inevitably arrive at false conclusions if he omit from his review the effect on the public mind of the erection of the Pump Room and Baths. At once Leamington was placed on a

level with the most fashionable health resorts of England, and on the part of the few who provided the funds, it was a policy of energy, forethought, and liberality. Their names, given by Hopper, will never be mentioned without respect by all who admire public spirit, nor without gratitude by the friends of Leamingron. They were 15. B. (Jreatheed, John Tomes, and H. W. Tancred, Esqs., and Mr. Parkes, of Warwick. The share of the last-named gentleman had, in 1842, fallen into the hands of Mr. Tomes, and the whole establishment, at that period, was in the possession of the three gentlemen firstnamed. The following description is from the *Warwick Advertiser,* July 2, 1814:—

"The *grand desideratum* is at length accomplished — anil LEMlNGTON, in addition to the many other attractions which it possesses, has now to boast of its Pump Room and Public Baths, which, for convenience, elegance of structure, and beauty of design, are perhaps unequalled in this or any other country. Much inconvenience has been experienced from the want of these Public Edifices, the Old Baths having of late seasons leen found completely inadequate to the accommodation of the increased numbers of fashionable company who annually resort thither. Every well-wisher to the prosperity of this charming retreat will, therefore, rejoice to hear that this defect no longer exists, and that the visitor will now find, in the room of censure, much to excite his admiration and applause. Leamington is indebted for this, as it is for many other of her public works, to the enterprising spirit of a few individuals who reside in the neighbourhood—their taste and liberality are too well known to need from us any comment—of which, if any proof were wanting, an honourable one presents itself in the building we are now describing. It is pleasantly seated on the north bank of the Leam, and but a small remove from the main road leading from the Old to the New Town. The building consists of two principal parts; the Pump Room forming the most prominent feature in the centre. It presents a noble contrast of native stone, extending upwards of 106ft. in length and 30ft. in height, and is surrounded on three sides by a spacious colonnade, supported by duplicated pillars of the Doric order. The roof is in the cottage stile, and is remarkable for its taste and simple elegance. Entrance is had into this splendid apartment by two doors, placed at either end; that on the left leads immediately to the pump, which, with an ornamental pedestal and bason of Derbyshire marble standing in the centre, is enclosed with a neat mahogany balustrade. The room is lofty and of noble proportions; it is lighted on one side by seven windows, the intervals being filled with Doric pilasters; the opposite side is adorned with a handsome painted window, and underneath, at equal distances, are two elegant chimney-pieces of Kilkenny marble. The ornamental part of the ceiling, cornices, and other embellishments of the interior, strictly correspond with the stile of the building without. At the extremity of the colonnading that runs to the right and left of the Pump Room are two wings, extending upwards of 30ft. in length and 20ft. in height, which form the two principal entrances into the Public Baths. They are built in the Grecian stile of architecture, and strictly accord with that part of the structure which is more conspicuously to view. There are 17 hot and 3 cold Baths, which are well constructed and neatly fitted up—everything that is essential, or that can in any way contribute to the pleasure of the luxurious, or the comfort and convenience of the invalid, is provided with a liberal hand,— nor are the blessings which here present themselves solely confined to the rich, for we learn, and it is with no ordinary feelings of satisfaction that we mention it, that the proprietors have very benevolently directed three out of that number to be appropriated to charitable purposes. This elegant building was designed and executed under the direction of Mr. C. S. Smith, architect, of London, and the cost of it is estimated at little less than _£30,ooo."

The great expense incurred in building and furnishing, did not cause an increase in the terms for bathing and drinking the waters over those at the other wells. The provision was extensive, and included every mode of bathing in vogue, namely, hot, tepid, vapour, cold, plunging, shower; hot and cold douche baths.

A storm of unusual severity, attended with considerable damage to property, visited the town on Thursday, July z8. The description of it says that " a fire ball, accompanied with a tremendous peal of thunder and lightning, but providentially succeeded by a violent torrent of rain, fell into the picture gallery belonging to Mr. Bissett, and in its progress forced the rafters from the roof into the centre of the room, leaving an aperture in the ceiling of upwards of 100 feet square. The doors ol the room were knocked down with considerable violence; several panes of glass were broken, and the interior arrangements were thrown into the utmost confusion. A few paintings were rent and peeled from the canvas, but the more valuable part has fortunately escaped injury."

On August 10, the first Summer Hall of the Master of the Ceremonies (Mr. J. Heavisides) took place at the Assembly Rooms, and proved a great social success. It was attended by six hundred persons, and dancing was kept up till four o'clock in the morning.

The celebration of the restoration of peace in 1814, when Buonaparte was subdued by the allied armies, took place in Leamington in August. A subscription list was started by the principal inhabitants, and, in lieu of giving the poor a dinner, the sum was distributed in sums ranging from 5s. to 15s. per cottage, and zs. 6d. to each labourer in agriculture. Desirous of sharing their joy with each other, the poor extemporised a fete of their own, had a tea-drinking at the Bowling Green Hotel, "where happiness, hilarity, and concord seemed to be the order of the day. Some of the gentry in the village distributed cakes to the attendant children with a liberal hand, and a fiddle played country dances to the younger females who tripped it gaily on the enamelled green.

" When the company were in the height of their merriment, Mr. Simnis appeared and invited them into the theatre—a kindness of which they readily availed themselves.

The " burthen" of taxation weighed heavily on the shoulders of the inhabitants in 1815, and on the 30th of January a public meeting was held at Mrs. Smith's, the Bath Hotel, to consider the best means of obtaining relief. No report exists of the result, and the event is chiefly remarkable as showing that at this date the name of the New Inn had given way to that of the Bath Hotel, and also that taxes were as unpopular in 1815 as in 1897.

In March was established the third of the modern hotels for which Leamington has ever been famous—the Crown, High Street. On the 3ist of that month, Mr. Joseph Stanley, grandfather of Mr. Sam Stanley, hon. sec. to the Warwickshire Naturalists' and Archaeological Field Club, Mr. Herbert Stanley, who was for many years a member of the Board of Guardians, and Mr. Joseph Stanley, of Sydenham Farm, advertised that he had taken and entered on the premises, adjoining Mr. Read's Baths (late in the occupation of Mr. Probett), "which is now converted into and called the Crown Inn." The "house warming," the universal custom of the time when new publichouses or hotels were opened, and frequently when they changed hands, took place on April 26.

It has often been the fortune, or misfortune, of great movements to encounter, at some time or other, dissensions and divisions within the ranks of their supporters. The Leamington Charitable Institution, founded by Satchwell in 1806, was no exception to the rule, though it was the last and most unlikely of all soils in which the weeds of discontent might have been expected to flourish. A rival "Leamington Charitable Institution" was started in April, supported by Drs. Lambe, Johnstone, Pegge, Kerr, Pennington, Chauner, and Middleton; Surgeons Birch and Franklin; the Rev. Edward Trotman, Curate at the Parish Church, being its Chaplain. An appeal to the public for support was issued, but it contained no allegation against the older institution, nor any statement of the cause of the difference. A counter-appeal, signed by Sir G. Skipwith, Bart., and ten others, was published in May, apprising the public that "the original institution still exists," and that Mr. George Birch having relinquished his "situation" as Surgeon to the Institution, Mr. John Wilmshurst was appointed to succeed him. Mr. Wilmshurst was a retired Army Surgeon, residing at Warwick. lie was medical attendant to the then'Earl of Warwick and his family; he also held the appointment of Surgeon to the Warwick Militia, was Mayor of the Borough twice, and was presented by the inhabitants with a handsome and costly service of plate, in recognition of his public work, and in token of the esteem in which he was universally held. His grandson, Mr. J. J. Willington Wilmshurst, is Clerk to the Kenilworth Sanitary Authority, and in May, 1897, was elected Coroner for Central Warwickshire.

The instinctive philanthropic tendencies of Leamington, first elicited by Satchwell and Walhouse, assumed a gratifying character in connection with the very earliest management of the Pump Room. On June 2, the proprietors stated that they had appropriated a distinct wing of the building, with hot and cold baths, "for the benefit of poor persons not able to pay for, but requiring the use of the waters," and every Monday and Thursday morning a room was set apart for the accommodation of those medical gentlemen who might wish to give advice and assistance to the poor gratis. The offer was immediately accepted by Amos Middleton, M.D. , Messrs. George Birch and F. Franklin, surgeons, who promised to attend on the days named, when they would be pleased to meet " our medical brethren " from the neighbourhood of Warwick.

This year, Charles Matthews, the popular comedian, appeared on the boards at the Bath Street Theatre. We have been unsuccessful in our researches, both as to the play and the character he represented, but the following description he gave of his visit, in a letter to a friend, will be accepted as an excellent substitute for what we have lost by the absence of a newspaper report.:—

"The arrangements were horrid; and no musician.could I get far or near till seven o'clock, when one wretched country dance fiddler arrived from a distance of five miles. I soon found that he could not play a note, and began my performance with an apology, stating that I had written forward to request that all the musicians in the town might be engaged, and that request had been complied with. 'Ladies and Gentlemen, said I, 'strictly *all* that are to be found arc now in the orchestra: lie is all. I hope, however, that the defects of the singing may be compensated for by the ability of the musician, and *vice versa*; and if the kindness of the audience will but keep pace with my anxiety to please, my friend and I cannot fail of success.' This produced a great laugh, and when we came to the first song, he in vain attempted to scratch a note or two, and he was literally not heard the whole evening, except between the two acts, when, to rescue his fame, he boldly struck up a country dance, which he rasped away to the no small amusement of the audience. I had all the visitors, I believe, in the place, and to my amazement they produced me *£2-.*"

While these mutations had been taking place in the Old and New Town, the Parish Church had remained almost stationary. The improvements of 1800 affected the character and not the extent of the accommodation. Leaving out of question the addition of the north gallery and the three pews added in 1781, the Church was as it had been for centuries. But all around it was changed, or was changing, and at length the conclusion had forced itself on the inhabitants that a substantial enlargement was urgently needed. Probably no congregation which has been gathered together in Church or Chapel in England ever presented such a strange compound of types and varieties of life. Lords and ladies, from whose minds the proud feeling of Norman descent was never absent, gratefully shared seats and books with the humblest farm labourers. The idea of making the Church larger had been under discussion for several years, but it was not till December, 1815, that the matter was taken in hand in earnest. The difficulty was one of ways and means. On the 20th of that month a vestry meeting was held, "to consider of the propriety of enlarging the Church and erecting new seats, according to a plan and estimates already made, and of entering into contracts for the completion of the work, and of applying for a faculty to enable the Minister and Churchwardens to do so, and to confirm the seats to the several persons whose names are inserted in such plan as purchasers (pursuant to the notice for that purpose given in the Parish Church two Sundays previous to such meeting)." As the result, an agreement was entered into between the Rev. John Wise, clerk; John Campion, of Newbold Comyn; and Thomas Abbotts, of Leamington Priors, churchwardens, on the one part; and Matthew Wise, the younger, of the Northgate, in the Borough of Warwick; the

The Upper Assembly Room, opened September 24, 1S12, stood on the site of Mr. E. T. Gamage's Drapery and Millinery Establishment, "The Louvre," 94 and 96, The Parade, and extended back along Regent Street to the Imperial Vaults, Bedford Street and Regent Street. The property was sold in 1878, and converted into the present range of shops.

Rev. John Willes, of Newbold Comyn; Isaac Wilkinson, of Leamington Priors, Esq.; and William Freeman, of Heathcote, in the County of Gloucester, for the sale of the following pews, at the prices quoted, the money so obtained to be applied in carrying out the new works."

The schedule of the pews and prices referred to specified the following:—In the body of the Church: Matthew Wise, numbers 22, 23, 24, 25, and 26, price £350; Thomas Potterton, 34 and 35, £85; William Alder, 38, *£bo*; Richard Cattell, 39 and 40, *£120;* William Treadgold, 27, £40; Thomas Walker, 33, £35; William Perkins, 29, *£5;* William Shaw, 30, £40; John Russell, 31, £35; Elizabeth Smith, 38, £50; Richard Smallbones, 37, £55; Stephen Peasenall, 32, *£30.*

In the gallery: Edward Willes, 3, *£60*; Mary Elizabeth Edwards, 5, *£to*; John Garrard, 27, £50; Richard Brown, *i,£$o* Edward Treadgold, 8, 9, and 10, £145. "John Campion and Thomas Abbotts, churchwardens, agreed tc pay out of the parish rates £100 for number 11 in the gallery for the singers."

John Wilkinson purchased numbers 4 in the galler', and 36 in the body of the Church, for the total sum of £150. Purchasers of pews were to pay the amounts due by two equal instalments, into the bank of.Messrs. Whitehead, Weston and Greenway, Warwick, the first by MSrch 1, and the second by September 29, 1816.

Many versions having appeared of the nature of the enlargement of the Church at this period, we cannot do better than supply the particulars from the specificaticns of the several contracts. These were "to take down the south front wall and extend the the Church into the churchyard 27 feet, 4 inches, exclusive of the turret or porch to form an entrance into the body of the Church, hereby enlarging the Church 39 feet from east to west, by 27 feet 4 inches from north to south" The prices paid were: John Morris, Warwick, stone mason, £731 7s.; Edward Treadgold, carpentry work, £590; and William Badams, Warwick, plumbing and glazing, *£112.*

An examination of the old records, for the time and circumstances of the foundation stone laying, and the re-opening services, is almost negative of result. Bisset, in his manuscript memoranda, says that he had the honour of laying the foundation stone himself, and that the ceremony took place on April 18, 1816, on which occasion he presented the builder with a silver medallion of his Majesty, which was placed with all due solemnity beneath the stone. The new wing afforded double the accommodation of seats for the congregation. It is worthy of remark that the illegal practice of selling pews commenced at

this date, with the sanction of a faculty, granted by the Consistorial Court of Lichfield. By a few happy literary and artistic touches, Eginton, Field, and Bisset, have given the old Church, the demolition of which had now commenced, a permanence more enduring than stone. "It had all the humble exterior of a country church, with plastered walls and low tiled roof. It is, however (1815), neatly fitted up. One of the windows is venerable for its antiquity, and affords no mean specimen of the fine pointed style which prevailed in the fourteenth and the following century. At the west end is a good old square tower, furnished with four bells. Against this was *once* a clock." Bisset, who always preferred to express himself in rhyme, thus described its dimensions:—

"The Church then was small, from North to South wall, Perhaps about Thirty feet wide;
Its length 'twas not great, yet the use of a Seat,
The Verger was sure to provide."
CHAPTER XXI.

OLLOWING, or accompanying, this first response of the Church to the needs of the growing population, was another religious movement, in no sense less remarkable, and historically as important, as the enlargement of the fabric just described. While the Vicar and Churchwardens were actively carrying on their work, Nonconformity was preparing to vacate for ever its cottage accommodation, and to build for itself the first Leamington chapel.

After the death of the Rev. James Moody, of Brook Street Chapel, Warwick, in 1806, the founder of the Congregational movement in Leamington, his widow left the borough and came to reside at No. 6, Clemens Street. His successor in the pastorate was the Rev. William Williams, but he remained at Warwick only from 1807 to 1809, when he removed to Edmonton. We mention this circumstance for the strong probabilities which exist in support of his having been the second Congregational Minister who preached to the young cause in Leamington. Nothing is more unlikely than that the old Church at

Brook Street should have neglected, for the space of two years, the fledgling which had been nestling under its wing during the Rev. Mr. Moody's ministry. But there is no doubt as to who was the third. The Rev. Joseph Wilcox Percy was ordained at Brook Street in 1810, and there is ample evidence to show that shortly afterwards he was in regular attendance at meetings held at the Blenheim Hotel, preaching to the score or two of villagers and visitors, who, at that time, formed the nucleus out of which have arisen three Independent Churches, two of which are still in existence. The original cause was poor, at one time, in fact, so poor that there was not a single member of the congregation who could afford to offer the Minister from Warwick the hospitality of a cup of tea. In consequence of the room at the Blenheim being required for another purpose, the services were threatened with an interruption, the inconvenience of which was avoided by Mrs. Moody promptly placing her house at the disposal of the friends of the rising cause. This event must have taken place about 1814, for it was in that year her name first appears on the rate book as the occupier of a house in Clemens Street. The offer was gratefully accepted, and until the building of the new chapel in 181 b, the meetings were held in her house, the Rev. Mr. Percy preaching occasionally on Sundays, and regularly on Thursday evenings. It was doubtless out of this circumstance, and the increased numbers attending the services, that the desire arose for a permanent provision »for the future. There were several unoccupied plots of land in the street, and immediately over the way, one which seemed to be waiting for the new chapel. To build thereon was an inspired wish that the

Church and congregation at Warwick fanned into a flame with words of encouragement and promises of assistance. With the approbation of the local public, Mr. Percy and his friends commenced a subscription, and from London, Bristol, and other towns, such aid was received as placed them in a position to purchase the land and build the first chapel in Leamington. It was opened on Wednesday, July i o, 1816, and the advertisement notice is curious, as announcing two sermons, and mentioning the Rev. I. J. James, of Birmingham, as engaged to preach only " one part of the day." Who was the second minister was not stated, but Sibree says it was Mr Hartley, of Lutterworth. The name of the first preacher, John Angell James, it will be observed, is not correctly given. He was the great divine of Carr's Lane Chapel, Birmingham, and twenty years afterwards preached the first sermon at Spencer Street, where, singularly enough, his successor at Carr's Lane, Dr. Dale, afterwards became a member, and an itinerant preacher in the villages of Mid-Warwickshire. The principles of the Church, as between Conformity and Nonconformity, were of the accommodating kind, the Liturgy of the Establishment being incorporated with the service, and independent self-government, free from all external control, strictly reserved for the congregation. At first it was described as "the New Chapel," and afterwards as "the Leamington Chapel," but the official designation which interpreted its comprehensive character was "the Union Chapel." The result of this attempt to unite things which were essentially different was not encouraging to its promoters. The Rev. Arthur Bromiley, of Hoxton College, "a young man of considerable powers of mind, and generally acceptable as a preacher," was chosen pastor in 1817. His secession from the cause, acceptance of holy orders, and admission into the Church of England took place in the early part of the year 1824. The Rev. William Seaton, of Wandsworth, in the same year, succeeded Mr. Bromiley in the pastorate, and, in 1827, also followed him into the National Church. The third minister was the Rev. Charles Bassano, who was ordained in 1827, in 1828 withdrew, and, like his two predecessors in office, went over to the Establishment. At this time the use of the Liturgy was objected to by a number of the congregation, and on its discontinuance there was a larger secession,

which led to the building of Mill Street Chapel. Commenting upon the strangely chequered history of the New Chapel at this period, Mr. Sibree speaks disparagingly of its policy of expediency, and refers to the failure experienced as the inevitable consequence of such a compromise. But he omits any allusion to the more general aspects of the case, and treats within local limitations a subject which at the time was attracting much notice in Church and Dissenting circles. The Rev. Rowland Hill, the witty, wise, and eloquent minister at Surrey Chapel, London, preached his first sermon at Leamington in the Union Chapel, Clemens Street, in August, 1817, at which time he was in the habit of visiting the Spa for the benefit of his health. The adoption of the Liturgy at Clemens Street Chapel was most probably by his advice; otherwise it was the consequence of his example. His position in the religious world was epigrammatically described as "A Churchman amongst There was a fourth secession. The Rev. Mr. Powell, who followed the Rev. W. H. Sisterson, at Mill Street, also ioined the Church of England.

Dissenters, and a Dissenter amongst Churchmen." His own account of himself was that he was travelling through life with only one boot on, referring to his having been ordained a Deacon without succeeding in becoming a Priest or Presbyter. On the completion of Surrey Chapel, in 1783, he adopted the Liturgical service of the Church of England, but maintained the Dissenting principle of independence for each Church. The fashion, thus set by a popular preacher, spread, though not without provoking the hostility of both the parties it was designed to conciliate. The archers of the Establish

An Early Visitor, and the Founder of Mill Street Chapel.

ment drew their bows and discharged arrows such as this at the innovation: "If Dissenting ministers can conform to the Book of Common Prayer, we should like to An old resident has communicated to us the following, received by him from the late Dr. Hitchman: Mr. Hill was afflicted with eczema, for which

he found the Leamington waters highly beneficial. He was a patient of the doctor's, and, when in Leamington, resided at his house. The morning Mr. Hitchman set out for his marriage, Mr. Hill, who was unable to leave his bed, shook hands with him, wished him all happiness, and, as he was passing through the door, pelted him with some old slippers which he had secreted beneath the clothes for that purpose. The marriage proved to be as happy as the most artistic thrower of matrimonial old slippers could ever wish to sec. know what else there is in the Church of England to which, with equal ease and consistency, they might not conform?" And they pointed triumphantly to the secessions of the first three ministers of Clemens Street Chapel as supplying an answer. The experiment failed, and was not a permanent success at Mill Street, where, in 1829,, it was transplanted and renewed under circumstances more favourable to its stability.

The seventh spring, discovered in 1816, in Clemens Street, on the site of the premises, numbers 6, 7, and 8, in the occupation of Sleaths, Ltd., as boot, cycle, etc., stores, was announced in August, 1817, as open, under the title of the "Imperial Sulphuric, Medicinal, etc. , new Marble Baths."

At this time Wesleyan Methodism had not raised its voice in Leamington, nor were there any signs of its being heard in the immediate future. One church and one chapel were considered sufficient to meet every want of the parishioners, and if latitude in matters of faith and an accommodating disposition be the criteria, the popular judgment was no doubt correct. But the population was in a changeful, fusing condition, and every coach brought in fresh elements which modified, strengthened, or gave new variety to the cloudland of local thought. Some of the visitors, when pleasure had been gratified and health improved, filtered away to their homes and their friends, while others were permanently deposited in the village to share and influence its fortunes. There were, no doubt, a few Wesleyan Methodists in the village from the beginning of the century, but they appear to have met in a class at Warwick, conducted by " goode Mistress Prichard," in "a roume over a carpenter's shop in ye strete yclept Gerarde strete, ye haunte of thys peculyar peple." There is a notable similarity in the circumstances under which Methodism was inaugurated in Warwick and Leamington. "Aboute ye yere 1801, a man didde come for toe d welle in ye ancyente toun of Warwyke. In ye farre off countrie, yclept Yorkshire, from whyche he cam, he hadde holpen ye cause of God as a Lay Preacher. It therfor cam intoe hys herte toe begyn toe teache hys neighbores and frendes after thys waye. Wheras, noe other place coulde bee got, he didde preache in hys owne hous, or in ye open aire, as ye wynde and weather didde allowe." In 1810, the room over the carpenter's shop in Gerard Street was hired as a meeting house, and thither the "oon or tuo" Methodists at Leamington, according to tradition, "didde habituallie resorte" until 1817, when they established a place of worship for themselves in a loft in Satchwell Street. The following paper describes the inception and growth of the movement, and, although it travels far beyond the period we are now considering, its antique costume, quaint humour, and chronological value will prevent the thought arising that the space it occupies is needlessly wasted :—

"Ytappeareth from ye moste ancyente recordes thatle aboute ye yere of oure Lorde 1817, oon Maistre Scott, bye professione a Haire Dresser, cam, wyth hys goode Wyf, from ye grete Citic of London, toe dwelle in Leamingtoun. Thys Maistre Scott and hys goode Wyf, havynge bene taute ye truthes of oure This amusing and most interesting account of the origin of Wesleyan Methodism in Leamington is copied from an extremely humorous programme specially prepared for the Bazaar in the Portland Street Rooms, May 20 and 21, 1884.
holie fayth after ye maniere of ye Methodistes, didde suffer moche payne to fynde thatte ther was noe peple yclept bye thys name in ye town, nor anye pro-

visione for ye worshyppe of ye neighboures and frendes after thys waye.

"Howe bee it, ye Goode Lorde didde putte it intoc theyre hertes toe attempte toe gette ye peple togethere. Ye onlie place whyche could bee founde, was a Lofte sytuated in a certayne yarde yclept Barnacle's Yarde, in ye famous Strete yclept Satchwell Streete. This Lofte was onlie kepte for a lytel space, and ye nexte place was a roume in yc Strete yclept Brunswycke, hard bye ye spot where ye water waye dothe crosse; for thys roume, ye hondfulle of peple payede ye large summe of 30 Poundes bye ye yere. Ye Church atte thys tyme consysted of q pcrsonnes, and to yese ye goode Maistre Milliner, of sainted memorie, thanne dwellynge atte ye famous Citie of Coventry, didde comme toe preache on ye daye of ye Lorde.

"In ye yere of Grace 1824, ye Lorde's werke havynge prosperede, it was felt bye manie personnes thatte a Chapelle schulde bee buylded, and after moche thoughte and discourse, a pyece of lande was boughte for ye summe of 103 Poundes in Quarry Field, now knowen bye ye newe-fangled name of Portland Strete. Here ye fyrste Chapelle was buylded for ye total summe of 800 Poundes, and in ye Magazine for yc yere 1825, is dyscrybcd as a "commodyouse and elegante buyldynge." Thys Chapelle was opened bye ye Reverende Maistre Joseph Entwistle, ye yonger. But ye Trustees didde soone fynde yemselves in ye bad case bye reasone of ye heavie dcbte whych was upon ye Chappellc. It is even recorded toe ye lastynge dysgrace of ye cause, yat somme of ye sayde Trustees were imprysoned, and others didde leave ye town to save ye Constable from ye same trouble on theyre accounte. Ye hystorian dothe not vouche for ye truthe of ye foregoynge, but thynkes it maye bee a legende invented bye somme evyl dysposed personne.

"Howe bee it, it is sayde thatte after ye noble effortes of ye feeble folke, ye usury monie on ye debte was payde, and thatte oon Reverende Maister R. Melson, of saynted memorie, didde borrowe ye monie from somme goode man of

wealthe, and ye ryproche was wyped awaye.

"In 1832, bye ye grace of ye Conference, oon Reverende Maister John G. Wilson was sente toe Leamyngtoun toe preache ye holie faythc toe ye peple Ye Churche bye thys tyme numbered about sixty members, oon Maister Milliner and oon Maister Barton were Leaders, and tuo Classes ye good Mynystere didde mete hymself. In yere 1833 yese tuo Classes whyche ye mynystere didde mete were dyvyded, and ye Leaderes putte toe yese were Mistress Whitehead, Mistress Mellor, Maister Manning, and Maister Mellor, and bye 1834 ye memberes were 120, and a younge man yclept R. Coulson was made a Leader.

"In 1834, ye moche respected Reverende Maister Wilson lefte, butte before he departed he didde cause ye frendes to assemble in ye hous of oon Maister Toone sytuated in ye Upper Parade, and ther it was ryght hertylic agreede thatte greater provysione muste bee mayde for ye publycke worshyppe, and all didde unite in sayinge thatte it wolde bee seemlie and wyse to seeke for ye monie requyred for these purposes toe ye amount of *bco* Poundes. After thys cherefullc lyberalitie of ye goode peple ye Chapelle was made toe holde more peple by biyngynge out ye fronte. Besides ye monies spente, ye gencrouse herted folkes didde gyve of theyre werke toe ye value of 200 Poundes, and ye Chapelle was reopened bye ye Verie Reverende Doctor Newton, and ye Verie Reverende Doctor Bunting.

"In 1835 ye Chapelle was agayn made bigger atte ye backe, atte ye totalle outlaye of 811 Poundes.

"In 1837 ye state of ye Churche didde warrante ye heedes of admynystracioun in makynge Leamingtoun ye heede of a newe Circuyte, with oon Reverende Maistre T. P. Clarke as ye chefe mynystere, and ye seconde mynystere didde resyde atte ye worlde-faymed Stratford-on-Avon.

"From thys daye ye hystory is too well knowen for ye goode peple toe waste ye tyme in readynge, or ye Edytor in writynge ye same. How soe ever, for ye enlyghtenmente of ye ignorante, bee it knowen thatte in 1870 ye grete and moche renounde Chapelle sytuated in ye Strete yclept Dale Strete, was caused toe be buylded, atte ye coste of 7465 Poundes, and thatte in 1876 ye good Mistress Holy, of saynted memorie, didde atte her owne coste cause toe be buylded ye Trinity Chapelle in ye olde town.

"It nowe onlie reraayneth for all ye chyldrenne of God to praye and werke wythe alle theyre myghte, thatte ye gloryous cause maye prosper. So mote it bee."

In 1818, Mr. James Heaviside, the popular first Master of the Ceremonies, resigned, in consequence of having been elected M.C. at Bath. Captain Charles Stevenson succeeded him in the office.

The postal service was materially improved by a new Royal Mail Coach, which commenced running on the 25th of July, from the Swan with two Necks, Lad Lane, London, to Leamington and Warwick. It was "established for the express purpose of giving the long-wished-for accommodation to the increasing and flourishing" Spa and County town. The result of this new arrangement was that letters were delivered in Leamington between nine and ten o'clock in the morning, instead of between twelve and one, and replies could be posted up till four o'clock, in lieu of two, as was previously the case. To the exertions of Mr. Charles Mills, M.P., for Warwick, the public owed the advantages of the new system. This was the first advancement on the service established in the village by Ben Satchwell, and the beginning of those successive enlargements and changes which have resulted in the present Post Office with its most efficient management and extensive postal and telegraphic business.

In the year 1819 we have the completion of the last of the principal hotels which belong to the first quarter of the century; the first visit of Royalty; the establishment of the first School of Music. The consequence of all public improvements is to create a demand for further advances, and it was in this way

that the Baths of Abbotts, Wise, Robins, and Read paved the way for the Pump Rooms; and the Bath, the Bedford, and the Crown for the Regent Hotel. The foundation-stone of the Regent was laid on Saturday, July 18, 1818, and it was opened on Thursday, August 19, 1819. The earlier demonstration has been omitted from the "Guides," but it is an interesting page in the history of the borough, and helps to complete the story of this celebrated hotel. At the time of the ceremony Mr. Williams was proprietor of the Bedford Hotel, and he is reputed to have had the new hotel built for the larger accommodation of his guests. The proceedings commenced with the procession of "a select and highly respectable party" from the Bedford Hotel, among whom were Lady Rossmore, Mr., Mrs., and Miss Greatheed, Mr. Wynne Belasyse, Mrs. Wade, and Mrs. Siddons and her daughter, to the site, when the stone with a silver medal were laid by Miss Greatheed, amidst the acclamations of a numerous and fashionable assembly, the band at the same time playing the national air. "From the well-known liberality of the projector," remarks the *Warwick Advertiser,* "and the ability of the architect employed, we may anticipate a fabric which will add greatly to the ornament and advantage of this rapidly increasing place of fashionable resort. The cost is estimated at from £10,000 to £15,000."

The inauguration of the Hotel, on August 19, 1819, was a grand and imposing affair. Nearly two hundred gentlemen dined—as Leamington knew how to dine in those days—for the good of themselves and the hotel. Lords Glenberrie, Hood, and Dunsmore; the Lord Chief Justice Abbott, Sir Thomas Shepherd, and Sir John Sylvester (the Recorder of London) were among the guests. Mr. Greatheed was in the chair; turtle, venison, and wines were on the table; John Tomes, "a most zealous friend of the establishment," was at home, fashionably afflicted with gout. There were many toasts, including one to the Rev. Mr. Willes for the gift of a piece of land in the vicinity of the hotel, and a mighty bumper to Nelson

and Trafalgar, Wellington and Waterloo. The party separated at a late hour convivially.

The Bath Hotel, still remaining in the Abbotts family, was advertised for sale in February, as "A most eligible and much-frequented Inn, with pleasure ground, two good dwelling-houses, an apothecary's shop, stabling, yards, cottages, and other out-offices thereto belonging." But it does not appear to have been sold, for in May, Mrs. Potterton (late Mrs. Smith) returned thanks to the public for the very liberal and distinguished support she had for so many years experienced, and informed them that the business at the Bath Hotel would in future be carried on by her family. Hopper, in his "Guide" of 1842, makes mention of Mrs. Potterton as having assisted him with information respecting the early history of the village, and reports with deep regret her decease during the time his work was in progress. She was the fourth owner of the Bath Hotel, which, at the time of the second marriage, passed into the possession of other members of her family.

From the annual report of the new Charitable Institution, issued in April, we obtain an insight into the character and extent of the work it was carrying on, and the vast amount of benefit it was conferring on the poor. It is the earliest statement of accounts by the younger of the rival organisations, and was published to gain additional support. There were seventy-six subscribers; the total receipts £77 10s. 6d., which, with the balance of £4.3 6s. 4d. from the previous year, made a total of £110 16s. lod. The sum of £24. 10s. had been paid Mrs. Smith, of the Bath Hotel, for four hundred and ninety baths, and on the list of beneficiaries were thirty-eight patients, who had received allowances for periods of three four, five, and six weeks each.

It was in August that the Regent was opened, and called "Williams's Hotel" from the name of the proprietor. In September the Prince Regent (afterwards George IV.) was at Warwick Castle, on a visit to the Earl and Countess of Warwick. On Friday, the 10th, accompanied by the Countess of Warwick and the Marchioness of Conyngham, he drove through the principal streets of Leamington in an open carriage and took a view of the different public buildings. "He was received," says Moncrieff, "opposite Copps's Royal Hotel, by the whole population and visitants of the two towns (the old and the new), who hailed his presence with loud cheers, which he most gracefully acknowledged by repeated bows; the band playing 'God save the King,' the colours flying, and everyone on the tiptoe of hilarity. After visiting the Libraries, Pump and Assembly Rooms, and expressing the highest gratification, intimating at the same time his gracious intention of making a stay here at some future period, the Royal Visitor returned to dine at Warwick Castle, leaving his permission for Williams's New Hotel to be named after him 'The Regent.' In the evening the towns were brilliantly illuminated. Cullis gave a grand fete at the Ranelagh Gardens. The patriotic Mr. Bissett's Pegasus was put in requisition, and an additional verse to the National Anthem produced on the occasion The Messrs. Elliston, jun., who had in their childhood been much noticed by the Royal Family, from the high favour and popularity of their father, were also permitted to present a richly-bound copy of the first edition of this little work, which was also most graciously received."

Determined not to miss the opportunity of showing their loyalty, a public meeting was convened to be held at the Royal Pump Rooms on the following day, over which Mr. George Brooks presided. The following address was adopted:—

To His Royal Highness, George, Prince of Wales, Regent of the United Kingdom of Great Britain and Ireland.

The humble, loyal, and dutiful address of the inhabitants of, and visitors at, Leamington Spa, in the county of Warwick. May it please your Royal Highness:

We, his Majesty's most dutiful and loyal subjects, the inhabitants of and visitors at Leamington Spa, in the county of Warwick, highly flattered by your Royal Highness's arrival in this county and in our immediate vicinity, and impressed with the most lively affection and gratitude by your Royal Highness's condescension in honouring this rising watering-place with your Royal presence, humbly offer this our loyal and dutiful address, expressive of our sincere and heartfelt acknowledgments of your Royal Highness for this distinguished mark of Royal favour. At the same time, we gladly embrace this opportunity of assuring your Royal Highness of our unfeigned, devoted, and inviolable attachment and loyalty to your Royal Highness's illustrious person and family.—Signed, on behalf of the inhabitants, George Brooks, Chairman; on behalf of the visitors, Charles Stevenson, M.C.

On Monday, the 13th, Captain Stevenson took the address to Warwick Castle, and gave it to Sir Benjamin Bloomfield for presentation, and the same evening the announcement was made that the Prince had given permission for the new hotel to be called the " Regent" in commemoration of his visit, and for his Arms to be placed on the front. There was a general illumination in honour of the event. The reply to the address was received on Tuesday, the 14th. It stated that it had been most graciously received by his Royal Highness with good wishes for the prosperity of the rising watering-place of Leamington. The Prince terminated his visit to Warwick Castle on Wednesday, September 15, and on his return journey to London rode along High Street, past Copps's Hotel, where a large crowd of the inhabitants assembled, and cheered him heartily. Thus began and closed the first of the Royal visits to Leamington Spa.

Previous to the visit of the Prince Regent, the attention of the inhabitants had been thoughtfully directed to thu desirability of obtaining a form of local government f superior to that administered by the Vestry. There were several rates in force—one for the Church, a second for the poor, a third for the highways, and a fourth described as a "Composition on the Turnpike and Bye-roads."

The total amount they were estimated to produce was small, and this was further reduced by an irregular and feeble system of collection of the rate, named the composition. The wealthy people were allowed to pay at intervals of several years; the poor were excused on the ground of their poverty. Between these two classes there was a third who paid something on SOUTH-EAST VIEW OK THE PARISH CHURCH, SHOWING THE SOUTH TRANSEPT AND PORCH WHICH FORMED THE FIRST ENLARGEMENT IN 1816.

account. The public work consisted in the employment of a few labourers, who were remunerated at the rate of is. 6d. a day, to potter about the roads spreading gravel purchased from Mr. Wise and Mrs. Shaw, and, here and there, putting down some bricks bought from Mr. Mackie. The original effort to obtain enlarged powers of local government took place on October 26, 1818, when a public meeting was held at Copps's Hotel to consider the question of applying to Parliament for an Act for paving, lighting, watching, cleansing, and improving the town. A year afterwards (November 2, 1819) the subject was further discussed at a " Parish Meeting " held at the Assembly Rooms. The next step was a meeting on September 27, 1820, in Bisset's Room, Clemens Street, at which Mr. Matthew Wise was in the chair. A resolution expressing a qualified approval of the project was adopted, and a committee of gentlemen, whose names will be found in our chronological tables, was appointed to consider and report at an adjourned meeting. Probably, as a result of their deliberations, the following notice appeared on the 20th of October following. It is the first requisition for a public meeting in the history of the town, and, although it is addressed to nobody, it has very considerable value as furnishing the names of the men who, with the Committee were the fathers of local government in Leamington:—

We, the undersigned, Proprietors of Houses and Land in Leamington, do request that a Public Meeting of Proprietors and Occupiers of Land and Houses be held on Monday, the Thirtieth Day of October Instant, at the Vestry of the Parish Church of Leamington, at Twelve o'clock at Noon, for the purpose of considering and determining on the expediency of obtaining an Act of Parliament for Paving, Lighting, and otherwise Improving the Town.— Matthew Wise, John Russell, Thomas Kinlow, E. Willes, John Tomes, R. Sanders, Thomas Tidmas, John Hickling, for Self and Satchell, Joseph Baly, William Perkins, Nath. S. Baly, Edward Taylor, John Mott Farman, Joseph Brookhouse, John Williams, R. Hooton, John Campion, Thomas Thompson, John Russell (Bath Hotel), John Denn, M. Copps, Richard Hopton, Benjamin Smart, Thomas Heydon, Charles Lamb, Stephen Peasnall, George Elliott, Robert Webb, William Smith, R. W. Elliston, W. G. Elliston. James Bisset.

This strong desire for an improved system of government was delayed for several years by irresolution and timidity, and an indefinite postponement seemed imminent until a local improvement in the new town demonstrated the inability of the Vestry to hold the reins of authority any longer. From the junction of the Union Parade with Warwick Street, the road proceeded to Milverton along a lane, and commencing near the top of Dale Street there was a steep descent to the Milverton brook, and on the other side an ascent equally difficult and dangerous. In making this passage, vehicles were jostled and damaged, and teams drawing heavily-laden carts and wagons were distressed and exhausted. It was proposed in 1821 to widen the lane to fifty-four feet, raise the roadway, and build a bridge over the brook. To carry such a work into effect a sum of £1,000 at the very least was required, and if the whole of the rates had been appropriated for two or three years there would still have been a deficit. By a combination of contrivances the difficulty was overcome. Mr. Willes gave the land for widening the lane; he and Mr. Greatheed built the bridge at their joint expense. A sum of £350 was still required, to meet which it was decided to ask the farmers to do the haulage,

estimated to cost £150, free of charge, and to raise the remaining ,200 by public subscription.

The eighth mineral water spring was discovered in 1821, situated on land on the south side of Charlotte Street.

Leaving for a time this development of local government, we must notice three Royal visits which occurred before the first quarter of the century closed. At about four o'clock in the afternoon of Sunday, July 7, 1822, the Prince and Princess of Denmark arrived at Copps's Hotel, dined, visited Elliston's Assembly Rooms, the Pump Rooms and Baths, and, between six and seven, left for the Warwick Arms Hotel, Warwick, where they remained for several days. Their stay, though brief, was of sufficient duration to give them a place among the early Royal visitors to the Spa, and in the historical chain of events it borrows and reflects a fresh interest on the fountain in Bath Street, which a later generation, in a spirit of loyalty and welcome, erected in honour of the marriage of H.R.H. the Princess Alexandra of Denmark with H.R.H. the Prince of Wales.

The next patronage of Royalty was of a residential character—the first of the kind in Leamington—and, as might readily be supposed, it was accompanied with demonstrations of rejoicing in every way befitting an event so auspicious. On Tuesday evening, July 30, 1822, at precisely eight o'clock, H.R.H. the Princess Augusta arrived with a numerous suite, and proceeded to No. 9, Upper Union Parade, which was named Augusta House. A triumphal arch was erected in High Street, opposite Copps's Hotel; the streets were lined with spectators, and a large number of the leading inhabitants, in their carriages, met Her Royal Highness on her entry into the town, and a calvacade of the local gentry escorted her to her residence, amid continuous cheers from the assembled spectators. Arrived at her temporary home, the Princess was received by Mr. Francis Stenton, Master of the Ceremonies at the Upper Assembly Rooms, and Mr. H. Bevan, who held a similar office at the Assembly Rooms, Bath

Street; and a band—an indispensable adjunct on all such occasions—filled the Parade with the strains of the National Anthem. The evening was spent in a general illumination of the town, the inhabitants competing with a spirited liberality for the honour of producing the most brilliant transparencies. The next morning, Mr. Matthew Wise (High Sheriff), the Masters of the Ceremonies, and a deputation of the inhabitants had the honour of waiting on Her Royal Highness, and were most graciously received; on the following day a loyal address from the inhabitants was presented,, to which the Princess replied:—

"I feel deeply obliged to the gentlemen of the Committee, and to every inhabitant of the town of Leamington, for their attention and for the kind interest they take in my welfare, and I can assure them that I shall lose no time in acquainting the King with their expressions of loyalty to his Majesty and to all the branches of the Royal Family."

Further honours came three days after (August 2), their Royal Highnesses the Duke and Duchess of Gloucester arriving on Friday afternoon and receiving the same hearty welcome as had been accorded to the Princess. They were also escorted to their residence in Cross Street by a numerous assemblage of visitors and inhabitants in carriages and on horseback, and an immense concourse of pedestrians. In honour of the event the dwelling was named Gloucester House—a style it retained until a few years ago. It is now called "the Old Bank House," and is occupied by Mr. H. C. Pickering, manager at Lloyds Bank. The town was again brilliantly illuminated in the evening. The Royal visitors resided in Leamington upwards of a month, frequenting the Pump Rooms almost daily for the use of the waters and baths, and, on leaving, acknowledged the great benefits they had received.

The same year the Roman Catholics provided themselves with a place of worship for conducting services in harmony with their own views. A considerable number had come to Leamington—some of them families of distinction—and, not finding any provision for their religious observances, they left, or remained and complained of the serious inconvenience to which they were subjected. To remedy this state of things, one of the large rooms at the Apollo, Clemens Street, was hired, fitted up suitably to their requirements, and regular weekly services instituted, at which the Rev. B. Crosbie was the first officiating priest.

The year 1825 saw the renaissance of modern Leamington. It was the eventide of the village era, whose ancient shadows were being dispersed for ever by the brightness of the morning of the town. Imagination fails to picture the energy, the enterprising spirit of speculation by the builders, the general industry and the constant changes of that time. Wherever the eye rested; progress was seen; wherever the ear listened, the music of the trowel was heard. Shrubland Hall, "near Leamington," was shaping itself in the sequestered solitude of its own grove. The Bowling Green Inn was being demolished to make room for the valuable properties now standing on its site. On the Green the sturdy strokes of the woodman were heard, felling with his axe those noble elms which had been the pride of the village for centuries. The rooks, croaking bitter anathemas at the devastation of their hereditary homesteads, directed their sluggish flight across the river and founded new colonies in the Pingle and the Holly Walk. Regent Place was being formed out of the Green to connect Bath Street with Church Street and the Old Town Close, and to prepare for the future Russell Terrace. In a few months £izo.ooo changed hands in the sale and purchase of building plots, and at an auction sale at Copps's Hotel, 9,680 square yards of land in Brunswick Street found eager buyers. The Quarry Field, "containing excellent stone for building," was in the market, one plot of which was purchased by the Wesleyan? for their chapel in Portland Street, and another later on by Dr. Jephson for his residence, Beech Lawn. The foundations for fifteen villas were laid at the back of the Episcopal Chapel, and plans were ready for double the number on

the east and west sides of the building. The Parish Church was enlarged; Christ Church and the Wesleyan Chapel built.

But that which specially marks the year as its own, more than aught else, was the establishment of a new system of local government. On June 10, 1825, the Act 6, George IV., c. 133, for "paving, or flagging, lighting, cleansing, watching, and improving the town of Leamington Priors," received the Royal Assent. By this the town obtained a firm footing on the lowest rung of the municipal ladder, the top of which was reached exactly fifty years afterwards, when by the Charter of Incorporation the prize of a Royal Borough, with an endless succession of Mayors, Aldermen, and Councillors, was gained. CHRONOLOGY 1800. —The water at the Old Well had nearly disappeared, in consequence of Abbotts's Well having lowered the level.

A retired London harness maker, named Wrench, brought his wife, Janet, to Leamington for the benefit of her health, and left an interesting description of the village at the time.

1801. —Population 315. 1803. —Rev. James Walhouse, commenced a movement for enclosing the Well by public subscription.

Benjamin Smart, junior, registered proprietor of "one cotton mill," in the parish of Milverton.

Earl of Aylesford induced to visit Leamington.

1804. —The well enclosed at his lordship's expense. 1805. —William Abbotts died, March 7, aged 69.

Mrs. Abbotts continued the business at the

Inn and Baths.

1806. —Tombstone erected over Abbotts's grave in the

Churchyard.

Read's Baths opened in High Street.

Mrs. Abbotts transferred business at the New

Inn, Bath Street, to her son-in-law, William

Smith.

First issue of Amos Middleton's Analysis of

"Lemington Waters."

Benjamin Satchwelfestablished the Lemington

Spa Charity.

Robbins's Baths, near the Bridge, opened.

Rev. James Moody died, aged 50.

1807. —Satchwell Buildings, afterwards known as

Hopton's Hoarding Houses, built.

Average value of land from £60 to £100 per acre.

1808. —First new private house in the Old Town elected at the south-west corner of High Street and Clemens Street.

Clemens Street commenced.

William Smith, of the New Inn, died, April

6, aged 42.

Mrs. Smith became landlady of the New

Inn.

First house in New Town built by Mr. Frost,

of Warwick. George Stanley, mason, also of Warwick, laid the first brick, October 8.

Rev. James Walhouse, Mr. John Tomes, Warwick, and Benjamin Satchwell, laid three stones connected with the first building in the New Town, September 20

Duke and Duchess of Bedford and family visited Leamington.

Bells rung to celebrate the inauguration of the New Town, September 20.

FROM 1800 1808. 1809. TO 1825.

"Building of the Bridge commenced.

John Toonc, builder, settled in Leamington.

Bridge completed—Mr. Couchman, builder.

Visitors numbered 1,500.

Two acres of building land, opposite Wise's gardens and baths, High Street, offered for sale.

1810. —Pump Room Spring discovered.

Supposed time of sale of a farm of 65 acres, on which the Parade is built. The Leamington Building Society, a Warwick institution, began to purchase land and build houses at Leamington.

Master and Miss Smith, "the celebrated musical phenomena," gave a concert at the

Bowling Green Inn.

The Duchess of Gordon and the Duke of

Manchester's daughter visited Leamington.

A row of twenty houses built by a company in the Parade.

Benjamin Satchwell died, December 1, aged 77 1811. —Bedford Hotel opened by John and Sarah

Williams.

Lord Middleton settled in Leamington

House warming at Bedford Hotel, December

4-

Kanelagh Gardens established by Mr. Mackie.

Dr. Franklin came to reside in Leamington

James Bisset, of the Museum, New Street, Birmingham, visited Leamington and stayed at Fisher's Boarding House.

Population 540.

1812. —Thomas Abbotts, senior, farmer and grazier, died, aged 82.

Sinker advertised his business for sale.

Golden Lion, Regent-street, sold by auction.

Two houses in High-street for sale, with "gardens in front."

A half share of No. 26, Union Street to be raffled for; 100 tickets, £5 5s. each.

Assemblies held at Mrs. Shaw's, the Old

Bowling Green Inn.

Benjamin Satchwell's tombstone erected.

Upper Assembly Rooms opened September 24.

First Edition of Pratt's Guide published.

CHRONOLOGY FROM 1800 TO 1825.— *Continued.* 1812. —Read's Baths, High Street, advertised for sale.

Bisset returned to Leamington and opened his Picture Gallery and Public Exhibition in Clemens Street.

Stoneleigh Hotel built.

Accounts of Churchwardens and Overseers began this year. Mr. Franklin, surgeon, commenced practice at No. 8,

New Town.

The Earl of Aylesford died suddenly at Packington Hall, October 20; aged 61. Church rate at 4d. produced £28 12s. 6d.

1813. —Assembly Rooms advertised to be let.

Earl of Aylesford claimed cottages in possession of the parish. Referred to parish officers and his lordship's agent (Mr.

Wedge) for settlement; March.

Public Market established in High Street,

May 5.

Theatre, Bath Street, opened October 26.

First list of householders entered on the rate book.

The principal centres of attraction were Bisset's establishment in Clemens Street and Olorenshaw's Library in High Street.

A rate at 6d. in the £ levied.

Reported enlargement of the Old Well

House.

Sarah Medley's "Beauties of Leamington"

published.

1814. —Michael Copps, from Cheltenham, succeeds

Sinker.

Assembly Rooms opened for balls, card assemblies, and promenades. A rate at 6d. produced £tx) 7s. J. C. Rackstrow, of the English and French

Circulating Librr.ry, moves from High

Street to more commodious premises at the top of Union Street. Assembly Rooms thrown open to the fashionable world, when 80 persons "of the first distinction" were present. The New Pump Rooms and Baths were opened in July. J. Cullis, proprietor of Ranelagh Gardens, planted the trees forming the Linden

Avenue.

Average value of building land £1,000 per acre.

William Merry's "original hunting and livery stables," near the Blenheim Hotel, High Town.

Great storm; fire-ball fell in Clemens

Street,

July 28. First Edition of Bisset's Guide. 1815.—Public meeting at New Inn, " to consider the burthen of the taxes."

Joseph Stanley established Crown Hotel in

March; house warming on the 26th.

New Charitable Institution started by seccders from Ben Satchwell's Charity. 1815. —Notice issued to the public by Sir Grey

Skipwith and others, stating that the original institution, begun in 1806, was still in existence. Third Edition published of Dr. Middleton's

Treatise of the Waters, the author describing himself as "resident physician at Leamington." Announcement in June that the proprietors of the Pump Room had set apart a distinct wing of trie building for the free use by the poor on Mondays and Thursdays. R. W. Elliston, of Drury Lane Theatre, played at the Theatre in July, August, September, and October.

The first edition of the Rev. W. Field's

History of Warwick published, in which will be found a valuable description of Early Leamington.

James Heaviside, of Bath, elected Master ot

the Ceremonies.

Michael Copps filled up the duck pond in

High Street.

1816. —First enlargement of Parish Church; foundation-stone laid by James Bisset, April 18.

Pews sold of the value of,£1,560 to pay the cost.

Clemens Street Chapel opened July 10, on which occasion sermons were preached by the Rev. John Angell James, of Birmingham, and the Rev. Mr. Hartley, of Lutterworth.

A brilliant ball at the Assembly Rooms; 500 present; August 15.

The largest number of visitors in the town ever known; every hotel crowded, and lodgings scarcely procurable at any price.

Thomas Rackstrow, who had been lessee of the Assembly Rooms, and resident there; became tenant of the "New

Hotel" in Clemens Street, which he opened at Michaelmas, under the name of the "Blenheim Hotel."

Rev. John Wise, Lillington, lets to Luke Harris "all that messuage, or tenement, called the Parsonage," situated and being in, or near, and opening into Church Street, at £15 yearly.

Smart's Spring discovered on the site of Sleaths' Limited, boot, cycle, etc., stores, Nos. 4, 6, and 8, Clemens Street.

First Edition of Loudon's "Dissertation" published.

1817. —Mr. Newbold was advertised as "renter" of the Assembly Room.

Mrs. Elliston and the two Misses Elliston commenced their instructions in dancing at their house "at the corner of Clemens Street, having engaged the Public Room in that street for their Academy days."

Rev. A. Bromiley, of Hoxton College, chosen first minister of Clemens Street Chapel.

CHRONOLOGY FROM 1817. —The Wesleyan cause commenced by holding meetings in a "Lofte sytuated in a certayne yarde yclept Barnacle's Yarde. in ye famous Strete yclept Satchwell Street."

Rev. Rowland Hill preached his first sermon in Clemens Street Chapel; August.

Smart's Baths, Clemens Street, advertised as open from 6 o'clock till 12, daily.

James Bisset completed Belle Vue Place, at the corner of Brunswick Street.

1818. —James Heaviside elected Master of the Ceremonies at Bath in February; resigned his office in Leamington in March, and was succeeded by Captain Charles Stevenson.

T. Rackstrow improved the Blenheim Hotel, and described it as " pleasingly situated on an eminence in Clemens Street, High Town."

Oliver Mills established the first wine and spirit vaults under the Assembly Rooms, Union Parade.

Mr. Newbold, Upper Union Parade, arranged for quadrille rehearsals at the Pump Rooms, two mornings each week.

Foundation-stone of Regent Hotel laid by Miss Greatheed, July 18; Mrs. Siddons, the famous actress, and her daughter were present.

Mr. Henry Jcphson came to Leamington. First Edition of MoncriefTs Guide published by William Gore Elliston.

Anniversary services at Clemens Street Chapel; the Rev. William Jay, of Bath, was one of the preachers.

Mr. Booth, of Covent Garden Theatre, played *King Richard III.*, at the Theatre, Bath Street.

"Barford Buildings," five freehold front houses, adjoining Copps's Hotel, sold by auction by J. and R. Loveday, at Copps's Hotel.

The proprietors and occupiers of houses and land held a meeting at Copps's Royal Hotel on October 26, "for the purpose of considering of the expedience of an application to Parliament for an Act for paving, lighting, watching, cleansing, and improving the town."

The first friendly assembly, held at the Apollo Rooms in October; the Rev. J. Walhouse presiding as steward of the evening.

Waterloo House, Bath Street, now occupied by Wackrill and Sons, Limited, built.

1819. —Bath Hotel, described as " eligible and much frequented," advertised for sale; February.

Messrs. Marshall commenced an Academy of Music at Church Street, Warwick, and also at Leamington, for teaching music on Mr. Logier's new system.

1800 TO 1825. —*Continued.* 1819.— Annual report of the Leamington Charitable Institution published.

Mrs. Potterton, formerly Mrs. Smith, daughter of William Abbotts, landlady at the Bath Hotel.

Foundation-stone of Bisset's Picture Gallery, High Street, laid by Captain Stevenson,

M.C.

Williams's Hotel (now the Regent) opened, July 19. Tickets for dinner, £ 1 ns.6d. each.

Grand Concert at the Assembly Rooms, under the direction of Mr. Marshall.

Mr. Munden, of the Theatre Royal, Drury Lane, played three nights at the Theatre.

The Prince Regent, afterwards George IV., visited Leamington and gave permission for Williams's Hotel to be called the Regent, Friday, September 10; town illuminated in the evening.

Public meeting in the Pump Rooms to adopt Address to the Prince, Saturday, Sept. II.

Captain Stevenson, M.C, presented Address to Sir B. Bloomfield, at Warwick Castle, Monday, September 13.

Mr. Cross succeeded Mr. Williams at the Bedford Hotel.

Supposed date of removal of the Methodists from Satchwell Street to No. 4, Brunswick Street, now occupied by Mr. William Olorenshaw, furniture dealer.

W. G. Elliston became "renter" of the Upper Assembly Rooms.

R. W. Elliston played at the Old Theatre.

"The Leamington Spa Ale and Porter Brewery," occupied by Mr. Parris, and the "Birmingham Tavern," in the occupation of Mr. Hanson, both in Wise Street, offered for sale.

Ten plots of land sold at the Bath Hotel by John Margetts. Lot 1, "intended to front a street to be called Smith Street;" 2, 3, and 4 adjoining. Lot 5, "intended to front Bath Place, on the west of Smith Street." Lot 6, "intended to front the street to be called Abbotts's Street on the south and Bath Place on the west;" 7, 8, 9, and 10 adjoining.

Seven lots of freehold land on the south side of Charlotte Street sold for building; locality described as "South Ville, Leamington Spa."

The "Pingle," the land on which the New Town Hall and Theatre Royal stand, sold by private contract.

Advertisement by Mr. John Cross, of the Bedford Hotel, stating that a turtle would be dressed on Monday, November 8; orders received for any part of the county.

About 30 lots of building land sold at an average price of 5,000 guineas an acre.

CHRONOLOGY FROM 1800 TO 1825.—*Continued.* 1820.—John Russell, son-in-law of Mrs. Smith (afterwards Mrs. Potterton), purchased the Bath Hotel and became the landlord. House-warming May 4; tickets £1 1s. each. Dr. Amos Middleton, president; there were 80 present.

Churchwardens paid the Clerk £1 for tolling the bell 14 days for his late Majesty, George III.,

Several " tenements " in the " Bazaar," consisting of a shop, back room, and one bedroom each, advertised by George Carter, to let.

J. Cross, of the Bedford, established in Bedford Street the first horse repository; first sale, July 31.

EUiston played at the Theatre in July. Dr. Hume Weatherhead's analysis of the waters published, a copy of which was presented by him to the King, at the Levee in July.

First Gala Night at the Ranelagh Gardens, July 25; when there were " pyrotechnicks;" solos on the harp and violin; "montgolfier, or night balloons;" and a remarkable Pandian, who performed on six instruments at once.

The Rev. Rowland Hill preached in the "Leamington Spa Chapel" on July 30, August 6 and 13.

Mr. Henry Twiselton Elliston, son of Mr. R. W. Elliston, appointed organist at the Parish Church.

Meeting of inhabitants at the Bath Hotel to consider the questions of nuisances and encroachments on private property.

Grand Gala at Ranelagh Gardens.

Mr. Chambers, surgeon, removed from

Gloucester Street to No. 11, Union Parade.

The Rev. J. H. Monk, B.D., Regius Professor of Greek in the University of Cambridge and Fellow of Trinity College,
preached at the Parish Church in aid of the Society for Promoting Christian Knowledge.

Grand Cabinet of Curiosities, known as "The
Leamington Museum," sold by Mr. Hodgson.

Edmund Kean engaged by Elliston to play
Shylock at the Old Theatre, on Saturday, September 23. The pit on this occasion was lined with green baize and appropriated to box company. Prices: Boxes, 7s.; upper ditto, 5s.; gallery, 3s.

Rev. Henry Forster Burder, MA., Fellow and Philosophical Tutor, Hoxton Academy, London, preached at "the Leamington Chapel" in September. Collections, realising £20, were made towards liquidating the debt of £800 remaining on the building.

1820. —At a public meeting held in Bisset's room,
Clemens Street, on September 27th—Mr.
Matthew Wise in the chair—it was unanimously resolved "That a Paving and
Lighting Act, under Proper Conditions and Restrictions, would be highly beneficial to the interests of Leamington."
The following Committee was appointed:
B B. Greatheed, John Tomes, Matthew Wise, Edward VTilles, John Russell, R. W. Elliston, R. Hooton, W. G. Elliston, J. Campion, W. Hunter, B. Smart, Mr. Booth, T. Wilkinson, M. Copps, R. Hopton, Joseph Stanley, Mr. Thompson,
James Bisset, J. Brookhouse, Mr. Dean, Mr. Finlow, Mr. Kinsnell, J. Edwards, John Russell (Bath Hotel), John Williams
(Regent Hotel), "to report to a future meeting."

Mrs. and the Misses Elliston gave their first annual ball at the Assembly Room,

October 18.

Meeting of parishioners in the Vestry at the Parish Church, October 30, for considering "the expediency of obtaining an Act for paving, lighting, and otherwise improving the town."

Freehold building land, containing 6,036 square yards on the south side of Charlotte Street, sold by Mr. J. Booth at the Castle Inn.

Died at Newbold Comyn, on Sunday evening,
December 10, the Rev. Edward Willes. "He expired most peacefully, in the 74th year of his age, sincerely regretted by many friends, beloved and lamented by his own family, to all of whom he was endeared through a long life."

Bisset opened his Paragon Picture Gallery,
High Street.

The Rev. Arthur Bromiley, minister at
Clemens Street Chapel, married at Bolton to Miss Mary Lomax, of Harwood.

1821. —A loyal Address, signed by 101 residents and visitors, presented in January to the King (George IV.), "who was pleased to receive the same in the most gracious manner." Captain Charles Stevenson, M.C., resigned his office through failing health in January.

Isaac Wilkinson, Amos Middleton, Richard
Hooton, William Collins (Warwick), and
Charles Harris (Coventry) convened a meeting of "subscribers to the dress balls for
Jany. 31," to elect a successor.

Mr. Francis Stenton elected third M. C.
Isaac Buxton and Henry Bevan unsuccessfully contested the appointment.

Joseph Stanley and John Russell, surveyors of highways, convened a vestry meeting for Feb. 27, "to determine a proposition for keeping in repair the new streets, roads, and ways, and for indemnifying (if necessary) the Surveyors in respect of their repairing and mending the same." CHRONOLOGY FROM 1800 TO 1825.—*Continued.* 1821. —In March, Mr. and Mrs. Hopton "greatly enlarge and improve" Satchwell Buildings.

"The situation is particularly pleasant—private rooms looking out into a beautiful flower garden" (now George Street).

William Smith (probably a grandson of

William Abbotts,) manufactured "the genuine Leamington Salts," at the Pump Rooms. Bath Street.

R. W. Elliston erected and opened the New

Royal Library and Assembly Rooms, Bath Street, at a cost exceeding £25,000.

George Carter, the first local auctioneer,

announced in May his intention to commence very shortly as an auctioneer. Address, No. 3, The Bazaar.

Mr. Power, late of Hinckley, surgeon to the late Duke of Kent, Surgeon Extraordinary to H.R.H. the Duke of Cambridge, and Fellow of the Royal College of Surgeons, came to reside in Booth's Terrace, Clemens Street, and commenced practice.

The "lane," leading from Warwick Street into Milverton, widened to 54 feet, and the bridge by the " Star and Garter" erected at the joint expense of Edward Willes and Bertie Greatheed, Esqs.

Horatio Palfrey, auctioneer, sold,the stockin-trade and effects of Mr. Barnwell, builder, Satchwell Street.

The hotels and boarding houses, and the town generally, brilliantly illuminated on July 19,

in celebration of coronation of George IV.

Francis Smith's "Descriptive Guide to

Leamington " published.

A new Assembly Room established at the

Parthenon, Bath Street, by William Gore

Elliston. H. Bevan elected M C. First ball, Tuesday, August 21.

Sale of 2,000 square yards of building land,

on the south side of Charlotte Street, "with the saline spring and well newly discovered," sold by auction at the Cas-

tle Hotel, Brunswick Street.

Madame Catalani gave a concert at the Upper Assembly Rooms, on Wednesday evening, October 10, "at nine o'clock," when she sang the "favourite variations of Rode's Violin Concerto." Tickets 10s. each; upwards of 400 present.

Pew No. 30 in the Parish Church, containing 8 sittings, sold by auction, at the Bath Hotel, by Margetts & Co.

A new walk made by the side of the Leam, and the foundation laid of an orchestra at the back of the Royal Baths.

Population 2,183.

1822. —Public meeting, at the Bath Hotel, on

January 8, "to consider the propriety of applying for a mail bag for Leamington," "to prevent the delay and inconvenience arising from Leamington letters passing through Warwick Post Office."

1822.—Mr. Hopton's Boarding House sold by auction, by George Carter, at the Crown Hotel, Jan. 14.

The Roman Catholics fitted up a commodious Chapel in Clemens Street, in

May.

The Prince and Princess of Denmark, passing through Leamington, dined at Copps's

Hotel, and, before leaving, inspected the Assembly Rooms and Pump Rooms; Sunday, July 7.

Three plots of building land on the south side of Gloucester Street sold by Nathan

Izod at the Bath Hotel.

H.R.H. the Princess Augusta arrived on

Tuesday, July 30, and stayed for several weeks at No. 9, the Parade. She was the first Royal resident at the Spa.

Their Royal Highnesses the Duke and

Duchess of Gloucester arrived August 2,

and resided at Gloucester House, Regent

Street, now occupied by Mr. H. C. Pickering, and known as " The Old Bank

House."

Concert at the Assembly Rooms, August

24, at which Mr. Braham sang. This was his second visit; dateof first, Sept., 1818.

Mr. Betty at the Theatre, August 31, September 4 and 7.

Public notice of an application to Parliament for a local Act; September. Adjourned Vestry meeting for considering the same, October 28. Warwick Gas Company announce their intention of supplying Leamington with gas; November. Shambles for the sale of meat established at the top of Wise Street. Auction sale at the vaults under the

Assembly Rooms, in the notice of which the present Regent Street West was described as " Wellington Terrace. "

Hopton's effects advertised for sale by auction, but were purchased at a valuation.

Pew in the front of the north side of the old gallery, containing 6 sittings, sold by auction at the Bath Hotel by Margetts and Co.

Joseph Parsons becomes tenant of the Bowling Green Inn.

Ten shares of £100 each, being one equal

moiety "of that flourishing and improving concern, the Leamington Gas Works," for sale.

John Dowler, cabinet maker, builder, upholsterer, paperhanger, etc., commenced business in High Street, opposite the

Royal Hotel.

The Brewery in Wise Street named "The

Regent Brewery."

National School established at the Parsonage

House, Church Street.

CHRONOLOGY FROM I 1813.—The Warwick Gas Company advertised 80 shares of £50 each, as having been reserved for the inhabitants of Leamington.

Read's Baths again for sale.

H.R.H. the Princess Augusta, the Duchess of Gloucester, the Dowager Duchess of Rutland, the Dowager

Duchess of Newcastle, the Duke of Grafton, and the Archbishop of Canterbury were in the list of subscribers to the Leamington Charitable Institution.

George Carter commenced business in Wise Street as auctioneer, house agent, and accountant.

Branch of Messrs. Tomes, Russell, Tomes and

Russell's Bank at Warwick (known as the

Warwick Old Bank) opened in Bath Street, May 1.

W. C. Macready at the Theatre for one night only; July 16.

Gas mains laid from Warwick Gas Works to

Leamington; July.

Workmen employed widening "the lane'

from the top of the Parade to Union Road.

Milverton.

The Regent Brewery, Birmingham Tavern,

public slaughter-house and established meat market, Wise Street, sold by auction.

Movement began in August for building the

Church now known as Christ Church.

Prince Kiataira, son of the reigning King

Paroa, a New Zealand chief, died, aged 18,

and was buried in the churchyard; August.

Public gas lighting introduced; 18 lamps in

Union Street (the Parade), October 29.

Residents in the Parade, between Victoria

Bridge and Warwick Street, to pay £63 per annum for ditto.

Petition to the magistrates for Petty Sessions to be held in Leamington; October.

Monthly Petty Sessions established at the

Apollo Rooms, Clemens Street; Nov. 6.

The Rev. Robert Downes succeeded the Rev.

John Wise as Vicar of Leamington.

1824.—Meeting at the Apollo Rooms of the Leamington Association for the Prosecution of Felons and Suppression of Nuisances.

In consequence of the inhabitants of the parish having very considerably increased in number, the Parish Committee resolved

"that ten guineas instead of five lie allowed for the annual parish dinner"; March.

Mrs. Hickin succeeded R. Hopton at the

Boarding House, Satchwell Place.

Green, the aeronaut, ascended from the

Bowling Green in the Coronation ballxm;

May 18.

TO 1825.—*Concluded.* .—Building land for sale; 864 yards; fronting Wellington Terrace, Bedford Street anil John Street.

Public meeting at the Apollo Rooms to petition against Window Tax.

Theatre advertised to be sold by auction at the Bath Hotel by George Carter; August 29.

Miss Stephens, a celebrated soprano, sang at a concert given by Messrs. F. lliston; September 13.

Foundation stone of the "Leamington Episcopal Chapel" (now Christ Church) laid; November.

The Parish Committee increased the Police Force by appointing four assistant constables at 10/-a week each; December.

5.—Claremont House, Charlotte Street, occupied by the late Colonel Blackburn, sold by auction at Copps's Hotel by Henry Jacob; March 2. It was occupied by John Phipps, at £150 per annum, as an academy for young gentlemen.

The old Bowling Green Inn demolished and the elm trees cut down.

Two new windows added to the Crown

Hotel.

The Theatre opened under the management of Mr. Bennett.

Mr. John Russell established the second

Leamington Market at the rear of the Bath

Hotel.

Miss Stephens sang a second time at Messrs.

Elliston's concert.

The parish presented at the Quarter Sessions for not having provided a pair of stocks;

October. Stocks immediately ordered by the Parish Committee.

Parish Church re-opened after enlargement;

May 22.

Wesleyan Chapel, Portland Street, built by

John Toone, opened by the Rev. J. Entwistle, junior. Cost of site and building,,£800; September.

Madame Caradori and T. Harper, the celebrated trumpet player, took part in a concert in the Assembly Rooms; September 22.

The Leamington Episcopal Chapel opened;

October 16.

The organ supplied to the new Episcopal

Chapel was played for the first time on Sunday, December 4.

The new organ at the Parish Church oened on Christmas Day.

CHAPTER XXII.

IGOROUS and successful as had been the development of the town in material wealth down to 1824, its advance in institutions was sluggish compared with the fruits of the next six years—a period in which we have the establishment of municipal government; a novelty in the revival of the ancient Court Leet and Court Baron; the adoption of a new kind of Charity in the Hospital and Dispensary movement; the commencement of the work of the Warneford Hospital; the second enlargement of the old Church, and the erection of a new one; the building of three new Chapels; the formation of two Musical Societies, and the founding of the Press. For a handbreadth of time, extending only from 1824 to 1830, these heavy sheaves of public utility cannot be considered a scanty harvest.

Chronologically, the Parish Committee takes precedence of all the rest. It was the old, constitutional form of parochial government under which the affairs of the village had been controlled for centuries; in its origin, coeval with, and possibly antedating the foundation of the ancient Parish Church, but now, for the first time in local history, beginning to develop signs of decrepitude and decay. The Committee was the outcome of the Vestry, at the annual meetings of which it was customary to appoint a number of parishioners to serve as a governing body for the ensuing twelve months, and a Rating Committee, whose duty it was to assist the Church-wardens and the Overseers in the preparation of the valuation lists. For the management of the parish business, the former held meetings once a month, always, in deference to the source from whence they derived their authority, assembling in the first place in the vestry at the Parish Church, and then adjourning to the Apollo Rooms in Clemens Street. Their powers were comprehensive, and the social status and importance which membership conferred were valued as much as those of an Aldermanship or a Councillorship of the present Corporation. All the secular affairs of the town were in their care, including the supervision of the first Poor House, which was situated near the site now occupied by the Warneford Hospital. The earliest records we have of their transactions are dated 1823. From these we learn that George Carter, who afterwards became the first resident auctioneer, was the Assistant Overseer and collector of Land and Assessed Taxes, the amount of which for the half-year ending Michaelmas, 1823, was £1,444 is. 4d. The popular Dr. Jephson, who rose to be one of the most famous members of the medical profession, was, in the following year, Parish Surgeon, in conjunction with his partner, Mr. Chambers, at a salary of *£10* 10s. per annum. The Committee continued to exorcise some of their former power long after the establishment of the Improvement Commissioners, but the general effect of the Act of 1825 was to make them more parochial and less municipal. Such privileges as they were allowed to retain were preserved with zealous care, and barricaded against the encroachments of innovation by a lofty and dig-

nified demeanour, an uncompromising attitude, and a phraseology, magniloquently tumid. When a material alteration in Upper Union Street was made without the consent of the Surveyor, the Committee "could not refrain from expressing their reprobation of so improper an usurpation of the duties of the constituted authorities.'' Gloriously " porochial " as was Mr. Bumble, he could not have said more. Under their regime the first increase of the police force was made, four additional assistant constables having been appointed in December 1824 at a remuneration of 10s. a week each. They rented a seat in the Parish Church to Mr H. T. Elliston at 6d. a year in recognition of his services as organist and directed the agreement "to be deposited with the Churchwardens in the parish chest "; purchased a strait waistcoat " for the use of the parish," supplied the town with stocks, and resolved that no public meeting should be convened by notice in the Parish Church without their sanction. Very important people were those old Parish Committee-men.

The ascent by Green, the aeronaut, from the Bowling Green on Tuesday, May 18, 1824, exceeded in the number of spectators it attracted, and the enthusiasm it created, all previous demonstrations in' the town. The balloon was the one used in the festivities with which the Coronation of George IV. was celebrated. The words "Coronation Balloon" were inscribed upon it in large letters, and the embellishments with which the car was decorated greatly enhanced its appearance. It was brought to Leamington and exhibited at Elliston's room to thousands of visitors from May 10, to the day of the ascent, when the town was full of excitement and from an early hour w ith sightseers from all parts of the surrounding neighbourhood. By mid-day the windows, roofs and balconies of the houses in the immediate vicinity of the Bow-ling Green, together with the main streets were crowded to excess, the total number of spectators being estimated at from fourteen to fifteen thousand. The balloon was inflated under the direction of Mr. Roberts, "

Superintendent of the Leamington Gas Works," and shortly after four o'clock it rose from the Green, a band playing "God Save the King" and the people applauding. It sailed due east until passing Southam when it took a south-easterly direction, and after having been travelling in the air for thirty-two minutes, it descended at Milton, a parish about three miles from Northampton. Mr. Green returned to Leamington the next morning with his balloon at nine o'clock.

Nearly a year before the resolution was formed for enlarging the Parish Church a second time, the decision to build a church in the New Town was adopted. On August 6, 1823, a special vestry was held—Mr. John Campion presiding—for the purpose of considering the question of the existing church accommodation in Leamington. Unanimously, it was resolved that the Parish Church being totally inadequate, a new chapel should be built. Mr. Willes, who was present, and at There were small gas works in Leamington previous to the present establishment in the Tachbrook Road.

the time was High Sheriff of the county, then proposed to build " a chapel of the Church of England under license to be obtained from the Bishop of the Diocese." His generosity was accepted with warm thanks, and Mr. Greatheed supplemented this munificent gift by presenting the land necessary to extend the road from the " top of Union Parade" (the point where it formed a junction with Warwick Street) "to the site fixed upon for the erection of the chapel." Thanks, equally sincere as those which had been voted Mr. Willes were returned by the Vestry for the local improvement he had thus effected in the principal thoroughfare of the town. The site was happily chosen, the position being on the south side of Beauchamp Square, the front commanding a view of the whole length of the Parade, and the Church itself standing out prominently from all the surrounding buildings. It was built in 1825, from designs furnished by Mr. Robinson, of London, who, in 1826, was the architect of

Copps's Royal Hotel. The opening services were held on October 16, 1825, at which time it was known by the name of " The Leamington Episcopal Chapel. " Two sermons were preached and collections made towards defraying the expenses of the organ and the painted windows. The Church, erected by Mr. Willes, became the private property of the Rev. Mr. Downes, who, with his curate, conducted the services. The novelty of charging for admission, for which tickets were sold, was introduced and continued until the Rev. John Craig succeeded Mr. Downes in 1839, when it was abolished by his direction.

The extension of the Parish Church in the year 1825, the second great development in the fabric, was the consummation of the work begun in 1816. In the intervening years the Church had been almost constantly in the hands of the builders for alterations and improvements; like a mass of plastic material it was continuously being moulded into different forms under pressure of an ever-increasing influx of visitors. The decision to add a transept north of the Church was arrived at in June, 1824, and in December, arrangements were made for holding the services in the Pump Room, for which purpose that building was licensed, at a cost of £4 4s. The proposal for the new work appears to have emanated from the Rev. Robert Downes, who, in 1823, had followed the Rev. John Wise as Vicar of Leamington. At a vestry meeting on June 1, 1824, Mr Downes offered to bear the whole of the expense " on certain conditions." The land on which are built the present choir vestry; the clergy vestry; the north porch, and all that part of the Church north of the Evangelist Columns, was partly churchyard, the remainder being a garden belonging to Mr. Matthew Wise, but in the occupation of Farmer Abbotts. This land he gave to the parish for the proposed additions to the Church. Mr. Downes's contract with the Vestry was to make an enlargement which " will give accommodation to about 400 Persons including 260 free and open sittings, the same to be made in manner following, that is to

say: To take down the North wall of the said Church and extend the Church into the Church Yard and the said Ground belonging to the said Matthew Wise, Esq., 28 feet 6 Inches, besides and exclusive of the Buttresses, and to extend the same from East to West, including a staircase to the Gallery and a side entrance: To sink that part of the

Church Yard which will be inclosed by the enlargement of the Church to the level required of the Foundation and to remove the soil therefrom and inclose the remains of those who are there interred in Brick Graves." (After giving the details of the building, and the materials to be used, the specifications provided that fifteen Pews and seats were to be appropriated to the persons entitled to the twelve Pews and three sittings removed from the North Wall:; "To remove the present Gallery from the North side of the Church and place it with two additional rowes of Pews against the New North Wall and to continue the said Gallery along the West side of the Church

The Parish Church, showing the enlargement on the north side, in 1825. to connect with the Gallery already built at the South side: To raise the lower part of the Present Gallery on the West side to the same level as the South and North Gallery: To make an Entrance into the Church from the Tower." In consideration of his carrying out this contract, the Vestry resolved that Mr. Downes sell or let all the pews except those reserved, and retain the proceeds for his own use. He was also to have all such contributions as he might be able to obtain from the Society for Enlarging Churches, or from any other source. Such was the scheme adopted in June, on the proposition of Mr. Downes. But in the following month of July a larger plan was submitted and accepted. He explained that, subject to the approbation of the parish, he intended to extend the enlargement " so as to make 278 additional sittings in pews, and 290 free seats, the said 278 additional sittings to be at his disposal in the same manner" mentioned in the order of the previous meeting as to the seats specified and agreed to be

made and subject to the exceptions in such order mentioned. The permission he sought was granted. As the Churchyard had been encroached upon by the south transept in 1816, and the space being still further diminished by the additions contemplated by Mr. Downes, the Vestry resolved to construct vaults under the new building, at a cost of £244 10s., the revenue to be derived from the sale of spaces to belong to the parish, after allowance of the Vicar's fees. In consequence of a difficulty in borrowing the money, Mr. Downes was permitted to defray the expense, and have the whole of the emoluments accruing from sales and fees for his own use, without any control by the parish. These improvements were augmented in April, 1825, when Mr. Downes arranged to raise the tower, put a spire on the same; raise the clock, recast the bells, add two new ones, and supply a new organ, the old one to be his property. For these purposes he was voted by the Vestry £1,328, to obtain which the church rates were mortgaged for that sum to Mr. William Taylor. As the result of these transactions, Mr. Downes became the owner of several hundred sittings, the whole of which were offered to the public at *£10* 10s. each, A large number found ready purchasers, and from such as' were not disposed of the Vicar received the rents. Their value as commercial investments is shown by the fact that within a period of three years the purchase price increased nearly 229 per cent. In 1828 the Churchwardens bought for the parish forty-one, for which they paid Mr. Downes about *£ji* 6, the average being £17 8s. 8d. each sitting. The same year they sold out by private contract and public auction, and realised £1,418 1 is. 8d. for the lot, being at the rate of £34 per seat.

The statute of 1825, the foundation stone on which historically rests the whole superstructure of our modern system of local government, was principally supplementary to the ancient authority vested in the Parish Committee; it was also the commencement of a process of evolution, in the course of which all that was valuable in the old was gradually absorbed into the newer forms, and the effete and useless rejected. It's title has been quoted. By its provisions, a new electorate was created, and public work, distinct from much of that in which the Parish Committee was engaged, specified as being necessary in the interest of the town. All residents, rated at not less than £bo per annum, were qualified to vote for, and eligible to be elected on, a Board of Twentyone Commissioners, by whom the affairs of the town were to be managed. The first The size of the vaults and the number ot the new sittings obtained are subjects on which there is great diversity of opinion. Moncricff (1829) says the catacombs were capable of containing 184 bodies; but Beck (1851) mentions 180 as the number for which spaces were provided. There is nothing on the minutes supporting these or any other figures. As to the new sittings, Moncrieff (1829) places the total at 568, consisting of 27S belonging to the Vicar, and 200 free; and in another edition (1833), he makes the aggregate 577, the Vicar's share being 278, and the free seats 299. Merridew (1837) asserts that there were only 560 new seats, of which 290 belonged to the Vicar, the remaining 270 being free and open to the public.

meeting was held in the Petty Sessions Room, at the Apollo, Clemens Street, on June 28, and adjourned to July 11, when the following were elected on the first staff of town officials: Treasurer, William Russell; Clerk, W. F. Patterson; Assistant ditto, E. W. Percy; Assessor and Collector, George Carter; Surveyor and Scavenger, John Russell, of the Bath Hotel. The effects of the change which had been made in the method of governing the town were soon visible in the improved state of the streets. In August the Commissioners advertised for contracts for lighting with "gas or oil" the town for one year; in September they raised their first loan on mortgage of the rates, the amount of which was 1,500, and in November they invited tenders for the beginning of the work of paving footpaths and crossings.

The general Hospital and Dispensary of 1826, grew out of the Charitable In-

stitution founded by Benjamin Satchwell twenty years before, and was the connecting link between that earlier manifestation of a regard for the afflicted and necessitous poor, and the Warneford Hospital of later times. Leamington has always been noted for its philanthropy, and it is satisfactory to find that at the time when the village had fairly developed into the town, Satchwell's humble endeavours were expanded into a form more adapted to the increased demands of the poor. The objects of the Dispensary were to give advice and medicine gratis to those who were not in a position to pay for them, and medical attendance at their homes when they were too ill to apply at the Dispensary. There was also a hospital or infirmary on a small scale for the treatment of in-patients. The Institution had the benefit of the most distinguished patronage, including that of H.R.H. the Princess Augusta, and H.R.H. the Duchess of Gloucester. With this movement the Warneford Hospital originated, the minutes of which date from 1826, though the name of Warneford was not given to it till some time afterwards. At the annual meeting, held on May 7, 1827 the surgeons retired from office, as they were giving up business and leaving Leamington, and Mr. William Middleton was appointed to succeed Mr. Chambers; Messrs. Jones and Cottle were elected in the place of Mr. Franklin, and Messrs. D'Arcy Bolton and Pritchard as successors to Dr. Jephson. In 1828, the ladies organized a bazaar, splendid gala and ball in aid of the funds of the Institution, the total receipts of which amounted to £904 2s. 6d., leaving, after payment of all expenses, a profit of £669 us. 3d.

Campanology could never have advanced far towards a state of perfection in the days of the village, for there were at the old church only four bells, which for all but chiming purposes, must have been practically useless. They were however of great age, and as examples of the bell-founder's art in the early part of the seventeenth century, were not altogether without interest. The treble was inscribed with the following, the date of

which shows that they must have been tinkling in the old gothic belfry for upwards of two hundred years, when the Vestry decided, in 1825, to have

'Both the former Charitable Institutions are believed to have been merged into this new movement, which probably was influenced by the efforts of.Mr. Smith, of Southam, to establish Provident Dispensaries, and the success of his views at Warwick in February, 1820.

a new set:—" Cvm sono si non-vis venire; Xvnqvam ad preces cvpies ire, 1621," of which the subjoined has been given as a translation:—

"Come when I sound, or il will shew, To Pray'rs you never wish to go."

In fulfilment of his agreement with the Vestry, the Vicar had the old bells recast by Mears, of Whitechapel, and two others were added, making altogether a peal of six. This increase of the compass, though small, was a public improvement of no slight value. The original set allowed only a very limited number of changes, and the chiming at its best could have been neither bright nor particularly melodious; but the new one was more musical, and by rendering possible an extensive series of fresh combinations of sounds, it brought the church more into harmony with the progressive spirit of the times, and the improved condition of the town. The bells, which were in the key of A, were rung for the first time on Monday, March 27, 1826.

At the time the question of selling pews at the Parish Church was before the Consistory Court in 1870, it was contended by the Rev. John Craig and other purchasers, that the system could not be interfered with, as the additions made in 1825 had never been consecrated. Hut in that view they were clearly mistaken, for the Bishop of Lichfield and Coventry consecrated the new portion on June 8, and preached a sermon, after which a sum of nearly £io was collected. The previous visit of his lordship was on August 24, 1824, when he confirmed four hundred candidates.

The formation of the first Leamington Musical Society, an event which cannot be viewed with indi.Terence in these days of high-class vocal and instrumental concerts, belongs to 1826. From the minute book, scrupulously kept by the late Mr. E. Enoch, we are able to glean the particulars of its objects and methods, and at the same time to preserve the names of many of the early local musicians. At a meeting of Professors and Amateurs, held in Elliston's Rooms, Bath Street, on Thursday evening, October 12, it was resolved to form " The Leamington and Warwick Philharmonic Society." The first list of members, each one of whom signed his name in the minute book, comprised the following: "H. T. Elliston, John Marshall, John Hewett, James Satchell, Thomas Wells, John Elston, W. G. Perry, Charles Elston, E. Enoch, G. Wells, W. L. Meyrick, W. H. Lewis, C. Marshall, William Clemens, F. Marshall, S. Flavell, John Merridew, H. Marshall, S. Whitehead, J. J. Gillman, J. Rees.

The strength and composition of the band, and the glee element observable in the programmes, are the principal subjects which will interest musicians now, and in future time, when considering the circumstances under which the earliest musical Association was founded in 1826. The former are thus described on the minutes of the Society:— Violins, Messrs. J. M. Marshall (leader), W. Meyrick, and — Wilkins; Violas, W. Lucas and T. Elston; Violoncello, W. H. Lewis,; Contra-bass, H. T. Elliston; Pianoforte, W. G. Perry (conductor); Flutes, J. Hewett and E. Enoch; Oboe and Clarinetto, C. Elston and W. Clemens; Horns, G. Wells and — Hosiaux; Trumpet, T. Wells; Trombone, S. Whitehead; Tympani, J. Satchell; Vocalists, Miss Bernard; Messrs. S. Flavell and C. Marshall. Glees made a considerable part of the programmes of the Society. They were forms of musical expression adapted to the times, and in the rural villages of England fostered a love of music under circumstances where choruses and even part songs were impossible for lack of sufficient number of voices. With reference to the first concert of the Society, it should be stated that the audience numbered about sixty

persons, "the greater part of whom were honorary members," each contributing to the funds £ 1 is. per annum. The Countess of Warwick was the Lady Patroness. Miss Bernard, of the Royal Academy, encouraged the Society by giving her services free of all charge, and Mr. Joseph Stanley, of the Crown Hotel, showed his interest in the success of these early musical efforts, by hospitably entertaining her at his establishment, during her stay in Leamington, without cost to the Society or herself. Other items of interest in the history of the Society are: An original arrangement of " God Save the King," by Mr. Satchell, which the Committee considered " highly creditable to his musical talent, but not sufficiently simplified "; the presentation to M. Francois Cramer, the eminent violinist, of an honorary member's ticket, "as a trifling mark of their (the Committee's) estimation of his talents," his courteous acceptance of the same, and announcement that he should feel happy in " lending the Society his assistance at any time his professional engagements might bring him to this part of the country "; the very large library of symphonies, overtures, etc., the Society accumulated; the nomination of "Master Mander," in 1829 as a member of the Society, and the numerous items in the financial statements of charges for candles and oil, gas not then having been introduced into the concert rooms. The following is the programme of the first concert which was given in Elliston's Rooms, January 25, 1827:—

Part I.

Symphony (in C.) Mozart.

Recitati Ve And Air, "The Moment of Victory" Rook.

Mr. Flavell.

I Violin, Mr. J. Marshall. c,,.., SOLO u. r. A ". »f D 1 SpAUNOLETTl.

I Pianoforte Accompaniment, Miss Bernard J

Glee (Three Voices), "The Witches" King.

Messrs. E. Enoch, V. G. Perry, and C. Marshall.

BALLAD, "The Bonnie Wee Wife," Miss Bernard

Overture, " Prometheus" Beethoven.

Part II.

Symphony (no. 3) Haydn.

Sono, "When Battle's Conch is sounding" Winter.

Round (Three Voices), "The Indian Drum" Bishop.

Messrs. E. Enoch, W. G. Perry, and C. Marshall.

Song, "When forced from dear Heht," Mr. Flavell Arne.

Overture, "Don Giovanni" Mo/.art.

TO COMMENCK AT HALF-1'AST SKVEN O'CLOCK PRECISELY.

CHAPTER XXIII. ONVERGENT developments in the Old Town contributed to the impetuous current of events in the New, where the speculative spirit of the building trade was concentrated on the Willes's estate, and was expending its energies in the formation of the Willes's Road, the erection of the bridge, and the construction of Newbold Terrace, Lansdowne Circus and Crescent, and other valuable properties in that locality. The most notable movements in the original parts of Leamington were the removal of the Wesleyans from Brunswick Street to their new chapel in Portland Street, the provision by the Catholics of a comfortable home for themselves in George Street, the improved position of Congregationalism in Clemens Street, and the erection of a new chapel in Mill Street.

In the amplitude of its accommodation, the grandeur of its front elevation, the perfection of its appointments, and the sumptuous wealth of art which distinguished each detail of its architecture and furniture, Copps's Royal Hotel surpassed every building of the kind which had been erected in Leamington. The Regent Hotel, the Upper Assembly Rooms, the Pump Rooms, and the Parthenon in Bath Street, compared but poorly by its side, and each and all were dwarfed by its majestic proportions. Every visitor admired it, and some declared that it was the finest hotel in the kingdom. As the result of the enterprise of one man, and of his confidence in the future greatness of the town, founded on an experience of some twelve years, it was one of the most remarkable events in the early history of Leamington. The property stood on the south side of High Street, and extended from the north-east corner of Clemens Street nearly to Court Street. Michael Copps, the spirited proprietor, succeeded Sinker at the Dog in 1814. He soon afterwards purchased Fisher's Balcony Boarding House, and in 1826 embarked in the erection of this celebrated building. The foundation stone was laid on November 13, by his daughter, Miss Maria Copps, a large number of the residents and visitors being present to witness the interesting ceremony. Miss Copps was "supported by several of her young female friends, and many other persons of the highest respectability in the town and neighbourhood." In the hollow of the stone were deposited numerous souvenirs of the period—silver coins of the reign; a medallion of George IV., struck in honour of his accession to the throne; a "Jubilean " medal, containing on the obverse side a representation of the head of the late Princess Charlotte; and several others of excellence and local interest, presented to Mr. and Mrs. Copps by Bisset, expressly for the purpose. The following description from the *Warwick Advertiser,* of June 23, 1827, worthily preserves the particulars of this, the most attractive structure in Leamington within the present century, which the railways in after years dissolved like the baseless fabric of a vision, leaving not a rack behind:—

"Among the most important additions which have been made to this class of Buildings since last season, that of the Royal Hotel decidedly holds the in st distinguished place. The front of this spacious edifice displays a most elegant specimen of Grecian architecture: and has been allowed by some of the best judges of the day to be unsurpassed by any similar building in the kingdom. It measures 111 feet in length, and with the old portion of the Hotel remaining, presents to the High Street a line of frontage upwards of 155 feet in extent. It comprises a centre and two wings; the whole being faced with Roman cement, in imitation of stone. Projecting ten feet from the former is a noble portico, supported by four fluted pillars of the Doric order of architecture; the pediment of which is surmounted by the Royal Arms, beautifully executed in stone. To the height of the principal story, the building is rusticated, and an highly ornamented balcony runs on a level with the second floor, from one extremity of the front to the other. Each wing is, or rather is intended to be, embellished (for one is not yet completed) with four fluted pilasters of the Corinthian order, which, springing from the level of the second floor, terminate at the top ol the third, and support an entablature extending the whole length of the building. The enrichments

Copps's Royal Hotel, High Street; foundation stone laid November 13, 1826; inaugural dinner,

June 21, 1827.

of the entablature, and the flowers, foliage, etc., in the capitals of the pilasters are executed in a manner at once expressive of the delicate richness so peculiar to the Order, and of the ability of the artist employed.

On the parapet above the attics, are to be placed over each wing, four ornamental vases, and the tablet now occupying the highest point in the centre of the building, and in which the name of the Hotel is inscribed, is to be surmounted by an highly enriched scroll. —The architect to whom Leamington is indebted for this splendid addition to her public edifices, is Mr. Robinson, of Brook Street, London. »

"The interior is exceedingly handsome, and the disposition of the principal apartments so judiciously contrived as to conceal that portion of the building appropriated to servants. The *coup d'aril,* on entering the house from the portico, is extremely fine. The Entrance Hall, 44 feet long by 14 wide, is decorated with sideboards, supported by Grecian ornaments in bronze, china erfume jars, antique vases, figures in plaster of Paris, and several bronze lamps of the tripod form, mounted on pedestals and elegantly worked. Fronting the entrance doors is a beautiful Window of coloured glass, to feet by 5, executed by James Freeth, of Birmingham. In the centre compartment, on a chaste fawn-coloured mosaic ground, are the Royal Arms richly emblazoned, and around the window is an elegant border, of a purple ground with gold scroll-work, embellished with medallions representing views of Warwick Castle, Stowe, Kenilworth Castle, Stoneigh Abbey, Guy's Cliffe, Coombe Abbey, and other distinguished edifices. At night a lamp is usually placed behind this "storied window, richly dight," which produces a very beautiful effect. The staircase is also lighted by two interior lights, placed in niches. Close to this window runs a geometrical staircase, comprising 21 steps, nearly 6 feet in width, and very easy of ascent; the handrails are composed of line mahogany, and the balusters are of bronze, beautifully wrought and of exquisite pattern.

"On the right of the Hall is the Public Dining Room, an apartment of noble dimensions, being upwards of 50 feet long by 24 wide, and capable of accommodating 150 persons with ease. The ceiling is supported by four handsome Ionic pillars, and as many pilasters of the same order of architecture embellish the walls. It is lighted by 6 windows, three of which command a view of the street, and the remainder at the opposite end, look into the garden, where

Various trees compose a chequered scene,
Glowing in gay diversities of green.

Above this apartment, is another of the same dimensions. This we understand is the Public Drawing Room. On the same floor are a number of Private Sitting Rooms, each of ample dimensions and lighted by two windows. The walls which are all battened and covered with canvas, consequently entirely free from damp, are enriched with Paper hangings of French manufacture, which in vivid beauty of colouring, approach nearer to oil painting than anything we have yet seen. The classical, allegorical and mythological subjects which are depicted on them cannot fail to be highly gratifying to the eye of taste. Among others we particularly noticed were various Passages from the History of Marc Anthony and Cleopatra, the Triumph of Bacchus and Ariadne, Telemachus and

Calypso, The Seasons, Luna and Aurora, Meleager and Atalanta, and a representation of the Grecian Games, Votive Sacrifices and ancient Nuptial and Funereal Rites. The bedrooms are all tastefully fitted up and comprise every necessary appendage. In this department we understand no less than 100 beds can be provided with ease. Some idea may be formed of the ample dimensions of this Hotel, when we state that on the second floor there are no less than thirty good sized bedrooms and a matted gallery, nearly 100 feet in length, which is terminated with a beautiful window of stained glass."

The house-warming dinner on June 21, 1827, was, like the hotel, on a scale of magnificence. Two hundred and fifty patrons filled the large drawing room, and the public dining room. Mr. John Tomes was in the principal chair, and the menu included "turtle, turbot and venison; an abundance of delightful dessert, and an excellent quality of wines." The feast was one of the jolliest of the time, and when the party broke up, after several hours of good fellowship, all danger of an inundation of wine in Michael Copps's cellars had been removed.

On Monday, April 14, 1828, after a lapse of more than ninety years, the Earl of Aylesford, as Lord of the Manor, revived the ancient Court Leet and Court Baron at the Bath Hotel. Since the previous Court, two local Acts had been passed— one in 1768 for enclosing the Commons, and the other in 1825 to appoint a Board of local Improvement Commissioners. In the former all the rights of the lordship of the Manor were preserved without diminution, and neither in the latter nor in any of the subsequent statutes, under which Leamington is governed, is there anything prejudicial to the ancient manorial dignity and privileges of the lordship. The Court Leet and Baron may, therefore, as we understand, be re-established at any time. At the Court, in 1828, upwards of nine hundred householders answered to their names and paid their fines, and several town officers were chosen and sworn.

A second Musical Association, entitled "The Leamington Choral Society," was started this year by Mr. F. Marshall, organist at the Episcopal Chapel. Its object was the study of sacred music, for which there were weekly rehearsals at the old Parish Church. Their first concert was given on Thursday, June 10, 1830, in the Episcopal Chapel, with oigan and band accompaniments.

The commencement of the advantage of having a local Press, the Borough owes to the year 1828, when *The Leamington Spa Courier* was founded on a durable and firm basis. In 1826, an effort was made, with equivocal success, to introduce a paper from Warwick, entitled *The Warwickshire Chronicle,* the first number of which was dated April 19. It contained a report of a social dinner at the Blenheim Hotel, Dr. Amos Middleton presiding, of which it was said that the superabundant supply of fish, flesh, and fowl, gave place to a delicious "desert." There was also an advertisement of a new paper, to be called *The Leamington Herald,* which never advanced beyond the prospectus stage. The first issue of the *Courier* was on August 9; it was printed in Wise Street, and was then the property of a company of shareholders. Mr. James Sharp was the editor, and with him was associated Mr. John Fairfax, one of the deacons at Clemens Street Chapel, and a man of great influence among the Nonconformists.

To meet the requirements of their increasing congregation, the Roman Catholics, in this year, erected in George Street, the building now belonging to the "Leamington Boys' Mission," as their first chapel. It was dedicated to St. Peter and was the work of John Russell, who was commended by Moncrieff for his consummate judgment in selecting as his model for the front elevation, the portico of that celebrated work of antiquity, the Ionic temple on the banks of Ilissus, near the city of Athens, built in honour of the mother of Christ. Merridew, who was not inferior to Moncrieff as an authority on ancient architecture, was of opinion that it was " after the order " of the portico, but not an

imitation. It was composed of a pediment supported by four Grecian Ionic columns, in a niche between the two centres of which stood a finely-executed composition statue of St. Peter, with the keys in his hand, after the antique by Clarke, of Birmingham. On the summit of the elevation was placed a large gilded cross of most elaborate workmanship, a plainer one being fitted on the east end of the roof. The sanctuary, a very beautiful work of art in the early Italian style, was from designs by Pugin, and the altar, which was composed of a peculiar stone, was the generous gift of Sir E. Mostyn, Bart. The superstructure, or tabernacle, was in every way deserving the blaze of artistic and costly material with which it was accompanied. It was made of the purest marble, and was supplied by Mr. Joseph Fletcher, for many years in business as a lapidary, at 13, Lower Parade. The inauguration took place on Thursday, Oct. 2, when High Mass was celebrated by Dr. Walsh, Bishop of the-Midland District, who preached standing before the altar, holding a golden crook, wearing his mitre, and robed in purple and gold. The serv ice was chanted by a choir, assisted by an orchestra. The first Priest was the Rev. Mr. Crosbie. One of the early organists was Signor Aspa, who for nearly forty years officiated at the Church in George Street, and at the present one in Dormer Place.

The following year saw the erection of a new place of worship in Mill Street by those who had withdrawn from that in Clemens Street. Our former reference to Clemens Street Chapel brought the history of its affairs down to 1828, when the secession of members and the formation of a new organisation took place. An effort was made by the trustees to preserve unity by submitting the question of the maintenance or rejection of a Liturgical form of worship to a general meeting of the

Mill STREET Chapel (now the Palish Church Men's Club) opened August 27, 1829.; known as Lady Huntingdon's Church; sold by auction March 31, 1887; purchased for Church purposes, 1807.

subscribers, but the Rev. Charles Bassano, who had been a student at Blackburn College, and was appointed minister by Mr. William Hunter, a powerful member of the church, refused to entertain the proposal. The trustees, however, convened the meeting, and the decision being in favour of Congregationalism, Mr. Bassano declined to remain in charge of the church, and, with his friends, adjourned to the premises in Clemens Street, formerly occupied by Mr. Brierley, printer, and now being part of the establishment of Messrs. Sleath, Ltd., cyclists, etc. There they formed the nucleus of a new cause, and held services according to their own views. Their action in this respect appears to have had the warm approval of the Rev. Rowland Hill, who, as we have seen, was a Liturgist to the core of his nature. He designated them "liberal minded Dissenters "; acknowledged the value of their support of his views, and on their appealing to him for assistance, he promptly responded. Thus encouraged, the Chapel in Mill Street was commenced in April, and opened on Thursday, August 27, 1829. In 1831, Mr. Hill purchased the property, completed the building, and furnished the Minister's house, at a total cost exceeding,£2,000, and to prevent his views being misunderstood at any future time, he caused a tablet to be placed under the gallery, with this inscription:—

"I, Rowland Hill, clerk, having purchased this Chapel for the express purpose of introducing the Liturgical Service of the Church of England (after the said Service was excluded from Clemens Street Chapel) do hereby declare it to be my Will that the said Service shall be adopted and continued herein, without any material alteration, so long as it forms a part of the Service of that Church—as now by law established."

Rowland Hill, *Proprietor.*

November 2, 1831.

edward Bates, *Minister.*

John Hitchman, *Surgeon.*

Charles Goring.

The vacancy in the pulpit at Clemens Street Chapel, caused by the refusal of Mr. Bassano to remain in the position of pastor, was filled by the Rev. Alfred Pope from the date of whose arrival in Leamington, a more prosperous era commenced for local Congregationalism. The immediate cause of his coming, which was as singular as any that ever occurred in the history of pastoral appointments, was thus described by the Rev. W. J. Woods, B.A., in the funeral sermon he preached in Spencer Street Chapel, on Sunday, January 6, 1878, in connection with Mr. Pope's death. After stating that he was studying at Highbury College for the ministry, Mr. Woods said: "His college term was near its expiration, when on a wintry Saturday, in February, 1828, he walked with a fellow-student as far as the Coach Office. His friend had been selected by Mr. Joshua Wilson to preach next day at Clemens Street Chapel, Leamington, but in the hurry of starting had forgotten his overcoat. To travel on the top of a coach for a hundred miles was not to be thought of in such weather. And although Mr. Pope would gladly have lent his 'Dreadnought' to his friend, they were of such unequal build that even this could not be done. In the emergency Mr. Pope agreed to take the journey in the stead of his companion; and thus he began with an act of brotherly love his long and kindly career in this town. Reaching Leamington he was met at the Bath Hotel by Mr. Frost and Mr. (afterwards the Hon.) John Fairfax, one of whom, in answer to his enquiry concerning the congregation he would be expected to address on the following day, said, 'We can depend upon five and there may be more.' On Sunday, February 10th, 1828, he preached for the first time in the old chapel at Clemens Street, to a congregation of twelve persons. He continued to preach on successive Sundays to increasing audiences, and on the 17th of July, in the same year, a little church was formed who received the Sacrament for the first time from the hands of Mr. Percy, of Warwick. About the same time Mr. Pope was requested to accept the A Colonial title, obtained by Mr. Fairfax after his emigration to Australia. pastoral oversight of the rapidly increasing church and congregation. He consented to do so for a period of twelve months; and then finding the sphere was one which was congenial to him, he signified his entire acceptance of the trust. He was ordained on the 28th April, 1829, Messrs. Jerard and Sibree of Coventry, Percy of Warwick, and Dr. Redford of Worcester, taking part in the service. In the same year he married Anna Maria, a daughter of Mr. Thomas Crosby, of Westbury, in Wiltshire." The after history of the church was one of continually increasing progress. The cause, which had dwindled into insignificance, began to show signs of expansion, until at length, in 1836, it was found necessary to erect the present chapel in Spencer Street to accommodate the greatly multiplied number of members of the church and congregation.

Cottage formerly standing at the corner of Mill Street, on the site of Brighton House.

We must not omit to mention in this place the name of a clergyman who made his first visit to Leamington in 1828; whose writings are to be found in every collection in the kingdom of standard authorities in ecclesiastical history and law, and who, besides erecting many churches for others, built up for himself a reputation and popularity, more than national, for learning, zeal and eloquence in the service of the Church of England. The Rev. Walter Farquhar Hook, MA.., Chaplain-in-Ordinary to George IV., and, at the time. Perpetual Curate of Moseley, preached two sermons on August 24—in the morning at the Episcopal Chapel, and in the afternoon at the Parish Church. Collections were made in aid of the National School, the amounts received after the services, being £30 2s. 8£d. and £1g 17s. jjd. respectively. Dean Hook, who was father of the Rev. Cecil Hook, B. A., the present Vicar of Leamington (1898), was the second preacher of eminence in the Parish Church after the enlargement in 1825.

An application in May, 1829, to the Postmaster-General for the establishment of a local Post Office, was courteously declined, but a promise was given that it should be reconsidered after some prospective developments in the service had taken effect.

A Royal visit in 1830, exceeding in local and national interest all that had as yet occurred, surrounds that year with a special halo. The tide of patrons from the commencement of the century had been one continuous flow, free from any recurrent ebbings—a wave without subsidence, crested with the sparkling hues of an everincreasing prosperity. In 1827 the town might almost have been described as swarming with coronets, and no sooner had the bells rung in one illustrious visitor than they had to commence a reverberating welcome for another. On April 5 of the year named, the Marchioness of Wellesley, acting on the advice of the leading physicians in Ireland, arrived at the Regent from the Vice-regal lodge, to take a course of the mineral waters, and on the 17th of the same month the Duke of Wellington, "the greatest captain of the age," reached that establishment on a visit to his noble sister-in-law. The Duke and Duchess of St. Albans were amongst the arrivals on June 3, and the following day the Earl and Countess of Bradford also joined the brilliant circle staying at the hotel. In August, the Duke and Duchess of Grafton hired a house in the Union Parade for the season; his Excellency the Dutch Ambassador was at the Royal, and in November, the Marchioness of Bute was occupying a residence in Charlotte Street, which has been known ever since as Bute House. Such marks as these of public favour were continued through the years 1828 and 1829. But the most illustrious of all visitors came in August, 1830. On Monday, the 2nd of that month, a party of travellers set out from the King's Palace, Kensington, on a journey to Malvern. There were four carriages in all, the occupants being H.R.H. the Duchess of Kent, and her daughter, H.R.H. the Princess Victoria; Lady Catherine Jenkinson, the Baroness Lehzen, Sir John Conway, and a numerous suite. Reaching Stratford-on-Avon on the following day, a detour was made

for Leamington, the fame of whose waters, we may rest assured, had been a familiar topic in Court circles since Dr. Weatherhead presented George IV., in 1820, with a copy of his Analysis. At about half-past six o'clock in the evening they arrived in Leamington, and proceeded through a dense mass of delighted spectators to the Regent Hotel. Three expensive triumphal arches, richly ornamented with evergreens and surmounted by the Crown, were erected near the hotel, which was most effectively illuminated during the evening. The welcome by the inhabitants was a right loyal one, and that the Princess, who was described as "a very interesting child between eleven and twelve years of age," warmly appreciated the devotion of her future subjects was evidenced by her appearance several times at the windows with smiles, bows, and other signs of gratification. The next day the party resumed their journey to Malvern.

About the time of this memorable visit, the Baptists appeared as an organization, and assumed what, though small, was a prominent and dignified position. We first meet with them in 1828, but it was not until 1829 or 1830 that they had regular stated services of their own and assembled for worship in a chapel. This was in Grove Place — not Grove Street, as erroneously stated in one of the "Guides." From the room in Grove Place, which is now connected with St. John's Church, they removed to the chapel in Brunswick Street, vacated by the Wesleyans in 1825, and in 1830, requiring larger accommodation, they migrated to Guy Street, in the New Town, where John Toone had built for them a new chapel. It was at this period that the Rev. George Cole settled among them and was elected their first pastor. Originally, he was a Wesleyan, but, changing his views respecting infant and adult baptism, he joined the Baptists, and was ordained to the ministry at King's Lynn, from whence he came to Leamington. He was never at college, and probably was no "Latiner," but he was a fluent, acceptable, and successful preacher, and a great force in

moulding those circumstances which led to the building of the chapel in Warwick Street. His efforts in this direction, it is interesting to learn, were ably supported by the Rev. James Phillipo Mursell, Baptist minister at Leicester, and father of the Rev. Arthur Mursell, the popular lecturer and preacher. The elder Mr. Mursell was one of the original trustees of the church, and always manifested a warm interest in its prosperity. Though services had been held in Grove Place, Brunswick Street, and Guy Street, two years elapsed before a church, consisting of pastor, officers, and members, was formed. At a meeting held on November 28, 1830, steps were taken for the regular constitution of a society in accordance with the principles of the denomination. Two years afterwards (October 14, 1832) the ordinance of adult baptism by immersion was administered for the first time in Leamington. The service was held at half-past seven in the morning; the Rev. George Cole was the officiating minister, and of the six candidates thus admitted to Church membership one was Mr. Richard Greet, father of the late Mr. John Greet, of 7, Church Terrace. Towards the close of the year a movement was commenced for erecting a more commodious place of worship, and ultimately the site of the present chapel was selected. It was a kitchen garden, owned and occupied by Squire Hooton, a member of the Parish Committee, and was bounded by a wall extending along Warwick Street to the corner where the Metropolitan Bank stands, and a considerable distance down the Parade and Satchwell Street. The new edifice was built from designs furnished by W. Thomas, an architect with an extensive business, who planned Lansdowne Circus, notable for its healthy situation, its restful seclusion, and its sylvan aspect; of which Nathaniel Hawthorne, himself once a resident there, happily remarks in "Our Old Home," "There is a small nest of a place... Lansdowne Circus... one of the cosiest nooks in England, or in the world." He also designed Lansdowne Crescent, whose bold and graceful sweep may be seen from the top of the Parade, and among other of the principal buildings of the new town most of the villas on the west side of Brandon Parade, in the architecture of which are combined something of the grandeur and strength of the Grecian and Tudor Gothic styles. The new chapel, erected by John Toone, was opened in 1833. Of the character of the structure we have found no description beyond the statement that the style was elegant and Gothic. The second minister was the Rev. D. J. East, of Stepney College, who was ordained to the pastorate on August ib, 1837. He resigned in 1839, and was succeeded by the Rev. Octavius Winslow, "late of New York; " afterwards Doctor of Divinity, and celebrated both as a preacher and an author. He commenced his ministerial labours on the second Sunday in June of that year.

At a disadvantage, when compared with the many other public buildings which preceded and followed its erection, the old Town Hall has a history permeated with the varied traditions of the several branches of public life in Leamington. The time of the transfer of the seat of local government from Clemens Street to High Street, in the sequence of events, demands a place. Granting that the date is chiefly of chronological value, when we reflect that the Town Hall was the first building provided by the Commissioners, and also that it has been the Parliament House of every administrative body that has exercised authority and control in Leamington, its claims will appear by no means unreasonable. It was built in 1831, at a cost of £2,000, and Leamington then supporting its own poor, the second of the two poor-houses it has had was erected near it in Court Street, by Edward Treadgold, at an expenditure of £650. For a short time previous to the building of the Hall, Gloucester Cottage, situated at the south-east corner of the walk through the Churchyard, was occupied by the Commissioners, the Parish Committee, and the Justices, for holding therein the Petty Sessions. As the Parish Committee assembled in the

Apollo Rooms for the last time on March 22, 1830, and in the Town Hall for the first time on June, 27, 1831, the arrangements for the meetings in Gloucester Cottage could have been only of a temporary character.

CHAPTER XXIV. ALEIDOSCOPIC, would not be an inappropriate term to apply to that constant change, and variety of form, colour and life, exhibited by Leamington in every phase of its early career. From 1830 to 1840, there were the same impulses of energy and public spirit as in the period we have just reviewed, but they occasionally branched out into new paths, and produced fresh results.

The erection of the Warneford Hospital in 1832 was a much-needed novel departure in the cause of local charity. The habitation of the old Hospital and Dispensary in Regent Street had long proved unsuited for the beneficial work there carried on for the benefit of the poor. How to provide funds was also a source of constant anxiety. The annual average income was £150; the expenditure ranged from £300 to £400. Such relief from pecuniary pressure as was obtained from time to time bv bazaars and large donations proving only temporary, the adoption of a new scheme was discussed at a meeting of the Governors, on May 12, 1829. On the proposition of Dr. Loudon, it was decided to introduce the provident system of contributions, originated by Mr. Smith, of Southam, and advocated by him with success throughout the Midland Counties The substantial change made, related to the recipients who previously participated in the benefits of the Charity gratuitously. By the new arrangements a payment of a weekly sum, equal to 6s. 6d. a year, constituted membership, with the right to choose any resident medical man to attend in sickness. After defraying all expenses the balance was divided among the practitioners according to the number of cases each had attended. Besides the adoption of this system, there was also a movement in progress for building a more commodious Hospital, the origin of which was in 1828. In addition to being too small, the premises

in Regent Street were inconveniently situated and lacked provision for future enlargements. The Building Committee, appointed in 1828, were joined in 1830 by the Rev. Dr. Warneford, Rector of Bourtonon-the-Hill, Gloucestershire; a Prince of Philanthropists, who in the course of his life dispensed about £200,000 of his wealth in support of various charities, and to whose liberality are largely owing the splendid proportions and the character of the present Warneford Hospital. There were three sites under consideration—one immediately adjoining the old Town Hall in High Street, another in the Kenilworth Road, the third being that on which the Hospital stands. An acre of ground was purchased from the Earl of Aylesford, at a cost of £boo, and the foundation stone laid on April 10, 1832, by the Hon. Charles Bertie Percy, the President of the Dispensary. The ceremony was performed with Masonic Honours, the members of the Guy's Lodge, and numerous others of the Brethren from various Lodges in the Warwickshire Province, being present in their attractive official plumage. Bisset, an artistic and skilful medallist, presented two medals, which, with three gold, eight silver, and three copper coins, were placed in a box and deposited in the stone, the inscription being as follows:—" This, the first stone of the Leamington Hospital, was laid by the Hon. Charles Bertie Percy, April 10, 1832." Towards the cost Dr. Warneford and his sister were munificent donors, and as a record of their generosity the new building was named "The Warneford Hospital." While the works were being carried on George Christopher Liebenrood was the secretary. He was the first schoolmaster at the National School, established at the Parsonage House, Church Street, in 1822, and afterwards was proprietor of the *Leamington Courier.* In 1833, we find Dr. Warneford staying at the Stoneleigh Hotel, frequently visiting the works in the Radford Road, and aiding the Committee with his constant supervision and advice. Early in 1834 the central block was finished, and two out of the six wards were opened for the reception of patients. The beginning thus made stimulated local effort to remove a debt of £1,000 then remaining on the building, and in September a bazaar was held, from which a profit of £400 was realised. Amongst those who interested themselves in bringing about this exceedingly satisfactory result were the Misses Manners-Sutton, daughters of the late Archbishop of Canterbury, and sisters of the Speaker of the House of Commons. The reduction of the debt, and the prospect of its extinction at an early date, produced a general feeling that some further recognition should be made of Dr. Warneford's liberality and service to the institution. He was accordingly entertained at two complimentary dinners, one given at the Regent Hotel by the nobility and gentry, of whom there were between seventy and eighty present, and the other by the tradesmen, at the Bedford, about the same number being in attendance. The Leamington Charitable Bathing Institution was allied to the old Infirmary, but was independent in its origin and management. In 1835 it was wisely amalgamated with the Hospital, and Mr. John Hitchman, the principal manager, was added to the Hospital Staff under the title of " surgeon-elect." Mainly through the exertions of Di. Jephson, two additional wards were furnished and opened, after which no material change ensued during the following twenty years.

Paganini, the unrivalled violinist, of whom it has been remarked that "none but himself could be his parallel," exhibited his talents in the Royal Assembly Rooms, on August 10, 1833, to an audience of about five hundred, consisting of the principal families in Leamington and the county. His most admired performance was the *Sonata Militaire,* played entirely on the fourth string. The price of the tickets was 7s. 6d., and his fee *£n.o.* He was again at the Assembly Rooms on October 22, but Dr. Warneford gave ji, 2,050, and Miss Warneford, his sister, £500 towards the building fund; various other donations by him to the same object

amounted to an additional sum of £1,000. In his Will, he bequeathed £,xo. ooo, in trust, for the benefit of the Hospital.

the novelty had worn away, and there were only about two hundred and thirty present. Still, he was heard " with intense delight," especially in his rendering of *S/. Patrick's Day.*

A proposal, in 1833, to amalgamate Leamington and Warwick for Parliamentary electoral purposes, elicited an indignant protest in which the town was more nearly unanimous than has generally been found to be the case in regard to other questions. The objections to the projected union, formulated and adopted by resolution at a public meeting, in the Town Hall, on May 29, were that it " would deprive Leamington in a great degree of the county vote, and make this peaceful place a partaker of the feuds, animosities, and dissensions which time has matured in the borough of Warwick." The Bill for thus uniting the two towns was thrown out by the House of Lords in August, 1834, in celebration of which the bells of the Parish Church were rung.

Music, represented in the two Societies by a combination of professional and amateur talent, won its first honours in 1834, by an invitation to join the Birmingham Musical Festival. Both the Philharmonic and the Choral had rendered excellent service in providing a new variety of harmony which made it no longer indispensably necessary in order to enjoy a musical treat, to listen to the larks of song, trilling and warbling sky-high in the gamut, or a basso profundo, descending many fathoms into the depths of the register, and electrifying his audience with distant subterranean murmurs. The names of the local musicians who assisted in the Festival of 1834 we have not obtained, but the requisition was repeated in 1837, and the following formed the contingent from the Spa at the Festival of that year:—W. Meyrick (violin), J. Elston and J. Hewett (violas), H. T. Elliston (double-bass). Semi-chorus: treble, Miss J. Hewett (afterwards Mrs. N. Merridew); counter-tenor, F. Marshall.

Chorus: trebles, Miss Cox, Master Hewett, and Miss Russell (afterwards Mrs. Archer); counter-tenor, T. Archer; tenors, J. Beck, W. Green, and — Sharp; basses, J. Brown, R. Croydon, and W. Reading.

In 1834 was founded the present Leamington Gas Company, with a capital of £20,000, in 1,000 shares of £20. The plant in Leamington, of the Warwick Gas Company, was purchased, and the works in the Tachbrook Road commenced.

The first bank entitled to be regarded as of local origin, was established in 1834, under influential patronage, and had for its name, "The Warwick and Leamington Bank." Its nominal capital was £250,000 in 11,000 shares of £25. At a meeting of the subscribers and members of the Provisional Committee, on June 5, Dr. Jephson presiding, it was decided to commence banking operations on July r. Messrs. John Russell and William Thompson were appointed joint managers, and it was stated that arrangements had been made for the purchase and transfer of the Warwick and Leamington Bank of Messrs. Tomes and Russell. The premises, where the new institution first opened its doors, were those at the corner of Regent Street and Parade, belonging to Lloyds Bank, Ltd., and it is from this early germ that Lloyds has always been known as the Old Bank.

The second was started in March, 1835, with a nominal capital of £200,000, in 10,000 shares of £20. It was called the "Leamington Bank." Mr. Ransford was appointed Manager, and the doors were opened for business, for the first time, on May 12, in premises in the Lower Parade. It failed about a year after, and the assets are believed to have been purchased by the Old Bank.

The Leamington Priors and Warwickshire Bank was also commenced in 1835. It acquired the branch Bank, in Bath Street, of Messrs. Tomes and Russell, and began business there. Mr. John Russell, the first manager, was succeeded, in 1843, by MrT. H. Thorne, who filled the post till 1887.

The course of events at the Parish

Church since 1825 are thus briefly detailed by Merridew (1837):—"In 1829 a third enlargement was made by the Churchwardens, who erected pews at the south end capable of accommodating 170 persons. The architectural style of this enlargement is equal to the best portion of the ancient edifice. Mr. Russell, of Wise Street, who was the architect, presented the handsomely painted window, at the north end of the church, containing the arms of the Earl of Aylesford, the Lord of the Manor, Edward Willes, Esq., Matthew Wise, Esq. , Rev. H. Wise, of Offchurch, and the Rev. Robert Downes, vicar. In 1832 a further alteration took place by the present vicar, who added 200 free sittings, and the fifth enlargement was also made by the vicar, in 1834, when 480 sittings were added on the east side, half of which are free seats."

The temperance movement in Leamington began on November 20, 1835, with a lecture in the Pump Room by Mr. Chapman, of Birmingham, "a gentleman who has sacrificed much time and property in the service of Temperance Societies." This was followed by a public meeting on January 7, 1836, in the Upper Assembly Rooms, to found a Society. Sir John Mordaunt, Bart., was in the chair; the speakers were the Rev. A. B. Campbell, of the new Episcopal Chapel; the Rev. John Angell James, of Birmingham; and Mr. W. Mellor, "a most respectable Wesleyan Methodist local preacher." The Bishop and the Earl of Denbigh were in the list of patrons. A second public meeting was held in March in the National School, Kenilworth Street, when there was a disturbance, in the course of which the stove and the piping were argued out of their places, and the two camps retired from the room in what military critics would not call good order, and perhaps not in quite the best of tempers. The new Society held weekly meetings in the building in Guy Street, previously occupied by the Baptists, and in five years about seven hundred members were enrolled. From the time they went into possession, it became known as the Temperance Room.

The Improvement Commissioners, in May, directed their attention to the state of the river, and the inconvenience caused by the narrow approach to the bridge on the south side. At a public meeting in the Town Hall, June 13, their decision to clean out the one and widen the other was approved, and a public subscription for £1,500 started towards the 5,500 required. The contract, given to William (keen, was to "widen the road at the northernmost end of Bath Street, take down part of the present bridge, widen and improve the same, excavate certain parts of the bed of the river, and make and lay new culvert and sewers." The road was widened twenty-nine feet, and on October 6, 1837, Mr. Hitchman laid the first stone of Victoria Terrace, an improvement which followed the action of the Commisioners in regard to the bridge, the road, and the river.

On February 29, 1836, was formed The Temple of Peace Lodge (1059) of the Manchester Unity Order of Odd Fellows. No reliable materials for compiling a history of the Friendly Societies of Leamington are available from 1777, the time of Satchwell's Fountain of Hospitality, until the dawn of the new era of sound insurance principles this Lodge introduced. But it must not be supposed that Ben Satchwell's teachings had been wasted, or that the desire of the labourers to provide something for the rainy days of affliction had been extinguished by the failure of his Society. As a matter of fact it is not clearly established that it did fail, for very early in the century there were several independent Friendly Societies, holding their meetings at the Golden Lion, the Angel, Oak, and Fox and Vivian, and some one or other of these may have been a late development of Satchwell's Club. It is not, however, our purpose to enquire into the history of his scheme. What is exceedingly more important is the establishment of a movement on a satisfactory footing. The Temple of Peace Lodge is the oldest of the affiliated Societies in Leamington, and was the first to adopt the federative plan which has given the Odd Fellows, the Ancient Order of

Foresters, the Hearts of Oak, and other similarly constructed Associations, solidity and an irresistible strength against the winds of misfortune. It was started at the Rose and Crown, Kenilworth Street, where the meetings continue to be held. To those who lightly value the work of such societies as this, and especially the ratepayers who reap in reduced poor rates an annual harvest of benefits, it may be useful to mention that, in sixty years, the Lodge has enrolled nine hundred and sixty members, and received in contributions £24,761. Of this it has paid back to its members £19,818 in benefits, and has £4,943 securely invested, at an average rate of 4J per cent. interest. Facts like these require no argument to enforce the utility of Lodges such as The Temple of Peace.

Affairs at Clemens Street Chapel having been remarkably prosperous since the choice of Mr. Pope as minister in 1829, in 1835 it was found necessary to build a larger and more central place of worship. The choice of a site lay between a plot of land in Dormer Place, then a fashionable resort and known as the Promenade, and the present situation in Spencer Street, at the time unmade and un-named, and extending from Bath Street only as far as the Lower Avenue, where a rustic gate thrown across the way stopped all further progress in the direction of what is now the Avenue Road. All the Those statistics relate to the close of the financial year, 18y6.

land beyond was pasture, the principal part being the Avenue Field, so-called on account of the beautiful avenue of elms, which left the Old Warwick Road and proceeded along where the bridge now crosses the two lines of railways, and passing round in front of the old Manor House, returned along the Lower Avenue to the Warwick Road, opposite the bottom of Tachbrook Road. The view from the Manor House was over an expanse of mead adorned with vestment of perpetual green and unbroken by any other obstruction than those of trees which flourished in the locality in great abundance. On July 21, 1836, Spencer Street Congregational Chapel, one of the most popular and influential centres of Independency in the Midlands, was opened by two services, at which the Rev. John Angell James, of Birmingham, and the Rev. James Parsons, of York, were the preachers. As the details of the provision made by the original edifice are of interest in connection with the history of the cause, we quote the following report from Merridew's *Leamington Chronicle* of July 21, 1836:—

"Having promised some account of the Independent Chapel, we now perform the pleasing task, and feel great satisfaction in being enabled to lay before our readers a general description of this edifice. To compliment our respected townsman, Mr. Russell, on the architectural taste and skill displayed, would be superfluous, but we must be permitted to congratulate the inhabitants of Leamington on the acquisition of another public building, simple, yet elegant, in design, and from its situation forming a great ornament to this town. Nor can we here omit to notice the classic effect imparted by the fine group of trees on the West side, which we sincerely hope may long remain as graceful appendages to this structure. We could have wished that the houses on the East side of the Chapel had been kept back to range with the Facade so as to give full effect to the projection of the Portico. The South front consists of a Portico of four Ionic Columns, placed on a platform of two steps, each column standing on a deep plinth. To our eye these columns are slender in proportion, but this probably contiibutes to the graceful effect produced. The Cornice is continued along the wings, which are each lighted by one long circular-headed window, the whole being surmounted by a balustrade concealing the roof. The flank elevation comprises the entrances to the staircases, and the six windows on the side are simply divided by pilasters. A central vestibule affords access, on either side, to the body of the Chapel, or to the staircases which are conveniently placed in the wings. The body of the Chapel is lofty, and exceedingly well-proportioned. It contains on the ground floor, side aisles and a central body of pewing, capable of accommodating 600 persons. A gallery, supported by light enriched columns, runs round the East, South, and West sides of the Chapel, which will contain 470 persons, and above this on the South side, a children's gallery is admirably contrived, which will hold 200 children, all in the full view of the minister. The pulpit, of an octagonal form, enriched at the angles with columns, is centrally placed at the North end of the Chapel, having behind it three slender ciicular-headed windows, which are filled with stained glass. The design comprises a running oak leaf as a border, with rosettes down the centre of each window. The Chapel is lighted by 12 windows, separated by pilasters surmounted by a cornice having a large single leafed enrichment next the ceiling. This is divided into thirty panels, formed by flat sinkings, and enriched with twelve rosettes. The interior of the Chapel has an exceedingly chaste and elegant appearance. There is a commodious vestry room with school mistress's room below, and under the Chapel is a capacious school. There are also catacombs for burial. We conclude our description with a hope that the highly esteemed pastor may long continue to instruct his congregation in the edifice thus happily completed by his and their exertions."

The collections at the opening amounted to *£170,* and on the following Sunday the inaugural services were continued, the Rev. James Parsons preaching in the morning and evening, and the Rev. J. W. Percy, of Warwick, in the afternoon. On each occasion the congregation filled all parts of the chapel, and in the evening it was estimated there were fifteen hundred persons present, while several hundreds crowded the doors unable to find even standing room. The total collections in the two days reached the sum of *£301.*

These interesting proceedings at Spencer Street Chapel were immediately followed by the opening of another place of worship. On Milverton Hill, overlooking the whole of Leamington, and commanding a series of magnificent views, in which Guy's Cliffe, Warwick Castle and Church, and Newbold Hills, were conspicuous objects, the Episcopal Chapel for Milverton was drawing near completion at the time of the assembling of the first congregation within the walls of the new Independent Chapel. As an addition to the ancient Parish Church of St. James's, at Old Milverton, it was designed to accommodate that portion of the Leamington population which was just beginning to flow over the boundary into Milverton parish. At the time of building, its situation was isolated compared with the position it occupied a few years later on, when the surrounding villas and houses were numbered by hundreds, and the population by thousands. The site was that on which have since been built the Milverton Hill villas. The cost was borne by the Earl of Warwick, the owner of a large portion of the land in this locality; the Rev. Alexander B. Campbell, the first incumbent, and a number of friends who contributed liberally to the building fund. Mr. J. S. Jackson, a local architect and surveyor, prepared the designs. The opening service was held on August 5, 1836, and the preacher was the Venerable Archdeacon Spooner. Subjoined is the description published by the *Warwick Advertiser* on June 11 of that year:—

"We mentioned in our last paper that this new chapel was nearly ready for opening. This week we are enabled to lay before our readers the particulars of the building. The Grecian architecture has been adopted, and although some anomalies are visible, they for the most part result from its adaption to existing circumstances. The following are its dimensions:—Extreme length, including portico and altar end, 115 feet; extreme width, 54 feet; area of chapel, exclusive of altar, 72 feet by 50 feet; and height, 26 feet. The chapel affords accommodation for about 650 perons, including the children in the gallery, and the free sittings on the ground floor. The entrance front has a portico of four Doric columns, 25 feet high and 4 feet in diameter. Two wings are attached to this portico, forming the side entrances, and containing a staircase to the organ and children's gallery. The regular entablature and pediment of the portico are surmounted by a circular ball tower, 15 feet 6 inches in diameter, surrounded by pilasters, carrying an entablature and flat dome, terminated by a cross; the whole height from the floor of the portico to the top of the cross is 70 feet. The flank walls of the chapel are plain, and will be much concealed from view by the houses to be built on either side. A small vestry room is attached to the western side of the altar. From the centre of the portico, a square vestibule is entered, communicating with the side doors opening into the chapel. The interior is divided into side aisles, with a centre aisle to a portion of the seats commencing from the altar end. It is lighted by four windows on either side, plain in character, and the altar end (from the suggestion of the Incumbent, the Rev. A. B. Campbell), is circular in form, with a dome terminated by a concealed top light. The pulpit is placed at the back of this circular end, and the reading-desk in the minister's pew on the light of the altar; on the left side, a pew is appropriated to the Earl of Warwick. At the opposite extremity are the children's and organ gallery, the latter central and projecting sufficiently for the reception of a fine organ now preparing by Messrs. Hill, of London. The chapel will be heated by hot air flues, will have proper ventilation, and the pews are variously and commodiously arranged as to the number of sittings. The clerk's desk at the opposite extreme from the pulpit is a novel feature, and the free seats are placed in front of it under the gallery. Plainness, simplicity, and, it may not perhaps be presumption to add, neatness, have been attempted throughout the design. In the interior, an enriched cornice is connected with the ceiling by a frame moulding, containing a running enrichment, with the addition of pateras, or rosettes, at intervals, and three large centre flowers for chandeliers. The domical ceiling of the altar is divided into five long panels, and the circular altar and altar piece are in a similar manner decorated with

pilasters and panels. In those of the altar piece will be contained the Creed, Lord's Prayer, and Commandments."

The year 1836 was the age of Mechanics' Institutions, and Leamington was not slow in adopting the new scheme. At a public meeting in the Royal Assembly Rooms, on March 23, Sir Eardley Wilmot presiding, the Mechanics' Institute of early Leamington was opened. During the first quarter a hundred and thirty members were enrolled, and a library established, containing two hundred volumes. The meetings were held at the Assembly Rooms every evening, from nine till ten o'clock. Daily and weekly newspapers, and weekly and monthly periodicals, were supplied for the use of the members. The President was Chandos Leigh, Esq.; Chairman of the Committee, Dr. Lloyd; Mr. A. S. Field was its honorary Secretary; and Mr. James Bird filled the office of Treasurer. The institution had a long and prosperous existence, and introduced the system of popular lectures. Compared with modern agencies of the same kind, its work was limited, but in the ancestry of the Philosophical Society and the Free Library, it occupies the first position.

There were grand doings on May 24, 1837, when the Princess Victoria, being eighteen years of age, attained her legal majority. That year she was emphatically " the Queen of the May" in all England, and in no place more so than in Leamington. At an early hour, the bells began clanging their loyalty, and the inhabitants turned out in their thousands. A procession of residents, clubs and schools, a mile in length, marched through the streets, the Warwickshire Yeomanry band giving them a good start with a version ot the National Anthem, played in splendid style and with plenty of-wind. For the time being the town had the appearance of fairyland. Bells and band made merry music throughout the day, which was a general holiday; flowers, and evergreens decorated the balconies; flags and banners were suspended from many of the windows, and the beautiful Victorian medals, struck in honour of the event,

from the necks or waists of the children. Scarcely a resident appeared in the streets without a white rosette, scarf and medal. All the school girls wore bonnets and tippets of the same style and pattern (presents from the promoters of the festivities), which made them look so much alike that their parents, after dining extensively, may easily have found some difficulty in sorting out their own at the close of the day. Two thousand and fifty of the working classes were entertained at dinner in "Mr. Willes's grounds" (the Jephson Gardens), the fare consisting of roast and boiled beef and plum pudding, with one quart of ale for each man, and one pint for each woman. The principal toast was proposed by Dr. Jephson—"The Princess Victoria, and may she have many happy returns of the day, and be a source of great happiness to her country," a twofold hope which has been realised to a far greater extent than any one at that period could have anticipated. In the afternoon, one thousand two hundred children were provided with tea, and while at their repast, a Montgolfier balloon, the production of Mr. S. Gore and Mr. J. Hordern, junior, watchmaker, Clemens Street, ascended from a field at the back of Victoria Terrace, and floated over the grounds. The event was also the subject of an address of congratulation on the part of the town, which Lord Eastnor, the Hon. Captain Somerville, and Dr. Jephson, were appointed a deputation to present. Equally patriotic but more magnificent, was the demonstration on June 28, of the following year, the date of her Majesty's coronation. The gracious concession of the Queen in 1838, entitling Leamington to the prefix of " Royal," caused much rejoicing in the town. At the levee on Wednesday, July 18, a deputation, composed of Lord Eastnor, Major Hawkes, M.C. , and Mr. John Hampden, attended and presented an address expressing loyal sentiments from the inhabitants of Leamington Priors, on her accession and coronation. This, we are informed, " was most graciously received," and the two last named gentlemen had the honour of being formally presented. The application for the new dignity was made by Major Hawkes on the 3rd, in a letter addressed to Lord Melbourne, to which the following reply was received:—

"Umbttcball, I9tb July, 1838.

Sir, Discount Melbourne bavmg placed tn mp banbs 'tbe Xetter wbicb pou aobresseo to bun on tbe 3co instant, 3 bave bao tbe "Ibonor of submitting to *TLbe*

Queen tbe respectful IRequest of tbe Sn-babitants of

Xeamtngton tbat tbeg map be permittee to call tbat

Spa in future tbe IRogal Xeamington Spa: Sub 3 am to inform sou tbat 1ber /lbajestg bas been graciously pleaseb to acceoe to tbe "IRequest of tbe Jnbabi-tants of Xeamtngton.

3 bave tbe bonor to be,

Sir

H)our ©bebtent Servant, ADaJor Dawhes, flb.C,

Xeamtngton Spa.

Leamington was nearly beside itself with joy on receipt of the news that the Queen had granted its request. Hoarse with its loyal shoutings at the coming of age and the coronation of her Majesty, it still had power enough to make the welkin ring with its present jubilation for itself. The deputation, highly pleased with the success of their mission, returned on the 24th, and reached the town shortly before ten o'clock in the evening. A crowd, brimming over with enthusiasm, awaited their arrival at the old Town Hall, for whose benefit rockets were sent up as soon as the approach of the embassy was seen in the Radford Road. At the Town Hall they were greeted with cheers, and the horses having been taken from the carriage, Major Hawkes and Mr. Hampden delivered congratulatory speeches from the steps, the former stating that the privilege of styling a town " Royal" was one possessed by no other place in the United Kingdom. They then re-entered their carriage, which was drawn by the crowd to the Regent Hotel, the cheering rolling along the streets like volleys of thunder. From the balcony at the south end they again addressed some thousands, both

felicitating the town on its good fortune in securing a royal favour, unique in history. Mr. Hampden's ancestor was John Hampden, who, in the Civil War, fell at Chalgrove in a skirmish with the troops of the fiery Prince Rupert, and of whom Macaulay says that his history, more particularly from the year 1 40 to his death, is the history of England. His descendant resided in Clarence Terrace, was one of the most popular men in Leamington in his time, and during his residence here was foremost in all movements for the good of the town.

In 1839, Leamington was again sunning itself in the smiles of Royalty, the visitor being the Dowager Queen Adelaide, then a guest of the Earl and Countess of Warwick. Complying with the loyal request of the inhabitants to favour the Spa with her presence, she left Warwick Castle shortly before two o'clock on Monday, November 4, with her suite and a retinue of the County nobility and gentry. She rode in an open barouche, drawn by four horses, preceded by two outriders, and with her were the Countesses of Warwick and Denbigh, and Lady Clinton. On reaching Myton Toll-gate they were met by a local Committee, with wands, white gloves and rosettes, and some hundreds of residents on horseback, in carriages, and on foot. These accompanied her Majesty into the town, which was beautifully decorated for the occasion. "The appearance of Bath Street was astonishingly splendid," and on entering it "every carriage became stationary for a few moments, that its inmates might enjoy the sudden effect of the brilliant spectacle." At the Royal Pump Room a halt was made, and her Majesty alighting was conducted by the Earl of Warwick into the building, where Major Hopkins, K.H., Drs. Luard and Jephson, were introduced. After a short stay she resumed her progress up the town, as far as the Clarendon Hotel. Pleased as she had been with all she had seen, "the most interesting spectacle of the day was presented to her view in the assemblage of all the school children of every denomination, arranged under their respective banners on a platform," in front

of the Episcopal Chapel. "A more gratifying sight, as the Queen Dowager herself acknowledged to the Rev. Mr. Craig, who was introduced, by special command, to her Majesty, could not possibly have been afforded. The tender voices of more than fifteen hundred of these young loyalists uniting in acclamation of welcome, and afterwards in a hymn, produced an effect beyond description: Her Majesty, with tears in her eyes, pronounced the scene to be equally exhilarating and affecting." Shortly afterwards, she returned to Warwick with the happiest memories of Royal Leamington Spa.

With the erection of St. Mary's Church in 1839, began the process of disintegration which in the course of time has contracted the original parish of All Saints to less than half its ancient dimensions. When built, it had to encounter some opposition, but the promoters of the project triumphed over every difficulty, and, as will be seen from the details given below of the district assigned to it, obtained advantages of a most important character. Like the Episcopal Chapel on Milverton Hill, it stood alone in the fields. This circumstance was made the groundwork of the first objection to the building. If, it was argued, the Church Building Commissioners had sent down their surveyor to have named a place for an additional church, he never would have selected a site so remote from the thickly populated parts of the town. The greater contest, however, was over the district, to the grant of which there was a feeling in the vestry, strongly antagonistic; and when Mr. John Cullis was re-elected Parish Churchwarden in 184.0, it was mentioned as one of his special qualifications that he "would fight for every inch of ground " forming the territorial inheritance of the old parish of All Saints. Such force as these arguments might have had at the time, was speedily abated, for in a few years, houses, streets and terraces spread over the meadows, and the Church, from being the most conspicuous object in the landscape, was almost concealed from view by costly villas and other residences.

With scarcely any ceremony, the work was commenced on October 5, 1838, by the laying of a memorial stone, in the presence of a considerable number of friends. It was inscribed: "St. Mary's Church. First stone laid by John Walter Sherer, A.d. 1838, in the second year of the Reign of Queen Victoria. 'Other foundation can no man lay than that is laid, which is Jesus Christ.' 1 st Corinthians, 3rd chapter, 11th verse." Mr. Sherer, who was assisted by the Rev. Dr. Marsh and Mr. Edwin Woodhouse, was an intimate friend of the former, shared his views, and reciprocated his enthusiasm. He had been Accountant General, and was brother-in-law to Bishop Corrie. The expense of the edifice was defrayed by the Rev. Dr. W. Marsh, Official of the Peculiar of Bridgnorth, and Rector of St. Thomas's, Birmingham, and a number of friends. Failing health and impaired eyesight compelling him to resign the arduous parochial duties inseparably connected with the rectorship he held at Birmingham, he sought a sphere of labour where the work would be lighter and more proportioned to his strength. The opening services and the consecration took place on Saturday, Julv 27, 1839, the sermon being preached by him, and Bishop Ryder, then the Diocesan, consecrating the building. Dr. Marsh settled in Leamington the same month, and took up his residence at Lansdowne House, but he did not at once enter upon the duties at St. Mary's. In consideration of his father's health, the Rev. W. Tilson Marsh filled the incumbency for a time. In " Beck's Directory" for 1851, the details are thus given:—

"This new district Church, erected from the designs of Mr. J. G. Jackson, is situated a short distance eastward of the Warneford Hospital, and in a field south of the High road leading from Leamington to Southam. The site is the gift of E. Willes, Esq., and the architecture of the building is the ecclesiastical of the 15th century. It contains six windows on either side, ornamented with tracery, and placed between buttresses, additional light being supplied by a large altar window. The tower at the west end rises to the height of 75 feet, and is ornamented with battlements and pinnacles. The interior consists of a nave and side aisles, the former being separated from the latter by a series of arches. The ceiling is divided into panels, having also enriched spandrels. The altar below the east window is decorated with panels, surmounted by ornamented canopies, pinnacles, etc. A very handsome stained glass window, placed at the east end, is the munificent gift of a member of the congregation, and contains in the upper central compartment the episcopal mitre surrounding the arms of the diocese, quartered with those of the late venerable and respected diocesan, Dr. Ryder. The remaining compartments are occupied by the arms of the trustees, viz., Edward Willes, Esq.; the Rev. W. Marsh, D.D. (the then incumbent); and Alexander Gordon, W. Sherer, and Edwin Woodhouse, Esqs. The whole presents a highly creditable specimen of the skill of Mr. Holland, of Warwick, by whom this and many very clever specimens in pictorial glass have recently been executed. A handsome font of Darlaston stone is placed in front of the reading desk; it is octagonal, and around the bowl are carved the emblems of our Saviour's sufferings. The body of the church is 80 feet long by 67 feet in width, and the height 30 feet. It was opened for public worship on the 27th of July, 1839, under the ministry of the Rev. Dr. Marsh, who, with several private individuals, have liberally endowed it. Mrs. N. Merridew is the organist."

Despite the influential opposition which existed, and a letter to the Bishop from the Rev. John Craig, protesting against the creation of an ecclesiastical district "in green fields," on Tuesday, February 11, 1840, the Venerable Archdeacon Spooner, with the Rev. Archer Clive and the Rev. B. Twistleton, met the Churchwardens in the vestry, and mapped out the following as the new district. This afterwards received the sanction of the Diocesan Consistonal Court, but St. Mary's did not attain what may be described as complete and independent autonomy until the death of Mr. Craig, on Saturday, June 30, 1877, from which date the parochial rights and privileges of all residents within the prescribed area were transferred from All Saints' to St. Mary's. The parish was constituted by a Deed, signed June 22, 1840.

' The said district parish commences in the centre of the Kenilworth Road, at the north-west angle of the junction of the parishes of Leamington and Lillington, from thence running southward along the centre of the road to the point where Clarendon Street and the Holly Walk meet, from thence westward to the east end of Regent Street, opposite the Angel Inn, and from thence southward down the centre of Newhold Street, across Newbokl Terrace, and down the footpath to the Mill; thence eastward to a a boundary stone at the north-east coi ner of the garden of Hope Cottage, thence southward, and between Hope and Brook Cottages, into Leam Terrace, and southward, along the east side of land conveyed in one thousand eight hundred and thirty-seven to Mr. Tuhcrville Smith, and thence to a boundary stone in the Mews road, south of Leam Terrace, from thence westward to the passage on the east side of the new Burial Ground, and round the Burial Ground on the cast and south side, and by the south end of Gordon House; from thence southward, along a passage on the east side of the Roman Catholic Chapel into the centre of Russell Terrace, returning eastward along the centre of Russell Terrace, to the centre of Korlield Place, down that place southward, and thence across the road from Warwick to Southam, and from thence in the same direction along the Watery Lane and the footpath to Whitnash as far as the junction of the parishes of Leamington and Whitnash; from thence eastward along the boundary of the said parishes to the brook forming the boundary of Leamington and Radford, and thence northward along the brook to its junction with the river Leam, and by the course of the river to the south-east angle of the grounds of Newbold Comyn House; thence northward to the boundary line belonging to the Earl of

Aylesford as far as the north-east angle of a coppice, which is bounded on the north side by the parish of Lillington, and thence westward along the northern boundary of the parish of Leamington to the spot in the centre of the Kenilworth Road whence the line of boundary commenced."

This form of St. Mary's district was continued until the creation of a parish for St. Paul's, on June 29, 1878, when it was materially changed and reduced in extent by the new parochial delimitation. The boundary stones referred to are still;'// *situ,* and may be seen, the one at the bottom of the tree near the Mill boat house, and the other in New Street, at the corner of the wall enclosing the burial ground. The footpath to and by the Mill has been altered, though not in a material degree. In the proceedings of the Paving Commissioners for May, 1847, reference is made to "the old foot road by the Mill" having been rendered useless by "the recent diversion, which is wider and more convenient to the public." The variation may be thus explained. In 1846, Mr. Oldham enlarged the Mill to nearly double its size by erecting, on the east side, a cottage, a large engine house, and additional rooms for his business as miller and corn factor. These closed that portion of the ancient footpath which, after leaving the bridge, proceeded over the site of the new buildings into the Mill yard, and as a substitute the present road was provided.

From a Photo by F. L. Spicer Lansdowne Ci"cus, Leamington Spa. CHAPTER XXV.

F the occurrences between 1839 and 1850, some, in the special influence they had on the prosperity of the town, were of epoch-making importance. In this class must be mentioned the rebuilding of the Parish Church on a cathedral basis, the erection of the Leamington College, the establishment of the Jephson Gardens, and the introduction of the railway system. The coaching service, which had been a favourite institution from the commencement of the century, was in a flourishing state, but its decline began

as soon as it was placed in competition with the more powerful and unwearied steam-fed iron steeds of George Stephenson. Nearly a hundred and twenty stage coaches arrived at, and departed from, the Royal, the Bath, the Crown, and the Stoneleigh hotels in each week.

In 1839, the connection of the Rev. Robert Downes with Leamington as its Vicar was brought to a close. On Sunday. June 9, he preached two farewell sermons to "exceedingly crowded congregations"—in the morning at the Episcopal Chapel, and in the evening at the Parish Church. His experience in the Vicariate had not been that of one luxuriously reclining on a bed of roses. Briefly stated in his own words, he had laboured in the parish for eighteen years, through evil report and good report, and " of the former there had been rather an undue proportion." To his memory it is only just to say that during his term of office, the Church had been enlarged four times, and though it is doubtful if he defrayed any considerable portion of the cost, as frequently stated in the "Guides," he threw himself heart and soul into the work, and carried it to a successful issue. His resignation of the living was followed by a circumstance of a ver-gratifying character. On the nthof October, 1839, he was entertained at a banquet at the Crown Hotel, and presented with a valuable gold watch and a massive silver candelabra, weighing two hundred ounces, and rising to the height of two feet six inches. Three figures representing Faith, Hope, and Charity, were on the base, with the following inscription: "Presented to the Rev. Robert Downes, M.A., in testimony of his faithful service, during eighteen years, as Curate and Vicar of the parish." This "olive branch" of good will having been subscribed for by those who were opposed to him, as well as by others who concurred in his opinions, greatly enhanced its value and acceptability, and led the rev. gentleman to fairly conclude that both parties respected the integrity of his motives and the sincerity of his intentions.

'Mr. Downes had as fellow students

at Winchester School, Dr. Arnold, of Kugby; the Right Hon. C. S. Lefevre, Speaker of the House of Commons; and Dean Hook. It was probably owing to this early association that the latter was induced to preach in the Parish Church and Christ Church on several occasions during the time he was Vicar.

The new Vicar was the Rev. John Craig, M.A. He was born at Fescati, County Dublin, his father being a Scotch clergyman, and his mother, an English lady related to Lord Melbourne. This triangular descent of birth and parentage, he was accustomed to turn to good account by remarking that he represented all that was best in the three countries—the English rose, the Scottish thistle, and the shamrock of Ireland. To Leamington he came from Fetcham, Surrey, the rectorship of which he exchanged with Mr. Downes for the living of All Saints'. His reception was as favourable as a clergyman could desire or an admiring parish give; for a time he was esteemed by all classes; *From a Photo by Bullock, Bros., The Parade, Leamington Spa.* The Rev. John Craig, M.A.,

Vicar of Leamington from 1839 to 1877.

by some almost worshipped with the passion of idolatory. Wealth had poured into his lap an abundance of its treasures; learning had awarded him one of its numerous chaplets; eloquence had touched the tip of his "subduing tongue" with the rod of its enchantment, and fortune had liberally strewn his path with flowers. Yet, in disappointment of all the bright anticipation of a long and happy ministry called forth by this many-hued rainbow of promise, he experienced every phase of sorrow, affliction, and bereavement, and spent much of his time in dissension, controversy and litigation. His riches took to themselves wings and flew away. Many early friendships were dissolved, and he became the target for a thousand shafts; the central figure around whom friends and foes were continually revolving, showering on higi and each other, diatribes of encouragement and praise; censure ami exasperating recriminations. Twice "in the interest of all parties," it was arranged that he should leave the parish, but heremained its ecclesiastical head to the close of his life, the serene setting of which resembled the golden calm of a summer evening following a day of elemental strife—of storm, cloud and tempest; of thunder, lightning and rain. To enter into the ceaseless disputes which gave to his term of office the character of a warfare—sometimes of a pitched battle—and to apportion blame where it was deserved, and commendation where it was merited, would be a task difficult under the most favourable circumstances; in the presence of that compact made at his bed side a short time previous to his death, extremely undesirable. He, and those between whom an estrangement had lasted for nearly a generation, asked and received mutual forgiveness. The reconciliation which then took place, the amnesty concluded, and the act of oblivion passed, are so many barriers opposed to even a most dispassionate and impartial review of events which kept the parish in the vortex of a" perpetual strife. Generally, however, it may be observed that there were faults on both sides, and that each party was at one time the aggressor, and at another the aggrieved. Mr. Craig was tall and sparely built, walked with rapid, tottering steps, and had a stoop which made him appear shorter in stature than he really was. In the street he talked much to himself—" thought aloud," as a quaint old writer expresses it — and at times gesticulated as though he was arguing with another. For the "archery of controversy" he never had the least aversion. He belonged to a former class of polemical divines who held the "once famous maxim that he who preaches the best and prays the best, can fight the best." If the churchwardens, or any others laid their coat tails at his feet, with gleeful alacrity he trampled them in the dust. Failing this, he had no objection to place his own before his opponents. He would even have done as much to oblige a near or a distant friend. His love of merriment was irrepressible, and of that degree which Dr. Johnson stern-

ly reprehended as "mighty offensive in parsons." But it was neither venomous, nor malicious. It was the quintessence of wit; light, polished and stingless. In the vestry, where he was paramount, he played the part of autocrat or that of an indulgent ruler, according to the humour of the moment and the direction in which his feathers were stroked. After being heckled hotly and acrimoniously for t wo hours, he would leave the chair shaking his sides with laughter, tickling his intimates and exclaiming, "wasn't it jolly?" He was an eloquent preacher, and though his voice, being thin and weak in quality, was not conducive to oratory, the disadvantage was overcome by exalted moods of intense and thrilling effect. On the political platform he was the most welcome of speakers. Wayward often, and frequently unmanageable, he yet possessed noble traits of excellence. His benevolence, his compassion for the poor, the impetus he gave to the cause of elementary education, and lastly, his service to Leamington for all time in planning and constructing the framework of the finest Parish Church in England, are ponderous weights to be placed in the scale against his numerous eccentricities. "I wish to speak with kindness and respect of the Vicar of Leamington. I have a great liking for Mr. Craig. I consider him a most excellent preacher; I believe him to be one of the ablest expounders of Holy Writ in this country; I know 'him to be a ripe scholar, and I believe him to be too good a lawyer for his own peace and happiness, but I do not consider him to be a very judicious or consistent politician," was the testimony given him by the Venerable Archdeacon Sandford. By way of explaining the qualifying expression of opinion as to the flexibility of his politics, it should be mentioned that this was said during the General Election of 1S68, when Mr. Craig, differing from Mr. Gladstone on the subject of the disestablishment of the Irish Church, left the Liberal Party, with whom the Archdeacon remained, and joined the Conservatives. The portrait we give is supremely a speaking likeness. With

rare fidelity it represents the concentration of mental power which always characterised him when interested in any question, and his general deportment " under fire" at the Easter vestry "vicar-baitings," searching for the weak joints in the armour of the enemy, and invariably finding them.

Mr. Craig, on his coming to Leamington, took a lease of the Episcopal Chapel from the Rev. Robert Downes, at a rental of several hundred pounds per annum, and one of his first public actions with respect to that property made him very popular. It had been the custom, we believe, ever since the chapel was built, in 1825, to pay at the door for admission to the services. The original tariff we are unable to give, but in 1837, the reduced terms of admission to each service for casual attendants were:— "Tickets to admit five persons, 2s.; four ditto, is. 6d.; three ditto, is. "; single admission, 6d.; servants, 3d." This practice had long been the subject of animadversion, and as early as 183/, Messrs. Robbins, Stanley, Smart, Bird, Oldham and Russell, of Wise Street, had waited upon Mr. Downes, as a deputation from the Parish Committee, and represented to him that "the mode of receiving contributions is objectionable to the public." His answer was " that he had no objection to sell or let the Chapel to the Parish, the Patron first declining, to whom he is bound to offer it in the first instance." Mr. Craig, on taking possession of the living, lost no time in abolishing the obnoxious charges. His next step was still more important. The National School, established in Church Street in 1822, he found, in 1839, to be cramped for want of better accommodation in a room in Kenilworth Street. At this time the Workhouse at the rear of the old Town Hall in High Street, was unoccupied, not for want of paupers, but because the Statute 4 & 5, Will IV., c. 76, had put an end to each parish separately maintaining its own poor, and had established Unions of Parishes, with Union Workhouses managed by Boards of Guardians. The old Workhouse belonged to the local Commissioners, and to them Mr. Craig applied and was granted its use for the National School, free of rent or any other cost excepting that of a lease. The School was thereupon removed from Kenilworth Street, and the late Mr. Robert Baker, of Church Street, became its first master. Under his management it entered on a new career of usefulness, which continued at the Apollo Rooms, and until its final removal into Bath Place, the particulars of which will be given in a subsequent part of this work.

The widening of the bridge, in 1839, was the completion of the most prominent public work with which the Paving Commissioners are to be credited. It was the last section of the local improvement commenced in 1837, when the road in Victoria Terrace was extended twenty-nine feet towards the church, and in addition to being a public convenience it was associated with a sanitary movement of no small consequence to the health of the town, the imperative character of which had been recognised so far back as 1831. At a meeting of the Parish Committee, on November 28, in that year, an Order'of the Privy Council was read respecting the formation of a Board of Health. On this the Committee adopted the prudent course of consulting the members of the

Musical Festival In The Upper Assembly Rooms, October 15 And 16, 1833.

medical profession, a precedent which has been followed on several occasions in the history of the town, and never without benefit to the inhabitants. Their opinion was that no new powers of government were then needed, but they advised constant and unremitting industry in abating nuisances which might arise, and particularly impressed on the Committee the duty of steps being taken " for causing a freer flow of water in the river." This advice was urgently needed. From the Mill to the bridge, the Leam was then scarcely more than half its present width. The sides and banks were lined with sedges, and overgrown with bushes, which intercepted the filth brought down by the stream and holding it there in accumulated masses, caused, in the hot The Festival was by the Cho-

ral Society, of which Mr. F. Marshall was the conductor. There were two performances, one being of a miscellaneous character, at which Miss Clara Novello sang, "Let the bright Seraphim," with trumpet obbligato accompaniment by T. Harper; F. Cramer led the band, among whom were Lindley (violoncellist), and Dragnnctti (contrabassi&t). The second concert was the " Messiah," considered, we are pleased to read, "a great card" in those days. season, smells which were offensive, if not pestilential. Notwithstanding this the health of the town was satisfactory, and a certificate that Leamington had never been more exempt from severe illness was signed by Drs. John Staunton, Amos Middleton, Henry Jephson, Francis Franklin, James Cave Jones, Charles Loudon; and Surgeons D'Arcy Boulton, Richard Jones, W. W. Middleton, John Hitchman, William Haines, J. M. Cottley, John Pritchard, E. A. Jennings, and William Fairweather. Not forgetful of the recommendation by the Faculty, the Commissioners, in their work of 1839, thoroughly cleansed the river, removed from the sides all obstruction, excavated the bed, and, by constructing a culvert for storm and surface water, with an outlet between the bridge and the Mill, gave to the water a motion which removed an admitted nuisance. The widening of the bridge was a matter of some difficulty. It was erected in 1809 by the county, and was still the property of the County Court of Quarter Sessions. The Court refused to sanction any interference, and for a time it seemed as though the enlargement could not be made. On reference, however, to their local Act of 1825, the Commissioners found they had power to proceed independently of the County Justices. In Section 122 it was enacted that it should be lawful " to make more commodious any Bridge or Bridges in the Town leading to or from the said Wells, or any or either of them, in such manner as the said Commissioners shall judge proper." Relying upon this, they proceeded with the work without interruption by the County Authority, and widened the bridge on the east side,

making the distance between the balustrades forty feet. The scheme was introduced and discussed in 1838, the year of the Queen's Coronation; the opening ceremony took place in May, 1840, Dr. Jephson officiating, and after laying the memorial stone, which may still be seen at the south-east corner, he formally declared the bridge open for traffic. The customary public rejoicings—bell ringing, flags, banners, garlands, music, etc., were not omitted. There was a large assembly to witness the ceremony, on the conclusion of which they sang, with ardent loyalty, "God Save the Queen," accompanied by Charles Elston's Military Band. The proceedings of the day were appropriately concluded with feasting in the evening, fifty workmen being entertained at the Angel Hotel, while a more select party dined at the Bath Hotel, under the genial presidency of Dr. Hitchman. Subjoined is the inscription commemorating the event:—" This stone was laid by Henry Jephson, M.D., on the 25th of May, 1840, in commemoration of the Extension and Improvement of this Bridge, and in celebration of the Birth Day of Her Most Gracious Majesty, Queen Victoria." From this time the structure became known as the Victoria Bridge, an appellation most happily chosen, seeing that in its commencement it was associated with an event of absorbing interest to the Queen, and that its completion and inauguration were coincident with a national celebration of her Majesty's birthday.

Beautiful beyond compare was the Holly Walk at this period; in native grace and luxuriance, perfection. No analogy can be traced between its appearance in 1840 and To prevent confusion arising (mm tin-date not agrcing with her Majesty's birthday, it may be stated that the 24th, the real anniversary, being Sunday, the proceedings were necessarily delayed until the following day-Monday, the 25th. its present day condition. The majesty of its oaks and elms, the vaulted roof, affluent with boughs interlaced in infinite variety of form and design, and the mass of holly trees at the point where the ΥVilles Road intersects the Walk, are now departed glories. A horticulturist then visiting the town, has, with an expression of admiration, placed on record some particulars of this singularly fine grove, the heirloom of many vanished centuries. The oaks and elms were on an average six feet in diameter, and the holly trees, two feet. According to this measurement made by an expert, the circumference of the latter would be at the least six, and the former from eighteen to twenty feet. From enquiries made we learn that few such oaks and elms are now to be found in Warwickshire, or in fact in the Midlands. What might have been their exact age cannot definitely be stated, but the authority we have quoted says they were old, and bearing in mind the familiar lines of Dryden:

"The monarch oak, the patriarch of trees,

Shoots rising up, and spreads by slow degrees;

Three centuries he grows, and three he slays

Supreme in state, and in three more decays,"

the period of planting was probably not much later than the time of the Conquest.

On Tuesday, January 19, 1841, the Solemn Dedication of the Catholic Church, George Street, under the Invocation of St. Peter, took place in the presence of a large congregation. Thirteen years had elapsed since its erection and the first service held within its walls. The old complaint of Catholic families and visitors that they had no suitable place for worship had ceased, and there were no longer to be heard in their midst threats of leaving the town on that account. The building of the Chapel elicited from the Rev. B. Crosbie, the first Priest, a generous acknowledgement of the healthful spirit of toleration prevailing in Leamington. "Those prejudices," he remarked, in the announcement of the opening services, "against the professors of the ancient faith, which unfortunately exist in many towns, are not known here." The dissemination of this intelligence in

Catholic circles, far and wide, must be counted as one of the many attractions and influences that have conduced to the happiness and prosperity of the Spa. The Dedication services were of a highly ornate and impressive character. In the morning there was Pontifical High Mass, and a sermon by the Right Rev. Dr. Wiseman (afterwards Cardinal Wiseman), president of St. Mary's College, Oscott. Vespers commenced at four o'clock, and included a sermon by the Rev. W. Tandy, D.D. A new organ, by Bevington, of London, was erected for the occasion, and a choice selection of sacred music by Handel, Mozart, Mazzinghi, etc., was sung by an efficient choir. Collections made in aid of the fund for removing the debt incurred by extensive alterations and improvements, realised,£220. Signor Migliorucci was the first organist.

The dispersion of the effects at Copps's Royal Hotel this year was the largest auction sale of the kind ever known in Leamington. It began on Tuesday, June 8, and lasted twenty-nine days, or six weeks within one day, for no lots were offered on Saturdays. The auctioneers were Messrs. White and Son, who founded the business in 1834, now carried on by Mr. J. Anthony Locke, at his offices 166, The Parade.

The beginning of John Bright's apostleship of Free Trade, "a signal event in the annals of the Anti-Corn Law League," is another leaf in the volume of local history for 1841. In the autumn of that year he came to Leamington with Mrs. Bright, who was seriously ill. He had been a Free Trader from the origin of the movement, and occasionally lectured in support of the League proposals. But his position was that of a powerful auxiliary, or co-worker, in the ranks rather than an official leader and director of the gathering forces of that great organisation. After a residence here of a few weeks, he accepted an invitation to deliver an address at Warwick on the subject of

Free Trade, and an unsuccessful application having been made for the use of the Court House, in respect of which the Mayor said "that he did not feel

called upon to give any reason for his refusal," the doors of the schoolroom of the Independent Chapel, Brook Street, were instantly flung wide open. On Thursday, August 12th, Mr. Bright spoke there for about two hours to a crowded audience, estimated to have numbered five hundred persons, and at the conclusion of the meeting a branch of the League was formed in the old county town. Mrs. Bright died on the 10th of September, and on the 13th, Mr. Cobden, then on a visit to some relatives in Leamington, called to condole and sympathise with Mr. Bright in his bereavement. The meeting and Art, literature and philosophy were represented by Mr. Kuskin, whose visit is recorded to have taken place in 1841. He was one of Dr. jephson's patients, and spent six weeks in " tiny lodgings near the Wells." resolution to which it led were thus described by him in his speech at Bradford, July 25, 1877, when he unveiled the Cobden statue:—"The sufferings throughout the country were fearful, and you who live now, but were not of age to observe what was passing in the country then, can have no idea of the state of your country in that year At that time I was at Leamington, and I was, on the day when Mr.

Cobden called upon me—for he happened to be there at the time on a visit to some relatives—I was in the depth of grief, I might almost say of despair, for the light and sunshine of my home had been extinguished. All that was left on earth of my young wife, except the memory of a sainted life and of a too brief happiness, was lying still and cold in the chamber above us. Mr. Cobden called upon me as his friend, and addressed me as vou may suppose, with words of condolence. After a time he looked up and said, 'There are thousands of homes in England at this moment where wives, mothers, and children are dying of hunger. Now,' he said, 'when the first paroxysm of of your grief is past, I would advise you to come with me, and we will never rest till the Corn Law is repealed.' I accepted his invitation. I knew that the description he had given of the homes of thousands was not an exaggerated description. I felt in my conscience that there was a work which somebody must do, and therefore I accepted the invitation, and from that time we never ceased to labour on behalf of the resolution we had made." The battle of Free Trade was protracted, bitter, and obstinately contested; its victory was not without a vast expenditure of service, wealth, and devotion. Public opinion, which was then widely divided, is now practically unanimous in its favour. It is to Cobden and Bright the country owes its cheap loaf, and though the policy of Free Trade is still questioned by a few, none will deny their disinterested service, or doubt the sincerity of their desire for the public welfare. Leamington does not appear to have taken any decided action, one way or the other, in the great contest, but it has the honour of having been the place where Cobden and Bright, to quote the words of Mr. John Morley, in his "Life of Richard Cobden," "made that solemn compact which gave so strong an impetus to the movement, and was the beginning of an affectionate and noble friendship that lasted without a cloud or a jar until Cobden's death."

Commencing with the year 1842, and continuing till 1843, the Improvement Commissioners were constantly employed in the work of establishing a local police force to be paid and managed by them independently of the County Authority. There have been three kinds of police establishments in the history of the town, only one of which was subject to external control. The first was the parochial system, consisting of constables, headboroughs, thirdboroughs, and special constables, appointed at the vestry meetings, and acting throughout the year under the direction of the Parish Committee. The pay of the constables was about £25 per annum, and their office being an annual appointment, they were liable to be superseded at any vestry meeting by preference being given to other candidates. Two constables were regularly appointed, but the numbers of the other classes varied; sometimes no headborough was elected, on

another occasion there would be three. The tenure of the thirdboroughs was similarly precarious One year the vestry would leave the office vacant; the next they would choose two, and in the year following, content themselves with one. As a rule the force consisted down to 1825 of two constables, one of whom was the superior officer, a headborough, a thirdborough, and a pinner and crier, who was also sworn in as an assistant constable. The first of the two principal officers to whom reference is made in the reports was William Langham, who held office in 1824. In the year following, George Reading and John Hickling (probably a relative of the late Superintendent Hickling, of Warwick), were elected. Besides this appointing power of the vestry, the County Magistrates had authority, on receipt of a memorial from the inhabitants that such a step was necessary, to supplement the parochial force with a number of assistant constables. It was in compliance with such a representation, signed by five respectable inhabitants, stating that the Civil power was insufficient for the protection of the persons and property in the town that the Rev. James Coral Roberts, clerk, and Arthur Francis Gregory, Esq., increased the local force on December 8, 1824, by swearing in four watchmen. This was the first departure from the old parochial system, and may be regarded as the time when the foundation was laid of our modern borough police establishment. George Reading, who had previously been known as one of two constables, is described as head-constable, and particulars are given of the first police uniform and appointments. Each of the new men was supplied with a coat of dark grey pattern, with one to four stripes of white cloth on the right arm; a dark lanthorn, rattle, staff, and belt. Their wages, we have already stated, were 10s. a week. This dual scheme was expanded by some police powers conferred on the Paving Commissioners by the local Act of 1825, under which they also began to appoint their own police, the pay for whom appears to have been 15s. weekly. This state of things continued until

1839, when Sir Robert Peel's Constabulary Act (2 & 3 Vict., c. 93) was passed, and the policing of the town was merged into the County Constabulary arrangements. At this time the police force of the Commissioners had grown to sixteen members, and the office of head constable was held by William Shirley Roby, at a salary of £150. The Commissioners were willing to part with their control of the force on condition that he was appointed the new chiefconstable for the County, and Leamington made the head-quarters of the Knightlow Hundred; and as an inducement to the Court of County Quarter Sessions to acquiesce in this proposal, they offered the free use of the Town Hall, the large room, cells, offices, etc. It was decided, however, to advertise for candidates, and out of eleven applicants, including Mr. Roby, the choice fell on Mr. George Baker, R.N. He was the first chief-constable for Warwickshire, and by virtue of his office, also the third for Leamington. He commenced his duties in 1840, and at the same time the local police force of the Commissioners underwent a singular transformation, and the county force was instituted in their place. The Commissioners soon saw reason to be dissatisfied with the new arrangements. Leamington was one of a group of eight parishes, to which the Quarter Sessions had allotted seven policemen, so that, as Mr. Patterson explained, the proportion of the County Constabulary in the town consisted of seven-eighths of one constable, for whom they had to pay a police rate amounting on an average to about £500 per annum. It was considered advisable to keep up the old force on a reduced scale, and to give it another title. Mr. Roby, the head-constable, was appointed Town Surveyor, the office being vacant owing to the death of John Russell, of the Bath Hotel, and to clothe him with proper authority, the vestry made him parish constable. Several of the former police were retained as streetkeepers, with duties not very distinctly defined, and a position which Captain Baker regarded as irregular and interfering with matters under his care.

Constant bickerings arose between the rival forces. The Captain declined to acknowledge Mr. Roby, who, trusting to his vestry appointment, considered himself quite as good as the Captain. In the Parade they passed each other without speaking, one generally discovering something on the opposite side of the street which required his attention; the other finding an attractive article in a shop window, the inspection of which enabled him to show his back to his great rival. The street-keepers turned up their noses at the county constable, and he looked down on them with feelings of lofty contempt. The Commissioners did not stand aloof from the quarrel. They refused to allow the County the use of the Town Hall, but offered the Station House in Park Street, for which they charged a rental, and on Captain Baker refusing to pay, they gave him notice to quit.

It was clear that the only way out of the difficulty was to obtain a new local Act, and as the one passed in 1825 was no longer sufficient, to include in it a number of other subjects besides that of the police establishment; a large Committee, consisting of Commissioners and the principal residents and tradesmen, were elected to prepare the draft of the Bill, the outcome of whose deliberations was the Statute 6 & 7, Vict., c. 59, of June 27, 1843. In this the Commissioners were empowered to establish their own police force, but the dismissal or suspension from duty of any constable was a right reserved for the Justices. A Police Committee were appointed, and in August they reported having reinstated Mr. Roby as "head of the new police force" at a salary of *£13$,* and ten constables at *£1* per week each, subject to a deduction of 2s. weekly for clothing, and is. per week " to create a sick fund." Powers were taken in the Bill to establish a public market, and to cleanse and improve the Milverton Brook, and it was stated in the preamble that a sum of £ 10,000, raised on mortgage of the rates, had been expended in improvements since 1825. The question of the qualification of a Commissioner was included in the draft, the pro-

posal of the Committee being for a very large reduction. This was resisted by Dr. Jephson and a number of other influential residents, whose memorial to Parliament appears to have been successful, for the Bill of 1843 left the franchise as it was. An unavailing indignation meeting was held in Copps's yard, when the omission was made known.

An impression prevails, and it has been publicly said, that the qualification for a local Commissioner was reduced to *£10.* There is nothing in the Act to support this view, and on reference to a carefully prepared synopsis, published in the *Leamington Courier* on July 8, 1841, we find that a Commissioner, to be qualified, had to be a resident possessed of houses or land of the annual value of £60, or the tenant ot property assessed to the poor rate at ££0 per annum. The Isill encountered much opposition. What the opponents desired was the introduction of a clause allowing every householder to vote in the election of the "Twenty One," or the vote to be given to all £10 householders, and that the qualifications should be reducedj from £60 to £40, and from *£So* to £30 respectively. All these recommendations were rejected. CHAPTER XXVI. ORTICULTURE, or garden culture, from time immemorial, has been universally considered promotive of the pleasure and profit of mankind; soothing to the mind distraught with the cankering cares of business or professional avocations, "refreshing to the worn invalid, and a source of perennial delight to all, whether in health or sickness, burdened with poverty or abounding in wealth. It is not within the province of domestic legislation to provide a beautiful garden separately for every house, but happily, means are to be found for laying out public pleasure grounds for the benefit of all, and at a cost so trifling to each householder that the poorest need not complain. These have been applied in Leamington with eminent success.

We have now to state the circumstances attending the acquisition of the Jephson Gardens by the town in 1846, and in due order to refer to that popular and beneficent measure of recent date, which has

idealised the primary object of the general good by admitting on three days in each week the public free of charge. Any remarks respecting their value would be as superfluous and futile as an attempt to "gild refined gold, to paint the lily," or to invite art " to throw a perfume on the violet." None can visit them at any season of the year without feeling how greatly Leamington would be impoverished by their loss. The land, about thirteen acres in extent, belonged to the Willeses, of Newbold Comyn, and early in the century was partly pasture in the occupation of Farmer Court, of Lillington, a man of burly size, who used to ride about on a stout cob, and chase and chastise the boys with his whip, when he found them birdnesting, playing at rounders, or gathering mushrooms on his land. A path, commencing near the west end lodge, the exact point of which is not easy to state, led through the wood beyond the present Willes Road, and on to the Hall. Before the Willes Road was made, about the year 1825, it was continuous and formed the direct course from Newbold Comyn to the village and the Church. Nothing definite can be gathered as to what was the precise state of the place at this period, but as it was called the Newbold Wood Walks, or Gardens, it is probable that the management was in the direction of ornament. John George Jackson, architect, succeeded Farmer Court in the tenancy, and about the year 1834 he laid the ground out as a pleasure garden and gave it a more distinctly recreative character than it had ever possessed before. He resided in a small, very pleasant and attractive cottage, formerly standing on the site of the Hitchman Fountain. At this time, Newbold Terrace, though it had been in course of building many years, was not advanced one-fourth towards completion, and as late as 1839 it consisted of only two or three houses at each end. All the intervening space was unoccupied land in the market for sale. As the vendor of the land in Newbold Terrace, and owner of the Newbold Gardens, Mr. Willes entered into covenants with purchasers which must have enhanced the selling price of the former very materially. These were—(i) that the Gardens were never to be built upon, and (2) that the occupier of every villa should have the right in perpetuity of free admission. This agreement was fulfilled by placing gates along the whole length of the north side, and as the villas were built one after another, the occupiers were supplied with keys with which to let themselves into the Gardens. A writer to the *Gardeners' Magazine* was in Leamington in 1840, and from the curt manner in which he refers to the Newbold Gardens, we conclude that they were not then in an advanced stage of development, nor possessed of much artistic beauty He is pleasingly talkative about the gardens at Bradley House, Beech Lawn, The Priory, *From a Photo by F. L. Spicer, Lansdownc Circus, Leamington Spa.*

Old Timbered And Ivied Cottage, Formerly Standing At The Top Of Holly Walk. the Holly Walk, and Mr. Cullis's Nursery; tells us in fact, that Mr. Bradley's flower beds are too fanciful and angular, and that a surrounding architectural walk is wanted, after the manner of the mural colonnades in the town gardens of Pompeii; that Dr. Jephson has some beautiful specimens ot Turkey and Luccombe oaks of several varieties; that the rockwork at the Priory is good in idea, but not carried out in the best manner, partly from want of proper materials; also that Mr. Cullis has very ingeniously covered the roof of a portion of the house with a collection of low-growing saxifrages; that the Holly Walk is finely bordered with old oaks, elms and hollies, and that Mr. Cullis's Nursery, which extends over many acres in different parts of the town and neighbourhood, has the largest stock in England of Cupresuss torulosa. But of the Newbold Gardens, respecting which fuller particulars might have been expected if their improvements had kept pace with the prosperity of the town, not a single word of description appears. No flower beds or walks are mentioned, no rare trees or choice plants. "There is a piece of ground containing about 14 acres, which is intended to be laid out as a public garden,

and for which we have made a plan,"' is the sum total of his reference. In 1845, a popular movement was originated for presenting a testimonial to Dr. Jephson in recognition of the advantages Leamington had derived from his enlightened practice. Foremost among the promoters were Lord Somerville, then residing with his family at Newbold Comyn, Sergeant Adams, and Drs. Amos Middleton and John Hitchman. At a meeting held in the Assembly Rooms, on Thursday, May 7, Lord Somerville presiding, resolutions in favour of the project were adopted with the unanimous approval of all present, and at the conclusion of the proceedings, it was found that subscriptions to the amount of £250 had been promised. A Committee, appointed to receive further donations, and to consider the most appropriate mode of carrying this praiseworthy object into effect, was directed to report thereon at a subsequent meeting. On Tuesday, May 12, 1846, Leamington was once more in one of its exuberant moods. The weather was glorious, the bells were ringing without pause note or rest; flags and banners were flying from every point of vantage; garlands were on the balconies, and "the Parades from one end to the other were thronged with holiday folks." What it was all about nobody knew definitely, except that the Newbold Gardens from that day were to "be made more directly subservient to the best interests of the town, ornamented with walks, flowers and trees, and beautified so far as wealth and horticultural skill would permit. Whereat there were general hand-shakings and congratulations. A short time before the ceremony in the Gardens took place, a second gathering of the subscribers, again under the presidency of Lord Somerville, was held in the Royal Assembly Rooms, and at this, the character of the testimonial, and the scheme for managing the Gardens, were made public. After reporting that a total sum of £1,850 had been collected, the Committee proceeded thus to state the decision at which they had arrived. They were unanimously of opinion that if the Gardens could be obtained on reasonable

terms, to be hereafter dedicated to the use of the visitors and inhabitants, under such regulations as Trustees to be nominated in the lease should appoint, the Gardens to be called the Jephson Mr. A. S. Field, the venerable Clerk of the Pe.ice for the County and Clerk of the County Council, is the sole survivor of the 44 trustees chosen. He is now in his 86th year, enjoys excellent health, and is more active than are the majority of men who are his juniors by a quarter of a century. His connection with the Gardens began with the first meeting held to promote the testimonial to Dr. Jephson, and closed fifty years afterwards, when the Trust was extinguished by the local Act of 1896, and the property was vested in the Corporation. At no time during this very long period have his services been of a merely nominal or perfunctory character. He was one of the first committee elected at the preliminary meeting in 1845 to make arrangements for collecting subscriptions for the testimonial, and in the lease of the Gardens his name appears as one of the trustees. He was also one of the first Committee of Management to whom the work of laying out the Gardens, in 1846, was entrusted, and in 1847, he, with several other trustees, signed a guarantee to the Warwick and Leamington liank for an advance of *£570.* To him Leamington is largely indebted for half-acentury of hard work in bringing the Gardens to their present state of perfection. He and Alderman Bright, who is in his 82nd year, arc the only living representatives of the original list of subscribers.

Gardens, and a statue of Dr. Jephson placed therein, it would combine more effectually than any other of the proposed plans, the instructions they had received. They also stated that they had succeeded in negotiating, and now had the pleasure of laying before the meeting for confirmation, a lease of the Gardens for 2,000 years at the small annual rental of *£30,* such rental being redeemable at any time within ten years upon payment of *£600.* Mr. Hollins, the eminent sculptor, was recommended as the artist to be employed, and they invited the attention of the subscribers to the splendid bust he had already executed of Dr. Jephson as the best proof of his fitness for the undertaking. In conclusion, they mentioned that considerable cost would have to be incurred in laying out and beautifying the grounds, and referred to the prevailing enthusiasm and demonstration of rejoicing then being exhibited in the town as evidence of the popularity of the movement. On the motion of Sergeant Adams, who mentioned that one hundred and fifty poor persons had contributed £10 in small sums, the report was adopted. The party then marched to the grounds, where it was estimated upwards of seven thousand people were assembled, and after a speech by Sergeant Adams the National Anthem was sung and the Gardens formally given their new name. A beautiful medal, struck by Messrs. Bright and Sons, from a design by Mr. Ottley, of Birmingham, was generally worn by the inhabitants, suspended from their collars by a blue ribbon. It scarcely need be said that an event so auspicuous was not allowed to close without the customary banquet.

Two years after (1848) there was another demonstration, or rather a series of demonstrations, in the Gardens. The men employed by the Labourers' Fund, started by Dr. Hitchman in 1842, had for more than twelve months been constantly employed, under the superintendence of Mr. Cullis, in forming the walks, levelling the ground, putting in shrubs and evergreens, and excavating for the formation of the lake. By way of celebrating the completion of the first section of the improvements, it was decided to plant two rows of evergreen oaks about the central walk in the lower part of the Gardens, and to name them after local men entitled by their position or service to public respect and esteem. The ceremony, which was appropriately described by the *Courier* as " The Festival of the Oaks," was conducted on a most extensive scale. It was commenced on Monday morning, May 1, and continued with but slight intermission until Thursday evening, May 4. Dr. Hitchman, a kind, liberal and energetic

friend of Leamington, was Master of the Ceremonies, and being in a charmingly speechifying mood, right well did he discharge the duties. We have only space to give the titles of the trees, and to remind our readers that as it was just fifty years last May (1898) Peter Hollins was a Pirmingham man, and resided in Great Hampton Street. In a letter to Lord Somcrville, dated May 15, 1846, he said that his usual charge for a statue executed in Carrara marble, and of heroic size, was £1,000, and for a suitable pedestal in Sicilian marble. £100, with an extra charge for fixing the statue. In consideration, however, of the importance of the undertaking, the "beneficial effect it cannot fail to produce on my future professional career," and also the handsome and highly honourable manner in which the commission had been placed in his hands, his charge would be £1,000 for statue and pedestal. "Heroic size" he explained to be 7 feet high. His offer was accepted. The statue of Dr. Jephson is considered by qualified judges to be an excellent likeness; in pose, drapi ry, and general expression, faultless.

since they were planted, the present is the Jubilee year of the Oak Walk. They were called the Royal, Jephson, Wellington, Somerville, Stoneleigh, Russell, Chambers, Warncford, Greville, Abbotts, Satchwell, Willes, Patron, Finch, Guernsey, Adams, Percy, Cholmondley, Manners-Sutton, Downes, Dynevor, Carnegie, Marsh, Satchwell, Bisset, Angel, Hodgson, and Walhouse Oaks. Mr. Hitchman's name was not included in this generous distribution of honours, but his reward came later on in the more durable fountain in the north-west corner of the Gardens. A project for erecting a gallery of arts and science proved a castle in the air, like the Winter Garden scheme of another period. The rights of tenants of property in Newbold Terrace to free admission to the Gardens through gates on the north side was determined by the new arrangements, but they were still allowed to enter by the two lodges without payment. Miss Dawson, who resided at No. 6, now occupied by Mr.

F. Foster, architect, resolved to test the legality of the action of the Trustees in closing the gate opposite her house, by causing it to be broken open. Thereupon they brought an action for wilful damage and trespass, which was tried at Warwick Assizes in September, 1848, before Mr. Justice Maule. The Court held that in the covenants Mr. Willes had not specified any particular place for entry to the grounds, and *so* long as the residents in the Terrace were permitted to pass through the lodges without subscriptions, there was, practically, a fulfilment of the obligation. A verdict was given for the plaintiffs, damages 40s., and 40s. costs, with power to the defendant to move for a nonsuit. An unsuccessful appeal followed, and, as a consequence of this litigation, the custom established by the Trustees has remained in force to the present time. The task of perfecting the Gardens was arduous. A committee of Trustees, appointed for three years, were authorised to act according to the best of their judgment. Among these were Dr. Jephson, Messrs. A. S. Field, R. Whitehouse (father of Mr. Robert Whitehouse), E. Woodhouse and . Haddon. Several thousand pounds were spent, and in a brief period what was almost a bare field was tastefully embellished with walks, flowers and trees. Of the poor and the nonsubscribing part of the public, the Committee were not unmindful. One of their earliest resolutions was to open the Gardens free every Sunday afternoon. They instituted horticultural fetes of the finest character, and introduced music of the best quality. In 1873, Mr. William Willes complained to the Trustees that the change of the name from the Newbold to the Jephson Gardens was unjust to his father's memory. Without admitting that the founders of the Gardens had exceeded their powers, or had in any way slighted Mr. Edward Willes, it was decided to erect the obelisk in the central walk, whereon the gratitude due to him for "the site" is conspicuously acknowledged. There was no doubt generosity on the part of Mr. Willes, but in the opinion of every inhabitant who remembers the state of the land, it was not of such a character as to entitle him to a retention of the old name. Further, the Trustees could not have been actuated by any unkind feeling towards him. All were his friends, and one—Sergeant Adams—had been his schoolfellow. The Committee received much voluntary assistance, and a resolution records their appreciation of the gratuitous services of the late Mr. John Hart, father of Messrs. George and Charles Hart.

Exterior And Interior Views Of The Wesleyan Methodist Church, Dale Street, ERECTED 1869.

The marriage of the Queen and Prince Albert was celebrated on February 10, 1840, by the hoisting of the Royal Standard on many of the public buildings. Bath Street was particularly gay with flags, banners, etc., as it always was on such occasions. The bells of the Parish Church were rung at intervals throughout the day. The Rev. John Craig, Vicar, entertained the children of the National School at his own expense, and an excellent dinner was provided for them in the School, while those attending the Infant School were regaled with tea and cakes. A committee of ladies, among whom were the Countess of Farnham and Viscountess Eastnor, superintended the arrangements. Those attending the Victoria School of Industry were indebted to Mrs. Young for an enjoyable entertainment. The managers of the various charitable institutions in Leamington also gave treats to the inmates. In the evening there was a grand ball at the Music Hall, attended by a large and fashionable company, who danced with great energy up till six next morning. The town was also illuminated in the evening. Devices of "V. A." were numerous, and the buildings most conspicuous for the brilliancy and success of the displays were the Assembly Rooms, the Music Hall, the Post and Stamp Office, the establishment of Mr. Ashmore (Queen's saddler), the office of the Warwick Brewery Company, and particular mention was made of the "old-established wine vaults of Mr. Johnson in Bath Street, on account of the chaste splendour produced by lighting with gas." It was also remarked "that those who adopted the same method had an advantage over the consumers of oil, the lamps of which were in various quarters extinguished by sudden gusts of wind." The shop " of Mr. Roby, in Regent Street, the private mansion of Sir Edward Mostyn, and the residences of the Misses Manners-Sutton in Lansdowne Place and Mr. Hampden in Clarence Terrace," are named as having been specially meritorious. An address of congratulation was adopted at a town's meeting held at the Town Hall on Tuesday, February 18, at which there were present Lord Teynham, Rev. Dr. Marsh, Revs. John Craig (Vicar), Campbell, Marsh, Otway; Dr. Luard, Captain Musgrave; Messrs. Matthew Wise, J. Hampden, J. W. Sherer, F. Lambert, Thos. Verner, N. L. Torre, J. Russell, E. Woodhouse, J.White, Owen White, G. C. Liebenrood, William Green, T. Oldham, J. G. Jackson, G. Cundall, Rousham, Cullis (Churchwarden), Croydon (Overseer). Two addresses were adopted— one to the Queen's Most Excellent Majesty, and the other "To Field Marshal His Royal Highness Francis Albert Augustus Charles Emanuel, Duke of Saxe, Prince of Saxe-Coburg and Gotha, Knight of the Most Noble Order of the Garter."

The event in the history of the Parish Church to which the public mind has, and ever will, revert with feelings of admiration and gratitude, was the commencement of the building of the present fabric in 1842 and its continuance with uninterrupted zeal, energy, and munificence, until 1849. All previous extensions and improvements were so many clumsy pieces of patchwork in comparison with the grand design which was then adopted. The idea of demolishing the old church and erecting a larger one was first broached in 1834, but the parochial climate was then too cold for its germination. The Parish Committee were in favour of the project, and Mr. Downes was willing to give his consent as soon as they could satisfy him that a new church was necessary. In the vestry the objection was of a commercial character. More pews and sittings meant lower rents, and if the accommodation were doubled, the monetary value of those which had been purchased would deteriorate to the great loss of the owners. On September 15, 1842, Mr. Craig explained to the Vestry his intention to proceed with the erection of a new nave and bell tower, the estimated cost of which was £10,000. Not a farthing of this expense, he said, was to fall on the parish. The Vestry having sanctioned the scheme, as a preliminary, several of the cottages were demolished, and the first stone of the projected new lantern tower was laid on September 13, 1843, with Masonic rites. The proceedings of the day commenced with the opening of the Provincial Grand Lodge at the Music Hall, after which there was a successful procession round the town, nearly forty clergymen, and a considerable number of residents joining the Masons. A special service was held in the Church, at which the Rev. Prebendary Gresley preached the sermon. The stone, ceremoniously laid, had this inscription:— "Laus Deo. This first stone of the Lantern Tower of the Parish Church of Leamington Priors was laid on the 13th day of September, 1843, by Thomas Henry Hill, Esq. , G. Register, acting as P.G.M. for Warwickshire. God save the Queen." In the evening, the Masons dined at the Bath Hotel, Mr. Nicholas Torre, deputy Provincial Grand Master presiding. The speed with which the work was carried forward was remarkable. In twelve months from the date of the laying of the stone, Dr. Hook, of Leeds, was in the pulpit preaching the opening sermon, and a crowded and fashionable congregation lost in wonder at the magnificence of that building which had risen, as if by magic, on the ruins of the old. Four evangelist columns marked the outline of the village church, and though not complete, two were already soaring aloft and spreading out their strong arms for the reception of the beautiful Lantern Tower which never came. This inauguration took place on May 9, 1844, and on July 17, 1845, there was another special service for the formal opening of the Chancel, when nearly fifty clergymen were present. The preacher was the Rev. R.Parkinson, 13.D., Canon of Manchester; the offertory realised about £200. On the conclusion of the proceedings, Mr. Craig again displayed his love of hospitality on a large scale by entertaining nearly four hundred people at a banquet in the Music Hall. The last of these great improvements at this period was the erection of the north transept and the clock tower, the foundation stone of which was laid on June 16, 1846, by the Rev. Vaughan Thomas. The ceremony and service were similar to those we have been describing. The Rev. T. Short preached the sermon; a sum of £210 was realised by the offertory, and Mr. Craig exercised his hospitable disposition by giving a generous banquet tor the third time to a very large number of clerics and laymen at the Music Hall. These improvements and enlargements, carried forward with astounding energy, were followed in 1847 by a movement for completing the fabric, and at the Easter Vestry in that year Mr. Craig expressed his willingness to finish the whole of the work as soon as he received a sum of £2,500. This liberal offer was readily accepted; collectors were appointed to canvass the town, and a sum of £1,366 18s. zd. raised. A legacy of £1,000 by Mrs.

Elizabeth Charlotte Burgess, which, however, was not paid until 18+9, and a few other contributions, brought the total up to the required amount. At this time something occurred which changed the whole aspect of affairs. What was its nature has never been explained, and probably never will. But it may have been the boundary wall question, about which there had been a long and fruitless correspondence between the Vicar and the Commissioners. Finding his own views were not approved, he gave up the contest by recommending them to change the name of Priory Terrace to Magpie Square, in commemoration of the endless talking and letters to which it had given rise; and after chaffing them on their official dignity, retorted with the ironical answer of Job to his three comforters: "No doubt but

ye *are* the people, and wisdom shall die with you." Be that as it may, the Vicar retired sulkily to his tent, as Achilles did of old, or to quote the words of the memorial to the Bishop in 1854, he "became very lukewarm and indifferent as to proceeding with the same." The work was stopped, and the building remained for many years in an unfinished state—a monument of high resolve paralysed by local misunderstanding. But that which had been accomplished was sufficient to mark the period as one of great activity and liberality, and also as that in which was condensed all that was best and happiest in Mr. Craig's ministry. The whole plan was his copyright, and though necessarily he had to call in the services of a draughtsman, it was to delineate his own ideas, not to supply others. The space at present disposal is not ample enough for all the details of these improvements. The illustrations, however, on the next page will convey to the reader a more vivid appreciation than could be derived from a copious assemblage of technicalities, figures, and measurements. The first exhibits the Lantern Tower projected by Mr. Craig. In the opinion of experts the Evangelist columns were incapable of sustaining the weight, and it was consequently never erected. The nave, compared with the height of the tower, lacks the harmony of proportion, but this defect would have been removed by its extension several bays, which from the first was in contemplation. In the second are displayed the manifold architectural beauties and merits of Mr. Craig's ideal— his ambition to build a church which should be national in its form, instead of parochial. How well he succeeded may be gathered from the testimonies of Bishops and Archdeacons, church architects, visitors from far and near, and from the universal sentiment which has readily ascribed to it the grandeur and sublimity of a Cathedral. At the luncheon following the laying of the Memorial Stone, on June 30, 1898, two speakers, competent to estimate his work, made reference to Mr. Craig's labours. Alderman Sidney Flavel, ex-Mayor, and Vicar's Warden for many

years, elicited the applause of a large and distinguished company by observing that it was to Mr. Craig's magnificent conception that they were indebted for the beautiful design they had in tlu; Parish Church, and the Rev. Cecil Hook, Vicar, also mentioned the name of Craig with a deep sense of gratitude, as he had laid the foundation of that which they were privileged to follow. However widely opinions may differ respecting Mr. Craig, few, we think, who are acquainted with this part of the history of the Church will dissent from the meed of praise thus bestowed on his memory.

IUTEKIOK OF THE PAKISH CHURCH, FROM THE DESIGNS OF THK REV. JOHN CRAIO.

Casual allusions to the state of the old Post Office in New Street, occurring in the local literature of this period, remind us of the duty of bringing forward the story of the changes which had taken place since it was last under notice. In February, 1829, and in January, 1830, an agitation took place for the establishment of a separate and independently constituted office for the town. Cogent arguments were fortified by statistics of great weight, and the Department, after enquiry by the Surveyor, granted the application. A few lines by the facetious Bisset, written in 1828, may be usefully quoted at this point as indicative of the status Leamington had acquired in public estimation:—

"Some time ago the letters sent To this (since days of Garrick),
Were superscribed thus—with a dash—
To Leamington, near Warwick.
The public of its consequence
A happy pressage draw,
As letters oft directed are
To Warwick, near the Spa."

The date of the Order for the new Post Office was February, 1830, and about the middle of that month the business was transferred to the shop in Bath Street, now numbered 29, and occupied by T. Maycock & Son, hairdressers, etc. The first postmaster was George Bevington. Only a portion of the shop was allocated to the postal business, the door into which was so narrow that a portly personage had to squeeze himself into small proportions to gain admission. The amount of business transacted at this date could not have been considerable, for the rates of postage were strictly prohibitive to all except business men and wealthy people. The penny postage system introduced by Sir Rowland Hill, came into operation in 1839, and the postal transactions in Leamington immediately rose to one third in excess of the former average. The effect of the reductions may be estimated from an authenticated circumstance which transpired at the time. A Leamington gentleman wrote four letters to various members of his family in Ireland, and transmitted them in one envelope. The postage was 4d. A few days before, the charges not then having been reduced, the cost would have been 16s. The office was next moved along Bath Street to 41 and 43, the present premises of Mr J. Bennett, confectioner; and Mr. W. E. Beckingsale, outfitter, and Mr. E. Enoch became the second postmaster. There was an ascent of two or three steps into the office, which lacked the necessary accommodation for a rapidly increasing trade, and in addition it was ill ventilated and dark, owing to the obstruction of the light by the heavy portico in front, pulled down in 1871. Such was the state of the postal arrangements at the time of which we are now writing. A break occurs in the history of the Post Office from 1820 to 1830. It has been generally supposed that the Hoptons continued the business in New Street until the date of the new Order, and that it was then transferred into Bath Street. But this could not have been the case, for in the first named year Satchwell Place was to let, and with it "the thatched cottage, lately occupied as a Post Office." Richard Hopton afterwards went to reside in Clemens Street, where he may have conducted the Post Office arrangements until 183o. CHAPTER XXVII. OUNG Leamington, for such it still was, according-to its growth in the principles of local government, was remarkably active at this period of its history. Counting the years from the local Act of 1825, we find it had now

nearly attained its majority; a time when the perspective of life is invariably accompanied by redundancy of strength, sinewy resolutions, fertility of enterprise, glowing ideals, and robustness of purpose. In individual experience these characteristics frequently raise high hopes which lead to bitter disappointment, but here every expectation was justified by a rich harvest of results. To proceed:

Music is another subject we must now bring up to date for it would never do to allow the early musical friends of Leamington to be eclipsed by any or all of the many topics to which in the course of this work we have alluded. The Philharmonic founded in 1826, sweetly sang its last Amen about the year 1830. Its life was short, but it was both merry and useful. As is the case with musical societies all the wide, wide, world over, it had quite its share of ups and downs; summer and winter; prosperity and adversity, and sometimes met with that peculiar kind of "contrary motion" which musical composers never put down in their parts. Musicians, the most harmonious of the great human family, have been constantly upbraided for their jealousies, their rivalries and dissensions. The psychological problem is beyond solution, but they may retort with a happy propriety that it was not the singers nor the instrumentalists, but the talkers who were responsible for the great Babel of tongues. The minute book of the society is now lying before us and out of twenty-three members we find there was one secession and one exclusion before the first concert. So it was not all harmony in those days. Talk about discipline, why our modern musical societies would crumble to dust in six months under the rules of the first Philharmonic. A fine of is. was imposed on every member absent from rehearsals at seven o'clock, the time for commencement; 1/6 at the end of the " first Act"; 2/6 if not present during the evening; is. for tuning during the performance of a piece; and 5s. for not returning in time for practice any part of music borrowed. Altogether, the society gave fourteen concerts, one of which

(on December 1 ith, 1827) was at the Court House, Warwick, and as the attendance was the smallest ever present at a concert in the United Boroughs, we quote it in the hope of preventing despondency in these days when our concert rooms are not more than half full. The audience, we are informed " was exactly as numerous as the members composing the orchestra," of whom there were twenty. The society never made a return visit, and the committee at their next meeting vented their indignation by liberally distributing votes of censure on those who left their places in the orchestra during the concert, and "particularly those who annoyed the members during the performance of a piece by conversing in the room." After the dissolution of the Philharmonic, F. Marshall's Choral Society was the sole occupant of the field, and its public concerts appear to have commenced about the time those of the old society were discontinued. Probably an amalgamation took place. There were regular practices in the Parish Church, and occasionally, performances of sacred music in the Episcopal Chapel, with organ and full band accompaniments. At one of these (June ioth, 1830), the strength of the latter was, four violins, two violas, two 'cellos, two contra-basses, two flutes, two bassoons, two horns, two trumpets, one trombone and double-drums. While the Choral Society were then pleasing the public with their sacred and secular concerts, a town band was formed. The leaders of the movement were Charles Elston, for many years bandmaster of the Warwickshire Militia; his nephew, George Elston Ball, who had been musically educated by G. Tatton, bandmaster of the Royal Horse Guards; and J. Cox, landlord of the Guards Inn, High Street, and also a military bandmaster. Their promenade concerts were successes, and as will readily be assumed from their experience, worthy of being recognised as the precursors of those grander performances we are now privileged to hear. Between 1840 and 1850 there was a remarkable growth of musical agencies and a manifestation of cultivated taste beyond all local precedent. Its range extended from the Parish Church choir to the orchestra in the Jephson Gardens, and its influence was felt in every department of harmony— vocal and instrumental. The Rev. John Craig commenced this new departure by encouraging Elliston to introduce the best music, by establishing a school for the choir boys in Grove Place and engaging from time to time competent teachers to train them in their duties. The cost of this work in twelve years was £1,711 1 is. sd., the whole of which he defrayed out of his own private purse. Mrs. Merridew, an accomplished singer, and her husband, the late Mr. N. Merridew, organised a series of high-class concerts on which was lavishly bestowed the cream of fashionable patronage. These increased the attractions of the Spa and brought before Leamington audiences the most popular artists of the day. A Glee Society established by Henry Marshall revived an old form of musical art which had been declining since the discontinuance of the Philharmonic. A prominent member of this society was the late Mr. John Beck, whose voice, a light tenor, was of such flexibility and range as enabled him to sing "Every Valley" with a distinctness of vocalisation and expression that won applause in the crowded concert rooms. Adhering steadfastly to the central idea of making the Jephson Gardens the loadstone for Leamington's prosperity, the Committee at an early stage of their career began to consider the question of providing open-air concerts for the visitors and residents. The intention was to establish concerts excelling all which had as yet been heard in the town and to make the gardens as celebrated for music as they were becoming for trees and flowers. The arrangements for the first band were made in June, 184S, under the guidance of "Mr. Godfrey, the Queen's Bandmaster." It was a London band consisting of thirteen performers, including Mr. Irwin, the conductor. To meet the expenses the town was canvassed and something like £200 raised as a band fund. The concerts, which were splendid, were continued for nine

weeks at a total cost of 235 9s. In the following year a local band was engaged (probably Elston's), supported by contributions from the proprietors of the Pump Rooms, private subscriptions, and donations from a Town Improvement Committee, then holding meetings at the Regent Hotel. In the summer of 1850, the celebrated Cologne band came to England specially to fulfil an engagement of fifteen weeks in the Jephson Gardens, made with them, on behalf of the Committee, by Mr. A. Berens, of London. The fame of the band having preceded its arrival, expectation was raised to a high pitch, and without disappointment. Finer playing has *From a photo by ff. P. Robinson, Tunbridge Wells.*

Patrick Brvne, The Blind Irish Harper. seldom been heard, and its visit remains one of the pleasantest memories of musical Leamington. The expenses were defrayed in the same way as the cost of the first band, Mr. Henry Bright (now Alderman) and the late Alderman John Bowen being the deputation from the Town Improvement Association to confer and arrange with the jephson Gardens' Committee. Only one other subject remains to be noticed in this connection. Patrick Byrne, the blind Irish harper, was a brilliant player who visited Copps's Hotel regularly. Seated in the grand hall, he discoursed the sweetest music, to the delight of the fashionable companies always staying at that establishment, and at the same time provided a treat gratuitously for passers by, many of whom lingered long in admiring crowds round the doors in High Street, charmed with those rich and beautiful harmonies which swelled from his instrument under the influence of his genius and taste. The orbless old musician was a general favourite, and an object of sympathetic interest, especially when taking his daily constitutional up and down the Parade without assistance. On one occasion he had the honour of appearing before the Queen and Royal Family at Windsor Castle. He was frequently at Beech Lawn, the welcome guest of Dr. Jephson, who in after life was himself

deprived of sight. After the demolition of Copps's Royal Hotel, he transferred his services to the Manor House Hotel, which had been opened by Isaac Curtis, formerly the proprietor of Wise's Baths in High Street.

No provisions had been made down to 1844, for the social convenience and daily intercourse of the nobility and gentry who were resident in Leamington and the neighbourhood in large numbers.-Their only means of association were the hunting field, balls, or assemblies as they were then called, and parties. To supply this want a movement was started in this year for providing a Tennis and Racquet Court. The first meeting was held on April 25th at the Upper Assembly Rooms when the scheme was adopted and a resolution passed to raise the requisite funds by shares. The following noblemen and gentlemen were constituted a provisional committee to give effect to the decision of the meeting: Lord Brooke, Lord Somerville, Lord Leigh, Lord Guernsey, Lord Lewisham, Sir Charles Douglas, M.P., Messrs. C. N. Newdigate, W. H. Wilson, H. C. Wise, Matthew Wise, E. Greaves, Hyde Clarke, R. Ramsay Clarke, Walter Gowan, E. T. Warde, W. C. Russell, E. Musgrave, B. Granville, J. Saunderson, J. B. Hanbury, G. E. Baker, and Dr. Jephson. Their first duty was to select a site, of which there were three offered. One was near the Old Bowling Green (probably the garden in Church Street and Regent Place now in the occupation of Councillor Purser), another at Lillington, and the third, a plot at the back of the Holly Walk the property of Mrs. Barber. It was decided to purchase the last for £1qj 10s., and Mr. Jackson was instructed to prepare plans. Before, however, the work was commenced attention was drawn to the present site in Bedford Street, and considering the situation more central, the committee paid £80 to Mrs. Barber for non-fulfilment of the contract to purchase and bought the land in Bedford Street from Mrs. Bishopp foroo. The work of building was at once commenced, the late William Ballard being the contractor, and Mr. Jackson the architect. The funds were raised in *£10* shares. The total cost, including furnishing was £4,211. The first trustees were Lord Brooke, Messrs. Charles Earle and H. C. Wise. The Club premises, substantially the same as when erected, though some improvements have recently been made in the Courts, consist of two billiard rooms, tennis and racquet courts, reading, smoking, committee rooms, etc., each and all being suitably furnished. The Club is very select, and the election of members, of whom there are two hundred and eighteen, exclusive of honorary members and visitors, is by ballot. The first secretary was Mr. Sanders. He was succeeded by the late Mr. W. J. Spicer, who held the office for a very long period; Mr. W. R. Wiggins is the present secretary.

The Leamington College in Binswood Avenue, erected in 1847, was the early harvest of an educational seed-sowing experiment, which took place some three or four years before. Either in 1843, or 1844, a company was formed to provide "for the sons of the nobility, clergy and gentry, a sound classical and mathematical education in accordance with the principles of the Established Church." Leamington was at this period of its history sadly deficient in scholastic arrangements suited to the requirements of the classes named. Public approbation was on the side of the new movement, and it was hoped that by the means to be employed, Leamington eventually would have a Public School which would place it on a level with Rugby, Winchester, Harrow, and Eton. Among the local leaders of this important work we find the names of Jephson, Marsh, Hitchman, and Dr. Amos Middleton. Mr. A. S. Field was the Secretary to the Company. The first home of the College was one of a fine row of houses, called Eastnor Terrace in honour of Lord Eastnor. The whole of these buildings have long since disappeared from local topography, and the site is practically unknown to modern Leamington, notwithstanding that it is visited daily by more people than perhaps any other spot in Leamington. It occupied the land of the Great Western Railway Station, for which it had to make way a few years later on. Here the young institution flourished, and it very soon became evident, from the increasing number of pupils, that a new building of large proportions would be necessary. In 1846, the land in Binswood Avenue was purchased, and on April 7, 1847, a large concourse of influential residents proceeded from the Regent Hotel to the site, where Dr. Jephson, in the presence of several thousands of spectators, laid amid general rejoicings, the foundation stone, which had an inscription of which the following is a free translation:—" Henry Jephson, M.D., laid this foundation stone of Leamington College, an Institution dedicated to Sacred and polite literature—a work long desired and long needed—on the 7th of April, 1847, which undertaking may the Almighty bless and prosper."

About the year 1847, the water for domestic purposes—a thorny question which kept the town in a state of agitation for the next twenty-five years—began to occupy the attention of the Commissioners by whom measures were at once considered for its improvement. Mr. Oldham, the tenant of the Mill, was the contractor, and his system was to convey the river water into filter beds in the old Innidge field, from whence it flowed into a cistern out of which it was pumped by the water wheel into the tank, still to he seen on the top of the Mill buildings. The distiibution to the town was by gravitation through a service of pipes laid down by him. There appears to have been at the time some question as to the wisdom of using the water from the river, but Mr. Hawkesley, who was consulted in 1847 and again in 1849 approved of it and in his later report said " I am still of opinion that the river Leam is the most suitable source from which to procure a large supply of water at a moderate cost. " During the three years the subject was under discussion, three schemes were propounded for acceptance. One was to build new waterworks on two acres of land at Stareham Hill, which Mrs. Willes was willing to sell for £400; an-other was to erect the works at Blakedown Mill, for which purpose Mr. Jordan offered one acre at £600; the other was to adopt Mr. Hawksley's report. He advised that £14,000 should be borrowed on security of the rates for the construction of a reservoir on the Rung Hills, and the placing of the works in a meadow, belonging to Lord Aylesford, suitated at the foot of the elevated ground on which the storage reservoir was to be placed. At a meeting of the Commissioners on September 10th, 1849, convened by Messrs. John Hitchman, G. A. Cundall, A. S. Field, John Bowen and John Goold, a resolution approving this plan was adopted, but only by the casting vote of the Chairman, a circumstance which perhaps explains why it was never carried into effect. This was the first phase of that question which became the very Marah of local politics in after years.

When the first half of the present century was drawing to a close, two new churches had been added to those we have noticed, and opened for public worship. One was Trinity Chapel, built in Beauchamp Square in 1847, and the other, St. Luke's, in Augusta Place, 1850. Both were Chapels of Ease to the mother Church of All Saints', and each had Episcopal License. The first was erected at the cost of the Vicar, who was praised for the beauty of the design, and who exercised great hospitality. It would seem from the circumstances of the time that after the dispute respecting the very ample district granted St. Mary's in 1840, a counter-policy was adopted of erecting proprietary chapels to prevent the parish of All Saints' being further reduced by the formation of new districts. The inaugural service at Holy Trinity took place on All Saints' Day (November 1), 1847. Mr. Craig preached the sermon, and in the evening he entertained, at the Town Hall, between sixty and seventy persons, the majority of whom were workmen who had been engaged on the building. The style of architecture was what is known as Early English decorated, and in the opinion of the *Courier* it is the most perfect specimen of the kind. The windows are large and splendid, the mouldings and tracings being of the richest description. The length from east to west is seventy feet, and the shape being cruciform the transepts are nearly of the same proportion. The height is from forty to fifty feet, and the elevation, the idea for which the Vicar derived from the plan of the Cathedral at Rouen, is particularly unique. The organ was supplied by Mr. H. T. Elliston, the organist at the Parish Church, and the Rev. William Young, D.C.L., was the first incumbent.

The Vicar's Grammar School, in Priory Terrace, now occupied as a furniture store by Mr. Jones, of "the Priory," was the second of several great projects which engaged Mr. Craig's attention during the first ten years of his ministry. One would have thought he had on hand at the Parish Church quite sufficient for all the time he could spare from his strictly clerical duties, but he was a man of great energy and liberality, and with the temperature of his nature raised to white heat by the praise he was daily receiving for his zeal, there was no scheme for the public advantage from which he could stand apart with folded arms. The special purpose of the school was to fill a void which the erection of the College had made more palpable than ever. The sons of the trading community were not then eligible for admission into that institution, and in the private academies, they could not obtain, economically, a good commercial training with some practical knowledge of the rudiments of a classical education. When the Leamington College closed its doors against the trades people of the town, Mr. Craig stepped forward and built the Grammar School, the site being land on which "Priory House" stands (Mr. Aspa's) and the furniture stores of Mr. Jones. Mr. Craig's idea was to found a Grammar School worthy of the Spa, and he very nearly succeeded. The foundation stone was laid on September 15 th, 1847, by the Free and Accepted Masons, whose services, by the way, have been of signal advantage to Leamington. Earl Howe, at the time Provincial Grand Master of the War-

wickshire Grand Lodge was to have performed the ceremony but was prevented doing so by indisposition. The Lodge was opened at the Regent Hotel, and after the customary ceremonials had been observed, there was a procession to the Parish Church, led by the fine band of Prince Albert's Regiment of Hussars, then stationed at Coventry. There were altogether about one hundred and thirty members of the craft who walked in the procession. The sermon at the Church was preached by Brother, the Rev. G. C. Fenwick, Grand Chaplain, after which the procession was again formed and proceeding to the ground the stone was duly laid by Dr. Bell Fletcher, Deputy P.G.M. The Vicar having delivered an address, the Old Hundredth Psalm was sung. There was a very large attendance of the public. The proceedings of the day were concluded with a grand banquet at the Bath Hotel at which ninety members of the Order were present. Dr. Bell Fletcher presided, and amongst those who supported him was Dr. O'Callaghan who attended as a member of Grand Master's Own Lodge, Ireland, and who afterwards took a leading part in the founding of The Leamington Philosophical Society.

St. Luke's Episcopal Chapel, Augusta Place, was built in 1850, on land which had previously been used for two important and at the time most prosperous local trades. About the year 1832, Stephen Peasnall, a plumber in a very large way of business, had his establishment there, and he was followed by Mr. Hoadley, a coach builder. The Rev. Edmund Clay, purchased the property in 1850, demolished the manufactory and with the sanction of Mr. Craig and the licence of the Bishop, St. Luke's was erected and opened on St. Luke's Day (October 18) in the same year. The adjoining schoolroom, now the printing and publishing office of the *Leamington News,* was built at the same time. An early and somewhat scarce illustration of the Chapel shows that neither the large circular window now to be seen in the front elevation nor the doors formed part of the original design. The entrance

was by a side door between the Chapel and the 1 The Rev. Mr. Clay was, in doctrine and ceremonial, what is known as Low Church, but in Spiritualism, table turning and table rapping, he was high enough for the most enthusiastic believers in that hazy faith A lecture delivered by him in 1850 attracted general attention on account of the extraordinary statements made of alleged transactions at seances in America and in England. Mr. liright (father of Alderman Bright) publicly offered to give £100 to the Warneford Hospital if Mr. Clay and his friends would cause a table to move without the application of physical force. The challenge was not accepted, and the Hospital lost a valuable contribution.

School. We quote the following description of the arrangements from the *Leamington Courier,* October 19th, 1850.

"The Chapel which has been erected in the Early English style, is calculated to accommodate about four hundred persons, there being three rows of pews, which will eventually be closed with doors, in the body of the building, and a gallery extending along the west and north sides in which about one hundred and fifty sittings will be provided, many of them let at reduced rates, and several at a mere nominal charge to suit the means of the less opulent classes, who will thereby have insured to them the exclusive right of their occupation. There are three lancet windows on the north end of the building, and eight in the east or principal front facing Augusta Place, which is surmounted by an enriched cornice terminating with a battlemented parapet, the external facings and ornaments of the Chapel being finished in Roman cement with a neatly-executed cross introduced at each gable. Both the Communion table and pulpit are, from the peculiar position and dimensions of the Chapel, placed in the south, the enclosed area of the former being paved with Minton ornamental encaustic tiles. The principal timbers of the roof and the internal fittings, which are of stained deal varnished, are completed with tracery to suit the general style of the building; the north and west galleries are supported by six clustered pillars of like material, and the floors of the aisles and lobbies are composed of partly coloured tiles. Ample provision has been made to warm the building by means of flues, and effective ventilation secured by four ornamental perforations in the ceiling from which is suspended a twelve-light chandelier. A neat and suitable organ occupies a portion of the north side of the gallery, to which is a separate entrance by a flight of stairs. The principal mode of access into the interior of the Chapel is from Academy Place through a convenient lobby which is lighted by a window formed of neatly stained glass. A vestry of adequate dimensions and replete with the usual accompaniments, communicates with the Chapel by a door on the west side, near to the Communion table. We understand the entire cost of completing this new place of worship has been incurred by the resident minister."

The opening services were plain and consisted of a sermon in the morning by the Rev. J. Craig, and another in the evening by the new clergyman, with congregational psalmody on each occasion.

A new Nonconformist place of worship was being finished about the time St. Luke's was commenced. This was the Congregational Chapel in Brandon Parade, Holly Walk. Its origin was a dispute at the mother church, Spencer Street, which led to the secession of some members, and the holding of separate meetings in the Music Hall, Bath Street. The event was a forcible exemplification of the crisis which inevitably arises in the history of every free church when the pulpit becomes empty, and of which Mr. James says nothing can happen that places its interests in greater peril. The Rev. Mr. Pope, having resigned the pastorate, removed to Torquay, and it was during his absence that the unity of the church and congregation was broken. A more eligible site than that chosen for the building could not easily have been found. The surroundings were pleasant, and the neighbourhood thickly populated; and the

structure itself was an agreeable contrast in its external appearance to the stereotyped plaster, or stucco work, so characteristic of every other sacred edifice in Leamington, excepting the Parish Church. The style of architecture belongs to the period of Henry VII. The front elevation is composed of pressed red brick, relieved with diagonal lines of blue, and Bath stone dressings for the windows, doors, buttresses, and walls. There are two entrance doors—one on each side—and in the centre of the elevation a fine window of five traceried lights. Two substantial ornamental buttresses, separating the windows from the doors, are continued to the roof, where they terminate in crocketted pinnacles and fineals. The gable is surmounted with an enriched stone cross The length of the building from north to south is seventy-two feet, including the schoolroom, and the width from east to west forty-seven feet. The interior was most comfortably fitted up with open seats, and with the gallery at the north end, provided accommodation for about six hundred persons. An ornamental desk, placed on a dais, approached by five steps on each side and in front, was the pulpit. The Rev. Henry Batchelor, of Chadshunt, was the first minister. Mr. D. G. Squirhill, to whom must be awarded special commendation for designing the most cheerful and comfortable edifice of the kind in Leamington at that period, was the architect. The foundation stone was laid in April, 1849.

The Original Station At Milvekton, erected in 1844, when it formed the terminus of the new line from Coventry to Warwick and Leamington.

CHRONOLOGY FROM 1836 TO 1850. 1826. —Satchwell Place, "the original licensed

Boarding house," and the thatched cottage "lately occupied as a post office," to let.

New peal of bells at the Church rung for the first time, March 27.

First issue of the *Warwickshire Chronicle,* April 19.

The Bishop consecrated the new por-

tion of the Parish Church, June 8.

House-warming at Copps's Royal Hotel, June 21.

York Terrace commenced, and Warwick Street formed.

First code of bye-laws published by Commissioners.

Braham, the great tenor, sang at Elliston's concert in the new Assembly Rooms, September 29.

First stone of Copps's Hotel laid by Miss Copps, who was afterwards Mrs. Busby, November 13.

Petition to Parliament in favour of the Bill for making turnpike, the branch road from Oakley Wood to Leamington, adopted at a public meeting.

Negotiations between Mr. Edward Willes and Parish Committee for land on which to build houses for the poor.

Poor Rate at is. in the £ granted and "notice given thereof in Church." 1827. —The Marchioness of Wellesley and Duke of Wellington, the Duke and Duchess of St. Albans, the Duke of Grafton and family, the Dutch Ambassador, and the Marchioness of Bute, were among the visitors this year.

F. Marshall, organist of Rugby Chapel and the Episcopal Chapel, Leamington Spa, published " Benedictus," a trio for three voices.

Miss Foote played *Rosalind* in "As You Like It," at the Theatre, August 20 and 21.

Dr. Loudon published "A Sketch of the History, Position, and Medicinal Properties of the Springs of Leamington Spa. "

Miss Foote at the Theatre, October 27, as *Miss Hardcastle* in "She Stoops to Conquer."

Mr. Fairweather succeeded Smart at the Marble Baths, Clemens Street.

Vestry purchased 16 pews, contain-

ing 97
sittings, from Mr. Downes, for £657.

Upwards of 7,000 yards of land on the south side of Newbold Square (now Beauchamp
Square), and the east of Upper Union Street, sold.

1827. —The Willes bridge built. While excavating the ground to lay the foundation of the abutment walls, there was found at the depth of 14 feet from the surface, "nearly in a line with the river, and about 13 feet from the edge of the stream, a human skull, which, notwithstanding it must have lain there for some centuries was in an excellent state of preservation. An oak tree upwards of 26 feet in length and an elm tree 20 inches in diameter, were also found lying in a longitudinal direction, near the same spot, and at about the same depth in the earth; the latter was in a complete state of decay, but the oak was quite sound."

York Terrace commenced.

1828. —Clemens Street Chapel repaired and reno vated; Rev. J. A. James preached at the re-opening service.

Rev. Alfred Pope arrived in Leamington,
February 9.

Preached his first sermon in Clemens Street
Chapel, February 10.

Dr. Staunton elected physician to the Leamington General Hospital and Dispensary,
in the room of Dr. Davie.

The Leamington Charitable Repository established at 55, Clemens Street; manageress Miss Tatnall.

Charles Kean played *Romeo* in " Romeo and
Juliet," at the Theatre, July 10.

Miss Foote made her third appearance at the
Theatre in the following week, and Mathews and Yates played there in August.

Adoption of the Provident Dispensary principle at the General Hospital.

Leamington *Courier* started, August.

Rev. W. F. Hook preached at the Parish
Church and Episcopal Chapel, August

24.

Elliston's Rooms, Bath Street, re-opened by
Mr. Ebury, of the Italian Opera House, London.

At a cost of £2,000, it was proposed to erect a new theatre in George Street, on the site of Mr. W. G. Bloomfield's house.

The ancient Court Leet and Court Baron held at the Bath Hotel.

The old Well House further improved by the
Earl of Aylesford, and cottage in Church
Walk built.

The Catholic Chapel, George Street, opened.

Dr. Loudon's "Practical Dissertation" on the Waters of Leamington re-published.

Mr. John Haddon joined Mr. Woodhouse in partnership in the drapery business at Waterloo House, Bath Street.

CHRONOLOGY FROM 1828. —Covent Garden Market established.

Baptists began to hold meetings in Grove
Place

Miss Foote played at the Theatre, November 8.

1829. —Petition to Postmaster General for the estab lishment of a post-office in Leamington.

Joseph Stanley succeeded at the Crown
Hotel by Mr. Rogers.

"Te Deum" for the organ and pianoforte composed by H. T. Elliston.

Notice issued of the intention of the Vestry to purchase houses for the employment and maintenance of the poor.

Mr. W. Flavel, ironmonger, Bath Street,
advertised his "patent kitchener register cooking stove."

Benefit performance at the Theatre for Miss
Foote.

Military Brass Band established by Mr.
Sanderson, late Trumpet-Major in 13th Light Dragoons.

Rev. A. Pope ordained Minister of Clemens

Street Chapel, April 29. This was the first service of the kind in Leamington. "Several clergymen were present, and seemed to regard the proceedings with the most earnest interest."

Organ removed from the south to the north side of the Parish Church.

Several of the old cottages demolished.

Bells rung in celebration of the Leigh Peerage case having terminated in favour of
Chandcs Leigh, Esq., of Stoncleigh, June 18.

Mill Street Chapel commenced in April,
opened August 27.

Parish Church enlarged at south end.

Dr. Daubeny, Professor of Chemistry at Oxford, discovered Iodine and Brome in the mineral waters.

1830. —King William IV. proclaimed (July 2). The inhabitants, accompanied with a band,
marched round the town.

Visit of the Duchess of Kent and the Princess
Victoria, August 3.

Baptists removed into Guy Street, New
Town, and formed themselves into a Society.

Rev. George Cole, the first Baptist minister in Leamington.

1831. —Old Town Hall, High Street, built.

1826 TO 1850.—*Continued.* 1831. — Parish Committee object to poor persons out side Leamington being admitted as inpatients at the Hospital and Dispensary, Regent Street.
Population 6,269.

1832. —James Bisset died; buried near the south porch in the churchyard; aged 72.

General Alexander Campbell, of Monrie,
N.B., an officer who had seen much service in Canada and the West Indies, died,
February 24.

First stone of the Warneford Hospital laid,
June 10.

The ordinance of adult baptism by

immersion administered for the first time in Leamington. This was at the Baptist Chapel in Guy Street, October 14.

Parish Church again enlarged.

Lord Ribblesdale died, December 14, age 43 1833. —Paganini at the Upper Assembly Rooms twice—August 10 and October 22.

Baptist Chapel, Warwick Street, built.

Bochsa and Mori at the Assembly Rooms.

The Rev. Dr. Warneford, staying at the
Stoneleigh Hotel.

Fairfax's Guide published.

The Old Theatre, Bath Street, purchased by by Mr. Ind, wine and spirit merchant, and converted into wine vaults.

1834. —Parish Church enlarged for the fifth time.

Leamington Gas Company established; capital 20,000. Warwick and Leamington Bank formed; capital,£250,000.

J. G. Jackson renting Newbold Gardens and cottage where the Hitchman Fountain stands; rent of gardens, £6; ditto cottage, £26 13s. 4d.

1835. —The Leamington Bank started; capital ,£200,000.

Leamington Priors and Warwickshire Bank established.

1836. —First Temperance Society established.

The Temple of Peace Lodge commenced.

Inaugural Service at Spencer Street Chapel,
July 21.

Milverton Episcopal Chapel (the "Pepper
Box Chapel ") opened, August 5.

The lirst Mechanics' Institute established.

1837. —Rejoicings in Leamington on Princess

Victoria attaining her majority, May 24.

CHRONOLOGY FROM I 1837. —Madame Vestris and Matthews at the Upper Assembly Rooms, August 31. Rev. John Angell James and James Parsons

preached Anniversary Sermons at Spencer Street Chapel, September 23. Collections £126.

Mori, Thalberg, and John Parry, junior, at the Upper Assembly Rooms.

1838. —Permission granted by the Queen to call

Leamington, "Royal," July 19.

Charles Dickens, a visitor.

Foundation Stone of St. Mary's Church laid,
October 5.

Prince Louis Napoleon, afterwards Napoleon
III., resided in Leamington. On Sunday, November 25, with his suite, he attended
Divine service at the Catholic Chapel, George Street. The following Wednesday evening, a banquet in his honour was given by Mr. John Hampden, at his residence,
Clarence Terrace, to which many of the local nobility and gentry were invited.

1839. —Leamington visited by the Dowager Queen

Adelaide, November 4.

Rev. Robert Downes ceased to be Vicar.

Rev. John Craig succeeded Mr. Downes.

Testimonial of the value of 150 guineas made to Major Hawkes.

Dr. Winslow became Minister at the Baptist
Church, Warwick Street.

The work of widening the bridge near the
Parish Church commenced.

The Leamington Brewery erected.

1840. —Thalberg, Madame Balfe, Grisi and Mr. Balfc gave a Concert in the Music Hall, January 31.

The New Bridge opened and named "Victoria," May 25.

Lindley, Blagrove and Parry at a Concert in the Music Hall.

Inhabitants present an address of congratulation to the Queen and Prince Albert on their Marriage.

Rev. W. Jay, of Bath, preached at Spencer
Street Chapel.

1841. —Dedication Service at the Catholic Church, George Street.

A great flood.

The Holly Walk improved by the Commissioners, and ornamental pillars placed at the Parade end.

Lizt at the Music Hall.

Mrs. Potterton, daughter of William Abbotts, and grandmother of Mr. T. B. Potterton, rate collector for Milverton, died.

i26 TO 1850.—Continued. 1841. —Population, 12,812. 1842. —Hopper's Guide published.

Application to Parliament for new local Act.

1843.—First stone of Lantern Tower at Parish Church laid, September.

New local Act passed June.

Establishment of town police force.

Planting trees in the streets began.

1844. —New nave at Parish Church opened.

Leamington College founded.

King of Saxony visited Leamington.

Railway from Coventry to Milverton opened.

1845. —Chancel at Parish Church finished, July.

Meeting held to promote public testimonial to Dr. Jephson.

1S46.—Foundation stone laid of north transept and clock tower at Parish Church, June.

Jephson Gardens opened, May.

Tennis Court built.

New Post Office in Bath Street opened.

1847. —Visit of Prince George.

Dr. Amos Middleton died, April 25.

Foundation stone of Vicar's Grammar School laid, September.

Holy Trinity Church erected; first service
November 1.

1848. —The College and the Grammar School opened.

Oaks planted in the Jephson Gardens.

Leamington Advertiser started, October. Victoria Bridge widened on the west side; contractor, J. Hart.

Jenny Lind, Lablache, Bellini, and Balfe, at the Assembly Rooms, November.

1849—Foundation stone of Congregational Chapel, Holly Walk, laid, April.

Clemens Street Chapel opened as a

theatre,
February.

Mr and Mrs Charles Kean at the Theatre in
"The Wife's Secret."

Victoria Pavilion opened as Hengler's
Equestrian Circus.

1850.-St. Luke's Church, Augusta Place, opened on-St. Luke's Day, October 18.

Adelaide Bridge built; contractor J. Heritage, Warwick.

Extension of Railway from Milverton to
Rugby commenced; bridges in High Street, and at the bottom of the new River
Walk erected by J. Hart.

CHAPTER XXVIII.

RADUAL progress, originally by degrees almost imperceptibly slow, has marked the growth of the fame of the Leamington mineral waters from an age of ignorance and superstition, to one of faith, founded on reason and scientific intelligence. In this chapter we purpose making a brief change in our historical survey, to consider a subject which is the fountain source from whence Royal Leamington Spa derives its existence. We allude to the saline springs, whose story we shall endeavour to construct from the writings of historians, eminent medical men, and others, extending back over a period of more than four centuries. By a freak of fortune, not uncommon in the history of mankind, the man whose proper position is first among all those who have referred to these waters has been gently elbowed away into the background of forgetfulness, and systematically ignored. It is both a duty and a pleasure to restore him to his rightful place, and to give him back the insignia of his seniority. Camden, in honour of whom the Old Well has been named, was not the first, but the second historian who made mention of the spring. John Rous preceded him by about a century, and has bequeathed to posterity a far more interesting account of the locality. Something must also be said of the sources of supply, and those causes which have combined

to produce waters of such priceless value.

Leamington stands on two great subterranean rivers, or, as the reader might perhaps prefer to call them, vast and inexhaustible, underground natural reservoirs, one being constantly filled with mineral, and the other with fresh water. The first of these is chiefly beneath the old town, namely, the portion on the south side of the Leam, but it also extends a short distance beyond the north bank, probably as far as Newbold Terrace. There, or somewhere near, a fault in the formation separates the fresh water storage from the salt. The strata from whence the mineral water is obtained is called "saliferous," a name, the meaning of which is sufficiently obvious without explanation; that where the domestic supply is found, the "Keuper," or waterbearing stones. A knowledge of the existence of these formations is of infinitely greater importance than any number of hazel-sticks, twirled about between the thumbs and fingers of "water diviners." It might not be an easy task for any but an experienced geologist to draw an exact outline of the mineral water-bearing area of the town, but the following rough sketch may be accepted as approximately correct—a line extended westward from the bottom of Newbold Terrace to a point in the Pump Room Gardens opposite the Kiosk; southward over the river to the top of Tachbrook Street; eastward across Brunswick Street to the Whitnash footpath, and from thence northward to Newbold Terrace. Within this space all our principal springs have been discovered, and although the mineral water may be met with outside the line thus indicated, southwards and westwards, as in fact it was in 1872-3, when the Corporation were boring for fresh water near the sewage pumping station, the story of a saline spring having been found in the South Parade (now Clarendon Avenue) must be discarded as highly improbable and totally unsupported by any creditable evidence. Having regard to the strata and the abundance of fresh water in the locality, it would not be more irrational to believe that it was a spring of

champagne. Figure 1 in the diagram on the previous page shows that the source of supply is deeper according to the distance of the well from the river; for this phenomenon we have never seen any satisfactory explanation by those who have studied the question closely. It should be noticed also that the Original Well, marked in the diagram, but not named, is the shallowest of all; yet its yield has been as abundant as from any of those of greater depth. Smart's Well in Clemens Street is not mentioned; it was the most remote from the river, and in accordance with the law governing the other springs, it was the deepest—seventy feet. The one in Charlotte Street is also omitted, but no particulars are extant of this spring.

The following extract from Loudon's most useful work deals with a question inscrutable to the geologist; one to which imagination has been able to return only a dubious answer:—

"In what particular w ay the mineral waters of Leamington acquire their impregnations, is by no means known. Various borings in the fields around the town distinctly prove that the sources of the wells are confined to the strata underneath the houses, and at a very short distance around them—perhaps not more than a quarter of a mile. As to the depth that the mineral fluid is found, that varies in *every* spring. The water of the Old Well once flowed from a fissure in the rock, quite at the surface of the earth. While in the South Parade, it has been found at more than 100 feet below the houses. The difference between the temperature of summer and winter, may be owing to the fresh water descending from the surface to the deeper parts of the earth before it reaches the spot where the saline impregnations are acquired; and this opinion seems strengthened by the well-known fact, that the level of some of the mineral springs is higher than the level of the river and the water contained in the wells employed for domestic uses. It has been thought probable, that there exists, underneath the town of Leamington, beds of salt, or brine pits, such as those at Northwich, in Cheshire, and Droitwitch, in Worcestershire; and that in passing over these deposits, the fresh water, in descending from the surface, acquires at least a part, if not the whole of its saline ingredients; during which time it becomes cooled to the temperature which has been already noticed; but the existence of these saline beds, or brine pits, is, however, purely hypothetical. That the mineral waters acquire their solid contents brfore they become charged with the gaseous, is inferred from the small quantity and few kinds of aerial substances which are usually found in common springs. To explain the mode in which the Leamington wells acquire their gaseous contents, it has been supposed that there exists also, near the salt beds, a layer, or number of layers, of marine vegetable matter, from whence the iodine, brome, and gases are extricated by the fluid which has been already considered, as charged with saline particles. In advancing nearer the surface, the fluid, thus impregnated, meets with a stratum of porus ironstone, which is combined with the silica, and which, in digging Mr. Smart's well, has been found to exist under the town; and hence the ferruginous bi-silicatc. These opinions, however, much as they are strengthened by a series of synthetical experiments, lately published by M. Vogel, being unsusceptible of demonstration, must necessarily be considered as mere suppositions; and indeed, are of little or no importance in a practical point of view. It is even probable, that from the time the first impregnation is acquired, until the water reaches the surface again, several chemical changes take place which do not admit of demonstration."

Geology is much better understood in the present day than it was in Loudon's time, and though not sufficiently advanced to explain all the processes by which the gases are united in the water, the existence of beds of rock-salt beneath the old part of the town is not now hypothetical. It is generally accepted that from these the saline quality is derived; the rest is reserved for ingenious speculation. Another subject to be noted is that the expansion of the town since his work was published makes his description of the extent of the strata inapplicable.

John Rous, the "fader" of Warwickshire historians, was a Priest, who, dying at the Chantry, Guy's Cliffe, in 1491, left several important works for the benefit of his country, only two of which have been preserved—the "Chronicon de Regibus Angliae," and an account of the Earls of Warwick, commonly known as the " Rows Rol."" In the latter, published, it is conjectured, about 1480, is the following passage, singularly beautiful in its old world setting of quaint spelling and phraseology, and of special value as a picture of the Leamington saline springs more than four hundred years ago:—" Wyth in lytyll more then a mylle from Warwik is a salt well and many spernngys about hyt where myght be made many wells and have salt watyr rennyng therowt the yere and the Reuer of Lemyn that rynys by of time flows ouer hem." From this we learn that in the fifteenth century there were numerous springs besides the principal one now known as the "Old Well," and that the supply was considered sufficient to provide for several other wells without intermission. Walter Bailey, Queen Elizabeth's physician, who in 1572 was in attendance when she visited Warwick, published, in 1582, a description of the chalybeate springs of Newnham Regis without making the slightest allusion to those at Leamington. As the roads were in such a bad state that her Majesty could not pass through the village, his silence may be explainable by his having had no opportunity of inspecting them. After Rous came Camden, the "Varro, Strabo, and Pausanias" of his age, at the respectable distance of about a century (1586). In his " Britannia" he speaks of " Leamington (so called of Leame, a small brooke that wandereth through this part of the shire), where there boileth out a spring of salt water" *fUbi/ons salsus ebullit)*. Speed, the next historian of note quoted in this connection, carries the subject no further, but simply remarks in his "Theatre of Great Britain" (1606) that "at Leamington, so far from the Sea, a Spring of salt-water boileth up." At this time there was only a glimmering of light as to the medicinal character of the English mineral waters, but in 1636, Dudley, the third Lord North, in his "Exonerations," brought the subject prominently before the public, and in so doing materially advanced the healing and health-preserving art. "The use of Tunbridge and Epsom waters, for health and cure," he says, "I made known to London and the King's people. The Spa is a chargeable and inconvenient journey to sick bodies, besides the money it carries out of the kingdom, and inconvenient to religion. " "It were well," remarks Moncrieff, "if this consideration were duly weighed by travellers in the present day when seeking for health and pleasure across the channel," and to this opinion all will readily subscribe who know anything of the value of the Leamington waters. The next notice occurs in Dugdale's "Antiquities of Warwickshire," published in 1656, where, in this particular, our great county historian can only be considered as having approached the simple grandeur of Homer when he was in one of his nodding humours. After some valuable information respecting ancient Leamington, he proceeds, "All that is further observable touching this Place is that nigh to the East End of the Church there is a Spring of Salt-water (not above a stones-throw from the River *Learnt)* whereof the inhabitants make much Use for seasoning of Meat." Here Dugdale is in error as to the situation of the well, and the quality of the water, the former being at the west end of the Church, and the latter possessing no power such as that attributed. But assuming that he was in a drowsy state of mind when he thus blundered in his description, Moncrieff must have been snoring heavily at the time he attempted to correct him, for after quoting him as having said that the spring was " nigh to the *west* end of the Church," which would have been correct, he asserts that the statement is " inaccurate, the spring lying to the East of the Church." In 1662, Fuller in his "History of the Worthies of Great Britain," "with his usual originality of thought and singularity of phrase," thus alluded to the subject:— "At Leamington, two miles from Warwick, there issueth out, within a stride of the womb of of the earth, two twin springs, as different in taste and operation as Jacob and Esau in disposition, the one salt the other fresh. This the meanest countryman does plainly see by their effects which it would puzzle a consultation of physicians to assign the cause thereof." Following Fuller came Blome, who, in 1673, printed his "Britannia," and substantially repeated Fuller's words. Down to this period the question of the medical power of the waters had not been brought into the alembic of scientific investigation: to the historians they were only matters of curiosity, and to the Faculty subjects of general indifference.

There was a new departure in 1698. Dr. Guidot, a practitioner at Bath, had devoted his whole life to the study of the therapeutic effects of the waters at different places. "He was a man of industry," remarks the celebrated Dr. B. W. Richardson, "and I suppose in his day, of erudition; but I do not think he would stand much chance now in the grand scuffle. He wrote seven or eight treatises on waters.... From the remarks he makes of the spring at Leamington Priors, I have no doubt he had been there and had observed the quality of the water." As the result of a reported analysis, he declared the old well to be a nitrous spring. In 1730, the Rev. Dr. Thomas published an enlarged and improved edition of Dugdale's "Antiquities," wherein there appears the first mention of the waters being resorted to for medicinal purposes. Having corrected Dugdale's error by stating that "nigh to the West end of the Church" there is a Spring of salt water, he observed that the inhabitants used it for making their bread, "and strangers drink it as a purging water with much success."

As the author was a Warwickshire clergyman residing at Exhall, near Coventry, he would have excellent opportunities for acquainting himself with this dawning fame of the Old Well. Guidot's vi ew as to the water being of a nitrous quality was probably the accepted opinion until 1740, when Dr. Short wrote his "Treatise on Mineral Waters," and announced it to be a " brine spring, possessed of a considerable quantity of calcareous nitre." Dr. Rutty, who has been pronounced "the most profound and correct inquirer of all the early writers, into the nature and properties of mineral waters," in his "Methodical Synopsis of Mineral Waters, including a minute examination of all the most celebrated mineral springs in thisand other European countries, 1757," in some degree reconciled the difference between Drs. Guidot and Short by declaring it to be "A saline

Boating On The Lf.am; from an oil painting by A. Varney, Parade Leamington Spa.

nitrous spring." He also made an analysis, and found that "after careful evaporation a gallon of the water yielded 960 grains of sediment, 30 of which were calcareous earth, and the rest marine salt." Public attention was further directed to the subject in 1765, when Dr. Russell, in his treatise on sea water and salt-springs, concurred with Dr. Rutty in the conclusion at which he had arrived.

Besides the increasing interest thus manifested, some progress had taken place in regard to the higher and more important question of the healing, or alleviating power of the water, and locally, there was a rude faith in its efficacy, one phase of which nowonly elicits a feeling of amusement. Near to the old spring a tub is reported to have been placed in the ditch for bathing purposes, and also for the immersion of sufferers from hydrophobia. Moncrieffe says it appeared to have been used " more in cases of hydrophobia than any other; a regular dipper, Thomas Dilkes, having been engaged from the beginning of the eighteenth century for this express purpose

Of the persons thus cured of that dreadful disorder, an annual register was kept, attested by the dipper on oath, from these registers, it appears that from June, 1778, to 1786, eight years, no fewer than 119 persons, who had suffered from the bite of mad dogs, had been effactually cured by immersion in the water. This Thomas Dilkes, the dipper, was quite a character in his way; so jealous was he of the water, that he declared, if ever he should meet with a failure, he would not dip any one again, and, on a patient being brought, whose case was more than commonly desperate, he obstinately refused to perform his office, so that the friends of the sufferer were obliged to undertake it themselves, and were luckily successful, for says my authority, though the man was absolutely raving mad at the time he was brought, he very soon afterwards perfectly recovered." This story must be taken for what it is worth. The name of Thomas Dilkes does not appear in any of the registers, and Thomas Dawkes makes no allusion in his Memoranda either to Dilkes or the dipping process. It has been thought that Dawkes himself was the " regular dipper," and that the name of Dilkes is a printer's error. Considering that he resided close to the spring, the theory is not improbable, but in any case the story of the cures of hydrophobia is the most absurd of idle fables.

In the *Coventry Mercury* for September 29, 1788, reference is made to a Dr. Allen, who is said to have been a resident medical man in the village, and the first that "generally impressed the public with a proper feeling of the value and qualities of the Leamington waters." As to his residence here, we can express no opinion but that he very worthily occupies a position with those writers whose names have been given, and Drs. Lambe, Kerr, Johnstone, Middleton, and Loudon, is beyond all question.

A most important advance was made in 1794 by Dr. Lambe, who, as Mr. Field remarks, "practised as a physician, with great reputation and success at Warwick." Of him some interesting particulars have been supplied by the late Dr. Jeaffreson, father of Mr. Councillor J. R. Jeaffreson. His personal recollections of Dr. Lambe were "that although somewhat eccentric in his practical views, he was not the less a scientific man, an intelligent observer of nature, and an accomplished physician. He was, moreover, one of the most elegant medical writers of his day. The springs of the neighbouring villages, continues Dr. Jeaffreson, did not escape his observation, and having studied and analysed the waters, he published an account of them in 1797, in the fifth volume of the "Transactions of the Philosophical Society of Manchester "—a society embracing the respected names of Priestly, Dalton, and Watt, and not, perhaps, inferior to any contemporary Association in Europe." The chief results of Dr. Lambe's investigations were, a demonstration of the presence of iron in the Leamington water to some extent, and general analytical evidence that the same curative effects might be anticipated from its use as from that at Cheltenham. Such an opinion, expressed by one of great eminence in his profession, at a time when the fashionable world were flocking to Cheltenham, had a powerful influence in turning the tide in favour of Leamington.

Working in the same field of research, and with corresponding zeal, success, and enthusiasm, were two other medical men besides Dr. Allen, to whom we have referred; Dr. Johnstone, of Birmingham; and Dr. Kerr, of Northampton. They were contemporaries of Dr. Lambe, and the commencement of their services dates from a period closely following the discovery of the second spring in Bath Street, in 1784. Dr. Edward Johnstone was a member of a family, or rather a series of families, famous for their intellectual endowments, their devotion to science and the cause of the afflcted. He was one of the founders of the General Hospital, and became its senior physician, a post he filled with great distinction until March, 1801, when he resigned. "His influence," the late Dr. W. B. Richardson writes, "was second to none, and as he commanded an extensive practice in the most rising district of the Midland Counties, he contributed largely to results which he did not foresee." It was doubtless owing to his exertions that many Birmingham people came to reside in Leamington in the beginning of the century. His son, Dr.

James Johnstone, died in Leamington in May, 1864, at the age of sixty-four years, few being aware at the time of the signal service his father had rendered the Spa in its village days.

Greater credit has been given Dr. Kerr for bringing the Spa fully before the world than has been allowed Dr. Lambe. He was connected with the Northampton Infirmary, and Dr. Richardson characterises him as " one of the shrewdest practitioners of the last century. He was not profoundly scientific, but a gentleman of position and influence, and one who possessed a profound knowledge of the world, its weaknesses, and its wants—a knowledge nowhere wanted more than among practitioners of the medical art. He was accustomed to send his patients from Northampton to the Spa, and under the force of his recommendation, the 'Dog' and the 'Bowling Green ' had become widely known in the year 1785."

By this time the value of the Leamington waters was generally acknowledged, but something more was required to popularise them. This was supplied by Dr. Amos Middleton, in 1806, publishing his Analysis "Illustrated with cases to prove their efficacy in the cure of Scrofula and Scorbutic Humours, to which are added Instructions for cold and warm bathing." His work was the most practical on the subject that had been placed in the hands of the public, and its value remains undiminished to the present day. Lambe did immense good by writing specially for the profession to which he belonged; Middleton did much more by writing down to the capacity of the people. We append the results of his matured experience, the cream of his thorough acquaintance with the subject, in the hope that the afflicted will be encouraged and led to see that the efficacy of " even a sovereign remedy" may be frustrated if used indiscreetly, either by not allowing it sufficient time, or applying it in a manner, and under circumstances calculated to render its virtues a nullity.

MIDDLETON'S GENERAL RULES FOR TAKING THE WATERS.

"It will be at first necessary to reflect

that mineral waters, like other medical substances, are appropriated to certain diseases only, and that the more powerfully they act, the greater mischief they are capable of doing, if improperly administered; for, if it be asserted that they are capable of doing good only, without the power of doing harm, we may be satisfied that their qualities are too insignificant to merit notice. This consideration indicates the necessity of some caution in the use of all waters which are said to possess any sanative power, and suggests the propriety of consulting some professional man upon the spot, whose judgment may determine how far the water is appropriate to each individual case, and in what manner it should be employed so as to be most efficacious. There is, however, an advantage attending the Leamington waters, in common with very few others, that wherever their use may be of service they may be entered upon at once, without any danger or necessity for previous preparation, for, at all limes, and in all cases, they invariably act upon the bowels as a mild and gentle purgative. The season for drinking them is during the whole summer, and in the spring and autumn, from March to December. The water should, if possible, be drunk at the fountain head, and never kept long exposed to the open air. After a full dose, there is generally a slight determination to the head, which is manifested by a sense of drowsiness, and a little fulness across the forehead, but this speedily goes off of itself, or is immediately removed by a walk, or ride, or any gentle exercise; and, indeed, I should always recommend some sort of exercise after drinking the water, as it prevents the nausea and oppression which arises from a quantity of any fluid when taken into a stomach preternaturally weak and irritable. In general, for an adult, I should advise half a pint of the water to be taken first thing in the morning, while the stomach is empty, and the same quantity in half-an-hour afterwards. Should this be found insufficient to keep the bowels open, and to act as a diuretic, I should recommend a teaspoonful of the salts to be dissolved in a wine-glass of the water, boiling, and added to each half-pint when taken, this being far preferable to increasing the quantity of water to any greater extent, for common prudence, independent of medical information, dictates that the quantity of water taken into the stomach at one time, that some people require to act as a purgative must be highly improper. By pursuing this method for a few days, the bowels will invariably be brought into that relaxed state that ever after, a pint or three half-pints of the water will be found sufficient. But, if the stomach should be in such a debilitated state from age or disease as to reject this quantity of water when taken in the morning, which will often be the case, I should recommend it to be taken at night, as water gruel, and a small glass, (about a quarter of a pint), at eleven in the morning, after breakfast, as the irritable stomach will, at that time, better receive it, and it will be found much more grateful if a little warm. To do this, it is by far the best method to put water into a bottle, closely corked, and to immerse the whole in hot water, for by this means but little of the air can escape. With regard to the time requisite to continue the use of the waters, much depends upon the disorder and convenience of the patient. A month or six weeks is the time commonly allotted for a trial; but this term is much too short for any great constitutional change to be effected, and it may be observed in general that in those diseases for which the Leamington waters are famous-for scrophula, and cutaneous eruptions of any kind—the longer they are continued the more important and conspicuous will be the relief they are likely to afford. With children, I have always found it the most pleasant way to give them the waters at first with their meals, for they will take it at those times when you cannot persuade them at others; and it is wonderful how soon they acquire a taste for it, and really prefer it after to common water. The quantity taken at a time must depend upon their age and constitution, but it will always be found that they will take more in proportion than adults. As a warm bath the waters of

Leamington, artificially heated, are highly serviceable, particularly in stiffness of the tendons, rigidity of the joints, the effects of preceding inflammation, from the attacks of gout and rheumatism. Patients afflicted with paralytic affections often find most remarkable relief. It is well known that salt water, instead of losing its saline impregnation by being heated, contains a greater quantity than when cold, owing to the evaporation of part of the water in which it was dissolved. For this reason, the bath may be used at the highest point of heat which the skin can endure, and this, in palsy, is of much consequence. The combined use of the warm bath externally, and the internal exhibition of the waters, has been found an almost sovereign remedy for all diseases of the skin, not excepting some of those even of a most deplorable nature, many people having come to Leamington in a condition so miserable as to be objects of pity to all around them, and returned so free from all symptoms and appearance of disease as almost to stagger credulity in the relations of their former sufferings. The peculiar cases in which cold bathing should be avoided, and the nice shades of distinction which, at times, may render its operation salutary or otherwise, will be best learnt by consulting the opinion of some medical adviser, who has an opportunity of weighing the particular causes and symptoms, which alone can properly determine the judgment. When mischief occurs to people of weak and irritable habit from cold bathing, it is, in general, from the neglect of proper caution, and arises, not from the use, but the abuse of the bath. The tepid bath is, however, a most excellent application in itself, whenever the body has been over fatigued by long watching, or agitation and anxiety of mind. In these cases it may be carried to the verge of a warm bath, and will have an excellent effect in refreshing the strength and spirits, and invigorating the system. By its moist and softening powers, it is of singular service in promoting the growth of young persons, and retarding a too rapid approach to the firm and compact state

of manhood. For the same reason, it is strongly recommended by Dr. Darwin, and much used in the decline of life, for preventing that rapid condensation of fibre, and unyielding rigidity of the general solids, which cramps the freedom of action, and prematurely stiffens the sinews of old age."

Further progress is observable in "The Medical Powers of Mineral Waters," published by Dr. Saunders in 1810, wherein will be found a newer and more comprehensive view of the whole question. He was the first to point out the importance to invalids of a mild, pure and equable climate; of the refreshing and invigorating effects of surrounding scenery, richly diversified with hill and dale, and variegated with flowers and foliage of many hues and colours. Nor did he neglect the question of soil, how indispensable it was for all, that it should be of such a nature as to admit of dry, healthy dwellings being erected on its surface. Each and all of these belong to Leamington, and as we have already adverted to them in an earlier part of this work, we need not recapitulate their advantages. In 1810, Dr. Winthrop, who had succeeded Dr. Lambe at Warwick, made an elaborate analysis of the mineral water of the Old Well, of that yielded by Abbotts's Well in Bath Street, Robbins's Well in the Colonnade, near the Victoria Bridge, the one in High Street opened by the Rev. Mr. Read, and Wise's Spring, now the Alexandra Fountain. No examination could take place of the water of the spring in Clemens Street, as it was not at that time known. All his processes and tests are set forth in Field's " History of Warwick" with great minuteness and care, but as they are matters for the analytical chemist and the physician rather than the general reader, we must content ourselves with mentioning the work where those interested in such subjects will be able to collect all the information they require. Dr. Winthrop states that the waters in the whole of the wells were similar in the quality of their contents, and most of them agreed in their quantities, and expresses his opinion that "internally and externally they may be had recourse to with well-founded expectations of advantage in various irregularities of the digestive organs, comprised under the general term dyspepsia; in some diseases of the liver and gall ducts, arising from deficient action or obstruction; in several scrofulous, rheumatic, and cutaneous affections, and in many anomalous complaints, which have been termed cachectic, proceeding from, or connected with, morbid action of the abdominal viscera. He also extols the occasional use of the warm bath, and observes that the waters, drunk for months together, gradually, and often rapidly, restored lost appetite, looks, flesh, and strength. The next work was by a local practitioner—Dr. Loudon—who resided first in the Lower Parade, and afterwards in Clarendon Square. It was entitled a "Practical Dissertation on the Waters of Royal Leamington Spa," and came out in 1816. His design was to disseminate information among medical men in distant parts of the country, of the value of the mineral waters, and for their benefit he furnished an elaborate report of each analysis. One circumstance mentioned by him is curiously interesting, as confirmatory of the description given by Rous of the " many sperringys" there were about the town in the fifteenth century, most of which, if not all, seem to have existed down to a comparatively modern date. After enumerating the several wells, he observes, "Besides them, there exist in the fields around the town several other open mineral springs, none of which, however, have been analysed. They are all similar in their properties to those already described, with the exception of Bissett's Well, at the north-east corner of the Leam bridge, which is of a sulphuric-chalybeate nature, without being, like the others, combined with any of the neutral salts. It has not hitherto been employed medicinally." But that with which we are more particularly concerned is the opinion he entertained of the efficacy of the waters in the treatment of disease. On this subject, he concurs with Middleton and others that their value is very great, and mentions

numerous complaints in which their use would be attended with advantage. His directions for drinking and bathing render his work of scarcely less value than that of Middleton. The popularity of the " Dissertatation" carried it through several editions, the last of which appeared in 1831, and placed it in the rank of a text book. The volume of approbation thus accumulated was increased by Dr. Weatherhead's "Analysis" in 1820, and in 1841 Dr. Granville published his "Spas of England," in which he expressed a high opinion of the sulphureous water at Mrs. Lee's Baths, High Street, and remarked that it well deserved the attention of the medical men of the place for many of the cases in which a saline water of considerable power, charged with sulphurated gas, was required.

Beyond the following collective pronouncement by the medical staff of the Warneford Hospital, in favour of the curative effects of the Leamington waters, testimony can go no further, nor is it necessary that it should, for the authority is unimpeachable, and the opinion worthy of being "engraved in letters of gold, on pillars of alabaster." All those who signed had spent many years in Leamington, were held in respect by their professional brethren, by the townspeople, and by all who knew them, and in addition to the benefits they had seen at the Hospital accruing from the use of the mineral waters, each one had a large private practice in which to make observations among a class of patients, not admissible into any charitable institutions.

Leamington Hospital, 12th Dec., 1855. We, the Medical and Surgical Officers of the Warneford General Bathing Institution and Leamington Hospital, having been requested by the Committee to enumerate the principal maladies in which we find the Leamington Waters useful, beg to state that they are more particularly useful in the following maladies, whether used internally as a medicine, or externally in the form of baths, whether cold, hot, shower, or douche:—

Most forms of dyspepsia and con-

sumption; in derangements of the liver, especially in congestion of that organ, as also of the spleen and other abdominal viscera; in jaundice; in some forms of diseases of the central nervous system, especially in the sequel of acute attacks, such as paralysis, &c.; in epilepsy (occasionally); in cholera, hysteria, neuralgia; in many forms of deranged kidney; in gout; in most forms of rheumatism, more especially the sub-acute and chronic; in many periostial affections; in scrofula; in many cases incidental to females; in most sub-acute and in almost all chronic affections of the skin, especially eczema, herpes, lepra, psoriasis, &c. Henry Homer, M.D.; Saml. J. Jeaffreson, M.D., LLM., Cantab., Fellow of the Royal College of Physicians, the Royal Medico-Chirurgical Society, Sec.; William Miidleton, F.R.C.S.; R. Jones, F.R.C.S.; John Hitchman. To the Trustees of the Warneford Leamington Trust.

After this, nothing of special importance appeared until 1884, when Dr. Smith, of Milverton (now of Harrogate), published a most valuable work, entitled "The Saline Waters of Leamington, Chemically, Therapeutically, and Clinically considered, with Observations on the Climate of Leamington." The motive which led to this publication he explains to have been a determination to satisfy himself with regard to the actual condition of the water, for which purpose he called in the aid of some of the first analysts of the day—Professor Brazier, Professor of Chemistry in the Aberdeen University; Dr. Meymott Tidy, Professor of Chemistry at the London Hospital, and Analyst for the City of London; Dr. Wilson Hake, and Mr. Napier Hake, F.C.S., F.I.C., of Westminster Hospital. Prompted by a desire to benefit, even in the slightest degree, any poor sufferer, he simply puts before his readers " plain and honest facts— truths which have been brought under my notice in the cure and alleviation of disease by treatment by the saline waters, as observed in patients from day to day. In the Leamington mineral waters we have nature's prescription—a prescription that would baffle the most skilful chemist to compose, for, although the analysis of all the mineral waters is well known, the mode of properly assimilating the component parts can only be done in Nature's laboratory." It is by no means an easy task, so to condense the excellencies of this skilful monograph as to enable our readers readily to comprehend its full importance. The style in which it is composed is attractive, and information of the utmost value to the afflicted shines on every page. Besides the analyses, made by the professional gentlemen whose names we have quoted, Dr. Smith gives a table showing the comparative composition of the Leamington mineral waters with those of similar saline and carbonated waters at fifteen popular German and French Spas, including Marienbad, Baden, Kissingen, Homburgh, and Wiesbaden, on which he remarks that so far as the totals of the constituent salts go "Leamington will be seen to compare favourably with them all." His cases of the cures he had met within his own practice are very remarkable. Visitors arriving in Leamington, bankrupts in health, in spirits and in hopes, having tried all other remedies in vain, after a short course of the waters, extending from one to two months, had returned to their homes perfectly restored and free from every trace of disease. Other practitioners, doubtless, could swell this list of miraculous cures, the collection of a fair proportion of which would, as Dr. Amos Middleton pithily expresses it, "stagger credulity," and at the same time add new force to the following lines on Leamington, penned and published some sixty years ago:—

"If but one leper cured, made Jordan's stream,
In Sacred Writ a venerable theme;
What honour to thy sovereign water's due,
Where sick by thousands do their health renew!"

Encouraging to the afflicted as these reports are, one is singularly hopeful for aged invalids suffering from sciatica of an aggravated type combined with obstinate forms of rheumatism. It is the case of the late Mr. Hyde, of 15, Church Hill, whose hale and wonderful convalescence, after so serious an illness, was, at the time, widely known. His own version, as supplied to Dr. Smith, is as follows:—"About the year 1871, I had a severe attack of sciatica. I tried the baths and waters at Buxton, Matlock, the Isle of Wight, and the ozone baths at Llandudno, likewise galvanism; but all to no effect. This had been going on for seven or eight years, and I got worse instead of better. I had to carry a camp stool when I went out, and had frequently to sit down, the pain coming on suddenly. In addition to sciatica, I had rheumatism in my feet and hands, which were much swollen, and for weeks at a time rendered me quite helpless. I was told that the complaint was chronic, and at my age (eighty-one) I must not expect a cure. I was not satisfied with this verdict, and determined to try the Leamington Spa Water, which I did. I began a course and soon experienced benefit; and after persevering tor several months I was quite cured, and remain so, although this is now thirteen years ago." A subject on which Dr. Smith lays special stress is the longevity obtainable in Leamington. "It is surprising to what ripe old ages people live here, especially women, and as a medical man I can testify that many of my patients look upon four score summers as in no way near the goal to which they hope to attain."

Another meritorious contribution to the medical literature of the Spa was the paper read before the annual meeting of the British Medical Association, at Birmingham, on July 31, 1890, by Dr. Eardley-Wilmot, a local practitioner, who, like his colleague, Dr. Smith, has devoted much attention to the nature of the waters, and their efficacy in combating disease. For several years he filled the important office of Chairman of the Pump Room Committee, in which capacity he succeeded in impressing the public mind with the necessity of augmenting the utility of the Bathing Establishment, by supplanting an antiquated system with all those appliances which modern science and experience have recommended and approved. After acknowledging the eminent services of Dr. Jephson, "the *genius loci,* the remarkable man under whose strong individuality the unprecedented growth of the Spa, in the early part of this century, was attained," Dr. Eardley-Wilmot points out the bountiful supply of our mineral water, and consequently the special advantage Leamington has over some other Spas, the springs of which are so impoverished that "the water has to be stored in winter for use in the summer, and where a constant dread of failure of the supply limits the use to which the saline springs can be applied. Here the water gushes plentifully and perennially from the earth, and is as common to all as it is unlimited in quantity." Comparing the analysis of Loudon, in 1816, with those of Dr. Frankland in 1884, and Dr. Bostock Hill in 1890, he demonstrates the important fact that the quality of the waters has in no sense deteriorated; on the contrary, in their average strength and composition, they remain unaltered. To that marvellous, we might even say, miraculous, blending of salts, gases and minerals, mentioned by Dr. Smith, as surpassing the skill and ingenuity of science, he bears emphatic testimony, and acutely remarks that the perfection of the proportions is such as is " calculated to aid the individual action of each, and to increase the therapeutic value of the whole."

Our review of this work completes the history of the mineral springs as it appears in the pages of general and medical literature, and brings down to the present time the most important publications on the subject we have been able to collect. An examination of the local journals will furnish hundreds of testimonials to their powerful agency as restoratives and preservatives of health, while in pamphlets and special contributions to organs devoted to medicine and the divine art of healing, will be found many distinguished physicians—Gull, Braun, Christison, Graham, Richardson, and Clark—asserting with the convincing authority of science and reason, the extraordinary health-giving properties they possess. Brimful of enthusiasm on this subject was the late Dr. Hitchman, and in one of his occasional papers he has elegantly and even poetically, compared the refreshing and invigorating effects of a stay in Leamington, with the use of the waters, on the wearied mind of the statesman, the courtier, and the merchant,to that "sweet restorative "which "balmy sleep" always brings to"tired nature."

The Leamington salts, famous in the first half of the century, have, in these later times, somewhat declined in fashion, but there is no reason for believing that they are less worthy of patronage. In Reeve's Guide for 1839, it is stated that they were first manufactured in 1803, by Abbotts, under the superintendence of Dr. Kerr, of Northampton, "who, by a long series of experiments, discovered a process by which alone a salt could be prepared retaining all the properties of the Leamington waters." After the death of Abbotts, in 1805, they were made by his son-in-law, William Smith, and subsequently by the grandson, also named William Smith, until 1836, when the sole right of manufacturing them was sold to Francis Herring, chemist, Bath Street. They are now supplied by Fisher& Co.,who own the business formerly carried on by Nelson & Herring.

In illustration of this it may be mentioned that in 1801 the quantity of water issuing from the spout of the old salt spring during the space of one solar year was 4,174 hogsheads and 18 gallons, or 262 080 gallons, wine measure. The yield of the other wells is equally abundant, and no sign of the slightest decrease has ever been observed. CHAPTER XXIX. AVING brought the course of events down to 1850, and supplied the history of the Leamington waters from the fifteenth to the nineteenth century, we shall proceed by giving a short sketch of some of the principal changes which have taken place in the borough within the last fifty years, and then prepare to bring bur labours to a close by completing our descriptions of institutions, already mentioned, but not carried forward beyond the middle of the

century. In so doing we shall follow, as nearly as possible, the order of time in which they appeared, and introduce others of which nothing, as yet, has been stated.

It is a trite observation that a person who knew Leamington forty or fifty years ago and had been absent since, would, on his return, experience much difficulty in recognising the town as that with which he was once so familiar. Allowing for a modicum of hyperbole, more or less inevitable whenever it is desired to express or create a feeling of wonder, this statement does not altogether unfairly represent what would be his perplexity. In Clemens-street he would search in vain for the balcony and portico in front of the Blenheim Hotel, and in the present Stoneleigh Arms find no trace of the quaint old house, the curiously shaped roof of which made it look as though one side had, with the rapidity of a weed, grown up to maturity before the other had reached its teens. The transformation in other places has been on a larger and more imposing scale. The unoccupied space on the north side of High Street, between Packington Place and Church Street, has been filled in with shops, and on the opposite side, near the Old Town Hall, the cottages, the gardens in front, the blacksmith's shop and the wheelwright's yard, have passed away from the position they had filled during many vanished centuries, and on the site are commodious and handsome business establishments. Changes, still more extensive, are to be seen in the Radford Road. The Warneford Hospital has been more than doubled in size by the addition of two extensive wings, the beautiful kitchen gardens surrounding it, cultivated by the tradesmen with profitable industry and success, have had to make way, with the large open field opposite, for the erection of residential properties. The barracks in Clapham Terrace have been supplanted by tenements for the working classes, and the land on the west side is now covered with similar buildings and a Board School. St. Mary's Church, fifty years ago " in the fields," is now the centre of a vast and

thriving community. Bath Street has afforded no opportunities for variations such as we have just mentioned, but in two instances it has lost architectural ornaments which in the early days gave it a far more impressive aspect than it now possesses. The removal of the portico before the old Post Office, and the " handsome and lofty Arcade and Colonnade of the

Ionic order," originally projecting from the central division of the Parthenon, or Music Hall, with the beautiful cornice frieze, has detracted seriously from the "remarkably classical and commanding appearance" of one of the oldest and most interesting streets in the Royal Borough, while the absorption of Abbotts' baths by the establishment of Francis and Son has dissolved the special charm which local history had thrown over a building closely associated with the rise of modern Leamington. At the west end of the Parish Church nothing remains of the Leamington of fifty years ago but the old well; the wooden belfry, the snug cottages in Church Walk, and the four houses on the north side of the wellhouse have all been cleared away. Further on, additional lines have been ruled by the waves of progress of the last half century. The charming Priory Gardens have disappeared, and on the site stands the present extensive Post Office; the ford way to the river has been levelled and closed. On the north bank of the Leam the changes are equally extensive. The Pump Room fence, protected by wooden palisades, carried along the present pavement round the tree standing at the south-east corner of Dormer-place, and continued to Portland Lawn, is gone, and the gardens, formerly available only for a privileged few, now greatly beautified, enriched with beds of choice flowers in perpetual bloom, and in the summer months filled with excellent music, are free to the public as the Parade or any other of the streets. Equally numerous, and commensurate with anything that has yet been noticed are the evolutions in the Parade itself. The cottage *om6* in the north-west corner of the Jephson Gardens has been replaced by the Hitchman Fountain; the grounds in Euston Place have been l'aid under contribution to the public pleasure by the removal of obstructive shrubs and the substitution of ornamental flower beds. The Holly Walk, poorer in the grandeur and luxuriance of its trees, and with outstretched withered arms beseechingly pleading, but in vain, that its succession might be preserved by planting for future generations, yet retaining much of its former beauty, has been otherwise greatly improved by the disappearance of the dwarf wall and palisades separating it from Regent Grove, the sloping of the north side down to the road, and the exchange of the heavy stone pillars at the Parade end for the Bright obelisk and fountain. As far as the old Denbigh Villa property is concerned, all is new, and to the suppositious visitor, whose feeling of surprise we are endeavouring to describe " passing strange." A theatre, which in the completeness of its arrangements will compare favourably with any other in the kingdom; two large and well-appointed clubs, a fine row of shops, and a splendid suite of Municipal Buildings are now on the site which was known in ancient history as the " Pingle," and forty years ago contained but one residence—Denbigh Villa. The soaring elms, firs and other trees, the flourishing rookery in their topmost branches, bringing into the very centre of the town the "habitual rusticity" of country scenery and an interesting phase of rural life, and the dense masses of laburnam and lilacs, trespassing over the plain brick boundary wall, and diffusing fragrance and scattering blossoms all around, are lost treasures never to be seen again in this part of the borough. The tramway, representing increased public activity and convenience, and bringing Warwick and Leamington into closer connection than was practicable when the principal means of inter-communication were McGregor's omnibuses, and the transformation of the Upper Assembly Rooms into large business establishments, are other manifestations of that steady advance in local energy, thought and action the past half century

has brought in its train. Evidence to the same effect is plentiful in all the remote parts of the town, but nowhere are the many developments of recent years in greater contrast to the state of things in 1860, than in the Avenue Road. There, the Manor House, then an Academy for young gentlemen, conducted by Mr. Andrews, has been succeeded by the Manor House Hotel; the section of the old Avenue between the railway and the road, by a shrubbery neatly arranged and always kept in good order, and the Avenue Station, at the time hardly bigger than a moderately-sized cottage, by a.building with ample accommodation for the public and provision for expediting the transaction of such business as an important town like Leamington is certain to yield. The extinction of Perkins' Garden, through which the public were permitted to walk without charge, is the deprivation of a peerless picture. For the loss of its opening leaf and bursting buds in the early spring; its broad acres of flowers in the summer, "golden stars " Campbell calls them, and its luscious fruits in the autumn, no villas nor public buildings will be adequate compensation. Lastly, though by no means exhausting the category of these changes, we may direct attention to the encroachment of villas, houses and streets, on to the Old Cricket Field, the locality of the sports of early Leamington, and the formation of the Victoria Park, which, in a few years, will prove to be one of the most delightful recreations of the borough.

Our last reference to the Parish Church brought the course of events down to 1847, when the offer of the Rev. John Craig to finish the fabric for £2,500 was accepted by the parish. The money was raised in subscriptions and promises, but the Vicar was another man from what he had been; no longer leading with enthusiasm, but viewing with want of active personal interest what once had been the great object of his life. We have said that " the work was stopped and the building remained for many years in an unfinished state. " "Delayed" is the term better suited to a description of the state of things at

the time, for in 1849, the north transept was opened, and the chancel completed in 1851. The tension between the Vicar and the churchwardens was increased in 1852 by his foolishly claiming as his own the large brass eagle now used as a Lectern, and on being informed that he might have it, he still more foolishly demanded the beautiful and costly silver-gilt service plate—two antique silvergilt chalices, two silver-gilt patens, wainscott case for ditto, and an antique pattern silver-gilt flagon. The vestry, by this time, saw the necessity of making a firm stand somewhere, lest he should proceed still further and claim the church, and refused his demand. The Vicar blustered, and brought an action to recover the property, but the proceedings do not appear to have progressed farther than service of the writ. The storm, which had been brewing since 1847, burst with great violence over Mr. Craig's head in 1853. A statement to the Bishop by Mr. Owen White, churchwarden, that the Vicar did not appear to have applied any portion of the £i,8oo raised for the completion of the building to that purpose, led to a long and bitter controversy, the effects of which lasted for many years. Mr. Craig published accounts showing total receipts from legacies, benefactions, collections and subscriptions, £6,631 18s. 8d., and stated that the sum expended on the church was £15,000. At a vestry meeting it was resolved to present a memorial to the Bishop, asking him to require from Mr. Craig a statement of all moneys received by him in aid of the church; to compel him to restore, at his own cost, one hundred and thirty-five free sittings for the poor, which had been taken away during the several alterations; to direct him to pass over to the churchwardens a sum of £500, given by the Rev. Dr. Warneford for the erection of a Poor Man's Church in High Street; also that he be asked to account for £27 19s. 9d. collected in 1843 for a Font, and a bequest of £300 by Sarah Campion in aid of a Parish Female School; that he discontinue his action for the Plate Service, or be peremptorily ordered to try the same at the ensuing Warwick Spring

Assizes, and that he be required to place a lodge-keeper at the Cemetery to preserve the same in proper order and condition. This added fuel to the fire, and the Vicar brought an action against Mr. Matthew Wise for libel, that gentleman having signed the memorial in his capacity of chairman at the vestry. The trial was commenced at Gloucester Assizes on April 3, 1856, before Mr. Justice Creswell and a special jury, and after two days' hearing, on the suggestion of his lordship was referred to arbitration, a verdict being entered for plaintiff, with nominal costs of 40s. In accordance with this arrangement, Mr. C. L. Whitmore, Q.C., sat at the Bath Hotel on the 19th of the following month. The only question of interest to the public, and that which forms the principal justification for this brief recital, is the alleged misappropriation by Mr. Craig of public moneys, distinctly implied, though not definitely stated in the memorial. In the course of the proceedings, the balance sheet prepared by Mr. W. G. Dixon, accountant, 38, Waterloo Street, Birmingham, was handed in, and by this it was shown that while the receipts amounted to £10,695 I2s-tod., the total expenditure had been £14,186 17s. jd., leaving a balance of £3,491 4s. 9d. paid by Mr. Craig out of his own private means. To this were added £1,751 11 s. 7d., the amount disbursed by him for the Choir School, and £1,717 12s. 6d. for the Grammar School, making in all £6,960 8s. lod. These figures were not disputed; on the contrary, Mr. Sergt. Pigott, who appeared for Mr. Wise, accepted them, disclaimed any intention to impute to Mr. Craig misapplication of the funds entrusted to his care, and consented to the proposal that he should be remunerated for the excess of his expenditure beyond the amount of the subscriptions he had received. After sitting three days, the enquiry was closed on terms agreed upon by the parties, and in his subsequent award the arbitrator set aside the verdict, ordered each party to pay his own costs, and declared the Communion service to be the property of the Church. Respecting the Church accounts, he found that there were no

moneys in Mr. Craig's hands applicable to the Completion Fund, and directed that in the event of his resigning the living of All Saints within twelve-months, a sum of £1,200 was to be paid him "towards his outlay on the Church improvements." The arbitrator further appointed a committee to complete the church. Mr. Craig did not leave Leamington, and the remuneration consequently was never paid, but he obtained by his action that which was of far greater consequence—an avowal that the memorial was never intended to impute the application of public funds to his own use, and proof that the parish was several thousand pounds in his debt.

Three years afterwards, steps were again taken to complete the Church, and for that purpose several designs were obtained, one set being sent in by Mr. Craig, who had been assisted in all technical matters by Mr. Alex. Johnson, a local architect, and afterwards one of the churchwardens. There were no immediate results from this movement, but in 1866, the Vicar's plans were approved by the Vestry, and on May 1, 1867, the foundation stone of the south transept was laid by Lord Leigh "in solemn form and according to ancient usage," in the presence of a vast concourse of Free Masons and the general public. Mr. Marriott, of Coventry, was the builder, and Mr. T. C. Barry, C.E., the architect. The total cost of this section was £8,400. The opening ceremony took place on September 26, 1869, the Rev. R. H. Baynes (afterwards Canon Baynes), vicar of St. Michael's, Coventry, preached in the morning; the Rev. T. E. Franklyn, then curate, in the afternoon, and Mr. Craig in the evening. This was the last instalment of the progress towards completion that the Vicar was permitted to see. lie continued to hold the living until June 30, 1877, when, after a long and painful illness, he died at the age of seventy-two years. A few hours before his death, he repeatedly assured his sorrowing friends that he was at peace, and so tranquil and imperceptible was his dissolution that those who watched at his bed-

side were unable to say the exact time at which it occurred. In the course of his sermon at the Parish Church on the following day, the Rev. J. W: Johnson, a former head-master at the Leamington College, referred to the deceased as a remarkable man in body and intellect. Of the latter, the congregation had evidence in that church, which was the conception of his mind, and were it only finished in all the grandeur of his original design, it would stamp him as a man who possessed one of the most remarkable minds of the present century. He was also singular for the power he had in making friends and enemies, for his forbearance in uttering words of unkindness to those whom he deemed to be his foes, for his want of power to appreciate the value of money, and for his exemplary patience, fortitude, and submission when writhing in agonies of bodily pain. His funeral, on July 7, was the most impressive ever seen in Leamington. The Parish Church, where the first part of the service took place, was crowded, and several hundreds, desirous of sharing in this last token of respect to his memory, were disappointed of admission. The officiating clergymen were the Rev. J. W. Johnson and the Rev. W. Florv, Incumbent of Trinity Church. Bath Street, Clemens Street, and Brunswick Street, the route from the church to the cemetery, were lined with spectators, and, until the procession had passed, the majority of the tradesmen's shops were wholly or partially closed, and at many of the principal private residences the blinds were drawn down. During the conclusion of the service, the number of persons present was estimated at 10,000, among whom were representatives of the Corporation, the Burial Board, and Christ Church. The remains were interred in the family mortuary at the east end of the chapel in the old cemetery. The coffin was covered with beautiful wreaths and crosses of the choicest flowers, and for a very long time after the conclusion of the service thousands crowded round the entrance to the vault to take a last look of all that remained of him "who in life was in many wavs eminent and distinguished, and who in death will not soon be forgotten."

Mr. Craig was an advanced student in astronomy, for the promotion of which his liberality was princely. In 1852, he erected, on Wandsworth Common, at a cost, ruinous to himself, the great telescope shown in the accompanying illustration.

It weighed three tons, and had a maximum focal length of eighty-five feet, being fortyfive longer than that of Sir William Herschell at Slough, and thirty-two in excess of Lord Rosse's at Parsonstown. But its aperture was less by two and four feet respectively. The magnifying power ranged from 500 to 3,000. The existence of a third ring round Saturn, the most "extraordinary in architecture," of the planetary system, had long been a subject of speculation, and it was set at rest only in October, 1852, when Mr. Craig's telescope was brought to bear on the "remote wanderer," its "luminous appendages," and imperial retinue of moons and other satellites. The instant result is reported to have been the discovery of the additional ring, clearly defined in all its parts, and in harmony with the two other rings previously known to astronomers. Mr. Craig, who had not the support of a royal bounty, as Sir William Herschell had, nor the wealth of Lord Rosse, lost an immense sum by his enthusiasm in the cause of astronomical science, and though he had the satisfaction of knowing that he had extended the boundaries of its knowledge, he at the same time had seriously impaired his own fortune Notwithstanding its superior excellencies in many respects, the telescope had some irremediable defects.

Mr. Craig was succeeded by the Hon. and Rev. James Wentworth Leigh, youngest brother of Lord Leigh, Lord Lieutenant of the county. His previous appointments had been a curacy at Bromsgrove, the Vicariate at Stoneleigh, and the curacy of St. James's, Stratford-on-Avon. With the usual formalities he was inducted on August 20, 1877. His advent to office was the signal for the establishment of a time of peace and harmony at the Parish Church such as had not been known since the resignation of the Rev. J. Wise in 1823. Large-hearted and broad-minded, he won back many who had left, united those who had long been divided, stimulated the practical sympathies of all, and inaugurated that system of beautifying the interior of the church, the splendid results of which are to be seen to-day in whatever direction the eye is turned. Apart from Church work, he was a great force in everything appertaining to the public welfare. While Vicar of Stoneleigh, he manifested a deep interest in the agricultural labourers' question, which glowed with white heat in 1872, counselling moderation, at the same time that he suggested means for much-needed amelioration. In Leamington, the several hospitals and other charitable institutions, the School Board, the temperance cause, and the Poor Law system were all benefited by his continuous services. By marriage he is allied to the Kemble family, eminent in literature and the drama. Mrs. Leigh's mother, Mrs. Butler, was the celebrated Miss Fanny Kemble, daughter of Charles Kemble, niece of John and Sarah Kemble, and sister to Adelaide Kemble, a famous singer, and John Mitchell Kemble, author of the authoritative work, "The Saxons in England." Sarah Kemble, Mrs. Leigh's great-aunt, became Mrs. Siddons, to whom reference has been made in previous pages. During his ministry at All Saints, Mr. Leigh was appointed one of the Honorary Canons of Worcester Cathedral, and in 1883 was presented by Mr. Gladstone to the living of St. Mary's, Bryanstone Square, London. He afterwards became Dean of Hereford, a promotion popularly regarded as the forerunner of a still more important advancement. Brief as was his tenure of office, it represented a time of great activity and liberality, and the commencement of the " decorative period " in the history of the church. The following list of donations demonstrates the importance of the movement initiated under his influence:— Readers interested in this subjec t should call at the Free Library and consult ' The Illustrated London News" for August 28, and October ib, 1852, for further particulars respecting Mr. Craig's magnificent telescope. They will there see how he discovered the third ring of Saturn, after Lord Kosse and Professor Challis, of Cambridge, had searched for it in vain. They will also find a becoming homage paid to his genius by an impartial authority, for constructing the ' largest achromatic telescope in the world," "as a measuring instrument, unapproachable bv all others." and they will be able to appreciate his distinguished services in bringing into view starry depths, previously unnoticed by the most powerful glasses, and in lighting up the whole scenery of the heavens with surpassing brilliance.

Carved reredos, gift of the Willes family, £300; stone pulpit, ditto, Mrs. Matthew Wise, £40; new vestry and organ chamber,,£1,218 15s.; new organ. £1,000; additional stop for ditto, £50; brass altar railings, carved sedilia, £500; Credence doorway and marble steps, etc., gift of Miss McTavish, £500; altar cloth and pulpit fall, /.25; ditto, gift of a parishioner, £15; carved oak steps of Lectern, 5; two gas standards (collected by Mr. Joseph Glover, £26), £29; window in memory of the late Mr. William Lloyd, £50; ditto in memory of the late Mr. and Mrs. Stubbs, gift of Mr. and Mrs. Heath Stubbs and family, £225; oak Lectern, £2; re-seating, chiefly at the cost of individual subscribers, £341 5s.; font, gift of the Rev. Mr. Beaumont, £35; window, gift of Miss Dean, 70; ditto, in memory of Mrs. A. D. Prowse gift of Dr. Otho and Mrs. Wyer, £40; two baptistery windows, in memory of the late W. Jackson, gift of Canon Leigh, £10; fencing along Church Walk, £40; two brass altar crosses, £15; altar desk, £4; total, £4,515.

The Rev. Walter Coplestone Furneaux was the next Vicar. His father was the Rev. W. D. Furneaux, Vicar of Walton from 1843 to 1860, and afterwards Rector of Berkley, Somersetshire, a gift he received from the late Sir Charles Mordaunt, Bart. Mr. Furneaux was first curate under his father at Berkley, then filled a similar appointment at Leeds, under Dr. Gott, and, at the time he accepted the living at Leamington, was army chaplain at the Pro-Cathedral, India. He arrived in Leamington in February, 1884, and was inducted on the 6th of that month, the attendance of the local clergy and parishioners being very large. His efforts in advancing the policy of his predecessor were very vigorous, and, as will be seen from the subjoined enumeration of improvements, both extensive and successful:—

Work by Mr. W. G. Bloomfield, contractor, £58 10s.; new clock in tower, £120; purchase and demolition of cottages, 1888, £1,500; ditto, £1,100; restoration of choir, "gift of Alderman and Mrs. Sidney Flavel, £1,100; organ gas standard, £6; embellishment of side chapel, gift of Miss Hughes, £70; reseating ditto, £100; stained glass millett, £100; two baptistery windows, giftofMr. Beaumont, 1884, £100; two ditto, gift of Alderman and Mrs. Flavel, £300, 1887; heating apparatus, £700, towards which a legacy, by Miss H. Garrett, of /300 was applied with a special fund contribution of £205; work of reseating, re-paving, etc., £200; new choir vestry, gift of the Rev. Mr. Beaumont, £400; removal of brick porch and improvement of north porch, £32 10s.; new fencing, west end of church, erected, and given to church by Corporation in exchange for gift of land to the town by the church, £220; two folding stools, £10; repairs to heating apparatus, £40; alterations to clergy vestry, £50; remaining windows in baptistery, gift of the Rev. Mr. Beaumont, £20; side chapel reredos, £100, gift of the Rev. W. Furneaux and family; altar cloth, etc., and fittings, £100; Jubilee Tower fund, £771 13s. od.; choir vestry window, gift of Mrs. Beaumont, £100; memorial window to the late Mr. Frank Spinney, organist, £15; altar desk, £2; processional cross, £5; crimson hangings, £15; two oak panelled lobbies in baptistery, £129; brass altar rail in side chapel, gift of a parishioner, £20; electric light instalment, £280; total, £7,764 13s.

If, to the foregoing, the cost of the new vicarage in Leam Terrace, also purchased while Mr. Furneaux was vicar, be added, and allowance made for several unavoidable omissions from the above lists, the probable total expenditure from 1877 to 1896, may be accepted as about £14,000. In 1896, Mr. Furneaux was presented by the Dean and Chapter of Worcester to the living of Mortlake and East Sheen, on the Thames, and was succeeded by

The Rev. Cecil Hook, the present vicar, son of Dean Hook, the author of "The Lives of the Archbishops of Canterbury " and numerous other standard works, including the popular and valuable "Church Dictionary." He had previously been Vicar of the Parish Church, Oswestry. The ceremony of induction took place on October 2, 1896, the Bishop of Worcester officiating, and a crowded congregation, with many of the local clergy, being present. On Sunday, October 4, Mr. Hook commenced his clerical duties by reading the Thirty-Nine Articles of the Church of England and giving an address; in the evening he preached his first sermon. Much as had been done for the church, and munificent as were the sums poured into its treasury, the completion still remained to be accomplished. To this he immediately turned his attention, and having regard to the fact that his father was eminent for promoting the building of new churches and schools, he might be considered as possessing hereditary qualifications for such a task. However, no time was lost in forming another Church Completion Committee, of which he was Chairman; his Warden, Alderman Sidney Flavel, hon. secretary; and Mr. G. M. Fayerman, hon. treasurer. In March, 1897, Mr. Hook issued an appeal for " something under £20,000," to consummate a parochial aspiration of nearly fifty years standing, and to make All Saints "The handsomest Modern Parish Church in the United Kingdom." After stating that "the splendid designs of the talented Vicar of Leamington, Mr. Craig, were not carried out with corresponding technical knowledge," the Vicar pointed out that "it had consequently been found necessary to expend a large sum on the present fabric, a difficulty which had been met in part by the generosity of the parishioners. The west wall had been excellently repaired, and the congregation thereby saved from the piercing draughts which used to issue from the faulty window. The Clock Tower had been entirely restored at considerable cost, and the satisfactory nature of the work was assured, as it had been carried out under the able care and advice of Mr. W. Ilawley Lloyd. It remained, however, to complete the external repairs; to lay down uniform flooring in the Nave; to reseat the Church; to extend the nave westward three bays; and to erect a suitable Western Tower in which to rehang the bells. The Committee have obtained designs for a Central Tower, like that of F.ly, in timber and lead. To accomplish these ends, in a style suitable to that in which the church had been begun, would be a matter of great cost, but it was felt that the work was in good hands. Sir Arthur Blomfield, who would carry out the plans, had been the consultative architect of the Church Committees for the past 14 years, and his skill in the arrangement of the chancel had already been abundantly displayed." This energetic statement was accompanied with a list of subscriptions amounting to over -2,000, the amounts in eleven cases being for sums of £100 and upwards. The work, happily designed to be an expression of " gratitude for the Queen's Diamond Jubilee," was commenced on July 5, when Messrs. G. F. Smith and Sons, the contractors, began excavating for the foundations, and on June 30, 1898, Mr. Hook can boast a family connection with Leamington extending back to 1784, the year of the discovery of the spring in Bath Street by Satchwell and Abbotts. His mother was the eldest daughter of the late Dr. James Johnstone, and granddaughter of Dr. Edward Johnstone, an eminent Birmingham physician, who was in Leamington shortly after the new spring was made public, and rendered great service by promulgating the virtues of the waters. — *See fa(e JjJ.* the Memorial Stone in the west elevation was laid by Councillor Gordon Lyon Bland, Mayor, amid general manifestations of the most enthusiastic rejoicings. The procession from the Town Hall to the site was one of the finest within memory of the oldest inhabitants. As it is of so recent a date, and is fully reported in the local press, a description of it in detail becomes unnecessary; we may, however, say briefly, that it included the Bishop of Worcester and Bishop Mylne (of Bombay), the Mayor and many members of the Corporation; the Vicar and the Wardens—Alderman Sidney Flavel Jind Councillor C. I. Blaker; the Sidesmen, nearly all the local and neighbouring clergy, a large number of the principal inhabitants, and Mr. W. H. Bellamy, organist, and the choir. The display of the beautiful banners of the various Guilds was very effective, and the national flag appropriate to the occasion. The stone has the following inscription:— "To the *glory* of God and in the faith of Jesus Christ, this Foundation Stone of the two Western Bays of the Nave and of the Western Tower of this Church was duly laid on Thursday, June 30th, 1898, by the Mayor of Leamington, Gordon Lyon Bland, in memory of the long and prosperous reign of Victoria, Queen of England and Empress of India. Laus Deo." Upwards of three hundred dined at the Town Hall, and in the course of the many congratulatory speeches called forth by an event so auspicious, Mr. Flavel reminded the company of the extremely interesting circumstance that they were celebrating the stone-laying for completing the Church on the day which was the twenty-first anniversary of the death of Mr. Craig, the designer of that noble fabric.

With a few general remarks of a descriptive character, applicable to subjects not hitherto noticed, we must bring to a close our remarks on the Parish Church. The foregoing illustration, with the accompanying ground plan, supplies all necessary information as to the complete form of the building and the nature of the work carried into effect in commemoration of the Queen's Diamond Jubilee reign. No comments are necessary by way of pointing out the mani-

fold beauties of Sir Arthur Blomfield's design, for even to the technically uneducated eye, its harmony of detail, graceful ornamentation, and bold outlines will prove to be so many attractions. While on this subject of the fabric, a reference must be made to the exceptionally noble wheel window and triforium in the north transept, and also the unusually fine rose window in the south facade. For these the parish is indebted to Mr. Craig, who obtained the first from the Cathedral of Rouen, and the second from the Church of St. Ouen, and his own explanation of them was that, while opposed in ideas, they blended so as to produce an effect exceeding anything to be seen even in our English cathedrals. The interior is lofty, and closely assimilated to that majesty of dimensions which is popularly associated with the cathedral characteristic. Few chancels in the churches of England are so enriched with costly gifts, and none appeal more powerfully to the aesthetic faculty. The triple window of stained glass in the apse, with its varied lights softened and mellowed by age, is in affectionate memory of Diana, Frances, and Anna Maria, Manners-Sutton, three daughters of the Most Rev. Charles Manners-Sutton, D.D., Archbishop of Canterbury from 1805 to 1828. After the death of their father, they came to Leamington and resided in Lansdowne Place. Towards the expense of this the family contributed £500. The carved reredos, the gift of the Willes family, is in memory of the late Mr. Edward Willes, and is a fine copy of Leonardo da Vinci's celebrated painting, "The Last Supper." The artistic restoration of the chancel, including the very handsome screen, are portions of a series of munificent gifts by Alderman and Mrs. Sidney Flavel, of the aggregate value of several thousand pounds. As set forth in a tablet, the earlier part of this work was carried out several years ago:

"To the glory of God, and in thankfulness for blessings received, this Chancel was tiled and the stalls and screen erected by Sidney Flavel, jun., Mayor, and Gertrude his wife, October 24, 1889." The large screen placed on

the former, one of the most beautiful outside the cathedrals, was made by Messrs. Hart, Son, Peard and Co., of the Drury Lane Works, London, from a design specially prepared by Sir Arthur Blomfield. The material throughout is of wrought iron, and the style—gothic—has been chosen so that it might harmonise with the early gothic architecture of the Church. On February 11, 1899, it was presented by Mr. Flavel to the Vicar for the use of the Church, at a largely attended service, when the Bishop preached the dedicatory sermon. On the reverse side are the arms of the Flavel family in heraldic colours. At the bottom of the south side are the following inscriptions: " In the reverence of God, and in grateful memory of Elizabeth Flavel, Widow of Sidney Flavel (married in this Church), died June 29th, 1894, aged 76 years. 'Her children rise up and call her blessed.' This Chancel Screen is placed by her son, Sidney Flavel, Churchwarden since 1885 of this Church, and Mayor four times of this Borough. Sexagesima, 1899."

The Church contains no "storied urn," no "animated bust," nor trophy to the illustrious dead,

"Where through the long-drawn aisle and fretted vault
The pealing anthem swells the note of praise."

Still, religion, law and patriotism, are worthily, if not numerously, represented. Formerly a modest slab in the centre aisle marked the last resting place of the Rev. Dr. Greenwood, from 171310 1724 Vicar of St. Nicholas', Warwick; of St. Nicholas and also of St. Mary in that borough from 1724 to 1739, and the holder of the two livings of Solihull and St. Nicholas from 1739 to 1750. He was the author of " Essays on the Creation," and a "Harmony of the Gospels," in addition to which he prepared some notes on the " Paradise Lost" for Bishop Newton's edition. In the chancel is a marble tablet to the memory of the Right Hon. Edward Willes, at one time Recorder of Coventry and Attorney-General for the Duchy of Lancaster; afterwards King's Sergeant-at-Law, and finally, Chief Baron of the Court of Exchequer and of the Privy Council, Ireland. He was one of the promoters of the Leamington Enclosure Act of 1768, an abstract of which has been given in the early pages of this work, and father of Mr. Edward Willes, whose name is associated with the history of the town down to 1846. In addition to these, the remains of Admiral Fleeming, who was distinguished by his bravery in numerous engagements between the years 1794 and 1839, repose in the catacombs beneath the north transept.

The Register, the material parts of which have already been quoted, dates back to 1646.

To other subjects of interest allusion would be agreeable, but the exigencies of space compel us to conclude with the statement that nothing of the original Church remains except the stone in the vaults, previously described, and the small stained glass window in the north transept, containing the arms of the Willes' and other families.

In the strictly regular order of events, the local government of the town might be considered as inseparable from the history of the Parish Church, and therefore entitled to our next consideration. Were it not that there still remains for description another building, which was originally part of the Church itself, we should at once proceed to relate how the Board of Commissioners, in 1852, was superannuated by the Local Board of Health, and how the Board of Health itself, in 1875, was retired as a pensioner on the bounty of the gratitude of the inhabitants by the more powerful and capable Corporation. To these interesting topics we shall refer as soon as we have disposed of the following subject.

From a Photo by Bullock, Bros., The Parade, Royal Leamington Spa.
Christ Church, Clarendon Avenue, erected 1825; chiefly designed from the renowned Abbey de Jumieges, in Normandy.

As a substantial branch of All Saints' the growth of which in 1825 was stimulated by the lack of sufficient church accommodation, Christ Church, originally known as the Episcopal Chapel, now comes under notice. We have stated that it was built by the late Mr. Edward Willes, who also gave the site, and that it afterwards became the private property of the Rev. Robert Downes, Vicar. The style of its architecture has raised objections; the pillars (formerly twice their present circumference) supporting the galleries and separating the nave from the aisles, obstructing the light, contrasting The views of the Wesley Church, Dale Street, on page 228, are also from photos by the same firm. disadvantageous with the "reedy columns" of modern architecture, and detracting generally from the elegance and brightness now so popular in places of worship. In answer to these depreciatory criticisms, it should be explained that, at the time of its erection, locally, church decoration as it exists to-day, was not in vogue; and, further, that the building itself has for its authority the Abbey of Jumieges, near Rouen, founded in 661, and described as "splendid." Christ Church, therefore, is not devoid of interest, especially to the archaeologist, who may find within its walls traces of ecclesiastical architecture in existence some six centuries before the foundations of the original Parish Church of All Saints were laid. Its history may be briefly told. Mr. Downes, assisted by his curate, conducted the services from 1825 to 1839, after which Mr. Craig was its second minister. In 1840, Mr. Craig disputed the authority of Mr. Downes over the chapel, and intimated his intention to withhold the rent, but beyond the correspondence nothing further was heard of the matter. About the year 1856, his tenure, which had been fruitful of controversy throughout, terminated, and the Rev. Dr. Bickmore came into possession. He was a popular clergyman, and during his ministration the congregation increased and the influence and position of the church were raised to a degree they had not previously attained. He resigned in 1870, after filling the incumbency fourteen years, and it is worth mentioning that the text from which he preached his valedictory sermon on Sunday, December 18, of that year, was taken from the first verse of the second chapter to Galatians: "Then fourteen years after." The esteem in which he was held was shown by the presentation of £80, promptly raised, and his portrait, with a general expression of regret at his leaving the parish. The course and purpose of his ministry are best described in his own words: "I have tried," he said, when receiving the gifts, "to avoid every extreme, both of doctrine and ritual." He was followed by Dr. Bedford Hall, previously Afternoon Lecturer for Archdeacon Musgrave, at the Parish Church, Halifax, who commenced his duties on Sunday, December 25, 1870. In August of the following year, after a slight indisposition of several weeks' duration, his illness assumed a serious character on the 12th, and terminated in his death the next day. Brief as was his residence in Leamington, he had won the esteem of his congregation and was rapidly gaining popularity generally in the town. After this the appointment was vacant until the early part of 1872, when it was given to the Rev. F. Haden Cope, of Wimslow, who, however, retained it only two years. A constant disagreement between himself and Mrs. Philadephia Downes, widow of the Rev. Robert Downes, and owner of the property, respecting the rent he had to pay, led to his giving notice in 1873 to relinquish the tenancy. The dispute was patched up by a new arrangement, but in September Mr. Cope received six months' notice to quit, which took effect in March, 1874.

The next incumbent was the Rev. J. A. Nicholson, LL.D., the holder of a chaplaincy in Sweden. He commenced his duties in 1874, after effecting some The objections of the early writers only applied to the columns before they were reduced to about half the former circumference by Dr. Nicholson in 1874. extensive alterations in the interior of the edifice, including a reduction of the size of the columns by stripping them of an outer casing, the removal of the organ from the south gallery to its present position, and the renovation of the chancel by the erection of choir stalls. An advanced ritual was now introduced, in explanation of which Dr. Nicholson remarked: "Without casting the slightest reproach or stricture upon the worthy priests who have preceded me, I may say that, aesthetically and devotionally, the services of one generation do not suit another, and circumstances, I suppose, in times past, have kept the services in Christ Church in a particular stage." A large and fashionable congregation was speedily collected, and everything indicated a long and happy occupation. In 1880, however, Mrs. Downes, in accordance with a notice previously given, refused to renew the lease, and Dr. Nicholson with his congregation were practically ejected from the building. The text, "Arise, let us go hence" (St. John, fourteenth chapter and thirty-first verse), from which he preached his last sermon in the church, was as singularly appropriate to the occasion as that of Dr. Bickmore's, and aptly described the extraordinary and unprecedented situation in which he and his congregation had been placed. It afterwards transpired that the property had been sold to the late Mr. Thomas Bellamy Dale, an ex-Mayor of the borough of Warwick, who conveyed it to trustees for the purpose of being used for ever for Evangelical purposes. By him, the incumbency was given to the Rev. Dr. Edward Wilkinson, Rector of Snargate and Snave, Kent, who settled in Leamington in September, 1881, and continued to minister to a small congregation until 1896, when, through serious illness, he resigned, and the church was closed. He preached in a black gown, the use of which was at one time extensive in Leamington pulpits, and held the tenets of Calvinism; but, though courageous in his promulgation of the distinctive Geneva theology, and indefatigable in his exertions, it cannot be said that his connection with the church was prosperous. The trustees, in July, 1897, offered the appointment to the Rev. J. G. Gregory, who for nineteen years had been incumbent of Emmanuel Church, Brighton, and accepting the same, he took possession in September. Further improvements were carried out by the late Mr. William Dawkes, and, as will be seen from our

illustration, the result has been to bring the church into line with those of more modern date, and, in the way of brightness and comfort, to meet every reasonable desire. Mr. Gregory, who belongs to the Evangelical school, re-opened the church in January, 1898. CHAPTER XXX. O explain the several phases of local government from 1825 to 1875 is the duty we have now to discharge. Altogether, Leamington has had four forms of administration — the Parish Committee, the Paving and Improvement Commissioners, the Local Board of Health, and the Corporation—each growing out of the other in obedience to the special circumstances of successive periods. We have stated the nature and constitution of the Parish Committee, and have mentioned that the Board of Commissioners came into existence in 1825. On the 18th of August, 1852, after a not inglorious career of twenty-seven years, the Commissionerships were abolished, and the Local Board of Health established. Praise and blame have been liberally bestowed on the Commissioners for their management of the public business, but it is due to them to say that steady and continuous improvement marked the whole course of their period of office, and, having regard to their limited powers and slender income, they served the town well. They were a self-elected body, deriving their authority solely from property qualifications, not from the suffrages of the inhabitants. During their ascendancy there were no annual elections, such as the town afterwards enjoyed under the Board of Health, and now possesses-under the Corporation, and as a consequence there was more general dissatisfaction. It was not their fault, but their misfortune, that they were an exclusive oligarchy, representing only themselves and possessing no authority to speak and act for their neighbours. The dictum of the meeting held in Bisset's Room in 1820, that restrictions and safeguards were necessary, was embodied in the statute and hedged them in on every side. Another thing to be noticed is that the atmosphere of local thought at the time was unfavourable for the growth

of heroic measures. Not only Dr. Jephson, but nine-tenths of those who took an active interest in town affairs, believed that the welfare of Leamington depended in a large measure on quiet, and the absence of all excitement, especially of a political character. Notwithstanding some very obvious defects in their constitution, and many difficulties in their path, their work was not wasted. We owe to them the Victoria and Adelaide Bridges, the wide space in Victoria Terrace, the commencement of the work of cleansing the river, an elementary application of the principles of All the books and other official records of this period having been lost, or destroyed, the number of the Commissioners cannot now be ascertained. The only reliable information on the subject is the statement of Mr. A. S. Field before the Railway Parliamentary Committee in 1847, that there were about 200 of them. As the population in that year was something like i ,ooo it will readily be seiin how small was their title to be regarded as a representative body. sanitary science, the establishment of a local police force, a vigorous though not a successful effort to provide a satisfactory water supply, and an excellent bargain, by which they received £2,500 from the Great Western and £2,250 from the London and North-Western Railway Companies, for property sold and compensation, when those lines were carried through Leamington. Though it is but a small reward for labours so prolonged, and service so valuable, we may name the following as appearing from the reports to have been the most active and assiduous in their exertions to benefit the town at that period: Messrs. A. S. Field, J. Hitchman, Owen White, W. Watkin, John Haddon, E. Woodhouse, Joseph Stanley, J. B. Jeffery, R. Whitehouse, Henry Hackforth, John Bowen, S. U. Jones, John Cullis, D'Arcy Boulton, J. M. Cottle, and J. Meredith. On the same day that the government of the Improvement Commissioners ceased to exist the Local Board of Health was established. Acting on a memorial from the inhabitants, the General Board of Health, now the Local Government Board, having caused inquiries to be made into the sanitary condition and general circumstances of the town, by Messrs. G. T. Clark and W. Ranger, two of their superintendent inspectors, issued a Provisional Order on June 15, 1852, directing that the Public Health Act, 1848 (11 & 12 Vict., c. 63) should be applied to Leamington, and a new governing body elected, consisting of fifteen members. By the Public Health Supplemental Act (15 & 16 Vict., c. 69), dated June 30, following, the Provisional Order was confirmed, and August 18 appointed for the first election, Mr. William Carpenter, the Chairman of the outgoing Commissioners, being authorised to conduct the proceedings, and, in the event of his being unable to do so, Mr. John Bowen was to officiate in his stead. Before describing the circumstances attending the constitution of the first Local Board, we must notice the principal changes introduced at this time into our system of local government. The justifiable aspiration of many of the inhabitants in 1842, for such a reduction in the qualification of candidates as would make a larger number of the ratepayers eligible for election, was now met by lowering it to £30 rateability to the relief of the poor, or the possession of £1,000 in real or personal estate; but, as was proved afterwards by a prolonged experience, it was a great mistake to withhold from candidates the right of being present when the votes were examined and cast up by the returning officers. Many of the bitter controversies in after years had their roots fed and nourished by the practice which then obtained of closing the doors against those who were most deeply interested in the results, and if the presiding Aldermen of the present Corporation were to adopt a similar course, instantly a demand would be raised in every ward for the admission of the candidates or their representatives. The voting of the new regime was restored to the original vestry standard of household suffrage, under circumstances, however, which imparted to the gift only a nominal value. By an ingeniously-constructed slid-

ing scale a vote was allowed to occupiers and owners for every £50 rateable value of their properties, so that the total did not exceed twelve votes for the same property. Under this system, the villa residents, nearly every one of whom had several votes, were possessed of the ruling power to the exclusion of the holders of single votes, notwithstanding the latter were vastly in the majority. The scale was complicated, inconsistent with itself, and absurd, even from the point of view that a property qualification was necessary. Another change effected at this time was the enlargement of the western boundary of the parish from the Milverton brook back to the Avon at Portobello. For sewerage purposes only, all the land in the parish of Milverton, bounded on the north by the Warwick and Rugby road, on the west by the river Avon, and on the south by the-Leam, became the Leamington main sewerage district, for which an additional member was elected. Power was also given the Board of Health, with the consent of the trustees of the Warwick and Northampton Turnpike Trust, to contract for the removal of the My ton Turnpike Gate, the tollage of which, at that period, greatly restricted the free use of the Old Warwick Road to the inhabitants of Leamington and Warwick for vehicular traffic, and excepting to pedestrians, was a tax on the enjoyment of some charming sylvan scenery, and a limitation of the finest view obtainable of the worldfamed historic Warwick Castle. Under this authority, the Gate was abolished by the Local Board in 1853.

The first election of members of the newly-constituted Local Board of Health took place on the date named, Mr. W. Carpenter discharging the duties assigned to him in the Provisional Order, and Mr. A. S. Field assisting as his legal adviser. Mr. Carpenter, who had been a member of the old Board of Commissioners for several years, and was its last chairman, in his official capacity had the honour of representing Leamington at the grand banquet given by the Lord Mayor of London, in the Mansion House, on March 21, 1850, to

a distinguished party of friends and promoters of the great Exhibition held in 1851; on which occasion, H.R.H. Prince Albert, the Chief Officers of State, the leading members of both Houses of Parliament, the Royal Commissioners for the Exhibition, the principal members of the Corporation, the Masters of the City Companies, several large contributors to the Exhibition Fund, numerous other gentlemen of eminence, and nearly all the Mayors or chief Municipal officers of the corporate towns of the United Kingdom, were present. It appears that this was the first occasion of Leamington being invited to participate in a national movement of supreme importance, and it is worthy of remembrance to the credit of the Commissioners that the close of their career of unpretentious, but useful public service, should thus have been ushered in by co-operation with the Court, the State, and the Municipalities of the Empire, in an endeavour to extend the blessings of peace and commerce throughout the world.

The novelty of the election attracted a large number of candidates, but if the percentage of voting papers not returned, or returned not filled up, be a fair indication of the general feeling of the town, there was more enthusiasm among those who desired seats at the Board than was shown by those in whose power it was to confer Analyses were made in 1857, and again in 1872, the result being the same on each occasion. In the first-named year 1.500 ratepayers had single votes, while 430 had as many as i.3oo. At the election in 1873, it was shown that every defeated candidate had polled more ratepayers, but fewer votes, than those who had been elected.

such a distinction Fifty-eight candidates went to the poll, with the result that the following were elected as THE FIRST LOCAL BOARD OF HEALTH.

W. Carpenter, 1071 votes; J. Haddon, 991; J. Bowen, 876; E. Vandeleur, 780; T. B. Jeffery, 665; R. Whitehouse, 660; R. Russell, 620; J. Prichard, 619; S. U. Jones, 607; Dr. Jephson, 604; Owen White, 524; John Stanley, 513; Joseph

Stanley, 492; J. Page, 486; T. G. Dundas, 462; Member for the Main Sewerage District, John White.

Mr. Carpenter was elected Chairman of the Board, which took over from the Commissioners a mortgage debt of £17,000, and assets estimated to be worth £12,000, in addition to about £1. 200 in cash, still remaining of the railway money. At one of the early meetings the question of an official seal was considered, when a suggestion was made to the effect that it consist of the motto, " *Fama valetudo contingal abunde"* with a design in which the efficacy of the Leamington water should be personified by an artistic representation of the Goddess of Health, standing near the fountain and dispensing the life-giving and health-restoring cup to a decrepid sick recipient, with Canova's celebrated statue of Benevolence behind. Strange to say, the Board could discover neither poetry nor utility in this original and beautiful idea, and after much waste of time in unnecessary deliberations adopted a plain inscription informing the world that Leamington had a Local Board of Health.

It could hardly have been otherwise than that the new governing body should have had a course of smooth sailing for a few years, as in the immediate duties they had to discharge there was nothing to tax heavily the powers of men of ordinary business capacity, nor were there any reasons why a special opposition among the ratepayers should have to be encountered in the near future. Troubles, however, began to arrive in 1855, when the first Ratepayers' Association was formed, with the assistance of Messrs. R. A. Wallington and T. Muddeman, two active and prominent members of the Local Board; and in 1864, when the second organization of the same kind, far more active and persistent in its attacks than the first, took the field; and increased in battalion order until 1868, at which time the Court of Chancery sequestrated the whole of the town property, the result being, as Mr. Muddeman graphically phrased it, that "we were all frightened out of our wits." It is nothing more than

what is due to say that in respect of many of these difficulties, the Local Board deserved and received the sympathy of the ratepayers; but one, for which there was no justification, was manufactured by themselves and maintained for years, in spite of the knowledge that it was a fruitful source of discontent. The practice of casting up the votes in secret, and refusing to permit candidates to be present, caused much heart-burning among those who had been unsuccessful as to the equality of the scrutiny to which the papers of friends and opponents had been subjected. Mr. W. (Jascoyne added greatly to his popularity by abolishing the custom when he was elected Chairman.

There were 1,642 voting papers distributed, of which 312 were not returned, 315 were sent back blank, and 82 were spoilt. The actual number of parers correctly filled up was only 933.

It would be a serious error to suppose that because the Local Board was frequently in some difficulty or another, coming out of litigation or going into it, harrassing others, or being harrassed by them, that therefore the public work of the town was neglected or badly done. At the demise of the Board, in 1875, Alderman S. T. Wackrill referred to it as'" Illustrious," and the compliment was in every way deserved. In the short space of twenty-three years (1852 to 1875), the period of this form of government, there were several important advances made in the interest of Leamington, most of them costly, and some, exceedingly complicated.

The first of these was the establishment of the Free Public Library, an institution now flourishing, and containing an extensive and valuable collection of books, much appreciated by the public, and certain in the future to be the subject of further developments and increased usefulness. On December 15, 1856, the Local Board, in compliance with a memorial signed by one hundred and twelve ratepayers, convened a public meeting at the Town Hall. The late Mr. T. Muddeman presided, and the Rev. Mr. Craig, vicar, after a speech sparkling with characteristic humour,

proposed the adoption of the Free Libraries' Act, 1855, and Mr. A. Campbell having seconded the resolution, it was carried by ninety-four votes to twenty. The original home of the Library was the Board Room at the old Town Hall, and the committee to whose fostering care the young institution was entrusted were:—Messrs. Owen White (chairman), J. Davis, T. Muddeman, H. Bright, T. Page, H. Hackforth, J. Bowen, Joseph Stanley, T. Lane, and R. A. Wallington. The supply of books was necessarily small (estimated at from five hundred to a thousand volumes), and the accommodation far from being adequate. In 1858.it was removed to the premises at the south-west corner of Church Walk, formerly occupied by the Leamington Priors and Warwickshire Bank, and in the following year the borrowing of books commenced. The volumes for lending were stored in one small room on the ground floor, that on the first floor overhead being used for reading purposes. A second removal took place in 1873, when the ground floor of the Music Hall, Bath Street, was leased, and the institution was moved to that building. While occupying these premises, a beginning was made with a Reference Library, a Ladies' Reading Room was established, some gifts were received to form the nucleus of a museum, and a collection made of books for a juvenile department. The lease expiring in 1875, the Library was transferred to Denby Villa, Regent-grove, and in 1885, to the Town Hall, where, at the present time, it is accommodated with several rooms. Pans for a new building for the Library and a Technical School, to be erected on the site of Perkins's Garden, have been passed by the Council, and ere long the institution will have a home worthy of its work. The Lending and Reference Libraries contain llefore the proceedings closed, a vote of thanks to Mr. Richard Eve. for the valuable services he had rendered the Committee, appointed to promote the adoption of the Free Libraries' Act, was carried *item Coh.* He was an articled clerk in Mr. Field's office, took great interest in public affairs, and was hon. secretary to the first Ratepayers' Association. While resident here, be was initiated into membership of the Guy's Lodge of Freemasons (No. 305, Leamington), a position he still retains, in addition to which he ranks as a Past Grand Treasurer of the Grand Lodge. He is new in practice as a solicitor at Aldershot.

over twenty thousand volumes, mostly standard books, and comprehending an endless variety of subjects. To Dr. T. W. Thursfield, who has filled the office of chairman for seventeen years, and who has been unceasing in his efforts to improve the institution, warm and lasting thanks are owing. Mr. D. B. Grant, the Librarian for the past thirty-six years, in the discharge of his duties has won the esteem of the Committee and all the frequenters of the Library.

This forward movement into the domain of knowledge and mental recreation was immediately followed by another in which the public health and convenience were deeply concerned. From 1856 to 1859, the then officially beardless Board of Health were engaged in negotiations having for their object the improvement of the drainage and the prevention of floods, to which at that time Leamington was peculiarly liable. In the last-named year, Mr. A. S. Field, legal adviser to the Board, and Messrs. A. Alexander and Joseph Stanley, after encountering many difficulties, arranged terms with the landowners having interests in the land adjacent to the river, and at a cost of £20,000 the Leam from the Victoria Bridge to its confluence with the Avon was widened, straightened, and cleansed, an enlarged and efficient drainage system being at the same time introduced. As indispensable parts of this work, the Board paid to Lord Warwick £2,676 for the right to remove the old mill and weir near the Manor House, Edmonscote, and to Mr. Matthew Wise £2,075 for the land now forming the beautiful New River Walk and the site of the Pumping Station. In the sixties, the Board, in common with many other local authorities, were confronted with the great sewage problem. There were two methods then before the country of dealing with sewage—pre-

cipitation and irrigation. They chose the former, but the result was not satisfactory, and in consequence of the effluent water from the works fouling the Avon, the late Mr. Thomas Heath applied to Chancery for an injunction, Mr. Hitchman's sage advice, "the sewage to the land and the rainfall to the river," was unheeded, and in 1868 the Court of Chancery sequestrated the town property in consequence of the contumacy of the Board in regard to prohibitory orders issued; inhibited Mr. Summerfield, of Lloyds Bank, the treasurer, from paying any of the Board's cheques, and left the Board stranded high and dry, deprived of every shred of authority. At this juncture, Mr. H. C. Passman succeeded in the clerkship Mr. R. A. Wallington, who had resigned, and his first principal duty was to obtain a relaxation of the Sequestration Order. In this he was successful, and the new policy of irrigation having superseded the former scheme of deodorisation, satisfactory arrangements were concluded with Lord Warwick There are several names indissolubly associated with the Library by long or special service In the early years of its history, the Kcv. J. Hamilton Davies and Mr. J. Hujrh Hawley were suc cessful in raising the general standard of its merit by gradually introducing works greatly in advance of the original selections The Reference Library, with its thousands of literary treasures, a priceless boon to Leamington, is principally the fruit of many years' unremitting toil by Alderman I r. Thursfield. Alderman S. Flavel. as the hon. treasurer to the first School of Art, carried on in connection with the Free Library, materially assisted in preparing the way for the Technical Education movement of the present time, and the establishment of a separate department for musical works, a most valuable addition to the attractions of the Institution, was brought about entirely by the exertions of Councillor Oven 11.

for the pumping of the sewage on to a farm of his at Heathcote. The application of the sewage to the land in this form relieved the town of all further litigation, and though the cost of the build-

ings, machinery, mains, etc., amounted to about £16,000, the advantages gained were quite equal to the outlay. However sadly the Board blundered over the sewage question in its first stages—and the most indulgent of its friends will not deny their failure—the members retrieved their credit in the purchase of the Pump Room property in 1868 for £15,000, and in the sanction they ultimately extended to Mr. Bright's valuable scheme for obtaining an artesian supply of fresh water. It was customary to speak of them in the heat of party strife as "the woodenheaded Board," but at this distance of time we are able to survey the whole of their work, and remembering the brevity of their tenure of office, their measures in number and importance compare favourably with those of their predecessors, the Commissioners, and their successors, the Corporation.

The fresh water question, just mentioned, was one of the most important events in the modern history of the town, and though the Local Board did not in the first instance take kindly to the artesian scheme of Mr. Bright, from time to time he succeeded, by indomitable perseverance, in obtaining majorities which led to the establishment of the present excellent works. Nothing had been done since 1832 by way of improving the quality of the supply; Mr. Oldham's works at the old Mill had been enlarged, and in substitution for the small iron tank on the roof of the pumping house, capacious reservoirs on the Newbold Hills had been constructed. But the water was still taken from the river, passed through filtering beds in the Mill field, pumped up to the reservoirs, and from thence supplied to the town by gravitation. In, or about the year 1870, Dr. Frankland, one of the medical officers of the Local Government Board made an analysis of the water, and published a report which practically amounted to a declaration that it was unfit for use. A statement so serious, and emanating from such a distinguished authority, was certain to inflict irreparable injury on the fortunes of the town, unless an effectual remedy was at once applied. Palliative measures, in the shape of extra filtration, were suggested in opposition to Mr. Bright's more practical plan of obtaining a supply from the strata beneath the town, the yield of which he was confident would prove to be sufficient for every need. The struggle at the Board for the adoption of this proposal was long and bitter. It was ridiculed as visionary and dangerous, to which were added objections insulting to ordinary intelligence. The liability of so disturbing the rocks as that the fresh water would find its way into the salt wells, with ruinous consequences to the Spa, was seriously urged by some, whose education should have preserved them from such delusions, and too readily accepted by many who never could have given the subject a moment's intelligent consideration. Not without great difficulty and much importunity, did Mr. Bright obtain a small grant of £100, for an experiment which was to decide whether the future of the town should be one of progress or decadence. But confronted as he was, more in the early than in the later stages of the movement, by an opposition, irritating and obstructive rather than powerful, happily, at no time was he left wholly without support. From the first he had the loyal assistance of Mr. S. T. Wackrill, to the value of whose daily visits to the works during the long and anxious time they were in course of construction, careful observation, and checking of evils which, without his supervision, might have proved serious, he has paid a generous public acknowledgement. Constantly at his side also were Mr. Bishop, of the Regent Hotel, and Mr. Bradshaw, one of the early builders of Leamington, both enjoying the confidence of the ratepayers, and always giving him the encouragement of their voices and the benefit of their votes, "and last but not least," to use Mr. Bright's own phrase, he had the co-operation of Mr. Harding, who was generally understood to have been sent to the Board to thwart the scheme, but like the prophet of old, bestowed his blessing on that which he had been commissioned to curse. It may be further mentioned that two out of

the three newspapers then publishing in Leamington recognised in Mr. Bright's policy the only sensible and rational solution of the difficulty, and as was shown by the stubbornly contested election of 1872, when various forces were united to eject him from office, he had the approval of a substantial majority of the ratepayers, who placed him second on the list of the six successful candidates. The obstacles against which he had to contend were placed in his path by a minority of the Board, and it would be a reflection on the intelligence of Leamington to suppose that they represented the general feeling of the town as to the merits of his policy. They were sufficiently numerous to raise a clamour, to delay, and annoy, but for anything like a reversal of his desirable scheme, they were impotent.

In December, 1872, the first step for procuring fresh water from the strata beneath the town was taken by entering into a contract with Messrs. Docwra for a borehole near the pumping station at the end of the New River Walk. Owing to the presence, in small quantities, of saline water, the experiment proved a failure; but on a second search being made on the site of the existing works, his perseverance was rewarded by the discovery of a bountiful supply of wholesome water. Several years were spent in testing the quality and quantity of the yield, and both proving satisfactory, in 1877, Mr. Bright, who at the time was Mayor, the town having been incorporated, had the satisfaction of laying the foundation stone of the new works, on which appears the following inscription:—"This stone was laid by Henry Bright, Esq., Mayor, September 1 ith, 1877." The ceremony was accompanied with the customary signs of public rejoicing, and what was considered at the time to be specially appropriate to the occasion, and an encouraging augury of the success of the new water scheme— drenching showers of rain. Mr. Bright entertained a large number of the members of the Town Council, officials, and personal friends at luncheon on the conclusion of the proceedings. The water was officially turned on

by Mr. W. Harding, Mayor, on March 11, 1879, when there was another public demonstration, and a luncheon at the Regent Hotel. Of the Well it is sufficient to say that it has realised every expectation, for in the twenty years which have elapsed since Leamington first slaked its thirst at this spring, there has been no suspicion of contamination, and no poverty in the supply; in fact, so very successful has it proved to be that the Council have had no hesitation in providing for the growing needs of an increasing population, by constructing a second artesian well in the neighbouring parish of Lillington. The beautiful granite obelisk at the Parade end of the Holly Walk has an inscription which prominently expresses the public gratitude for a work of supreme importance to the health, comfort, and prosperity of the Spa:—" Erected by public subscription to record the services of Alderman Henry Bright, to whose untiring exertions this town is chiefly indebted for its supply of pure water, 1880." Mr. Bright, by his unwearied exertions, his intelligence, and his undaunted courage, has placed his name in the first rank of the benefactors of Leamington. The contest in which he played the leading and principal part was obstinate, but his triumph over every kind of opposition was perfect and complete, and he has the proud satisfaction of knowing that the present and future generations will never pass a day without enjoying the benefit of his splendid and disinterested work.

To the geologist, the subjoined details of the several strata met with in the formation of the Well and the borehole will prove of special interest, affording as they do, ocular demonstration of arrangements which otherwise could never have been known:—

The total depth of the well is 112ft. , 6in., composed in the following order:—Made ground, 5ft.; red marl, lift. ; grey sandstone, 1 ft.; red marl, 4ft.; blue bind, 4ft. 6in.; brown sandstone, ift.; blue bind, 2ft. 6in.; red rock marl, 3ft.; grey sandstone, 3ft. 6in.; marl and stone mixed, 6in.; red marl, ift.; white sandstone, ift. 6in.; soft white sandstone, 2ft. 6in.; hard blue bind, 3m.;

white sandstone, 5ft.; blue bind, 3m.; white sandstone, 2ft. 6in.; blue bind, 3m.; white sandstone, 2ft. 6in.; blue bind, 3m.; white sandstone, 6ft.; blue bind, 3m.; brown sandstone, 5ft.; ditto, rather softer, 5ft.; red marl, 6in.; bluish sandstone, ift. tin.; blue bind, 3m.; brown sandstone, 12ft.; streaky hard blue bind, 3in.; rag sandstone, 4ft.; white sandstone, 4ft.; brown ditto, 2ft.; raggy ditto, ift.; grey rag sandstone, 3ft.; white sandstone, 8ft.; ditto, rather darker, 2ft.; and grey ditto, 2ft.

The borehole, from the bottom of the Well, descends to a depth of 100ft., through the following series of strata, specimens of which were carefully taken at the time for Alderman S. T. Wackrill, and with the foregoing, collected from the Well, are now in his possession:—

White sandstone, 4ft.; hard ditto, 8ft.; white ditto, 4ft.; hard white sandstone, 3ft.; soft red marl, ift.; hard marl with layers of sandstone, 7ft.; very hard reddish stone, 10ft.; ditto yellow stone, 1ift.; red marl, ift. 6in.; hard sandstone, 6ft.; ditto red marl, 2ft. 6in.; reddish sandstone, 9ft.; red marl, 6in.; very hard stone, 5ft.; red marl, 6in.; sandstone, 3ft.; soft red marl, 4ft; red marl, 10ft. 6in.; red marl, 4m.; and sandstone, 9ft. 2in.

The water is obtained from the Keuper sandstone, on which the north part, or new town, of Leamington stands. It extends over an area of about five square miles, and provides an inexhaustible supply, the available yield, according to present arrangements, being estimated at not less than a million gallons per diem. Professor Tidy and other eminent authorities have pronounced it a wholesome water, and generally of excellent See diagram, page 2(7 quality. The contractors for the wells and boreholes were Messrs. King & Co., of Hull; and for the machinery, Messrs. Powis & Co., of Milwall. The total cost of the works was over £30,000. A smaller well recently constructed at Lillington has proved a success, both as regards the quality of the water and the amount of the supply.

While the water question had been sluggishly passing through its several phases, the project of applying to the Queen in Council for the grant of a Charter, was brought forward for the third time. As far back as 1855, a period only three years after the establishment of the Local Board, the subject of incorporation was in the air, and in 1858, a petition to the Privy Council was prepared, with the approval of upwards of forty of the most influential inhabitants, including Drs. Jephson and Jeaffreson, and *From a photo, by Bullock Bros., l'arade, Leamington Spa.*

Alderman S. T. Wackrill, J.P.,

First Mayor of Roval Leamington Spa, and Father of the Corporation. Fleeted 1875-1875-6, 1885-6, 1886-7.

Messrs. H. Bright, J. Glover, Joseph Stanley, J. Haddon, and T. Muddeman. Public opinion, however, seems to have been in an unsettled state, for Dr. Jephson withdrew his signature, and Mr. Muddeman, who had been a warm supporter of the movement, advised that no further steps be taken, as the majority of the ratepayers were opposed to the scheme. In October, 1872, the subject, which had never been wholly absent from the public mind, was revived, and at the request of a number of influential ratepayers, the late Mr. David Johnson readily obtained fifty-six signatures to a requisition, asking the Local Board to convene a town's meeting for the discussion of the proposal. Of those who, on this and the former occasion, thus played their part so well on the civic Runnymede of our local history, the following are (1899) still living, namely— Aldermen S. T. Wackrill, H. Bright, Dr. T. W. Thursfield, and W. Gilbert; and Messrs. J. Glover, H. Horncastle, Peter Spicer, F. White, J. Hawkes, W. Andrew,

G. Smith, and T. Welch. The memorial was presented, and on the motion of Mr.

H. Bright, seconded by Mr. Lyas Bishop, the Chairman, Mr. Philip Locke, was requested to convene the meeting. In due course this was held in the old Town Hall, the Rev. Mr. Craig (vicar) presiding, and after an animated discussion, it was decided, on the motion of Mr. S. T. Wackrill, to appoint a committee to enquire into the whole subject and report thereon to a future meeting: the following gentlemen were selected, with power to add to their number: Messrs. S. T. Wackrill, H. Bright, G. Wamsley, R. Leech, W. Overell, W. Heritage, B. Bradshaw, J. Tom Burgess, T. H. Thorne, and Dr. James Thompson. At the first meeting of the committee Mr. Wackrill was elected chairman, Mr. W. Overell legal adviser, and Mr. J. Tom Burgess secretary, the committee at the same time being enlarged by the addition of several members, amongst whom were Messrs. J. Glover, J. Beck, Lyas Bishop, T. Muddeman, W. Gascoyne, George Rogers, Dr. Thursfield, Dr. T. Thomson, and J. Watson. At a meeting of the ratepayers, held in the Public Hall in the month of December following, the committee made public the results of their labours. After an extensive and careful investigation, they reported in favour of a Charter being obtained, and the meeting approving of the conclusions at which they had arrived, steps were taken to give practical effect to the decision. The advantage thus gained brought into existence a three-fold opposition such as had never before been encountered in connection with the movement—an opposition possessing the resolution and all the means necessary for contesting every inch of the ground. The local dissentients, not to be despised, either in numbers, influence, or intelligence, led the attack, and in the second and third lines were Milverton and Lillington, excited to supreme efforts by the proposal to amalgamate those portions of the two parishes contiguous to Leamington. The prospect of success was by no means assured, and the effect of the certainty of the committee having to pay heavy costs, amounting to several hundred pounds, in case of failure, was seen in a decrease in the attendance of members, and temporary lack of enthusiasm in the project. What the ultimate result would have been, had not Mr. Wackrill generously taken upon himself the whole cost in the event of the Charter not being granted, it is impossible to say, but the probabilities are that Leamington to-day would still have been under the management of the Local Board, and have been lacking in all the dignity and prestige which belong to a Corporation.

The outcome of the memorial to the Privy Council and two counter petitions from Milverton and Lillington, was an official enquiry, held by Major Donnelly, R.E., at the Public Hall, in October, 1874, at which Mr. Motteram and Mr. Caches (instructed by Mr. W. Overell) were Counsel for incorporation and amalgamation, and Mr. J. S. Dugdale (instructed by Mr. A. S. Field) for the opposing parishes. In the course of the proceedings, which lasted three days, the following witnesses were called in support of theCharter: Messrs. Joseph Glover, proprietor of the *Leamington Spa Courier,* John Watkin, Chairman of the Local Board of Health, H. Bright, R. Davidson, C.E., Town Surveyor, S. T. Wackrill, David Johnson, A. Holmes, G. Wamsley, J. G. Wackrill, T. H. Thorne, and the Rev. J. W. Lake. The witnesses opposed to it were: Messrs. R. H. Burman, George Rogers, Clerk to the Lillington Local Board of Health, James Baly, H. Hunt, J.P., Rev. N. Milne, Messrs. J. Harding, S. U. Jones, Booth Mason, T. Muddeman, R. C. Heath, Clerk to the Milverton Local Board of Health, J. Panton Gubbins, J.P., Rev. Carus Wilson, Messrs. T. Bradshaw, M. Heath, W. Harding, John Beck, proprietor of the *Leamington Advertiser,* J. Fletcher, J. Ashton, A. S. Field, R. Jones, and E. L. Lucas. With regard to the question of opinion, the strength of the opposition to the Charter was as two to one, but on matters of fact the supremacy was decidedly on the side of the promoters. Frequent remarks by the Commissioner proved that the community of interest existing between the three parishes was clearly recognised by him.

In February, 1875, the Privy Council decided to grant the Charter for Leamington without including Milverton and Lillington. It was a victory for both sides, rather more so for the outlying parishes than for Leamington, but only

temporarily, for in 1890, by a special Local Act of Parliament, all that was sought in 1874 was obtained. The Charter itself, the object of so many agitations during the previous twenty years, created Leamington a borough and gave it all the powers, authorities, immunities, and privileges enjoyed by the Municipal Corporations of England and Wales. It directed that the Corporation should consist of a Mayor, six Aldermen, and eighteen Councillors. The first Burgess List was to be prepared by Mr. William Overell and Mr. Albert Overell, revised by Mr. Louis Gaches, or Mr. Hugh Eardley-Wilmot, Barrister-at-Law, and the Returning Officers appointed for the first election were Mr. John Watkin or Mr. Samuel Thomas Wackrill. In the case of any two of these gentlemen, each of whom is described as "our trusty and well-beloved," being unable to discharge the duties assigned to them, the Lord Chief Justice of the Court of Common Pleas for the time being was empowered to appoint someone in their place. Power was given the Corporation to purchase "lands, tenements, hereditaments, and all other possessions whatsoever to the value of three thousand pounds by the year." The first revision of the Burgess List was made by Mr. Gaches at the Town Hall early in June, and on July 2, the following, out of sixty-one candidates, were elected THE FIRST TOWN COUNCIL FOR LEAMINGTON.

South-East Ward.—J. Bloor, 419; B. Bradshaw, 369; W. Harding, 283; J. Staite, 259; J. Watson, 246; J. E. M. Vincent, 217. (17 candidates).

West Ward.—S. T. Wackrill, 406; W. Gascoyne, 378; Lyas Bishop, 314; G. Wamsley, 297; J. Bowen, 278; T. Muddeman, 269. (25 candidates).

North-East Ward.—H. Bright, 344 votes; J. Devis, 316; G. Eyres, 305; W. Colley, 300 H. Davis, 269; J.Lewis, 256. (19 candidates).

At the first meeting of the newly constituted Corporation, held in the old Town Hall on July 12, Messrs. Wackrill, Bright, Bradshaw, Gascoyne, Bloor, and Devis, were elected Aldermen, and the vacancies thus created

were filled by the return of the following at an election held on the 24th:— NorthEast "Ward: W.Brown, 360 votes; T. de Carle Jackson, 318. West Ward: P. Locke, 376; W. Overell, 327. South-East Ward: R. L. Francis, 367; S. Flavel, jun., 356.

The chief event of the meeting of the Corporation on the izth was the choice of Mayor, and it was in this selection that the interest of the public was most deeply concerned. Alderman S. T. Wackrill was unanimously elected, and as subsequent events proved, no better appointment could have been made. His known business aptitude, his arduous exertions to introduce the form of government now established, his popularity and wide-spread influence, were so many guarantees that the duties would be discharged vigorously and efficiently. These anticipations were so abundantly realised that, at the first annual meeting on the 9th November following, the Council readily and unanimously re-elected him to office, every speaker bearing testimony to his industry, intelligence, and impartiality. His hospitality was dispensed on a scale of magnificence in every way worthy the event and the festive annals of the Spa. In October, over a hundred of the leading burgesses were his guests at a sumptuous banquet at the Regent Hotel, and while thus " feasting the rich," he " ne' er forgot the poor," for in March, 1876, several thousands of the inhabitants were generously entertained in the Public Hall at most enjoyable concerts, organised by the late Mr Richard Ward and the members of the Philharmonic Society; and Mr. H. A. Heden, who had specially engaged for the purpose a high-class band. Refreshments, of which there was no stint, were provided. LIST OF MAYORS.

The Mayors, and the order of their elections since the Incorporation of the town, are:— Alderman Samuel Thomas Wackrill; 1875, ditto; 1875-6: Alderman Henry Bright; 1876-7: Alderman William Harding; 1877-8, ditto; 1878-9: Alderman Thomas Muddeman; 1879-80: Alderman H. Bright; 1880-1, ditto; 1881-2: Alderman W. Harding; 1882-

3: Alderman Sidney Flavel; 18834, ditto; 1884-5: Alderman S. T. Wackrill; 1885-6, ditto; 1886-7: Councillor John Fell; 1887-8: Alderman S. Flavel; 1888-9: Councillor J. Fell; 1889-qo: Alderman Joseph Hinks; 1890-1: Councillor John Doherty Barbour; 1891-2: Alderman J. Hinks; 1892-3: Alderman S. Flavel; 1893-4: Alderman Thomas William Thursfield; 1894-5, ditto; 1895-6, ditto; 1896 7: Councillor Gordon Lyon Bland; 1897-8, ditto; 1898-9:

A short statement of the work of the Council forms a necessary part of the present portion of this history. The desirability of providing a new Town Hall having been considered and reconsidered for more than twenty years, now assumed greater importance and urgency in consequence of the municipal dignity which had been obtained. In 1857, an effort was made to supply the want by two projects, neither of which was acceptable to the ratepayers. One was the purchase of the Public Hall in Windsor Street, and the other the acquisition of the premises in Lower Bedford Street, originally belonging to the Bedford Hotel, and in recent years used as the Leamington

The exceedingly beautiful Mace shown in this illustration was pr.ented to the Borough in October, 1896, by Alderman T. W. Thursfield. As a work of art it has won universal admiration, and as a gift, it will worthily preserve for posterity the name and services of the generous and publicspirited donor. The head of the Mace combines the Carlovingian Royal crown, with a restrained and harmonious vase head or bowl. This, with the Royal fillet, the cross pattees and fleur-de-lis, completes the decorative head, and typifies the delegated authority of the Sovereign. On the obverse are the arms, crest, and motto of the Borough, in heraldic blazon, and on the reverse, the Royal arms, crest, motto, and supporters in proper colours; at either side, the Royal emblems of the double rose and crown are shown in enamel, with the letters V.R. This band of the head is canopied with Tudor tracery. The lower division of the head is ornamented wnth a wreath of

Warwickshire oak. The Royal arms appear on the roundel of the head. The staff is relieved by rich projecting knops; the upper member, which forms the capital, being of bold embossed work. The two knops have bands, with Latin mottoes, in raised gold letters on a chased background. The borders on each side the lettered band are embossed guilloche pattern, with English roses in each leading centre of the ornament. The motto on the upper'knop is" *Nisi Dominus custodierit ci-vitatem frustra vigilat qui custodit earn"* (" Except the Lord keep the city, the watchman waketh but in vain;") and that on the lower one," *Facere judicium el diligere misericordiam et solicitum ambulare cum Deo tuo"* (" To do justly, and to love mercy, and to walk humbly with thy God.") Below the capital are two raised monograms of the Borough, surmounted by the Royal crown. On the leading division of the column is a winding band, recording important municipal events, and immediately above this, in connection with the higher knop, is a moulding with an ornament of laurel. Beneath the lower knop the form takes a rich curve, thus giving a highly ornamental terminal. On the obverse of the curve is a shield, bearing an enamelled inscription:" This Mace was given to the Mayor, Aldermen, and Burgesses of the Borough of Royal Leamington Spa, by Alderman Thomas William Thursfield, if.D., J.P., on the occasion of the completion of his second year of Mayoralty. Laus Deo." On the reverse are the arms and motto of the donor, in heraldic colours. In the interspaces are the emblems of the rose and crown. The lower division of this terminal has a chased decoration of Warwickshire oak. On the bottom of the Mace is enclosed a coin—a sovereign—of that year, to emphasise the date of presentation. Around the lower part is given, in very distinct and raised letters, the legend" Borough of Royal Leamington Spa." The Mayor entrusted this important work to Mr. R. S. Roberts, of 100, The Parade, Leamington, who had previously supplied the costly mayoral chain, the gold catket presented to H.M. the Queen, as well

as many other Royal, municipal, county, and public presentations. The whole is carefully cairicd out in a very elaborate style in sterling silver, lichly gilt, the workmanship being executed in a first-class manner.

Bicycle Works. Both these schemes were rejected, and the proposal remained in abeyance until 1875, when it was revived by Alderman Wackrill, moving, at the annual meeting of the Council, the appointment of a committee to consider the question of a site. The resolution was carried, and for several years what was known as the " Battle of the Sites " kept the town in constant agitation. One party was strongly in favour of the Pump Room Gardens, for which plans were prepared; the other, and the more powerful of the two, selecting the land near the Regent Hotel, on which the Hall now stands. It was erected by Mr. John Fell, to whom Leamington owes much for the vigour of its modern forward policy; for several of its principal public buildings; for the leading position it holds in regard to healthy athletic recreation and technical education. The late Mr. John Cundall, A.R.I.B.A., furnished the plans and design, to the artistic effect and success of which the structure itself bears suf-ficient testimony. The elevation, a hundred and fifty feet in length, and rising in the centre to a height of seventy, is very fine. On the ground floor are of-fices for the Town Clerk and the Borough Surveyor, and rooms for the Lending and Reference Libraries. A wide and noble staircase leads to the corridor in the upper storey, at the south end of which is a lofty and well-proportioned Council Chamber, and adjoining it is the Mayor's Parlour, comfortably and elegantly furnished. In the Council Chamber are two beautiful stained glass windows, one—the gift of Alderman Flavel during his first Mayoralty—being filled in with Shakespearian subjects, the other containing the names of several of the Mayors and their mottoes. At the north end is the Assembly Room, capable of seating between seven and eight hundred people. The offices of the Borough Treasurer, who is also the Assistant Overseer, are on this floor, and in the room above temporary provision is made for the School of Art. The tower at the south end rises to a height of one hundred and thirty feet, and is furnished with a valuable public clock, the gift of Alderman H. Bright. Its special merits are—(1) a gravity escapement which secures equal action whether the weight be heavy or light; (2) a pendulum absolutely compensated, whereby accurate time is obtained in all varieties of temperature; and (3) an electrical arrangement for instantaneously registering, on the dials in the offices throughout the building, the time recorded by the parent clock. The foundation-stone was laid by Alderman Bright, at the time Mayor, on October 17, 1882, in commemoration of which it is inscribed: "This stone was laid by Alderman Henry Bright, J.P., Mayor of Leamington, October 17, 1882;" and the event is further preserved in terms expressed on a beautiful silver trowel presented to him by the Corporation, and on a parchment, containing also a list of the members of the Town Council at the time, deposited in a sealed bottle with a number of coins of the realm, and placed in its cavity. On the conclusion of the ceremony, Mr. Bright entertained a large company at luncheon at the Regent Hotel. The official opening took place two years afterwards, and was performed by Mr. Councillor Sidney Flavel, then filling his first year of office as Mayor, to whom was given a valuable gold key, artistically engraved with the subjoined historic statement: "Presented to Sidney Flavel, Esq., junior, Mayor, on the occasion of his opening the New Town Hall, 1884." The exact date was September 18th of the year named. Mr. Flavel gave a luncheon in the Town Hall at the conclusion of the proceedings, and in the evening there was a fancy dress ball for children, of whom upwards of six hundred were present. For the land, buildings, fittings, and furniture, the total expenditure was upwards of £20,000.

In 1876, the year following the decision to proceed with the building of the new Town Hall, the Council had un-

der consideration the advisability of applying for a separate Commission of the Peace for the borough. The feeling was general that the dignity conferred by the Charter included the right of this additional honour, and at a meeting on January 11, a motion authorising Mr. H. C. Passman, the Town Clerk, to make such application was proposed by Alderman Gascoyne, seconded by Councillor Sidney Flavel, junior, and carried by eighteen votes to three. The request was granted, and the same year the local jurisdiction of the County Justices, which had been in force from a time " whereof the memory of man goeth not to the contrary," ceased. On August 10, Borough Justices were appointed, and the new Petty Sessional Court sat for the first time on October 18, 1876, at the old Town Hall in High Street. Mr. Passman was appointed Clerk to the Bench, and subsequently the sub-clerkship was given by him to Mr. A. Turner. Several additions have since been made to the original appointments, particulars of which are furnished in the subjoined roll of

The Borough Magistrates. 1876: Samuel Thomas Wackrill (Mayor), William Willes, Matthew Lyon, Thomas Henry Thorne, John Ford, Thomas Muddeman, Joseph Glover, Richard Jones, William Harding, John Bowen, Sidney Flavel, jun., Charles William Marriott, Lieut-Col. James Ashton, John Johnson Bradshaw, and Major Joseph Ernest Edlmann. 1881: Henry Bright, Colonel William Blackburne, Thomas William Thursfield, M.D., Samuel Harwood, William Marjoribanks, John Massie, and Richard Spraggett. 1887: Colonel John Machen, Surgeon-Major George Allen Hutton, Michael Grazebrook and John Fell. 1890: Joseph Wood, Frederick Harry Haynes, M.D. , and Frederic Augustus Muntz. 1891: William Chadwick Grimsdick and Joseph Hinks. 1894: Charles Richard Burgis, Frederick William Francis, and George Norris. 1897: John Bennett, Thomas Salmon Harvey, Thomas Latham, and Robert Eardley-Wilmot, M.B.

During the twenty-five years which

have elapsed since the town was incorporated, the work of the Council has been carried forward with remarkable energy, and in two instances only have its aspirations failed in realisation. These were—the proposal in 1876 to provide a Winter Garden, a scheme advocated by Dr. W. B. Richardson in 1865, in the *Medical Times and Gazelle,* as the one thing wanted to complete the arrangements of Leamington; and the effort made in 1879 to obtain for Leamington, Milverton, and Lillington independent Parliamentary representation. It is superfluous to say that in neither of these cases could the Council be blamed for the negative results of much hard and earnest labour on their part. The opening of the Pump Room Gardens to the public, free of payment for admission, is distinctly an honour standing to the credit of the new form of government established by the Charter. After the purchase of the property by the Local Board of Health, in 1868, a demand to that effect became a popular cry, and soon found expression in a numerously-signed memorial to the Board, forwarded by Mr. W. Colley, one of the originators of the movement. In 1871, the subject was introduced into the election, and in 1873, Mr. Bright proposed, Mr. G. Eyres seconded, and Mr. B. Bradshaw supported, a motion for granting the burgesses the untaxed enjoyment of their own property. The resolution was rejected by eight votes to three, and a demonstration by the working classes followed against the obnoxious restrictions in force, Messrs. H. Taylor, H. Duckett, T. Wager, and other prominent Trades Unionist leaders, proceeding from the Mill down the river in a boat, from which addresses, forbidden in the ground, were delivered to an applauding crowd of listeners who lined the bank. Had it not been for the Charter, it is doubtful if these gardens would have been free to the burgesses even at this day, for so far as regards an absence of active sympathy with popular measures the Local Board of Health were very slightly in advance of the old Board of Commissioners, from whom they inherited many old-fashion notions and some prejudices. With the Charter there came an entire change of view in this particular; the majority of the members were men more immediately in touch with advanced public feeling and sentiment, and therefore it was that when Alderman Wackrill in 1877 submitted a proposition for abolishing the "odious penny tax" and making the gardens free, his motion was welcomed by the whole Council and adopted without a dissentient vote. But the victory thus won was not finally assured until 1889, at which time the Pump Room Committee instructed the Surveyor to enclose with unclimbable iron hurdles that portion of the gardens extending from the main east walk to a line drawn across the grass plot from north to south, twenty yards west of the kiosk, and recommended that the Town Improvement Association should be empowered to charge a penny a head for admission into such enclosure during the band performances; children, unless under proper control, to be excluded at all times from the portion of the ground so enclosed. It was explained by Mr. Passman, the Town Clerk, that such a regulation would be illegal, as the motion of Alderman Wackrill adopted in 1877 had not been rescinded; and after Alderman Wackrill and Councillor Fell had expressed their opposition to the proposed change, Alderman Bright moved and Councillor Waring seconded the elimination of the clause from the Committee's report. In spite of the Clerk's opinion, the Council adopted the retrogressive report by eight votes to four; but it was not a largely attended meeting, and of those present there were four who abstained from voting. At the July meeting of the Council, Alderman Wackrill's motion of 1877 was rescinded, on the proposal of Alderman Dr. Eardley-Wilmot, seconded by Councillor A. Johnson. In the meantime the opposition to the "penny tax" among the burgesses had broken out afresh, and was, what it had never been before, defiant. Mr. C. Purser (now Councillor Purser) successfully insisted on his right to the free use of the gardens when the band was playing, and the late Mr. Ge-

orge Wamsley also rendered good service outside the Council. A public indignation meeting was held in the new Town Hall on the 19th, at which a resolution, moved by Mr. Purser and seconded by Mr. Rayner, protesting against the re-imposition of any charge for admission, was enthusiastically adopted, and in a few days the Pump Room Committee, assailed from without, and feebly supported within the Council, capitulated, and consented to terms satisfactory to all. By the new arrangement the free use of the grounds was preserved, a charge of one penny for the use of the chairs being substituted for the payment of the same sum for admission; and it was agreed that the band should have the privilege of making collections. Such were the final terms of settlement of a contest which had been carried on for twenty-one years with alternations of successes and defeats, and with which, in the ten years that have since elapsed, neither the public nor the Council have shown any signs of dissatisfaction.

While thus conceding the right of the burgesses to the enjoyment of their own property without taxation other than that imposed by the rates, the Council have not been indolent in the discharge of the kindred duty devolving on them of maintaining intact for public uses the beautiful rural walks outside the borough. In 1878, the Urban Sanitary Authority of Lillington and the Surveyors of Highways for Cubbington endeavoured to close the footpath leading from "the Red House" farm, past that aviary of wild birds, the Rungles, into the turnpike between Cubbington and Offchurch. This path, famous from time immemorial for its charming woodland and pastoral scenery, and the opportunities it affords for the study of bird life and the collection of wild plants and flowers, being wholly within the two parishes named, the approval by both of the projected stoppage rendered an opposition by private individuals doubtful of success. On the attention of the Council being called to the matter by the late Councillor J. S. Salmon, Alderman Bright moved and Alderman Devis

seconded that Mr. Passman take immediate steps " in the interests of the inhabitants of Leamington" to oppose the contemplated application to the Court of County Quarter Sessions for the necessary order. The proposition was unanimously adopted, and, being informed of this decision, Lillington and Cubbington took no further steps, although the usual notices had been issued. It is, therefore, to the Leamington Town Council the public are indebted for the presei-vation from enclosure of a walk with which Nathaniel Hawthorne must have been familiar, and which he probably had in his mind when he wrote in "Our Old Home" that the English scenery round Leamington was such as Tennyson immortalised in his idylls and eclogues.

Our references to the remaining work of the Council, and to those other public improvements, in the introduction of which it has either rendered assistance or granted permission, must necessarily be very brief. In 1879, an ineffectual effort was made to obtain a Parliamentary seat for Leamington, Milverton, and Lillington, and in 1881, the Tramway was established. The proposal to extend the boundaries was brought forward in 1882, and though, in 1883, it was defeated for the second time, it was carried by a Local Act in 1890, from which date, Leamington and the urban parts of Milverton and Lillington became one authority for Municipal purposes. The foundation stone of the new Joint Hospital at Heathcote for Contagious Diseases was placed in its position under circumstances and at a time described in the inscription it bears: "This stone was laid by Alderman S. T. Wackrill, Mayor of Leamington, and Chairman of the Warwick Joint Hospital Board, November 7th, 1887," and it was officially opened by him on May 29, 1889. The installation of the Electric Light took place in 1887. A great improvement in the Adelaide Road was effected in 1891, by removing the old bridge and substituting the present ornamental structure, the inauguration of which is thus described on the memorial stone:—" This bridge, having been rebuilt, was opened by the Mayor, Councillor J. Hinks. J.P., August 13th, 1891, W. de Normanville, Engineer," and in commemoration of the marriage of H. R.H. the Duke of York and H.R.H. Princess May, two years afterwards, the many beautiful walks in Leamington were increased by the addition of the York Promenade, and the Pump Room Gardens improved by the building of the York Bridge, on the memorial stone of which is the following inscription: "This bridge and Promenade were opened by Alderman J. Hinks, J.P., Mayor, July 6th, 1893. W. de Normanville, Engineer." The desirability of Municipalising the Gasworks was strenuously advocated by Alderman S. T. Wackrill in 1894, and in 1897, and under the Leamington Corporation Act, 1896, the necessary notices were served on the Gas Company in 1899, on the motion of Alderman Wackrill, for acquiring the property, if necessary, by compulsory arbitration as to price. The statute under which this decisive step was taken was introduced by Alderman Dr. T. W. Thursfield, in 1895, and passed in the following year. By its provisions the Council obtained enlarged sanitary powers and authority to grant subsidies out of the rates for providing free music for the public; an object urgently needed in the interest of the town, ahd now that it is obtained, much valued by visitors and residents. Since the passing of the Act the Spa has been rendered more attractive by free concerts almost daily either in the Pump Rooms or the adjoining Gardens, given by an excellent band provided by Mr. C. S. Birch, Musical Director. While the Bill was under the consideration of the Corporation, a suggestion by Mr. Councillor J. Heath Stubbs, Chairman of the Parks' and Gardens' Committee, affected the Jephson Gardens and led to their becoming the property of the town. His proposal that the acquisition of the Gardens should be one of the objects of the Bill, was accepted, and a guarantee being given by the insertion of a clause that the name of Jephson shall never be changed, all opposition on the part of the Trustees was withdrawn, and a

boon of inestimable value was secured in the free enjoyment of which the poor share equally with the rich. In 1897, the Victoria Park, consisting of twentyone acres, was purchased for a sum of £7,600, exclusive of £3,000 for laying out the ground for ornamental purposes. This great step forward in the work of beautifying the town and increasing its attractions and pleasures, was mainly brought about by the energy and persistent advocacy of Alderman Dr. Thursfield, who, as Mayor, officially opened the Park on the Diamond Jubilee Day of the Queen's reign in the presence of many thousands of residents. Further provisions for the inhabitants of a similar nature were made in 1898, by the acquisition of the Eagle Recreation Grounds, five acres in extent, at an expenditure of £1,300, and an additional £500 for improvements, and the buying of the Mill property, of eight acres and a half, in 1899, for £4,085, the desirability of acquiring the last named property having been first urged on the attention of the Corporation by Councillor J. Fell. Including, the thirteen acres contained in the Jephson Gardens, the Council have, within the past few years, obtained nearly fifty acres of free pleasure grounds for the public, and while this work is passing through the Press, they are contemplating the purchase of the gas works and the electric lighting system, the application of electricity as a motive power to the tramways, and the promotion of Leamington to the position of a County Borough is now the dream of wakeful men. To these assets of municipal enterprise must be added the decision to erect extensive buildings for the Public Library, the Technical and Art Schools, at an outlay of £ 17,700, including cost of site; the increase of the rateable value of the borough from £129,918 in 1890, to £173,395 in 1899; the decrease of the death rate from 18-3 in 1888, to is-4 in 1899, and the zymotic mortality in the same period from r6 to o-2; and also the commencement of a Freeman's Roll, on which appear the names of Lord CURTIS'S BATHS, HIGH STREET, ERECTED ON THE SITE OF WISE'S SPRING DISCOV-

ERED IN 1790. DEMOLISHED IN 1847.

Leigh and Alderman S. T. Wackrill, the latter of whom selected the borough motto, "Sola bona qua: honesta" (" Those things alone are good which are honourable "), and gave to the town the costly mayoral chain and official robes. Viewing the whole of these events, none can say the Corporation has proved a failure, nor that its policy and services have been feeble, or fruitless in yielding a new harvest of material, physical, and recreative advantages for the borough.

CHAPTER XXXI. HE modern history of Spencer Street Congregational Church dates frorr 1836, the year in which the present building was opened, under circumstances already described. Mr. Pope continued in the pastorate until 1846, at which time, a change being necessary for the health of his family, he resigned and accepted the charge of the Independent Church at Torquay. The climate there proving unsuited to him, at the earnest request of his former congregation he returned to Leamington after twelve months' absence and resumed his ministerial labours in connection with Spencer Street Church. There he remained without further interruption until 1863, when he had a paralytic seizure, from which he never recovered. The sad event occurred immediately after a public meeting held on January 10 to celebrate the extinction of a debt of £3,300, and it was attributed to the great excitement and joy he experienced on that occasion. The seizure left him a helpless invalid, and after submissively enduring fourteen years' suffering he died on the 26th of December, 1877, at his residence, Rochester Road, Camden Town, London, aged seventy years. At his interment, in South Norwood Cemetery, the Church were represented by Mr. John Hordern, the senior deacon, and Mr. Ebenezer Goold, one of the old members. The sudden deprivation of Mr. Pope's services in 1863 was a great blow to the congregation, whose affectionate regard for him was marked by the grant of a superannuation allowance sufficient to provide for every comfort he could desire or need. His mind was clear and unclouded throughout his long illness, and letters received from him occasionally by the deacons proved that Leamington and the Church at Spencer Street were to him ineffaceable, pleasant memories. Mr. Pope was the first in the order of time, and not the last in that of murit, of five preachers whose names are prominent in the histories of the Leamington Churches in the early and middle parts of the present century, and whose ministries were attended by crowded and fashionable congregations. He was not what is called a learned preacher, as was the Rev. John Craig, nor profound, like the Rev. Dr. Winslow; in the subject matter of his discourses he rather approached the practical and easily comprehended style of the Rev. J. H. Smith and the Rev. Dr. Marsh, at the same time retaining a peculiar charm of manner which distinguished him from both. His reading, which was as near perfection as can be imagined, won praise from Sheridan Knowles, who was one of his converts, and it was probably due to Mr. Pope's influence that the distinguished actor and dramatist forsook the stage and devoted the last fifteen years of his life to theology and the pulpit. During the time he James Sheridan Knowles joined the Baptists, and became a popular and influential minister of that denomination. was at Spencer Street (1836-1863) the congregation was unusually aristocratic, and included Earl Buchan, Sir James and Lady Carnegie, Lord James and Lady Murray, the Ladies Campbell (2), Lady Cartwright, Mr. Agnew, and many others. About the year 1861, the dwarf wall, iron palisades, and gates in front of the portico were erected by Mr. B. Bradshaw, and the school immediately at the rear of the building by Mr. E. Goold. The successor of Mr. Pope was the Rev. J. Morrell Blackie, LL.B. , and B.A. of New College, whose ordination took place on September 26, 1865, when the Rev. Dr. Halley (Principal of New College), Professor Newth, the Revs. T. Binney and J.W. Percy, Mr. John Fairfax, of Sydney, New South Wales, and several others participated in the proceedings and gave brief ad-

dresses. Mr. Fairfax, it will be remembered, was co-founder of the cause with Mr. Frost, both of whom met Mr. Pope on his arrival from London by the stage coach at the Bath Hotel on Saturday evening, February 9, 1828. His appearance on the platform gave a special interest to the meeting, and his recital of the story of the early struggles of the Church, in which he had himself borne a principal part, had a freshness it had never before possessed. The chief improvements in Mr. Blackie's time were the erection of a new school in 1866, by Mr. T. H. Jones, the memorial stone of which was laid on June 11, by Mr. R. Baker, of Walpole Villa, and the decoration and renovation of the interior by Mr. E. Goold at an expenditure of about £500. The pulpit was set back several feet and a dai's in front constructed. The decorations were most artistic, the walls being coloured with sage green, the columns lavender, and the ceiling bearing elegant designs copied from the apartments in the British Museum. Mr. Blackie resigned in 1873 and went to Everton Crescent Church, Liverpool, subsequently removing to Sudbury, and finally to Cheltenham, where he died. The Rev. W. J. Woods, also of New College, was the next minister. He settled in Leamington in 1874, and in 1878 declined an invitation from the congregation at Wycliffe Chapel, Hull, to become their minister, but in 1881 he removed to Manchester, where he succeeded the Rev. Paxton Hood. Subsequently he accepted the pastorate of the Congregational Church at Clapham, and eventually was elected Secretary to the Congregational Union, an important appointment he still holds (1899). The Rev. A. Holden Byles, of Heading!y, Leeds, followed Mr. Woods in May, 1882. He was an ardent Liberal politician and applied himself with great energy to the advancement of those principles, which he regarded as essential to the welfare and prosperity of the country. His frequent appearance at the meetings of his party, and his uncompromising speeches, were much resented by those opposed to him. He resigned in 1889 and went to the Taber-

nacle, Hanley. In 1890, the Rev. J. Sellicks, of Newton Abbott, Devonshire, accepted the invitation of the church to fill the vacancy, and settled in Leamington the same year. Throughout the whole course of his ministry the relations between himself and the congregation have been of the happiest; the progress of the Church within the same period almost phenomenal, and its liberality beyond precedent, the total sum raised within nine years for various purposes amounting to something like £13,000. A new Lady Agnes Murray Carnegie, widow of Sir David Carnegie, Bart., died in June, 1860, at Dynevor House, Newbold Terrace, aged 06 years. lecture room was built in 1891, on which occasion Mr. Fairfax, proprietor of the *Sydney Morning Herald,* and son of the John Fairfax just mentioned, being on a visit to England, attended and laid the foundation-stone. At the same time the interior of the Church was thoroughly renovated, artistically decorated, and the organ removed from the south gallery to its present position behind the pulpit. The whole of this work was carried out by Mr. John Fell, and for comfort, light, ventilation, elegance, and harmonious combination of colour, Spencer Street Church is not surpassed by any in the Midland counties. Mr. Sellicks takes his fair share of public work, and though not obtrusive in politics, occasionally discusses them with that moderation of sentiment and language which always commands respect and produces more lasting impressions than ultra views clothed in extravagant phraseology. He has been a member of the School Board for several years, during three of which he was its Chairman. In 1897 he had a pressing invitation to accept the pastorate of the Congregational Church at Johannesburg, South Africa, which, to the satisfaction of his Church and the Leamington public, he declined. Anonymous donations, amounting in the aggregate to the liberal sum of;£ 1,250, have been given to the cause during his ministry. Among the old members of the various religious bodies in Leamington, Mr. Ebenezer Goold, sen., occupies a position, probably unique. As a boy attending the Sunday School, he was present at the opening services sixty-three years ago, and his church membership is one of fiftynine years' standing. The modern system of assigning parishes to Free Churches for special work applies to Spencer Street Congregational Church.

From what has already been stated, the history of Wesleyan Methodism in Leamington from 1817 to 1835 is a subject with which our readers are well acquainted. We resume now the story of the progress of the cause from the last-named year when "ye Chapelle was agayn made bigger atte ye backe, atte ye totalle outlaye of 811 Poundes." and bring the events down to date. One circumstance connected with this enlargement must be mentioned as a relic of an ancient custom by which artisans and even labourers who could not subscribe money could give of their labour, and so reduce the expense of building. Thus we find Messrs. Mace, Jesson, Coulson, Hunt, and other operatives " prepared the galleries and made the whole of the pewing for the same," in their overtime without charging for their labour. The total value of their services, at the ordinary standard rate of workmen's wages, was £50. Samuel Turner, another working man, made the staircase and railing for the galleries, and fixed the same. The equivalent in money for his time, labour, and skill was £10. John Manning, one of the earliest temperance reformers in Leamington, practically contributed £5 to the building fund by making and fixing the front doors free of charge. Sometimes a member gave the materials and the workmanship for a portion of a new church, as John Toone, the builder of the original structure, did in this case. The materials for the roof, the glass for the windows, and the workmanship, were gifts from him of the value of £80. The amount collected at the reopening services was £t 11 10s. Previous to 1837, the year when the Leamington Circuit was formed, the Portland Street cause belonged to the Coventry Circuit, established in 1791, of which the Rev. John Gay Wilson was

one of its ministers. That he resided in Leamington is believed by those who have closely studied the local history of Wesleyan Methodism, but in any case his frequent presence in the pulpit at Portland Street is beyond all doubt. He is now stationed at Redhill, Surrey, and, after a ministry extending over sixty-seven years, his position on the roll of Wesleyan preachers connected with the great British Conference is that of being the oldest but one. It is not, therefore, without feelings of pleasure that the Wesleyans associate with the early years of their first Circuit the name of one who has attained such an enviable distinction in length of days and service. There was a second enlargement in the years 1845-6-7, in aid of which Dr. Jephson gave £21. The entire cost of the work, the principal part of which was carried out by Mr. J. Goold, was £811 8s. id.; and as the Rev. W. H. Clarkson, the Superintendent, had exerted himself successfully in furthering the object in view, the Enlargement Committee and Trustees placed on the minutes a resolution expressing their warm appreciation of his untiring labours, and the great advantages and benefits he had thereby conferred on the Society and the congregation. An important movement, having for its object the erection of a new place of worship, more commodious and better adapted to the altered circumstances of the town, was started in 1866. For this purpose negotiations were opened, and continued for some time, for the purchase of three very eligible properties on a desirable site, in Portland Street, but owing to some insuperable difficulty, the scheme, as regards that situation, had to be abandoned. Proceeding with their enquiries, the Committee ultimately selected the one in Dale Street, on which the present edifice stands. Cavendish Cottage, a detached villa, occupying the site, was purchased for the sum of £1,500, and, after the ground had been cleared, building operations were commenced. The project was an ambitious one, and, considering the whole circumstances of the case, such as might well have dismayed a congregation less resolute and

hopeful, for, in addition to the expense of the new church, a debt of £1.000 on the Portland Street property had to be paid off. In aid of this the Connexional Chapel Fund Committee lent £300, free of interest, for the repayment of which Messrs. Kelin England, Richard Hodkisson, Thomas Jenner Stratton, Richard Fletcher, Joseph Hankinson, and William Winterburn were sureties, and from the same source a grant of £100 was received. Mr. R. Hodkisson, whose name appears in the list, is the senior continuous member of the Wesleyan body; he has been one of the hardest workers in the cause, and is much weather-beaten in its service. His connection with the Society extends over the Jubilee period of fifty-seven years, and he has filled evenoffice open to a layman, including those of Superintendent of the Sunday Schools, and for eight years was Circuit Steward, the last named being the highest attainable.

On Wednesday, May 19, 1869, the two memorial stones of the new building were laid by Messrs Isaac Jenks, of Wolverhampton, and Thomas Davis, of West firomwich. The event, memorable as it was in itself, wa« increased in interest and importance by

"Since the above was in type we have ascertained that Mr. Wilson occupied No. o, Grove Street, in 1832.

the annual meeting, then held for the first time in Leamington, of the Birmingham and Shrewsbury Wesleyan District, at which there was an attendance of about a hundred and twenty ministers and friends, most of whom were present at the ceremony. A short service was held, in which the Rev. B. B. Waddy, Superintendent of the Circuit, the Rev. E. Polkinghorne, second minister, took part, and the Rev. W. Hurt, of Wolverhampton, delivered an eloquent address on the principles of Methodism. A sum of £199 16s. 9d. was collected, £25 8s. 7d. of which was contributed by the school children. At the last service held in the Portland Street building, on Sunday evening, June s, 1870, the Rev. E. Workman, who had followed Mr. Waddy in the Superintendency, made some interesting references to the history of the cause, mentioning, among other things, that the original structure was only about one third the length of the place as they knew it, and that the front elevation stood back some distance from the street. The dedicatory services commenced on June 9, the Rev. Dr. Jobson, President of the Conference, preaching in the afternoon, and the Rev. Dr. Waddy, of Bristol, in the evening. They were continued on three successive Sundays, the preachers being the Rev. T. Llewellyn, Chairman of the Birmingham and Shrewsbury District, the Revs. W. Davenport and B. B. Waddy, and the Rev. F. J. Sharr, of Manchester, and on Monday, the 19th, when the pulpit was occupied by the Rev. R. Roberts, of London. The total sum collected was £4.2u 3s. 6d. The late Mr. W. Green was the contractor, and the cost of carrying out the whole scheme, inclusive of £1,124 9s. lod. required for adapting the Portland Street property to its present purposes, was £8,770 bs. 8d. Towards this, the donations, of which we give a few examples, were numerous and unusually liberal:—Mrs. Holy, £1,300, and £500 towards removal of the debt on the Superintendent's house; Miss Harvey, £1,200, and £300 for debt on the same property; Mr. G. Hyde, £1,020; Mr. J. Brown, £500; Misses Holy £500, and Miss Holy an additional £200, and £400 for the organ; Miss Collins, £205; Miss Gardner, £200; Mrs. Cole's estate, £zoo; Mr. T. Mason, £200; Mr. W. Miles, £160; and Mr. F. Hurlston, £110. The following year (1871) brought a further improvement, but it was in Court Street, in the old town, where for a considerable time a preaching station had been established. By the generosity of Miss Harvey, who gave £1,000 for the purpose, a new building was erected, adapted for services on Sundays and for use on weekdays as a school. The cost of the gothic cottage residence adjoining (£300) was defrayed by Miss Holy. Messrs. T. Mason and T. Mills were the builders. In addition to this remarkable manifestation of the growth of Wesleyan Methodism, locally, five years afterwards, Trin-

ity Church, a commodious and elegant building, was erected in the Radford Road. At first the locality chosen was Brunswick Street, the charm of the early associations of the cause rendering it desirable to have a site near the humble structure to which the Society was transplanted from the loft in Satchwell Street probably in 1819. The cost of the new place of worship, including land, minister's furnished residence, and boundary wall, amounting to £4,568, was defrayed by Mrs. Holy, who also gave £432 in addition to make the munificent gift the good, round, and even sum 0f £5ooo. A memorial stone placed in the vestibule thus records the commencement of the work:—" This stone was laid, for Mrs. Holy, by James Wood, Esq., LL.B., B.A., July 3, 1876. " On September 20, 1877, the opening services were held, and the inaugural sermon was preached by the Rev. W. B. Pope, D.D., President of the Conference and Theological Tutor at Didsbury College. Another sign of the prosperity of the Society was the purchase of additional land and extension of the Court Street School premises about the same time, at an expenditure of £903 16s., contributed by Miss Harvey, Miss Holy, and Mr. J. Wood. Leaving our readers to make their own comments and reflections on the interesting facts we have collected relative to this part of the history of the Spa, and omitting many reminiscences of Wesleyanism in former years, we must close with the following list of ministers since the Leamington Circuit was established, premising, however, that the Portland Street Wesleyan Training Schools, for thirty-five years admirably conducted by Alderman T. S. Harvey, J.P., the Head-master, occupy a high position among the educational institutions of the borough, and to their efficiency the annual reports of H.M. Inspectors, the grants and the successes of the scholars bear conclusive testimony:— 1837, Thomas P. Clarke, George Russell; 1838, T. P. Clarke, George Mitchell; 1839, Charles Clay, Frederick F. Woolley; 1840, George Maunder, William Limmex; 1841, G. Maunder, Jesse Ed-

goose; 1842-3, Benjamin John, Samuel Cooke; 1844-5. William H. Clarkson, William H. Bakewell; 1846, W. H. Clarkson, John I. Dredge; 1847-9, William D. Goy, George Curnock; 1850, Elijah Morgan, Alexander T. Weir; 1851-2, James Allen, A. T. Weir; 1853, J. Allen, Joseph Sutton; 1854-6, Joseph T. Sanger, Francis J. Sharr; 1857, Thomas Collins, John Broadbent; 1858, T. Collins, Thomas Ratcliffe; 1859, T. Collins, William L. Appleby; i860, Ralph Stott, Samuel Naish; 1861, George Jackson, S. Naish; 1862, G. Jackson, John Pearson; 1863-4, William Davenport, George Kenyon; 1865, Samuel Walker, Joseph H. Hargreaves; 1866, Benjamin B. Waddy, Samuel Simpson; 1867-8, B. B. Waddy, George E. Polkinghorne; 1869-71, Edward Workman, Joshua Hawkins; 1872, Josiah Pearson, Charles F. Nightingale; 1873-4, J-Pearson, C. F. Nightingale; E. Blanshard Keeling; 1875, J-Lancaster Ball, Nehemiah Curnock, D. Arundel Hay; 1876, J. L. Ball, N. Curnock. John Leal; 1877, John L. Ball, N. Curnock, Timothy Wheatley; 1878-9, William J. Hutton, Charles Winters, T. Wheatley; 1880, W. J. Hutton, C. Winters, William J. Boole; 1881-2, Henry Pollinger, James Bransom, W. J. Boote; 1883, H. Pollinger, J. Bransom, John Thompson; 1884-5, Nicholas Boyns, Charles D. Newman, J. Thompson; 1886, N. Boyns, D. Newman, William Scarborough; 1887, Edward Knibbs, W. Scarborough, George Henry Shafto; 1888, E. Knibbs, W. Scarborough, G. H. Shafto; 1889, E. Knibbs, G. H. Shafto, Samuel B. Coley; 1890, Joseph Cranswick, Thomas Jenkin, S. B. Coley; 1891, J. Cranswick, T. Jenkin, S. B. Coley; 1892, J. Cranswick, T. Jenkin, Thomas Edward Brigden; 1893, William Oldfield, John William Genge, T. E. Brigden; 1894, W. Oldfield, J. W. Genge, T. E. Brigden; 1895, W. Oldfield, J. W. Genge, Josiah Hew; 1896, Samuel Thomas House, J. Flew, William George Dixon; 1897, S. T. House, J. Flew, W. G. Dixon; 1898, S. T. House, Daniel Bate, W. G. Dixon; 1899, William Burkitt Dalby, D. Bate, Henry V. J. Angel.

Amongst the foregoing, the Rev. F. J. Sharr and the Rev. J. Pearson were remarkable preachers. Mr. Sharr was preeminently silver-tongued, his discourses being richly tapestried with choice thoughts, beautifully expressed in a rich, copious, and splendid diction. As an artist in word pictures, he has never been surpassed in Leamington. While Mr. Sharr soared in the blue sky, Mr. Pearson searched in deep mines, where he found treasures which frequently supplied matter for half a dozen profound sermons on a single and simple subject. The Wesleyans, for the concentration and better organization of their work, have a parish, under conditions similar to those of the Churches at Spencer Street and Warwick Street.

Next in the order of time to the Wesleyans, are the Baptists, the origin and date of whose cause and the building of the Church in Warwick Street are described in previous pages. The Rev. D. J. East, the second minister, on leaving Leamington, went to Waltham Abbey. The reason of his resigning the pastorate was the great failure of Ransford's Bank, in the Lower Parade, a financial catastrophe not surpassed by the smash of the Greenway's Bank in 1887. Speaking of that event, in a letter to Mr. Hambly, one of the deacons in 1898, he says the effect was to bring the town almost into a bankrupt condition. In 1841, we find him writing from Arlington, Gloucester, to the *Nonconformist,* urging on Dissenters the importance of compiling for general use in schools, a catechism, in which the fundamental principles of Nonconformity should be clearly set forth, and pointing out the permanent good which would inevitably result from such a system. No Leamington minister has ever found a wider field of usefulness, or gained greater distinction than Mr. East in our colonies. He was chosen by the Baptist Missionary Society, in 1851, President of the Calabar College, in Jamaica, and in the following year, he was successful in establishing a Normal Institution for the training of teachers and a High School for all classes of the community. In 1864, the institution was removed to

East Queen Street, Kingston, and a Normal School Tutor and an English Mathematical and Classical Tutor were added to the staff. While under his direction, fifty native preachers and one hundred schoolmasters were trained and qualified for their duties and a large number of young men educated for respectable positions in the colony. He was a member of the Reformatory and Lunatic Asylum Boards, the Government Female Training College and of two Royal Commissions on vagrancy and education, and on the completion of the fiftieth year of his ministry, all classes and creeds in Jamaica celebrated his jubilee with presents and addresses, Sir Henry W. Norman, Governor, himself expressing his warm appreciation of Mr. East's untiring services in furthering education, raising the people of Jamaica to a higher standard, and promoting good government. Mr. East, who is now in his eighty-fourth year, is residing at Watford, and in memory of his life's labours and triumphs in the cause of humanity he has named his home "Calabar Cottage." A special lustre was conferred on the Church and the Spa by the erudition, the eloquence and the zeal of the Rev. Dr. Octavius Winslow, the succeeding minister; a lineal descendant of the Pilgrim Fathers, who, on September 6, 1620, sailed from Plymouth Sound in the Mayflower, and in the New World formed a colony, where civil and religious liberty, at the time unattainable in England, were firmly established. One of his ancestors was Edward Winslow, a pioneer in that famous pilgrimage, and one of the early Governors of Plymouth Colony; so named in affectionate remembrance of the port of embarkation in the Old Country, dear to the hearts of Englishmen as the place where Drake, Hawkins, and Frobisher, in 1588, fell upon the Spanish Armada and defeated it, and near to Torbay, where a century later William of Orange landed. Dr. Winslow's grandfather, when the American War of Independence broke out, was resident at Boston and possessed of very considerable property, all of which was confiscated in conse-

quence of his loyalty and attachment to England. His father was a captain in the British army, and his mother was the daughter of Dr. Forbes, who was related to Lord Forbes, of Aberdeenshire. Captain Winslow died in the summer of life, leaving Mrs. Winslow a widow with ten young children. Dr. Octavius Winslow was intended for the medical profession, but, after some studies in that direction, he selected a ministerial career, and passed in divinity at Stepney College. His mother *From a photo by Bullock Bros. The Parade, Leamington Spa.* WARWICK STREET BAPTIST CHURCH, ERECTED 1833.
emigrated to New York, at the University of which he took his M.A. degree, and in 1839, came to Leamington and commenced his pastorate at Warwick Street, but it was not until 1851 that the honorary degree of D.D. was conferred upon him by the Senatus Academicus of Columbia College (Episcopal), New York. This was in acknowledgment of his contributions to theological literature, and was a distinction very rarely granted to ministers outside the pale of the Episcopal Church. Before coming to Leamington, he married in New York, the only daughter of Colonel Ring, of the United States Army. He left for Bath in 1857, and in 1870 seceded and was ordained a priest in the Church of England by the Bishop of Chichester. As a writer and preacher he had few equals; the prosperity of the Church, while under his care, was great, and when he resigned a void was created in the pulpit and on the platform difficult to fill. The Rev. W. A. Salter, of Amersham, followed, and preached his first sermon on May 30, 1858, but remained in the pastorate only about two years, in consequence of some misunderstanding which led to his resignation. The Rev. David Payn, who had in 1844, in consequence of his acceptance of the views of the Plymouth Brethren, resigned the pastorate at the Baptist Church, Bridgnorth, and was for a short time a member of the Society of the Brethren, accepted an invitation to the ministry at Warwick Street in 1860, and remained there until 1868, when failing health

compelled him to relinquish the office. He continued to reside in Leamington until his death in 1888, his age being eighty years. Between the time of his resignation and his decease, he occasionally held services in one of the small rooms at the Public Hall, which were attended by a number of warm personal friends and admirers. Mr. Payn was Calvinistic, and a PreMillenarian, and according to Dr. Trestrail, who knew him intimately in his early ministerial career, "he was a devout good man, of more than average ability; a very acceptable preacher, and a choice companion and a friend." The Rev. W. B. Bliss, from Hemel Hempstead, succeeded Mr. Payn in 1869, and left in 1872 for Belgrave, Leicester, and from 1873 till 1891, the pastorate was filled by the Rev. S. T. Williams, who came to Leamington from Middleton-in-Teesdale, and on leaving went to Whitchurch, Salop. The present pastor, the Rev. A. Phillips, was a student at the late C. H. Spurgeon's Pastor's College, and on the cordial invitation of the Church accepted the pastorate in 1892. Under his ministry the cause has attained a position, surpassed only by that it filled socially when the Rev. Dr. Winslow occupied the pulpit. In 1893 a considerable increase in the congregation and Church membership necessitated the carrying into effect of an important building scheme. The work comprised the reconstruction of the pulpit, enlargement of the baptistery, removal of the organ from the north gallery to the rear of the pulpit, conversion of the schoolroom into class-rooms and vestry, a re-arrangement of the seats, whereby accommodation was provided for an additional hundred persons, and the erection of a new Sunday School, with vestry, on the site of the old burial ground. The work was commenced in April, 1894, by Messrs. Smallwood and Co., of Stratford-on-Avon, whose contract price was £1,200; on May 31, the memorial stone, inscribed as follows, was placed in front of the building: "Baptist Sunday School, erected 1894. 'Suffer little children to come unto Me, and forbid them not.' This stone was laid by Councillor J. Bennett." The re-opening services were held on August 30, the preachers being the Rev. W. Hackney, of Birmingham, and Mr. Dawbarn. To the liberality of the members, congregation and friends, and to the good taste of the architects, Messrs. Ingall and Son, Birmingham, the present state of the edifice is a most gratifying testimonial. The Rev. A. Phillips is locally esteemed, and his having filled the office of President of the West Midland Baptist Association demonstrates the respect in which he is held by the denomination. Under the Union of Evangelical Free Churches, Warwick Street has allotted to it a large parish in which a Parish Committee specially attends to the work of visitation, etc. In the "Church Manual" for the present year, Mr. T. Kennard, the Hon. Secretary, points out that the total membership is greater than ever it has been before, and that the honour conferred on the Rev. Mr. Phillips by electing him President of the denominational Association named is unprecedented in the history of the Church. The new arrangement of parishes for Nonconformists, it should be explained, is not of legal origin, and consequently is unaffected either in the way of recognition or prohibition by the existing ecclesiastical and parish laws. It is part of a system recently developed by the Federation of the Free Churches by which districts surrounding places of worship are marked on the map as parishes, for special work, without excluding any portion of the borough from such services as the ministers and members of either of these churches may feel disposed to render.

We now come to the recent history of the Roman Catholic Mission, established in 1822. There were three Priests following the Rev. Father Crosbie, the first who filled the office after the erection of St. Peter's, in George Street, in 1828. One of these was the Rev. Dr. Weedall; the others were the Revs. Macdonald and Fairfax. The subjoined extract contributed to the *Leamington Rambler,* June 1, 1892, by the late Mr. Tracy Turnerelli, an enthusiastic worshipper, throws an interesting light on the services, the congregation, and the building in 1850, the time he first came to Leamington, and two years before the arrival of the Rev. Canon Jeffries, "What is most important to mention connected with the Chapel, as well as the Presbytery adjoining it, is that both were built at the expense of Major and Mrs. Ann Bisshopp, his wife, two prominent members of the congregation, and two of the most kind and charitable beings that ever a congregation could boast of. This Chapel and Priesthouse cost them a little fortune, but they gave it willingly and joyfully, justly hoping that the Catholics who succeeded would revere their memory and respect their graves; for besides building the Chapel with its appurtenances, they bought a plot of ground adjoining the Chapel to serve as a burying-ground for themselves and their fellow Catholics, and therein later they were buried, a colossal cross marking their place of interment, some of the principal members—the first members—of the congregation lying around them. To return again to the little Leamington Chapel. It was piously fitted up, and had a devotional, inspiring look about it, which larger and more pretentious churches have not. The congregation was not at that time a large one, but it made up what it wanted in numbers in true piety and brotherly love; pure, plain, piety, not hysterical or ecstatic, but genuine, sincere and undemonstrative. I shall never forget that little chapel, or the small body of worshippers in it. Often, and often again in after years my memory reverted to it and to them. I have been in hundreds of chapels since, but I remember none with greater pleasure than Leamington's little Catholic Chapel as it was in 1850, at the time of my first visit, or the really good people who assembled in it. There was no grand organ, no gorgeous vestments, no well-trained choir, but the chants, often by children, were heartfelt and went to the heart. Can the same always be said of more efficient choral singing in our churches, where it becomes the fashion to discard the grand, solemn, almost divine, Masses of Mozart and Handel, and to substitute for them the trashy, theatrical French compositions, of modern, very mediocre composers?" Canon Jeffries was Priest in 1852, and in 1855, Father Bittlestone, formerly a curate at the Parish Church, was his *locum lenens*. Fathers Pannier, and Verney Cave Browne Cave, another convert from the Established Church, were associated with Canon Jeffries. The foundation stone in Dormer Place was laid May 1, 1862, by Bishop Ullathorne, Roman Catholic Bishop of Birmingham, who was also the principal officiating Priest at the opening services on August 18, 1864. On both occasions the attendances were very large. Dr. Manning, (afterwards Cardinal) Protonotary Apostolic and Provost of Westminster, preached the inaugural sermon. The architecture of St. Peter's represents the transition from the Basilika to the Lombard style, immediately preceding the Gothic. Simplicity, combined with majestic strength, are its characteristics. Mr. W. Gascoyne was the builder, and Mr. H. Clutton, New Burlington Street, London, the architect. The greater portion of the cost, which amounted to £8,000, was defrayed by Miss France, who also bequeathed funds for the tower, erected in 1878. Canon Jeffries died on January 3, 1880, aged seventy-five, greatly beloved by his people and respected by the inhabitants, and was succeeded by Canon Knight (subsequently Bishop of Shrewsbury), who was followed in 1883 by Canon Longman. A calamitous fire in December of that year destroyed the Church, which was rebuilt at an outlay of £6,000. Canon Longman resigned, through failing health, in 1892, and died a few months after, aged seventy-five. The Rev. Father Nary was the next Priest, and he was succeeded by Canon Souter.

After the Mill Street Church property was purchased, in 1831, by the Rev. Rowland Hill, the Rev. Edward Bates of Cheshunt College, was appointed minister. He resigned in 1841, and the buildings having been given to Lady Huntingdon's Connexion, the Rev. Alfred New, who subsequently became editor of the *Harbinger*, the official organ of the Society, was chosen his successor. He wrote two highly commended works, namely, "The Coronet and the Crown, or Memorials of the Right Hon. Selina, Countess of Huntingdon;" and "The Voice of the Bible to the Age," respecting which the Rev. Alfred Pope remarked that it was an honour to Leamington to have had two such books produced by one of its ministers. He left in 1858 for Wigan, the vacancy thus caused being filled by the Rev. W. H. Sisterson, whose ministry for the ensuing twenty years represented a period of uninterrupted success. A courteous, hardworking pastor, he was one of the first to assist in the establishment of the Public Hall Sunday Afternoon Services. In 1878, he accepted the pastorate of Christ Church, Exeter, and his removal from Leamington caused general regret. After brief ministries by the Rev. J. T. Powell, who seceded and entered Holy Orders; the Rev. W. H. Hannah, and the Rev. T. Mace Humphreys, the property was sold by auction on March 31, 1887, at the Crown Hotel, by Mr. Josiah Southorn (Cookes & Southorn), the vendors being the Society called Hackney College, who had obtained the sanction of the Charity Commissioners. It was afterwards occupied by the Presbyterians, and in 1897, the Rev. Cecil Hook, Vicar, purchased it for the Parish Room.

CHAPTER XXXII. OR the conclusion of the history of the Warneford Hospital in a manner suited to the magnitude of the subject, a goodly-sized volume would be required. A host of names deserve honourable mention, some for the splendour of their gifts, others for years of devoted, energetic and selfdenying service. An extensive survey of disheartening difficulties overcome, and of serious obstacles removed, would also be necessary. The direct benefits to the poor in more than one hundred parishes in South Warwickshire, and the indirect advantages accruing to the wealthy classes, from the opportunities the institution affords for studying, in its wards, every type of disease and method of treatment, are subjects which could not be overlooked. Inviting as the consideration of these questions is, under existing circumstances they must give place to the dry, but not valueless, statistics of growth from 1838, when two wards, as already mentioned, were added. In 1856, the two upper wards of the original building were furnished and opened, chiefly through the exertions and liberality of Dr. Jephson, and in 1857, the Committee erected the east wing, containing a spacious receiving room for out-patients, and consulting rooms for the physicians and surgeons. A Sanatorium was added in 1862, and in 1866, the Chapel was completed with funds provided by the bequest of Mr. T. Oldham, of Southam, A further enlargement took place in 1868, when the west wing was erected, and the children's ward fitted up for occupation. Although the Warneford Hospital had been known from 1832 as a bathing institution, it was not till 1872, that the saline waters were introduced within its walls. This improvement the Governors were enabled to make in consequence of the late Mr. Matthew Wise having, when he sold the land at the south-west corner of Bath-street to the railway companies, reserved the free use of the saline spring for the inhabitants, and especially for the benefit of the Hospital. Without specifying details of each and every addition, all of which are described in the annual reports, we may mention the following as the chief events in the history of the institution during the past quarter of a century: In 1877, trained nurses were first employed; new wards for children were opened in 1880 by Lady Leigh, in honour of whom they are named; the jubilee year of the Warneford was celebrated in 1882 by a special service and a luncheon, the venerable Archdeacon Holbeche preaching at the former, and Earl Percy, presiding over the latter; two acres of land on the east side of the Hospital were purchased in 1889; in 1891, Lord Leigh laid, according to Masonic ceremonial, the first stone of the new east wing, which was opened in 1892 by Mr. A. W. Peel (afterwards Viscount Peel), M.P., Speaker; in 1898, Lord Leigh, in laying the foundation stone, inaugurated the building of the Victoria Wing, designed to commemorate the Diamond Jubilee of the Queen's reign, and in January, 1900, H. R.H. the Princess Christian, well known throughout the Empire for her labours of love on behalf of the sick and afflicted, consented to perform the opening ceremony. The Princess, who had a loyal and most enthusiastic welcome, lunched with the Earl and Countess of Warwick and a distinguished company, at the Castle in the morning, afterwards visited Lady Warwick's Cripples' Home at Emscote, and arriving in Leamington shortly after three o'clock, drove to the Town Hall, where the Mayor (Mr. J. M. Molesworth), having been introduced by Lord Leigh, presented her with a loyal address on behalf of " the Mayor, Aldermen, and burgesses of the Borough," signed by himself officially, and the Town Clerk (Mr. Henry Consett Passman). In reply, the Princess briefly expressed her thanks. His Worship presented the Mayoress (Mrs. Molesworth), to her Royal Highness, and their son, Master Murray Molesworth, handed her a beautiful bouquet of choice flowers. She was accompanied by Lord Leigh, and a fashionable and representative party to the Warneford Hospital, where she unlocked the door and declared the Victoria Wing open. Afterwards, she gave the name of '"Victoria" to the large lower ward, and at the request of the Committee, bestowed her own, " Helena " on another. Publication in these pages of the following principal pecuniary aids to the Hospital, will, it is hoped, induce many others to make a similar bestowal of a portion of their wealth; and the list given of the officials from the time of the founding of the institution will assist in preserving from oblivion many names deserving the gratitude of posterity.

Lrgacies: 1855, Rev. Dr. Warneford, £10,000, in trust; 1844, J. Williams, £550; 1845, Mrs. Kemble, £100; 1853, T. Ford, £ 100; 1855, Miss E. Bilbie, £100; Miss Lovell, 200; 1859, W. Taylor, £500; i860, Mrs. E. Bisshopp, £100; Miss S. A. Martin, £330; 1861, Miss

France, £500; 1862, Miss Brown, £100; Mrs. Ryland, £100; 1863, Miss Grew, £200 (less duty); 1866, N. Phillips, £200; 1867, O. Pell, £105 (less duty); 1868, J. Oldham (Southam1, £1,115;,869, Miss Chetwoode, £100; E. Pershouse, £100 (less duty); 1871, Miss Alston, £100; W. H. Bracebridge, £100; Miss Cleaver, £200; 1872, S. W. Lewis, £500; E. Allenby, £500 (less duty); Miss Phoebe Fellows, £500; 1873, Mrs. Nugent, £200; Lady Wheler, £100; 1874, W. H. Skurray, £200; 1875; G. Jones, £100; 1876, Miss Mary Strettell, Share of Residue, £320; Miss Ellen France, £100; W. Bayes, £100 (less duty; 1877, Mrs. E. Young, £200 (less duty); 1878, Mrs. M. Gibson, £500; 1879, H. Pinches, £200; Miss Hall, £100 (less duty); E. Greaves, £100 (less duty); J Walker, £100; J. Oldham, £100; 1880, F. Manning, £300; Mrs. E. Holy, £100; E. Beere, £225 10s. 8d. (less duty); 1881, W. E. Buck, £100; 1882, Mrs. Pratt, £400; 1884, Mrs. F. A. Bennett, £300 (less duty); 1885, Miss E. Osmond, £500; Dr. R. L. Baker, £100; 1886, T. J. Jackson, *£200;* Mrs. Litler, £500; Miss Pinches, £100; Mrs. C. Greaves, £300; Miss M. Weston, £100; N. S. Du Moulin-Browne, £100; 1887, Mrs. Cumberland, £100; Mrs. Hyatt, £100 (less duty; 1888, Mrs. O. Pell, £100; Miss Woolley, £200; J. Jury, £1,000 (less duty); Captain Thursby, R. N., £500 (ditto); J. Whitehead, £125 (ditto); Miss M. T. Cobb, /300 (ditto); 1889, Miss Garrett, £300; Miss Ryland, £1,000; J. C. Harter, £500; 1890, Miss Galan, £200; Mrs. S. Wood, £300; J. Timms, £5,721; Mrs. Price, £400 (less duty); Miss Landor, £500; H. Curtis, £100; Miss M. Phillips, £1,500 (less duty); 1891, Mrs. F. R. Wallington, £1,000; Mrs. S. Hitchman, £2,000; Mrs. M. A. Turner, £100; Colonel Mac hen, £1.000 (less duty); Mrs. Colonel Machen, £500 (ditto); 1892, Miss Mellor, £5,956; W. Dean, £300 (less duty); Mrs. F. A. Bennett, £250 (2nd, less duty and expenses); 1894, J. Bailey, £100; Mrs. G. Hughes D'Aeth, £100; R. Hopkins, £500; 1895, F. W. Arkwright, £200; 1896, D. R. Thomas, £100; Miss C. A. Cobb, £300 (less duty); Mrs. E. G.

Welman, £300; 1897, Mrs. H. Hamilton, £3,000 (conditional, known as "Hamilton Faulconcr Trust Fund"); Colonel W. Blackburne, £ 1,000 (less duty); Mrs. F. O. Hyde, £100; J. K. Williams, £100; 1898, Miss Mozley, £500; Mrs. Welstead, £100; J. Fessey, £693 (legacy and share of residue); 1899, J. Hirons, £300.

Donations: 1831, Rev. Dr. Warneford, £2,050 (to Building Fund); ditto, £1,000 (various gifts); Miss Warneford, £500, ditto; Mrs. Arnold, £510, ditto; Rev. H. Wise, £100, ditto; 1842, Duke ot Northumberland, £100; 1843, H. Jephson, M.D., £1,270; 1848, Rev. J. L. Galton, £126; 1850, Rev. W. Hopkins, £200; 1856, Mrs. Lockett, £100; 1863, J. Mellor, £100; 1868, W. Hitchcock, £300; 1870, Miss Ryland, £126; 1872, T. Horley, £105; 1875, Mrs. Hitchman, £100; 1878, E. Beere, £105; 1879, "E. P.," per F. Wyley, £100; G. Welch, £150 (part of receipts for skating); 1880, Mrs. Greaves, £100 (for the late J. W. Greaves); C. E. Bickmore, £100; F. O. Hyde, £100; Miss Ryland, £100 (2nd); 1881, Miss Galan, £100; 1882, H. Pierce, 105; Lady C. B. Percy, £100; Mrs. Colonel Wallington, £100; T. N. Harris, £100; 1883, Mrs. Cumberland, £700 (in memory of the late Colonel Cumberland); Miss Ryland, £105 (3rd); J. F. English, £100; 1884, Miss Ryland, £300 (4th, for sanitary work); Miss Parker, per C. N. Newdigate, £100; Rev. J. A Beaumont, £800 (for the erection and furnishing of the "Herbert Beaumont Cottage Hospital"); S. Flavel, jun., Mayor, £105; Messrs. G. Nelson, Dale & Co., £100; 1885, Mrs. Jones, £105 (in memory of husband and son); Miss A. Terry, £105; 1886, Mrs. J. C. Blanshard, £105; a lady, per Dr. Haynes, £250 (for deficiency fund); Miss Ryland, £250 (5th); Mrs. Hitchman, £100 (2nd); 1887, Mrs. Grenfell and the Misses Low, £600 (in memory of Bruce Grenfell); 1888, a lady, per Dr. Thursfield, £500 (for land); Mrs. Hitchman, £200 (ditto); W. B. Gibbins, £100 (ditto); 1889, Mrs. Beaumont, £100 (for Cottage Hospital); J. F. G. Williams, £250 (land); 1890, Mrs. Grenfell, Mrs. H. Graham, and Misses Low, £700 (in memory of Andrew Low); Mrs. Newbould, £100; Anonymous, per Dr. Thursfield, £100; Mrs. Beaumont, for Cottage Hospital (2nd), £100, 1891, ditto (3rd); Rev. W. G. Wise, £105 (in memory of Mrs. M. Wise); 1892, Miss Gibbins, per Dr. Thursfield, £100; Miss Attye, £100 (in memory of Miss A. Attye); Mrs. Beaumont, for Cottage Hospital, £100 (4th); C. A. Smith-Ryland, £700 (in memory of Miss Ryland); 1893, Mrs. Beaumont, for Cottage Hospital, £105 (5th); W. B. Gibbins, per Dr. Thursfield, £120 (for Pathological Laboratory); 1894, Mrs. Beaumont, for Cottage Hospital, £105 (6th); 1895, Mrs. H. Pierce, £105; Miss Mozley £105; Mrs. Beaumont, £ 105 (7th); Miss M. H. Hewitt, per Dr. Wyer, £105; G. C. Benn, £300 (in memoriam of the Rev. W. H. Benn); a Friend, per Dr. Haynes, £105; executors of the late Mrs. S. E. Baker, £200; 1896, Miss Mozley, £1,200 (endowment for a bed to be used exclusively for cancer cases); Mrs. A. S. Palmer, £389, reversionary legacy; 1897, J. Page, per the Misses Page, £100; 1898, Major and Mrs. Marsland, £105 (building fund); 1899, Mrs. Thursfield, £500 (in memory of her father, the late Mr. Matthew Heath), the entire cost of furnishing the Victoria Wing; Mrs. Arthur Nugent, per Dr. Thursfield, 200 (for endowment of the " Nugent Cot);" 1900, J. Feeney, £105.

Special: 1895, Public Subscription, initiated by Dr. T. W. Thursfield, Mayor, £403 (to repair damages caused by the gale on March 24, 1895; 1898, Public Jubilee Subscription, started by Dr. Thursfield, Mayor and Corporation, £2,695 Cor tne completion of the Hospital).

Physicians: Dr. Amos Middleton, 1826—1847; Dr. Davie, 1828; Dr. Staunton, 1828-1835; Dr. Luard, 1835—1842; Dr. Homer, 1842—1882; Dr. Jeaffreson, 1847—1867; Dr. Carter, 1864—1884; Dr. Slack, 1867—1873; Dr. Haynes, 1873: Dr. Thursfield, 1882; Dr. Otho F. Wyer, 1884.

Surgeons: Mr. Franklin, 1827; Dr. Jephson, 1827; Mr. Chambers, 1827; Mr. R. Jones, 1827— 1875; Dr. Cottle, 1827—1849; Mr. D'Arcy Boulton, 1827—1836; Mr. Pritchard, 1827—1855; Mr. William Middleton, 1827—1856; Mr. Hitchman, 1832—1867; Mr. Male, 1856—1871; Mr. J. R. Jeaffreson, 1867; Dr. Marriott, 1871 —1891; Mr. Morris, 1875—1896.

Consulting Surgeons: Charles Marriott, M.D., 1891; Joseph Morris, 1896.

Dentist: Mr. A. Jepson, 1874.

Apothecaries: Mr. Treslove, 1826 — 1829; Mr. Gossage, 1829—1831; Mr. Horwood, 1831 — 1833

Resident Dispensers: Mr. Jenkins, 1833—1834; Mr. Alcock, 1834—1837; Mr. W. J. White, 1883—1884; Miss E. M. Swain, 1884; Miss Gertrude Mannox, 1895—1899; Miss Jessie A. Sutton, 1899.

House Surgeons: — Hulbert, 1837 —1841; J. E. Male, 1841—1852; H. J. Franks, M.D., 1852— 1854; T. Furneaux Jordan, 1854—1856; T. T. Gardner, 1856--1858; Otho F. Wyer, 1858-1862; T. S. Swinson, 1862-1863; Joseph Morris, 1863—1869; F. H. Haynes, M.U., 1869—1872; B. B. Floyer, 1872—1874; G. W. Crowe, M.D., 1874—1876; T. Lloyd Brown, 1876—1878; A. Lawson Heale, 1878—1880; A. Stewart Brown, 1880—1882; Bernard Rice, M.D., 1882—1889; Philip Hicks, M.B., B A., 1889--1891; George Dickinson, 1891 —1892; Andrew R. Mackinnon, M.B.CM., 1892—1893; E. J. P. Olive, M.B. (Cantab), 1893—1894; H. N. Crowley Atkinson, 1894-1895; F. W. Garrad, M.B., 1895; Arthur Trethewy, B.A. (Cantab), 1896-1898; W. G. Silvester, 1898; C. Dudley Bishop, 1900.

Sfxretaries: Captain Donald Harrow, 1832; T. R. Blayney, 1849; W. de la tour Blackwell, 1851—1874; W. Maycock, 1874—1890; J. Warren, 1891—1899; Richard J. Coles, 1900.

With the following remarks on the foregoing we must conclude our notice of the Hospital. Dr. Warneford's generous legacy of £ 10,000 depends on the management of the institution having the approbation of the trustees; a material deviation from the original plan might have the lamentable result of diverting the fund to another charitable object. The bequest of £5,721 by the late Mr. J. Timms, a tailor and clothier in business on the Parade, is the largest sum ever bequeathed to the Hospital by a tradesman. Dr. Amos Middleton, whose portrait hangs in the Committee Room with that of Dr. Warneford, was the father of the medical profession at the Spa, and a grandson of Sir John Lambert Middleton, of Belsay Castle, Northumberland, in memory of which relationship he named his residence in Bedford Street, Belsay House. The property, long since removed, stood a considerable distance back from the street, on the north side of the Tennis Court. The last tenant was the late Mr. C. E. Large, solicitor. Dr. Middleton retired from the Hospital in 1844, when his likeness was subscribed for and presented by a large number of grateful and admiring friends. The following inscription appears on the frame:—

Amos Middleton, M.D., *Æt* lxvi.,
Balneorum in hoc oppido
Pauperum Egrotorum Causa
    Institutor.
Hospitii Warnefordensis Medicus Senior.
P. P. Araici Compluris.
    M.DCCC.XLIV.

He died on April 25, 1847, aged sixty-eight, but in none of the obituary notices is any mention made of the place of his burial. William Gossage was the successor of Nelson & Co., chemists, Bath Street, and the author of several patents of great public utility. In 1855 he established the present famous soap works at Widnes, reported to be the largest in the world.. Captain Donald Harrow was a member of the old Parish Committee, and his name appears on the first list of voters after the passing of the Reform Bill in 1832.

The absence from the list of surgeons of the name of Mr. Egerton Allcock Jennings, one of the most promising medical practitioners in Leamington from 1827 to 1834, will no doubt be noticed by readers who have frequently seen his connection with the institution mentioned in print. Probably the explanation is that the Warneford has been inadvertently substituted for the Leamington Charitable Bathing Institution, in the management of which he was associated with Dr. Hitchman. The present position of the Hospital cannot be otherwise than gratifying to all its supporters. Few towns, if any, possess a building so noble, with arrangements perfect throughout, and dispensing benefits over so wide an area. It is satisfactory to find, and we refer to it as evidence of its popularity with the working classes, that from 1878 to 1899, the Hospital Saturday Collections have produced over £5.000, while those of the Hospital Sunday, from 1851 to 1899, amount to nearly 13,000.

The incumbency of St. Mary's Church by the Rev. W. Tilson Marsh, after the opening in 1839, appears to have been provisional for the convenience of his father, the Rev. Dr. Marsh, who, as regards intention, might be justly referred to as the first who really held the appointment. Dr. Marsh was a man of wide and solid reputation as an evangelical divine, a personal friend of the Rev. Charles Simeon, of Cambridge, whose views on doctrine and simplicity of service he shared; particularly resolute in his opposition to Ritualism and Apostolic succession, the last-named tenet being, in his opinion, the great root-error in the Church. He was tall and handsome, with a benign expression of countenance, and a voice singularly rich in persuasive power. He had a warm welcome in Leamington, and during the twelve years of his ministry there was probably no one more highly esteemed. On reaching, in 1849, the jubilee year of his clerical life, he was presented by his many ardent admirers with a congratulatory address and a horse and carriage, and when, in 1851, he resigned, through the weight of years and increasing weakness, he was entertained at a public breakfast at the Regent Hotel, and was given another testimonial and address. On leaving Leamington he went to reside with his-son-in-law, the Rev. Mr. Chalmers, at Beckenham Rectory, and in 1860 accepted the living of Beddington, where he died, August 24, 1864, aged eighty-nine years, sixty-four of which had been spent in Holy Orders. The vacancy at St. Mary's was filled by

the appointment of the Rev. D. F. Morgan, who made himself very unpopular in 1852 by dismissing Mrs. N. Merridew from the organistship because she was in the habit of giving and singing at public concerts. Mr. Morgan afterwards resigned, and became the English chaplain at Mentone. For some time the Rev. J. Nadin was curate-in-charge, and in 1856 the Rev. T. Bromley was appointed to the vacancy by the trustees. He effected many improvements, and the removal of a heavy debt on the school in the Holly Walk, the establishment of an infant school in Queen Street, the erection of the schools in the Radford Road and New Street, and the formation of St. Paul's parish with the building of St. Paul's Church, are so many permanent memorials of his energy and devotion to his work. He died at the age of seventy-two years, on the 22nd of September, 1880, and was succeeded by the Rev. Dr.

S. C. Morgan, formerly Vicar of Swansea, who retired in October, 1890, to take charge of the English Church at Mentone. His relations with the parish were clouded with a want of sympathetic support, many subscriptions being withheld on account of some singular doctrine he was supposed to hold. The present Vicar, the Rev. E. W. S. Kingdom, came from Lowestoft in 1891, and preached his first sermon in St. Mary's on Sunday, February 1. He has succeeded in restoring the harmony which was broken during the vicariate of his predecessor, and in bringing back the days of prosperity of Dr. Marsh and Mr Bromley. The purchase of a vicarage, at a cost of £1,500, the renovation and improvement of the interior of the Church, together with the maintenance in a state of efficiency of the various parochial institutions, are evidences of his zeal and the support and esteem of his parishioners.

The College in Binswood Avenue, built in the Tudor style of architecture, was opened in 1848, the Rev. W. Wright, LL.D., D.C.L., retaining the Principalship, held by him since the inauguration of the institution, in Eastnor Terrace, in 1844. His resignation, in

1851, was followed by the election of the Rev. T. Burbidge, LL.D., on whose suggestion the College was changed from a Proprietary into a Public School. Dr. Burbidge was a man of great energy, and besides enjoying the respect and confidence of all connected with the College, he won a large measure of popularity by the vigour with which he supported the Rev. E. Clay in his advocacy of the Early Closing Movement, and the enthusiasm with which he worked for the establishment of the Free Public Library. Of a volume of sermons, preached by him in the College Chapel, it has been said that a copy ought to be placed in the hands of every young student. He was also the author of " Hours and Days,'' a collection of poems favourably noticed in the Press. In 1862 he resigned, and the Rev. E. St. John Parry, of Winchester School, was appointed to the post, the duties of which he discharged until the College was closed in 1865 for the want of adequate support. While the property was in the market, and its future doubtful, Mr. S. T. Wackrill, by prompt action, succeeded in forming a Limited Liability Company, who purchased and started it again on a more comprehensive basis. The new Head Master was the Rev. J. W. Johnson, who commenced his duties in 1867, but in consequence of some disagreement, retired in 1870. From that year until 1 890 the College vas under the direction of the Rev. Dr. J. Wood, and many were the important improvements of that time, chief among which were the additions of the cricket ground, chapel, organ, library, gymnasium, sanatorium, fives courts, etc. Dr. Wood was appointed Principal at Tunbridge School in 1890, and his successor was Mr. W. J. Ford, of cricketing celebrity, who resigned in 1893, when the Rev. R. Arnold Edgell, M.A., of University College, Oxford, was elected, and a new era of prosperity commenced. He is also Chairman of the School Board.

On October 25, 1849, the opening sermons in the Holly Walk Independent Chapel were preached by the Rev. J. Sibree, Coventry, and the Rev. W. Forster, London. Mr. Batchelor, the first minister, having accepted the pastorate of the Congregational Church, Fetter Lane, London, resigned in 1853, when the Rev. J. Hamilton Davies, of Sherbourne, was elected. His ministry was of short duration, for in consequence of his views undergoing some change, he resigned, and on February 17. 1856, was ordained by the Bishop of Worcester, and in the following month he preached his first sermon as one of the curates at the Parish Church. It would be idle to deny that this unexpected event was a heavy disappointment to the young cause. Mr. Davies was a fine, gentlemanly-looking man, portly, with gifts and graces in the pulpit vouchsafed to few. He was a member of the Hebrew Literature Society, and generally his scholastic attainments were extensive and sound. With the exception of a period of sixteen months, during which he was acting as senior curate at Holy Trinity, Coventry, he remained at the Parish Church until 1872, popular as a preacher, a lecturer, an indefatigable worker for the good of the town, and especially useful as Chairman of the Free Library Committee. In 1874 he was presented to the living of St. Nicholas, Worcester, where he passed the remainder of his life. The Rev. J. Key, of Cheshunt College, succeeded him at the Holly Walk in July, 1856, but he retired in two years, and after Mr. Sibree had conducted the services for three months, the Rev. T. Slade Jones, of Rotherham College, was elected. The next minister was the Rev. C. S. Sturrock, B.A., who resigned in 1863, through failing health, and was followed by the Rev. W. Slater. In 1868 he removed to the Vineyard Chapel, Bath, and was succeeded by the Rev F. S. Attenborough, who came to Leamington from Uckfield, and preached his first sermon in the Holly Walk Chapel in March, 1869. Under his ministry the church prospered, and signal proofs were given of the esteem in which he was held. He was an attractive speaker on the platform, and an able preacher in the pulpit. For many years he was a member of the Free Library Committee1, and he originated the idea of the juvenile department, the literature

of which has always been a source of much enjoyment and instruction to young Leamington. For some time before Mr. J. E. M. Vincent disposed of the *Leamington Chronicle,* he was a regular contributor to the editorial department of that paper, and subsequently became its proprietor and editor, holding at the same time the editorship of the *English Labourers' Chronicle,* the organ of the National Agricultural Labourers' Union. His death, deeply lamented by all classes, occurred in October, 1879, at the early age of thirty-seven. During his illness arrangements were made for the transfer of the cause at Holly Walk to Spencer Street. A minority, however, dissenting from the plan of amalgamation, elected the Rev. Mr. Tuck to the vacant pastorate, and the services were continued for some time with slender support. In 1897 the property was sold to St. Luke's Church and Congregation, Augusta Place, and Independency retired, probably for ever, at any rate for irany years to come, from a most eligible position on the north bank of the Leam—the largest, the wealthiest, the most thickly populated and prosperous part of the borough, the seat of its local government, and the centre of its municipal institutions.

Tranquil as the course of events at St. Luke's, from 1850 to 1897, proved to be, its extinction in the latter year brought into unnecessary prominence the evils inherent in the Proprietary system. The Rev. Edmund Clay, founder and first minister of the Church, remained in office till 1856. He was an earnest advocate of early closing, and pointed out that, if the public would only agree not to purchase goods after a certain hour, tradesmen would soon close their establishments when that time arrived. On tableturnings and spirit-rappings, subjects of engrossing interest in the fifties, he appears to have been far too credulous, accepting as established and incontrovertible facts, the alleged extraordinary manifestations at seances, such as heavy tables rising from the floor and turning over without anyone touching them, hand-bells leaving the mantlepiece and ringing violent-

ly while floating about the room near the ceiling, chairs flying from corner to corner with a velocity which endangered the safety of all present, and answers to questions by knockings under the floor, remarkable for some successful efforts at emphasis and an appreciation of correct spelling. In one case the movements of a table could not be prevented, although "a heavy book, believed to be a dictionary," was placed upon it, but the moment "a small Greek Testament" was substituted its caperings gave way to a staid and motionless decorum. All this Mr. Clay believed, as did several other clergymen of that time, and scores of educated people besides, but he held the cause to be of Satanic origin, asserted that consulting familiar spirits was prohibited by scriptural authority, and, as a further deterrent, quoted statistics showing the large number who had found their way into lunatic asylums through their minds having become unhinged by such studies. During the six years he was at St. Luke's the building was enlarged and improved three times. Retiring in 1856, to the sincere regret of his congregation, who presented him with an affectionate address, he removed to Brighton, where he held the Incumbency of St. Margaret's for sixteen years. His death in 1872, at the age of fifty-two, was followed by a glowing eulogy in *The Rock* on his sound evangelical churchmanship, his arduous and effective ministry, and by a wide-spread feeling of sorrow at Brighton, in which Leamington joined. The Rev. Henry Fisher succeeded Mr. Clay at St. Luke's in 1856. Like his predecessor, he was a thorough evangelical, and throughout the thirty-eight years of his ministry he never deviated from the utmost simplicity in his manner of celebrating divine service. All ceremonies, ornaments, and everything having the least semblance of sacerdotalism were regarded by him as alien to the genius of the Church of England, and dangerous to her safety as a great Protestant institution. At the annual lectures of the Rev. Dr. Cumming, which always crowded the Public Hall, and at other enthusiastic Protestant meetings in the same buildings, he was a regular attendant and was often in the chair. He was Calvinistic, though probably not so extreme as the Rev. Dr. Wilkinson; preached extemporaneously, sometimes for an hour, but without producing a sense of weariness. To the Sunday afternoon Services in the Public Hall he rendered signal assistance by numerous addresses. The new school-rooms and formerly flourishing Day and Sunday Schools were established during the incumbency of Mr. Clay, and it is interesting to learn that the Rev. Dr. Warneford contributed £50 in aid of the building fund. Mr. Fisher died on the 2ist of June, 1894, aged seventy-nine years, and had as his successor the Rev. J. W. Dance, of Old Hill. A dispute arising respecting the tenure of the premises, the Holly Walk Congregational property was purchased for £2,000, and on Sunday, February 16, 1896, Mr. Dance and his friends celebrated divine worship for the first time in their new home. Their right to establish a church in St. Paul's Parish without permission of the Vicar (the Rev. J. Pargiter) was questioned, and led to an acrimonious controversy, but though the sanction was withheld, and the license of the Bishop refused, in the peculiar circumstances of the case, public sympathy was on the side of the ejected minister and his congregation. On May 29, 1899, Mr. J. A. Locke (late Locke, Gilbert & Co.) sold the property in Augusta Place by auction at the Crown Hotel.

Theatrical matters were greatly advanced in 1849 by the purchase of the old and disused Congregational Chapel in Clemens Street, and its dedication to the drama. At what time performances ceased at the Bath Street House is uncertain, but probably they were not continued after 1831. Small though it was, we doubt if any theatre in the provinces, at that time, had a more brilliant career. Among the "stars" who played there were Edmund Kean, Booth, Munden, R. W. Elliston, Master Betty, Macready, Miss Foote, Mrs. Waylett, Mrs. Davidson, Charles Kean, Mathews, and Yates. When dramatic representations were no longer possible at the original theatre, arrangements were made by Messrs. Henry and Charles Elliston for their continuance at the Upper Assembly Rooms, which became and continued to be the local temple of Thespis until the important development in 1849, just mentioned. The catering at the " extremely elegant temporary theatre, fitted up in the Assembly Rooms," was energetic, and occasionally Mr. H. T. Elliston, the organist at the Parish Church, won much applause by his realistic impersonations. The name given the Clemens Street House was " The New Elliston Rooms and Theatre Royal;" Mr. Charles R. Elliston was the Managing Director, and the opening performance took place on Monday evening, February 5, the pieces selected being the comedy of *The Wonder, or a Woman Keeps a Secret,* and Planche's comic drama, *Who's Your Friend, or the Queensbury Fete,* for which Mr. James Wallack, Mrs. Glover, and Mr. Webster were specially engaged. On the following evening, and on Saturday, the 10th, there were grand concerts, at which Thalberg appeared, and on the 31st. Jullien gave two concerts to crowded audiences. Mdlle. Alboni, then commencing her brilliant career, sang the part of Norina in *Don Pasquale,* in October, Benedict conducting; and Macready, at his farewell visit on December 1, played *Hamlet,* the building being packed, and Clemens Street a vast surging mass of disappointed applicants for admission. Buckstone, Mrs. Fitzwilliam, Mr. and Mrs. Charles Kean, Charles Matthews, G. V. Brooke, Sir William and Lady Don, Anderson, Madame Celeste, Sam Cowell, and many other celebrities might be quoted as having delighted Leamington from the footlights at this theatre. In 1859, a local A.B C. Dramatic Club, established by Captain Horton Rhys, were fashionably patronised in their amateur performances, and in the early sixties, entertainments of a similar character, given by the Rifle Volunteers for the funds of their Corps, were exceedingly popular. The principal characters, with one or two exceptions, were sustained by the officers and men of the company, all acquitting themselves creditably, and Colonel (then Ensign) Magrath, Lieutenant N. Merridew, and one or two others being particularly good. The Theatre was closed in 1866, after which dramatic plays were occasionally performed in the Music Hall, Bath Street, and the Upper Assembly Rooms. A new movement opportunely started at this time by Sergeant White, and first known as "The Leamington Amateur Dramatic Club," but afterwards as "The Garrick," supplied for fourteen seasons a most enjoyable series of entertainments. With him were associated Messrs. *J.* Heydon Sole and E. and A. Holmes, all of them possessing good histrionic ability and deserving well of the public for the admirable manner in which they catered and acted for its pleasure. In 1881, the Leamington Theatre Company was formed, and proceedings at once commenced for building the present charming theatre in Regent Grove. It was erected by Mr. John Fell at a cost of £10,000, from designs by Mr. C. J. Phipps, of London, and was opened on the 2nd of October, 1882, with a performance of "The Lily of Killarney," under the direction of Sir Julius Benedict. After changing hands several times, the property was purchased several years ago by Mr. H. Dundas, and under his experienced management, excellent judgment, and liberality, the dramatic art has reached a point in every way worthy of a Royal Borough.

The local Volunteer movement had its origin in 1859, the year in which General Peel issued his famous circular. Two meetings for the consideration of the subject having been held in October in the Town Hall with satisfactory results, Lord Leigh was in a position in November to offer the Queen the service of "a Company of Rifle Volunteers at Leamington and Warwick," and on January 11, 1S60, he was officially informed by the War Office that " her Majesty has been graciously pleased to accept the same." The enrolment of the corps took place without delay, Mr. J. Machen being appointed captain, Mr. R. C. Heath lieutenant, and Mr. E. Muntz, ensign, and before the month of January was out, sixty volunteers were sworn in at the Shire Hall, Warwick, before Mr. E. Greaves and Captain R. D. Vaughton, a Crimean hero. Words of encouragement and congratulation having been addressed to the men, certain baptismal or christening rites, in which the element of wine was substituted for that of water, followed, and after " trying their hands at the goose-step" for a short time, the newlyfledged Volunteers had a march-out to the martial strains of the Militia Band. Drills were held alternately at Warwick and Leamington; the first instructor was Sergt-Major Robertson, and afterwards, Captain and Adjutant Edwards, a typical soldier, who, as Sergt-Major, in the ist Scots Fusiliers, had seen active service in the Crimea, undertook and carried out to a successful issue the military training of the battalion. The butts at Milverton were erected in 1860 at a cost of £500, and in the same year the County Rifle Association was formed to promote good shooting, and encourage the volunteer spirit by offering prizes annually for competition. Foremost in this patriotic work was Lord Leigh, subscribing liberally to the funds and providing a target and range in Stoneleigh Deer Park free of all expense. The. first battalion prizeshooting in July, 1860, was attended by thousands of spectators, and had a most healthy and invigorating influence on the movement. At the subsequent yearly meetings, which have been continued to the present time, the Leamington Volunteers have had the honour of holding the first position for high-class firing, and chief amongst the band of crack shots who have thus won military laurels for themselves and the Spa the following must be named:—Quarter-Master-Sergeant (now Major) Cutting, Quarter-Master J. B. Stanley; Colour-Sergeants Metcalf, Doogan, Squires, A. Orton; Sergeants E. Holmes, H. Johnson, Peyton, J. Smartt, Walker, Whieldon; Corporal Haynes, and Privates Stoney and Slater. In 1860 the Company creditably took part in the great Volunteer Review in Hyde Park, and some time afterwards, in consequence of the number of recruits increasing, two corps

were formed—one for Warwick and one for Leamington. The want of a suitable Drill Hall and Armoury, which from the first had caused great inconvenience, was met in 1870 by the erection of the present building near the Adelaide Bridge, the cost being ultimately defrayed by shares, repayable by ballot according to a scheme proposed by the late Mr. John Beck. Sergeant-Major Hodge, connected with the Corps from 1861 to 1876, was a popular officer, and was the possessor of several medals and clasps. His successor was Q-M.-Sergt. Harwood, from Budbrooke, who, after serving eight years, retired, and was followed by ColourSergeant Davenport, the present holder of the office being Sergeant-Instructor Rogers. Captain Machen, the first Captain Commandant of the Detachment, was succeeded by Colonel Magrath, who joined in 1860 as a private, was made Ensign in 1862, Captain in 1869, Major in 1882, and afterwards proceeded to the ranks of Lieutenant-Colonel and Colonel. He retired in 1893, vvith full rank as Colonel, after which the office was filled successively by Major A. E. Overell, Major Frank Glover, and Captain Kendall. The following are among the prominent supporters of the movement in the early days as well as recent times, and sharers of its work by membership:—Ensign Sidney Flavel, Lieutenant J. W. Hassall, Lieutenant Dr. Collins, Captain C. I. Blaker, Lieutenant Dr. Thorne, Surgeon-Major Dr. T. W. Thursfield, Lieutenant J. R. Jeaffreson, Lieutenant Laurie Brown, Ensign Parsons, and Quarter-Master-Sergeant J. P. Beck.

S. Alban's, to which no reference has yet been made, has had a history more strange and eventful than any other church or chapel in Leamington. It is the survival of a corrugated iron building erected by the Rev. John Craig in 1861, on the site in Priory Terrace now occupied by Priory House, and was known in those days as "The New Opposition Church." Mr. Craig was caustically criticised in the Press and at the Vestry meetings for causing the Iron Church to be placed within a few yards of the Parish Church, and as it was

thought that he had some pecuniary object in view, his enemies did not hesitate to speak of it openly as "The Vicar's New Shop," one of them recommending him to dedicate it to St. Demetrius, and to have inscribed across the front elevation this motto, in bold characters, " Sirs, ye know that by this craft we have our wealth." At this time the Parish Church afforded sitting accommodation for nearlv 2,500. and in the Iron Church there was provision for about 1,000 more. In 1864 the new building was purchased by the Rev. T. S. Millington, Rector of Woodhouse Eave, Leicestershire, and transferred to the site in Warwick Street, which was then part of the large and beautiful garden belonging to Orleans House, now the Working Men's Conservative Club. The credentials of the new clergyman were, the authorship of a book of laborious research, high scholastic attainments, and sound churchmanship, "going to extremes in neither High nor Low directions." There was some change in the arrangements, including the erection of a chancel, designed to form part of an entirely new church, for which the Vicar had agreed to assign a district. Mr. Millington resold the property in 1865 to Mr. Craig, who, with clerical assistance, continued the services until February, 1871, when the Rev. W. Wilkinson, of Christ College, Cambridge, and Vicar of Sutton, St. Michael, Hereford, became the purchaser. Means were now adopted for building a new church, and the appeals to the public for support meeting with liberal responses, the present edifice was commenced on June 7, 1877. A special sermon was preached by the Hon. and Rev. J. W. Leigh, on the conclusion of which Mrs. G. Unett laid the foundation stone with a silver trowel she had used for a similiar purpose at the building of the Smethwick National Schools. The designs, which have been much admired for their many artistic merits, were prepared by the late Mr. J. Cundall, and the work was carried out by Mr. John Fell at an outlay exceeding £2,000. The name was now changed to that of "St. Michael's and All Angels." In 1881, there was another variation in the proprietorship. It will be remembered that in 1880 the Rev. Dr. Nicholson and his congregation had to leave Christ Church in consequence of Mrs. Downes refusing to renew the lease. The only building available was the Public Hall, to which they removed and there resumed their services. Early in the following year it was reported that Dr. Nicholson had purchased "St. Michael's and All Angels " from Mr. Wilkinson, and that possession was to be had as soon as the money was paid. Shortly after, Dr. Nicholson acquired the property, and gave the church the name of S. Alban's. In his financial statement for 1882, the price paid is set down as 5,600, and the total expenditure as £6,174 8s. 3d. The transaction gave rise to much discussion, for the particulars of which we must refer our readers to the local papers of that time. A splendid processional cross was presented to the Church in June, 1886, the font fixed in the Lady Chapel was given in October, 1892, and in 1887, the tower was erected as a memorial of the Jubilee reign of the Queen. After the sale of the church, Mr Wilkinson left Leamington, and in 1890, was rector of Burrough, Melton Mowbray, Leicestershire.

The next Proprietary Church to which we have to refer is that of Holy Trinity, Beauchamp Square. Dr. Young, the first incumbent, was licensed November 11, 1847. He was of Oriel College, Oxford, and came to Leamington from the Isle of Wight, where he had been Vicar of St. Helen's for several years. In 1850 he resigned, and was presented to the Rectories of Croxton and Eltisby, Cambridgeshire. For the space of nearly seven years there was no regularly licensed minister, but the services were continued, and in 1S56-7 the Rev. J. Hamilton Davies, then a curate at the Parish Church, was frequently preaching the Sunday morning sermons. On August 28, 1856, Mr. W. H. Hewitt offered the property for sale at his Mart, opposite the Bank of England. The first offer was £1,500, and the biddings having advanced as high as £2,680, the auctioneer's hammer fell, and the edifice was disposed of at that price, the fix-

tures, including the organ and communion table to be taken at £200. The Rev. W. N. Tilson *From a Photo by Graham, Royal Leamington Spa,* The Rkv. William Flory:
London College of Divinity, and Balliol College, Oxford.
First Vicar of the New Parish of Holy Trinity, Leamington.
Consecration of Church, November 16th, 1899.

Marsh was appointed incumbent on the 13th of August, 1857, and is reported also to have bought the property. He returned to Leamington from Ryde, Isle of Wight, where he had been rector of St. James's. The next minister was the Rev. A. F. Pettigrew, MA., of Trinity College, Cambridge. The Rev. W. H. Lambart succeeded to the incumbency in 1863, and in 1865, expended nearly £400 in enlarging and improving the edifice. From 1869 to 1876, the Rev. J. S. Ruddach was in office, and on his leaving for the Isle of Wight, the Rev. W. Flory, formerly curate to the Rev. Charles Dallas Marston, Vicar of St. Paul's, Onslow Square, South Kensington, was appointed his successor. Mr. Flory, who was ordained by the Bishop of Worcester to the curacy of St. Clements, Nechells, Birmingham, in 1870, and afterwards worked for a considerable time in St. Mary's district under the Rev. T. B. Bromley, preached his first sermon in the Church on Sunday, January 7, 1877. His appointment gave great satisfaction. In 1881, some extensive improvements, designed by the late Mr. John Cundall, were carried out by Mr. T. Mills, builder, including the addition of a new choir vestry and enlargement of the north and south transepts. On completing the twentieth year of his incumbency, in January, 1897, Mr. Flory was presented with an artistically-illuminated address, bound in morocco, and lined with white satin. The pages were of vellum, the first being embossed with his coat of arms, crest and motto, and the others containing the address and some beautiful etchings of the interior and exterior of the Church. He was also given, at the same time, a costly silver dessert service, consisting of an

epergne with two fruit and four hanging baskets, four bon-bon dishes, and six flower vases. Mrs. Flory was presented with a silver afternoon tea service, "in recognition of her faithful co-operation with her husband in his earnest and faithful ministry, unfailing sympathy, kindness, and courtesy." An event in 1898 exercised an important influence on the future of the Church, besides affording further evidence of the high esteem in which Mr. Flory was held. The living of Snitterfield was offered him by his Diocesan, and with the view of inducing him to stay in Leamington, an organised effort was made for obtaining the assignment of a parish to the Church. This was regarded by the Bishop and the Rev. Mr. Hook, Vicar, with favour, and as soon as the necessary endowment fund of £1,000 was raised, the application was granted, and Holy Trinity Parish, with Mr. Flory as its first Vicar, was the gratifying, result. The consecration service, at which there was a very large gathering of the clergy and laity, was held on November 16, 1899, the Bishop, who was attended by his chaplain, the Rev. A. Perowne. and the Registrar, Mr. Hooper, preaching a sermon special to the occasion. In the " Worcester Diocesan Calendar" for the present year (1900), reference is made to the formation of the new parish of Holy Trinity as a noteworthy event, and the portrait of Mi. Flory is given as one of six clergymen who have, in various ways, " contributed greatly to the advance of Church work in the Diocese." The creation of the parish, it should be stated, had the full consent and active assistance of the Vicar of Leamington and the patron of that living. The liberality of Mr. T. Ryland, of Moxhull Park and Erdington, and the congregation was exceptionally great; and it is extremely creditable to all that on one occasion the offertory amounted to £765 17s. 5d., while in the course of the year the magnificent sum of £5,000 was found for the purchase of the edifice, endowment, and necessary extensions and repairs. Mrs. and Miss Lee contributed £1,000 to the endowment fund, erected the chancel wall, laid the chancel with mosaics, and gave the handsome communion table. The font of alabaster is the gift of Mrs. Reloe. During Mr. Flory's ministry the Church has been greatly improved in many respects. His success is a matter of congratulation in the Borough, not less to the Nonconformist bodies than to Churchmen, with all of whom, including the working classes, he is immensely popular.

The absence of any reference to the Pump Rooms since our description of the opening ceremony in 1814, must not be attributed to a want of appreciation of the importance and influence of that institution on the prosperity of Leamington. The fact is, we have found few events in its history from 1814 to 1860 calling for special remark. One circumstance, however, deserves notice, relating as it does to an illustrious discoverer and public benefactor. Amongst those who were employed in fitting up and completing the property was William Murdock, the inventor, in 1792, of gas lighting.

It has been asserted that he introduced his system of using gas as an illuminant into the rooms, but Smiles, in his " History of Inventions," says he was engaged in erecting an apparatus of his own invention for heating water for the baths, and that, while so employed, a ponderous cast-iron plate fell upon his leg, above the ankle, and severely injured him. He remained a long while in Leamington, and when it was thought safe to remove him, the Birmingham Canal Company kindly placed their excursion boat at his disposal, and he was conveyed safely homeward. At this time he was connected with Boulton & Watt, of the Soho Foundry, with whom his name is honourably associated for the perfecting of the condensing steam engine. Bisset mentions that in 1815, a band played every morning for the delectation of visitors, and at a later period, Mr. Hitchman was active in raising a fund for the remuneration of a number of local musicians who supplied matutinal music to the crowds of aristocratic patrons, as they quaffed their goblets at the spring before breakfast, and walked

briskly round the grounds the regulation number of times. In its early years the establishment was extensively patronised, and proved a profitable investment to the owners, but at the commencement of the second half of the present century, through neglect, its popularity declined. How the property came into the possession of the town is a story of disinterested public service, and of great liberality on the part of the leading local men of that time. In 1860, it was known that the Hon. Charles Bertie Percy, then the sole proprietor, had determined to close the institution, and to offer the land for sale. To prevent what would have been a serious loss to the town, a number of the principal residents met at the Regent Hotel in May, and decided to raise a fund to purchase the Pump Room and grounds, improve them, and preserve the baths, etc., for the benefit of the town. The prospectus of a Joint-Stock Company was published in June, and for a time all was promising. These appearances turned out to be deceptive, and in May, 1861, the committee resigned, and the Company was dissolved. In the month of July following, the project was revived, and the " Leamington Royal Pump Room Company (Limited)" formed, with a proposed capital of £8,000, in. £5 shares. According to a valuation the property was worth £10,000, which the vendor reduced to £8,500, in consideration of the purchase being made in the interests of Leamington. At this price it was purchased, the Company taking possession in October, 1861, and improvements on a large scale were at once begun, bringing the total outlay to £17,361 4s. 8d. , at the close of 1863. After carrying on the business for several years without realising any dividends, the Company, in 1868, sold the Pump Rooms and grounds to the Local Board of Health for £15,000. In 1886, the Corporation wisely adopted a more vigorous policy of management, and having borrowed an additional £3,000, proceeded to renovate the institution and adapt it to the requirements of modern balneology. The total outlay was £2,983, a section of the work being carried out by Messrs.

Jenkins and Sons, for £1,556. On June 1, 1887, the Pump Rooms and Baths were re-opened by the Right Hon. A. W. Peel (now Viscount Peel), M P., and Speaker, in the presence of a distinguished company. Since then, numerous other developments have taken place, and the bathing establishment may now be regarded as thoroughly efficient. The Pump Room itself is of noble dimensions, and its walls are adorned with three portraits of great local interest—Dr. Jephson and Mr. John Haddon, painted by W. Gill, and presented by the town; and the Rev. Dr. Marsh, by Taylor, of Leicester, the gift of Mr. Joseph Glover. Space will not allow us to mention all, who, in the crisis of the history of the property in 1860, united to avert, what to Leamington would have proved an irretrievable disaster—the loss of the Pump Rooms—but among them, Mr. Glover was specially distinguished by his zeal and perseverance, despite many obstacles. Mr. Ravenhill is the capable Manager of this Institution.

Through the energy of the Rev. J. Sibree, the deserted theatre in Clemens Street was reopened on April 24, 1866, as "The Congregational Free Church," when sermons were preached by the Revs. Enoch Mellor, of Liverpool, and Clement Dukes, of London. Among those present were the Rev. J. W. Percy, then in his eighty-second year, the principal founder of the building in 18 16, and Mr. Jesse Johnson, aged ninety, one of the original trustees. The inaugural services were continued on the following Sunday, on which occasion the Rev. S. McAll, President of Hackney College, was the preacher. Mr. Sibree was the first pastor, and his successors in the office have been the Revs. W. Robertson, J. W. Bain, J. S. Beamish, J. Perkins, and Mr. G. Astbury. In July, 1900, the services were discontinued, the church disbanded, and the Sunday School closed, the number of Congregational Churches at the Spa thus being reduced from three to one.

To bring the history of the Jephson Gardens to date, a few facts must be added to those already mentioned. In

1854 the redemption money of £600 was paid, and from that time the rental of £50 ceased, and they became public property. The cottage referred to on page 223 as standing on the site of the Hitchman Fountain, and the land belonging to it, were purchased from Mrs. Willes in 1866 for £1,100 and added to the Gardens. For half a century — 1846.to 1896—the grounds were in the care of the Trustees, with a Committee of Management acting under them, and it would be ungrateful not to recognise their services in the public interest. Their horticultural and floricultural shows were the best of the kind in the Midlands; their concerts and fetes were unrivalled; and the archery meetings, admirably arranged in the first instance by the late Mr. N. Merridew, and afterwards by Mr. H. Bown, attracted archers from all parts of the kingdom. In 1896 the property passed into the hands of the Corporation, under the Act of that year, since when the public have been admitted free on three days in each week. The principal gardeners have been Messrs. Cullis, Aylott, and Dell, to each of whom praise is due for the culture which has characterised their services.

After the Rev. W. A. Salter resigned the pastorate at Warwick Street Baptist Church, as mentioned on page 303, he and some attached friends held services in Beck's Room, Upper Parade; and in August, 1860 (six months after the commencement of these meetings) he announced his intention to remain in Leamington. Steps were immediately taken to provide a new place of worship, the result being the purchase of a site in Clarendon Street, and the erection of the present edifice by Mr. B. Bradshaw from his own designs. The architecture is Early English, and the arrangements and treatment throughout "evince a rare combination of beauty and commodiousness." The entire cost, exclusive of the schoolroom, was 2,098 2s. 1 id. The late Mr. C. E. Large prepared the necessary deeds and gave valuable professional advice without any remuneration,and,among other helpers,Mr. T.H.Thorne and Mr. Philip Locke subscribed liberally and rendered much practical assistance. At the opening services, in June, 1863, sermons specially appropriate were preached by the Revs. John Aldis, of Reading; Newman Hall, of Surrey Chapel; and YV. Landels, of Regent's Park Chapel, London. Mr. Salter continued his ministrations with steadily increasing popularity until 1877, and his health then beginning to fail, the Rev. Henry Wright, of Regent's Park College, was appointed co-pastor, and on his subsequent removal to Manchester, the Rev. J. Butlin, B.A., was elected his successor. Mr. Salter died on the 29th of July, 1879, aged sixty-seven, and was interred in Warwick Cemetery on the 2nd of August. During his twenty years' residence in Leamington he had gained general esteem by his willing services to every good cause, and by his zeal, learning, and personal excellencies. When his death was announced, the " Athenaeum " mentioned, as a matter of world-wide interest, that he was one of the principal writers of the "Annotated Paragraph Bible," published by the Religious Tract Society, and that he had completed a new edition ot his notes on the New Testament, and with those of the Old Testament had made considerable progress, at the time his labours were finally interrupted. After his death the Rev. J. Butlin, who had been assisting him three months, was elected pastor. In 1884 he was succeeded by the Rev. G. A. Willis, of Regent's Park College, who resigned in 1896, and after staying in Leamington a few years accepted the pastorate at Henley-in-Arden. In the month of October following, the Rev. Francis Johnson, the present minister, was elected.

St. John's Church, dating from 1877, was the outcome of a feeling that the parochial system of the Church of England demanded the constitution of an ecclesiastical district for South Leamington. Among the early promoters of this project was the Rev. Canon Young, of Whitnash; and to Mrs. Matthew Wise special praise must be awarded for having given the substantial sum of £1,000 for the benefit of the church. At a pre-liminary meeting at the Crown Hotel, 1875, for the purpose of selecting a site, it was announced that there were eight offers, one being by Mrs. Hitchman, who, in addition to contributing liberally to the building fund, was willing to give sufficient land and convey it to the trustees free of all charge. This generous offer was accepted. The foundation-stone was laid by Lord Leigh, with Masonic honours, on April 3, 1877, and the building was erected by Mr. John Fell, from plans and designs prepared by Mr. J. Cundall. The style of architecture is the early English. On February 14, 1878, the church was consecrated by the Bishop. The Rev. E. T. Franklyn, who, previous to its erection, had been conducting services in a large room lent by Mrs. Hitchman, was the first incumbent and vicar of the parish. In 1882 he accepted the living of Kenilworth, and was succeeded by the present Vicar, the Rev. W. G. Wise, formerly of Leeds, and son of Mrs. Matthew Wise, whose signal liberality has just been mentioned.

The preliminary steps for erecting St. Paul's Church were taken in July, 1872, when the Rev. T. Bromley, Vicar of St. Mary's, issued an appeal for the necessary funds. In August, £3.212 had been subscribed towards the £5,000 required, not estimating the site, given by Mrs. Willes, and valued at £150. The foundation-stone was laid by Mr. William Willes on May 15, 1873, and the church was opened by the Bishop on May 14, 1884. The style of the building, which has accommodation for nearly 1,000 persons, is the 13th century Gothic. Mr. J. Cundall was the architect, and the contractor was Mr. Kibler, of Wellesbourne. At first the services were under the superintendence of Mr. Bromley, who had, as assistant ministers at St. Mary's, the Revs. J. H. Rogers and D. C. Hunt. In 1876 the Rev. W. Flory took the place of Mr. Hunt, and continued in office until his acceptance of the incumbency of Holy Trinity in 1877. Mr. Rogers resigned in 1876, and became incumbent of St. George's, Kemp Town, Brighton. After the transfer of Mr. Flory to Holy Trinity, Mr. Bromley carried on the services with the Rev. H. Macdonald as his assistant curate. In September. 1877, the Rev. J. Bradley, of Walsall, succeeded Mr. Macdonald as assistant curate, became incumbent-designate in October of the same year, and the church having been consecrated on the 25th of Apnl following, and on the 20th of June having had a district allotted to it, he was presented to the living in July. Mr. Bradley, after fifteen years' harmonious and prosperous work, resigned in 1893 through failing health, for the benefit of which he had been abroad for a considerable time, the Rev. J. Pleydell Driver acting as his *locum tenens.* He was succeeded by the Rev. G. E. A. Pargiter, formerly of Yarmouth, the present Vicar.

The supply of music from 1850, the date of our last reference to that subject, has been varied and abundant, occasionally ebbing and flowing in quality, but on the whole showing constant improvement. "The Royal Leamington Glee Club," under the conductorship of Mr. H. Marshall, were giving delightful concerts, at which the principal vocalists were Mrs. N. Merridew and Misses Hewitt; Messrs. N. Merridew, John Beck, H. Mayle, D. Hughes, Curtis, Page, and Taylor. Their rehearsals were held at the Crown Hotel, where, in 1865, the assets of the Society, consisting of "a very fine piano and an excellent selection of music," were lying unused. Contemporaneous with the "Glee Club" was " the Leamington Choral Society," of which Mr. F. Marshall was the conductor. This was probably the Association started by him in 1S28. Mr. Marshall, who had a very successful musical career in Leamington and the Midlands, died at Olney in 1857, aged sixty-seven. He was a pupil of Dr. Crotch, and, as a composer, a vocalist, and an instrumentalist, did credit to his master. The commencement of "the Leamington Philharmonic Society," in May, 1854, by Mr. Richard Ward, then organist at St. Luke's, was an interesting and signal departure in our local musical history, the importance of which was clearly recognised by the Rev. J. Montague, Mr. John Hitchman, Mr. H.

Marshall, and the *Courier,* In their opinion Mr. Ward was succeeding in the "bold and hazardous experiment" of cultivating a taste for good music among the industrial classes, or "million," as they were called, and in providing them with opportunities for study and practice, of which they had not previously had the advantage. Greater praise than this, no musician can desire nor merit. The Philharmonic lasted thirty-six years, holding its own against a succession of powerful rivals, with the wrecks of many of which its path was strewn; giving to large and gratified audiences on an average two concerts yearly, and securing for itself, among many other honours, the distinction of having on April 22, 1873, performed "Elijah" for the first time in Leamington. Mr. Ward died May 18, 1890, aged sixty years; and a memorial slab placed on his grave by those who had been connected with him in the work of the Society, and others, rightly commemorates his very valuable services. The commencement of a new "Leamington Choral Society" was announced in October, 1854, by Signor R. Aspa, a well-known local musician of cultivated taste and high professional qualifications. This Society, of which Mr. T. B. Gleadah, of the Music Warehouse, Victoria Terrace (now Bezant's), was secretary, gave pleasing concerts for a few years, and was then dissolved. Its conductor, Mr. Aspa, now (1900) the *doyen* of Musical Leamington, comes of a talented family, and is nephew to Signor Mario Aspa, better known in Italy as the "Maestro Aspa," whose works comprise no less than eleven operas. A pupil of Moscheles, the celebrated pianist and composer, he has earned and occupies an excellent position as a successful teacher, and has been warmly commended by the *Musical Times* for the beauty and originality of his numerous compositions. In 1867 he published a useful work entitled "Exercises for the Cultivation of the Voice," and in 1868 "A Collection of French Romances, Italian Ariettes, and English Ballads," respecting which the Press notices were complimentary. Mr. Aspa, it should be

stated, is the author of the article on "Leamington," published in the last (the ninth) edition of the "Encyclopaedia Britannica." His brother, the late Mr. Edwin Aspa, composed two cantatas, "Endymion " and "The Gipsies." At the concerts of this Society, Miss Johnstone, daughter of Major Johnstone, won general applause by her very fine singing of oratorio and ballad music. She married Mr. J. W. Elliott, the talented composer of the everpopular " Hybrias the Cretan," and many other favourite songs; who held in succession the appointments of organist at the Baptist Church, Warwick Street, in the Rev. Dr. Winslow's time, and Christ Church; he is now, and for nearly a quarter of a century has been filling the post of organist at St. Mark's, St. John's Wood, London. In 1857 an open-air concert was given in the Pump Room Gardens by Mr. John Cox, Mr. R. Ward conducting the first and Mr. T. E. Cooke the second part. The band, with a chorus of fully four hundred voices, rendered the Old Hundredth Psalm and Luther's Hymn, the latter being accompanied by the impressive trumpet obbligato part. About this time, Mr. Harold Thomas (son of Mr. J. H. Thomas, firm of Thomas and Coles, Lower Parade), whose success in the musical world had for some years been attracting attention, and who had been elected a Professor and Associate of the Royal Academy of Music, an Associate of the Philharmonic Society, London, and a Governor of the Royal Society of Musicians, had the honour of playing before the Queen and Prince Albert at Windsor Castle, and by the latter was highly complimented.

"The South Warwickshire Harmonic Society," started in 1869, and producing unfulfilled expectations of permanence, was more remarkable for the smartness of the minutes of the hon. secretary than for its concerts, excellent as undoubtedly they were. It was an aristocratic affair, with a phenomenally brief career and a list of performances all too few. The officers were: Sir F. A. Gore Ouseley, Mus. Doc, President; Mrs. Frank Gresley, Vice-President; Mrs. Graham Woodmass and Mr. H. Bowyer, treasurer; Signor Aspa, conductor; and the Rev. Marmaduke E. Browne, lion, secretary. The patrons included belted Earls, with many other titled people, and among the honorary members were the distinguished names of Benedict, Cummings, Santley, Stainer, Madame Sainton-Dolby, and Mons. Sainton. It had the best secretary-to be found in the musical annals of Leamington—the most practical, the most candid, and the wittiest. Minutes of musical societies are seldom or never consulted for entertainment or instruction, but Mr. Browne's sportive and sagacious pen lights up every page with laughter, philosophical reflections, and advice of the utmost value. As to the reasons which led to the early disruption of an organisation surrounded by circumstances so favourable to longevity, nothing distinctly is stated, but in June, 1870, several of the principal officers resigned, the rehearsals were discontinued, and the borrowed music called in. Revision of the rules and a reconstrucion of the Association followed, one of the changes being to dispense with the services of Associate members "who refuse to perform unless paid for every rehearsal as well as the concerts, and to engage in their places the members of the Birmingham Amateur Harmonic Society, who were better singers, and would attend on payment of their expenses and refreshment." Its last concert was given in January, 1 871. "The Concordia Choir," established in 1870 by Miss Rachael Gray, for several years gave attractive concerts under the direction of its energetic and gifted foundress—the only lady who has wielded the baton at a series of public musical performances in Leamington. She was organist at Christ Church, and, as principal soprano, frequently assisted at important local concerts. The Society was broken up on her removal to Shrewsbury; she afterwards emigrated to Australia, and in 1880 made her debut in the new world with marked success at a conversazione at the Sydney Academy of Art. In 1897, to the regret of numerous friends at Leamington and Warwick, she died at Les Angelos, after

undergoing an operation for tumour. The next organisation was of spontaneous origin. On November 5, 1879, there was an unusually fine performance of the "Messiah" at the Parish Church, by a band and chorus of over two hundred performers, comprising the best amateurs and professionals in the town and neighbourhood. In many quarters it was considered to be a favourable opportunity for establishing a new Association, and " The Leamington Musical Society" was the result. Mr. Frank Spinney, the organist at the Parish Church, was chosen conductor, and, until his health failed, he carried on the work most satisfactorily. His lamented death closed the Society, which at one time had the promise of a long career of usefulness. In the same year (1879), Mr. A. E. Gibbs, organist at St Paul's, started "The St. Paul's Choral Union," the first concert of which was given in the Holly Walk Schoolroom in January, 1880. From this comparatively small beginning the Society grew in numbers and influence, and for more than twelve years provided annual concerts at the Winter and Town Halls, remarkable for good chorus singing and orchestral developments. To this period also belong "The Leamington Choral Society," conducted by Mr. Piercy Watson, and later on, the " Orchestral Society," ably directed by Mr. Walter Warren, the former devoted largely to opera and cantata music, and the latter giving brilliant interpretations of the instrumental works of the best masters. After the demise of Mr. R. Ward, in 1890, the Philharmonic was amalgamated with the St. Paul's Choral Union, Mr. Gibbs continuing in the leadership; and at the same time a new Association was formed under the title of "The Leamington Musical Union," of which Mr. H. A. Heden, organist at Spencer Street Congregational Church, was elected the conductor. Between these two organisations there was a rivalry, which fortunately proved conducive to the interests of music, the concerts of each, for choral and orchestral effects combined, being greatly in advance of the most successful efforts of all previous mu-

sical associations in Leamington. Both conductors, by the power they displayed in the training of their singers, the excellence of their selections, and their extensive developments and application of orchestral resources, justified the confidence reposed in them, and produced a series of concerts which are, and will remain for many years to come, the high water-mark of chorus performances with band accompaniments. In 1897 tne tw0 organisations were amalgamated as " The Leamington Harmonic Society," the services of Mr. Heden and Mr. Gibbs (now Mus. Bac.) being properly retained for management and direction in alternate years. To the foregoing must be added the Leamington Charity Madrigal Society," started in 1898 by Mr. Roberts-West, organist at S. Alban's, the concerts of which form an agreeable contrast to the modern schools; and "The Parish Church Augmented Choir for the study of Church Music," conducted by Mr. Bellamy, organist at the Parish Church, commenced in 1900. This list, extensive as it is, would still be materially defective, if we failed to mention the high-class concerts organised by the late Mr. and Mrs. N. Merridew; also the very successful catering of Beaant & Son; and in recent years, the Jephson Gardens Concerts of the latter, and those of Mr. Birch, both of which have merited high praise. For fifty years, Leamington has been full of music, native and imported, and of the large harvest of honours which has been gathered, a fair share belongs to our own musicians.

A few words respecting the histories of the several banks are rendered necessary by the very brief notices of their origin on pages 199 and 200. At the Warwick and Leamington Bank, 73, Parade (now Lloyds), Mr. H. Sutnmerfield was appointed manager in 1843, and remained in office until March, 1869, when he died at the age of fifty-nine years. In 1866 the Bank was purchased by Lloyds, Limited. Mr. Summerfield was succeeded by Mr. Child, who was followed by Mr. Seymour, at whose death Mr. A. C. Pickering, the present manager, was appointed. The Leamington Priors and Warwickshire Banking Company remained in the premises at the south-west corner of Church Walk, Bath Street, until 1858, when they purchased the Bedford Hotel property, in the Parade, on the site of which the present Bank, 126, Parade, was built by Mr. W. Gascoyne. Mr. T. H. 1 horne retired from the post of manager in 1887, but remained on the Directorate until 1889, when the business was sold to the Birmingham and Midland Banking Company. His death occurred in August, 1890, his age being seventy-eight years. Mr. Sanders succeeded him as manager in 1887, after whom Mr. R. J. Hcnn was appointed, and on his promotion to a more important position in the Birmingham Bank of the Company the vacancy was filled by the present manager, Mr. Lawford. It is now the London City and Midland Bank. The Metropolitan Bank (of England and Wales), Limited, 33, Parade, is the successor of a branch started in January, 1863, by Smith and Greenways' Bank, Warwick. After the failure of the Greenways in September, 1887, their business was purchased by the present firm. Mr. G. C. Lake has filled the office of manager since the opening of the first Bank in 1863. The Midland Counties District Bank, 55, Parade, was opened in 1898, under the management of Mr. W. Stevenson.

The Friendly Societies' movement, started on Whit-Monday, 1777, by Ben Satchwell, under circumstances set forth at some length on pages 84-87, found in Leamington a soil and climate congenial for its development. Early in the century several associations for self-help were founded, but as these had to give way to the federative principle it is only necessary now to say that the chief among them were the " United Tradesmen's Friendly Society," the "New Town Friendly Society," and the "Royal Spa Philanthropic Society." In 1836 the sounder systems of the great affiliated societies were introduced by the establishment of the "Temple of Peace" Lodge (M.U.), and at sutsequent periods other Lodges of the same Order followed, bearing the names of the "Loyal Leamington Lodge," the " Loyal Guy's Cliffe Lodge," and the " Albion Lodge." In a comprehensive paper contributed to the *Leamington Courier* in July-, 1897, by P.P.G.M. J. Hudson, ex-valuer of Friendly Societies, the number of members of these four Lodges was stated to be 1,653, tne reserve capital amounting to £19,157. The kindred great Society, the "Ancient Order of Foresters," had in the same year two Courts, the "Royal Leamington" and the "Leamington Oak," with 460 members and £3,131 reserve capital; the "Nottingham Ancient Imperial Lhiited Order of Oddfellows," four Lodges, namely, the "Shrubland," "Aylesford," " Rose of Sharon," and "Hand of Benevolence," with 87 members and £1,282 capital. The total membership of these three Orders was 2,240, and the reserve funds £24,631. In addition to these there were two Juvenile Societies with 450 members and £810 reserve capital, and a " Tent of the Independent Order of the Rechabites," with 48 members and capital amounting to £1,061, making the aggregate total of members 2,498, and reserve funds £25,441. Mr. Hudson estimates that the total amount paid by these Societies in relief, during sixty years, amounted to £75,000, thereby effecting a saving to the poor rate equivalent to £496 per annum. Besides the above there are "The Druids," "The Hearts of Oak," and "The Rational Association Friendly Society," the funds of which are transmitted to headquarters.

The Public Hall, Windsor Street, built by a Company of shareholders, for the accommodation of the Royal Leamington Literary and Scientific Institution, was intimately associated with the literary, recreative, and religious life of the town from 1854 to 1884. Lord Leigh was to have laid the foundation-stone on May 23, 1850, with Masonic Ceremonial, but being unable to fulfil the engagement he voluntarily fined himself £25, a cheque for which amount he forwarded with an apology for his absence. The duty was ably discharged by Mr. J. W. Houghton Leigh, Deputy Provincial Grand Master, in the presence of a large concourse of spectators. The opening ceremony took place on February 20, 1854, when an excellent concert, arranged by Mr. N. Merridew, was given to a crowded audience. Financially, the speculation was not satisfactory, and after vainly endeavouring to sell the building to the town in 1856, the proprietors disposed of it to Mr. Ebenezer Goold. Until the opening of the new Town Hall it was the resort for all the Associations and Societies in Leamington, and the favourite room for concerts and entertainments. Some years ago the ground floor was let to Messrs. Mousell Bros., the well-known furniture removers, whose business, under the management of Mr. Cooksey, grew to such an extent that in 1897 they leased the whole of the extensive property, and the use of the Hall for public meetings, etc., ceased.

Associated with the Public Hall, is the origin of " The Sunday Afternoon Services for Carmen, Bath-Chairmen, Grooms, and Stablemen," the inaugural meeting of which was held in January, 1800. From the first, the movement was extremely popular, and for years it was difficult, and frequently impossible, for late arrivals to find even standing room. In November, 1896, the services were removed to the Royal Pump Room, and in January, 1900, to the comfortable and convenient Memorial Hall, Augusta Place, formerly St. Luke's Church. The Clergy and Nonconformist Ministers, together with the leading laymen of the several religious institutions in the town, have from time to time rendered valuable aid, and Mr. E. Goold, senior, on whom has devolved the burden of management, has, for forty years, provided a suitable supply of preachers and speakers. The " S.A.S." were introductory to the present day P.S.A."

The Educational work of the town in the opening years of the last half of the present century had several points of interest, of which only the briefest notice can be taken. The Rev. Dr. Brindley, a brilliant and versatile lecturer, conducted a famous academy at Knightcote House; the Rev. Dr. Bickmore had a private school at Highlands, extensively patronized by the gentry and nobility; Mr. Andrews, at the Manor House Academy, and Mr. J. Hugh Hawley, at the Brunswick School, were both successful, and among the elementary schools, several had acquired popularity for the efficient education they provided, and their very moderate fees. The National Schools, in Bath Place, were erected in 1859, after a prolonged and acrimonious dispute respecting the question of site, the proposed situations being: Copps' Yard, Clemens Street, the then unoccupied land at the corner of Church Street and Priory Terrace, and the land in Bath Place on which the Schools stand. The foundation stone was laid with the usual Masonic ceremonial, on April 12, by Lord Leigh, and they were opened on the 2nd of November following. Mr. R. Webb was the first master. He came from Cheltenham College in i860, and, in 1876, was followed by Mr. J. Gameson. On the retirement of Mr. Andrews, Mr. Webb succeeded him at the Manor House Academy, and when the lease expired, established Chorlton House Academy, Portland Street.

On April 7, 1881, the School Board was established. There were twenty candidates, and the following were elected

The First School Board.

These statistics give useful prominence to the astounding vagaries of the cumulative vote, and prove how fallacious, as tests of public opinion, are all returns of such elections from which the numbers of voters and plumpers are omitted. The Hon. and Rev. J. W. Leigh was chosen the first Chairman, Mr. C. I. Blaker the first Clerk, and Mr. T. H. Joyce, elected School Attendance Officer in 1877 by the Town Council, was continued in his appointment. Leamington had a strong desire to preserve the Voluntary system, but the " stars "—*i.e.,* the Lords of the Committee of the Privy Council on Education—in their courses, fought against and defeated the wish. Deducting spoilt papers, not 50 per cent, of the voters were polled, and although by so doing they put themselves to extra heavy expense, the managers of seven

Voluntary Schools refused to transfer them to the Board. Since its formation the School Board have increased the attendance of the children from 75 to 86 per cent., and have erected four fine blocks of schools which meet every requirement for the comfort and welfare of the children, and have originated Continuation Classes which have been of great service. The number of children now being instructed in the Board Schools is 2,293, and in the Voluntary Schools there are 1,662. In fairness to the managers and teachers of the latter, it should be stated that in the exciting discussions which preceded the establishment of the School Board, no complaint was ever made as to the inefficiency of the education they provided, and the allegation that the Order of the Department was the work of some two or three public men is totally without foundation. The determining cause was the amount of accommodation provided, which being below the required standard, the School Board followed, partly as a consequence of that deficiency, but primarily in fulfilment of the policy of Mr. Forster to have a School Board in every parish. The following were the first teachers appointed by the School Board: Messrs. Warner Simpson, J. Lamsdale, and W. Smith; Mrs. Mawer, Misses Baker, Jeans, Campbell, and Garley.

In our remarks on page 233, respecting the postal arrangements, we inadvertently omitted to state that the removal of the Post Office from Bevington's, in Bath Street (now Maycock's), to the premises occupied by Messrs. Bennett and Beckingsale, took place in May, 1846. Considerable alterations were made to the property, and an ornamental portico was erected in front, the cost of which was defrayed by the public, who also provided the new uniforms donned by the officials for the first time on May 25, the day on which the office was opened. It was a copy of the one chosen for the Metropolitan postmen, and consisted of blue coat and vest, scarlet collar and cuffs, and gold band round the hat. The Improvement Commissioners in 1851 applied to the

Postmaster General for improvement in the delivery and dispatch of letters, and in 1856 the premises were enlarged by adding a wing of the building which had been used as a shop. The business of the establishment and its public utility also were greatly increased by the Post Office Savings Bank Act of 1861, after which the necessity for much larger premises began to be felt, especially when the work of receiving and dispatching telegrams was added. The new General Post Office in Priory Terrace was built by Mr. W. Gascoyne, and opened in 1870. For several years the transactions of the Inland Revenue Department were carried on in the upper rooms, and the telegraph business was added the same year the office was opened. Mr. E. Enoch, after thirty-six years' service, retired on a pension, and was succeeded by Mr. E. S. Adams, who left in 1892 and went to Exeter. His successor was the present Postmaster, Mr. W. Clarke, of Worthing, a public official deservedly esteemed by all classes. In 1871 the portico at the Bath Street Office was demolished, the late Mr. Sidney Flavel, sen., purchasing the columns and erecting them in front of his residence, Edgeville, Newbold Terrace. Some idea of the magnitude of the work carried on at the Post Office may be formed from the following statistics: The staff number 170; there are 10 offices in the borough and 9 in the district; the sub-offices are 14; and the receiving boxes in the town and neighbourhood, 60. The letters amount to about 170,000 weekly; parcels, 5,500; money orders about 10,000 yearly; postal orders, 72,000 ditto: savings bank transactions, 10,000; and telegrams, about 200,000 ditto.

The National Schools, Bath Place; Wesleyan Training Schools, Portland Street; St Paul's, Holly Walk; St. Luke's, Augusta Place; and Guy Street, Church Schools; and the Roman Catholic Schools, New Street and Augusta Place.

The pre-eminently useful Institution, of which an illustration is here given, has special claims for support on the benevolent throughout the Midlands. It occupies the site of the old Leamington

Hydropathic Establishment (see page 58), a healthy, quiet, and pleasant position, in every way calculated to soothe the minds and alleviate the sufferings of those afflicted with incurable disorders. A glance at the views of the two buildings will show the great work which has been accomplished in extension and ornamentation since the property was purchased by the Committee sixteen years ago. The" Home." all the details of which are admirably arranged, admits a certain number of in-patients, and grants pensions of £zo yearly to others. Mr P. H. Couchman, both efficient and courteous in the discharge of his duties, is the Secretary, and General Radcliffe has been a tower of strength in promoting the prosperity of the Institution.

The limits originally prescribed for the completion of this work having been slightly exceeded, and every subject essential to a fair knowledge of the history of the Spa referred to, either fully or in concise terms, the opportunity for now bringing it to a close will readily be seen. In doing so, we have one or two explanations to make, and some highly appreciated services to acknowledge. Taking the latter subject as the first, we desire to express our indebtedness for the kind assistance received from all to whom application has been made, and for the liberal patronage which has exhausted the first edition of this History, and rendered a second necessary. Thanks are due for the privilege of inspecting and making extracts from several interesting documents in the office of the Clerk of the Peace for the County, and for permission to consult, as occasion required, the files of *The Warwick Advertiser, The Leamington Cornier,* and *The Leamington Chronicle,* readily granted by the proprietors of those journals; to Messrs. Burgis & Colbourne (Limited), for the loan of numerous illustrations, to Mr. H. Sherratt, for furnishing the artistic design for the Borough Arms, appearing on the cover, to Mr. S. S. Stanley, Vice-President, and Mr. T. W. Whitley, late Hon. Secretary of the Warwickshire Naturalists' and Archaeologists' Field Club, for much valuable aid, and also to the journals

named and *The Daily Circular* for numerous complimentary notices.

The curious old stone mentioned on page 104, found by the author while examining the crypt, he regards as a rare and valuable relic of an early gift, or bequest, to the Parish Church. It appears from the publications of " The Midland Record Society," and "The Records of Rowington" by J. W. Ryland.that bequests of sums of 6s. 8d.,for church, charitable, and other public purposes, were not uncommon in the sixteenth century. Among the Birmingham Wills published by the Society are four of this character, namely, one of 6s. 8d. "to Byrmyncha Church;" another of a like amount '" towards the reparacons of Seynt Kat'yne's Church;" a similar legacy for the "reparacon of Church of Hales owen;" and a further sum of 6s. 8d. for '" por peple." In the Rowington Wills, 6s. 8d. is several times devised for highway purposes, expressed in the quaint phraseology of the period as "mending Fowle waves." There can be no doubt that the stone in the vaults records a bequest of 6s. 8d. to the Church by R. Yardley, and that it originally formed part of one of the walls of the fabric.

I Iistorical productions are proverbially susceptible to error, especially first editions, on behalf of which the elder D'Israeli generously interposes a shield against criticism, vehemently hostile. Owing chiefly to misleading information and inadvertencies of the Press, in regard to which there is no protective formula of infallibility, the following corrections are necessary. On page 15, the Hearth Tax returns of the seventeenth century are represented as containing the first intelligence of the inhabitants of the village. This needs amendment by omitting the words " the first," for the Inquisition of Edward I., in the thirteenth, gives names and particulars of every resident at that time. The statement on page 27, made in reliance upon another writer, that the value of the estate of Leamington had increased from £4 to £533 15s..fd., is unreliable and confused; for, whilst £4 was the value of the manor in

1086,£533 15s-4d. remained the total revenue of the Mother Abbey of Kenilworth in 1535. The Rev. William Jay, of Bath, is said, on page 61, to have taken part in the opening services at Spencer Street Church in 1836. It was, however, at a later date he preached there. Reference is made on page 90, to a number of bonds mentioned in the Parish Register, (one of which is quoted,) which were believed to relate to the parochial system of apprenticing boys. The more probable view is that they were part of the Poor Law system, and were intended to prevent poor persons settling in Leamington unless they could give security against becoming chargeable to the rates. In the Valuation of Tythes of Newbold (pages 93-4-5) the sum of iod. , whenever it occurs, should be is. The Housewarming at Copps's Hotel, appearing on page 243, in the events of 1826, belongs to those of 1827, and " Dr. James Johnstone," page 268, should be " Dr. John Johnstone.-' CHRONOLOGY FROM 1851 TO iqoo.

1851. — Public meeting to petition for repeal of the window tax, Jan. 29. Rugby and Ieamington Railway opened, teb. 22.

Meeting of Grand National Archery Society, June 25 and 26,

Wesleyan Reform Chapel opened, Sept. 7.

The Manners-Sutton Medallion Window

placed in the apse at the Parish Church, Sept.

Lord Leigh initiated a Free and Accepted

Mason by the brethren of the " Lodge of Light,' Birmingham. December.

Population 15,723.

1 i?52 —Presentations to Mr. John Hitchman by the inhabitants and the working classes for his services to the town. January. Congratulatory address presented to Lord Brooke, on his marriage, March 4. 1853. —Nathaniel Hawthorne resident at No. 10, Lansdowne Circus.

Second Warwickshire Militia commenced

their annual trainings in Leamington. Telegraph Office established at the

Jcphson

Gardens Lodge. October.

1854.-Presentation of colours to Second Warwick shire Militia by Lady Skipwith. April. First public concert of the Leamington

Philharmonic Society, established by Mr.

R. Ward. May.

G. V. Brooke at the Theatre.

1X55.—Proposed amalgamation with Warwick for water and gas supplies.

Rev. Dr. Warnefoid died at Bouiton-on-the-

Hill, aged 92. January.

Public address presented to General Sir George Brown, G.C.B., on his return from the Crimea. July.

185b.—Jenny Lind at the Upper Assembly Rooms with Ernst and Weiss. The Swedish Nightingale's first visit was in 1848. March. Tickets for reserved seats, £ is. Demonstration in the Arboretum by the Oddfellows, in Celebration of the Peace, May 26.

Dr. F. R. Lees, the celebrated temperance advocate, lectured twice in the Public Hall. December.

1857. —Arrival of the Russian Gun.

The United Methodist Free Church commenced in the Teraerance Hall, Warwick Street, December.

1858. —Queen Victoria passed through Leamington on her way from Stoneleigh Abbey to open Aston Park, June 17. This was her Majesty's second visit to the Spa, the first having taken place on August 3, 1830.

Visit of Charles Dickens.

Grand evening concert at the Music Hall by the Brousil Family. August.

1859. —New booking office anil station erected at the Avenue, L. & N.W.

Foundation-stone of National Schools laid by

Lord Leigh; Masonic ceremony. April.

1860. —Visit of Empress Eugenie.

John Hampden, a descendant of the illustrious patriot of that name, died, aged 62 years. Nov. 12.

1861. —Sunday Afternoon Services at the Public

Hall commenced Jan. 19. Rev. A. Pope preached.

Charles Dickens at the Music Hall.

January.

Violent thunderstorm, and Parish Church

struck with lightning. July.

Population 17,352.

1862. —Midland Counties Sunday School Conference in Leamington, Good Friday. Completion of New River Walk and Sewage Deodorising Works.

1863.-Lecture at the Public Hall by H. Coxwell, on

Scientific Ballooning. February.

Celebration of the marriage of H.R. H. the Prince of Wales with H.R.H. the Princess Alexandra of Denmark. Foundation-stone of fountain under the bridge, Bath Street, laid by Dr. Jephson. March 10.

1864. —Volunteer Fire Brigade established.

Henry Twiselton Elliston, first organist at the

Parish Church, died April 21, aged 63.

Rev. C. H. Spurgeon preached in Warwick

Street and Spencer Street Churches, June 8.

Philosophical Society inaugurated.

1865. —*Leamington Chronicle* started by Messrs.

Vincent *Sc* Jones, November 4. Presentation of Dr. Jephson's portrait to the town.

Father Gavazzi at the Public Hall. Deccmler.

1866. —Important Conference on Sewage Disposal.

Lecture by Rev. E. J. Paxton Hood. Burial Board established.

1867. —Catholic Apostolic Church commenced in

George Street. October.

1868. —Earthquake.

Longfellow and Miss Longfellow at the

Regent.

Distribution of prizes at the Leamington College by Earl Clarendon.

Hitchman Memorial Fountain uncovered.

October.

1869 1870.

-New allotment of sittings at the Parish Church.

Death of Mr. Joseph Stanley, Chair-

man of Local Board of Health in 185S, when the Queen paid her second visit to Leamington. He was in his 49th year.

1871.—Titiens, Sinico, and Foli at the Music Hall.

Population 20,919.

CHRONOLOGY FROM 1872. —Thanksgivings for recovery of the Prince of Wales from serious illness, Feb. 27.

Notices issued for laying tramway.

1873. —Dr. Thomas Thomson died, aged" i, Jan. 21.

Clemens Street Hospital closed. April.

Albert Hall, Kenilworth Street, opened.

1874. —Mr. A. S. Field appointed Clerk of the Peace for the County.

1875. —Charter of Incorporation granted, Feb. 18. 1876. —Assembly Rooms in Chancery.

Opening of Skating Rink.

First Spelling Bee. l'ebruary.

1877. —Death of Mr. Philip Locke, aged 69 years January 28,

Congress of Sanitary Institute, October.

1878. —Victoria Coffee Tavern, Regent Street, opened by Lord Leigh, July 24. Upper Assembly Rooms sold by auction at the Regent Hotel for,£5.600, Aug. 28.

1879. —Gift of reredos to the Parish Church by Mr.

W. Willes. Januaiy.

1880.-The Hon. Gilbert Leigh elected M.P. for South Warwickshire, April 7.

Westminster Coffee Tavern, Clemens Street mow in Bath Street', opened by Lord

Norton, May 14,

1881. —First School Board elected. April.

Population 22,976.

1882. —Jubilee celebration at Warneford Hospital,

April 11.

1883. —Proposal to amalgamate Leamington, Mil verton, and Lillington defeated. Apiil. 1884. —First triennial report of School Board. March.

New Town Hall opened, Sept. 17.

1885. —First annual meetiqg of subscribers to the Midland Counties Home held in the

Arboretum, Jan. 24.

Death of Alderman W. Harding (ex-Mayor),

Feb. 2; aged 49.

1886. —Pachmann at the Music Hall, May 22. 1887. —Mr. J. Fell elected President of Allotments and Small Holdings Association, Feb. 15. Failure of Greenways' Bank, Sept. 6. Installation of electric light, Nov. 8. 1888. —Celebration at St. Peter's, Dormer Place, of the Pope's Jubilee, Jan. 1. Pachmann at the Royal Assembly Rooms, Jan. 24.

Tuesday's *Chronicle* started, January 10.

1889. —Borough boundaries beaten, April 30. 1890. —Opening of Mission Church, Satchwell Street, March 13.

Death of Mr. R. Ward, founder of the Philharmonic Society, aged 60 years; May 18.

Visit of British Medical Association, Aug. 2.

1891. —Consecration of Dr. Pcrowne, Bishop of

Worcester, Feb. 2.

851 TO 1900—*Continued.* 1891. —Leamington Orchestral Society gave their first concert, Oct. 21. Population 23,124. 1892. —Decision of Town Council to open Free

Library on Sundays, Jan. ri.

Death of Mr. B. Bradshaw, 78 years of age; May 4.

H.R.H. the Prince of Wales and the Duke of York passed through Leamington,

June 18

1893. —Celebration of marriage of H. R.H. the Duke of York and the Princess May, July 6.

Jubilee dinner at the Town Hall of the Guy's

Cliffe Lodge, July 11.

1894. —Death of Mr. John Beck, aged 81 years;

July 12.

Mr. Bellamy appointed organist at All

Saints. July.

1896.-First issue of the *Warwick, Leamington, and District Daily Circular,* June 20. Earthquake distinctly felt by scores of residents, December 17.

1897. —The members of the Press at Leamington and Warwick were entertained by the Mayor (Dr. T. W. Thursfield) at a banquet at the Town Hall, Feb. 5. *Daily Advertiser* commenced April 10. Celebration of the Diamond Jubilee Year of her Majesty's Reign, June 22. 1898. —H.R.H. the Duchess of York, on a visit to

Mr. Frank and Lady Eva Dugdale, arrived at the Avenue Station, Jan. 21.

Public presentation of an album, a gold minute repeater chronograph, a la-

dy's gold watch and chain, an ivory and silver-fitted suite case, and a set of four silver table candlesticks, to Alderman T. W. Thursfield, M.D., F.R.C.P. (London!, J. P., and Mrs. Thursfield, as marks of public esteem, and in recognition of their valuable services as Mayor and Mayoress, from the 9th of November, 1894, to the 9th of November, 1897.

1899. —Presentation in the County Hall, Warwick, of an address, signed by 500 subscribers, and a portrait painted by Walter Ouless, R.A.,

and a valuable brooch, to Lord and Lady

Leigh, in celebration of their golden wedding, and in recognition of half-acentury of public work in the county of Warwick. Jan. 2.

Freedom of Leamington conferred on Lord

Leigh and Alderman Wackrill, Nov. 9.

Councillor Molesworth elected Mayor, Nov. 9 1900. —Opening of the New Waterworks at Lilling ton, by Alderman Bright, Sept. 5. Re-opening of Parish Church on completion of Nave, Nov. 1. Alderman W. Davis elected Mayor, Nov. 9.

GENERAL

Lightning Source UK Ltd.
Milton Keynes UK
UKOW02f2209310713

214699UK00009B/493/P